Navigating *Deep River*

Navigating *Deep River*

New Perspectives on Shūsaku Endō's Final Novel

EDITED BY

MARK W. DENNIS AND
DARREN J. N. MIDDLETON

Cover design by Hugh Cowling.

Published by State University of New York Press, Albany

© 2020 State University of New York

All rights reserved

No part of this book may be used or reproduced in any manner whatsoever without written permission. No part of this book may be stored in a retrieval system or transmitted in any form or by any means including electronic, electrostatic, magnetic tape, mechanical, photocopying, recording, or otherwise without the prior permission in writing of the publisher.

For information, contact State University of New York Press, Albany, NY
www.sunypress.edu

Library of Congress Cataloging-in-Publication Data

Names: Dennis, Mark W., editor. | Middleton, Darren J. N., 1966– editor.
Title: Navigating Deep River : new perspectives on Shusaku Endo's final
 novel / Mark W. Dennis and Darren J. N. Middleton.
Description: Albany : State University of New York Press, [2020] | Includes
 bibliographical references and index.
Identifiers: LCCN 2019016745 | ISBN 9781438477978 (hardcover : alk. paper)
 | ISBN 9781438477961 (paperback : alk. paper) | ISBN 9781438477985 (ebook)
Subjects: LCSH: Endō, Shūsaku, 1923–1996. Fukai kawa. | Endō, Shūsaku,
 1923–1996—Criticism and interpretation.
Classification: LCC PL849.N4 Z78 2020 | DDC 895.63/5—dc23
LC record available at https://lccn.loc.gov/2019016745

10 9 8 7 6 5 4 3 2 1

For Van C. Gessel,
translator,
literary critic,
mentor,
friend,
and recent recipient of one of the highest non-Japanese civilian honors.
With abiding affection

Contents

ACKNOWLEDGMENTS   xi

FOREWORD
The Myths of Ganga   xiii
   Julian Crandall Hollick

INTRODUCTION
A Novel We Have Loved   1
   Mark W. Dennis and Darren J. N. Middleton

Part One: Historical and Comparative Approaches

CHAPTER ONE
Navigating *Deep River* through the Lens of Buddhist Thought   29
   Mark W. Dennis

CHAPTER TWO
A Gaze Turned Inward: Perspectives from the Orient   57
   Mini Chandran

CHAPTER THREE
Japan's Orient and Animal Theology in Endō Shūsaku's *Deep River*   73
   Zhange Ni

CHAPTER FOUR
Religion and Violence in *Deep River*   89
   Ronald Green

Contents

CHAPTER FIVE
Endō Shūsaku: The Long Road to the Deep River   107
   Mark Williams

Part Two: Literary and Theological Approaches

CHAPTER SIX
Catholic Convergences in *Deep River*   127
   Mark Bosco and Christopher Wachal

CHAPTER SEVEN
Shūsaku Endō and Flannery O'Connor on the Grotesque   149
   Elizabeth Cameron Galbraith

CHAPTER EIGHT
From "Catholic" to "catholic": Arriving at *Deep River*   167
   Maeri Megumi

CHAPTER NINE
Deep River as Endō's *Book of Job*: Gathering a Community of Sufferers at the Water's Edge   181
   Van C. Gessel

CHAPTER TEN
Mitsuko, That's Me: Autobiographical Space in Endō Shūsaku's Final Novel   197
   Justyna Weronika Kasza

CHAPTER ELEVEN
Imagining India: Traversing *Deep River* with Enami and Ōtsu   213
   P. A. George

CHAPTER TWELVE
Endō Shūsaku and Religious Pluralism   231
   Emi Mase-Hasegawa

CHAPTER THIRTEEN
Endō Shūsaku's Process Panentheism   245
   Darren J. N. Middleton

CHAPTER FOURTEEN
Japanese Sensibility and Transcendence in *Deep River*   261
    Dennis Hirota

AFTERWORD
Deep and Wide: Tourists and Pilgrims in the Shallows   287
    S. Brent Plate

FOR FURTHER READING   295

CONTRIBUTORS   305

INDEX   311

Acknowledgments

Several industrious, skilled, and kind people assisted us in publishing as well as assembling this book, our second anthology of essays on Shūsaku Endō's fiction. We would like to recognize them here; naturally, any errors remain our own: anonymous peer reviewers with SUNY Press; the Association for Asian Studies; the Conference on Christianity and Literature; Jenn Bennett-Genthner; Barbara, Brent, and Joe Dennis; J. Sage Elwell; Betsy Flowers; Andy Fort; Rob Garnett; Priscilla, Solomon, and Gladys Jaichander; Fran Keneston; James Peltz; S. Brent Plate; and Paul John Roach.

We value Christopher Ahn, our tirelessly attentive editor at SUNY Press. Chris is a gentleman and a scholar, a lovely human being, and we are sincerely grateful for his thoughtful and generous encouragement. To Hugh Cowling for our book cover's astonishing artistry, our thanks.

Permissions to reprint copyrighted material in this book are gratefully acknowledged:

> For nonexclusive English-language UKBC rights, print only, of Shusaku Endo, *Deep River*, translated by Van C. Gessel (London: Peter Owen Publishers, 1994), we deeply appreciate the helpfulness of Simon Smith, senior editor and rights manager, at Peter Owen Ltd. Copyright © 1994 the heirs of Shusaku Endo; English translation copyright © Van C. Gessel 1994—Peter Owen Publishers, UK.

> For nonexclusive English language world rights, excluding British Commonwealth, print only, of Shusaku Endo, *Deep River*, translated by Van C. Gessel (New York: New Directions Publishing Corp., 1994), we thank Christopher Wait, permissions editor, New Directions Publishing Corp. By Shusaku Endo, translated by Van C. Gessel, from *Deep River*, copyright © 1994 by Shusaku Endo.

English Translation © 1994 Van C. Gessel. Reprinted by permission of New Directions Publishing Corp.

For nonexclusive world, ebook rights to the English translation of *Deep River*, we value the kind permission of Ryūnosuke Endō, president and COO, Fuji Television Network, Inc., Japan.

An earlier version of Zhange Ni's work in chapter 3 was first published as "Japan's Orient and Animal Theology in Shūsaku Endō's *Deep River*," *The Journal of American Academy of Religion* 81, no. 3 (2013): 669–97. Reprinted by permission of Oxford University Press.

Mark W. Dennis
Darren J. N. Middleton
Autumn 2019

Foreword

The Myths of Ganga

JULIAN CRANDALL HOLLICK

I had never read anything by Endō Shūsaku until November 2017. I had certainly never heard of *Deep River*. It came as a revelation. I can honestly say I enjoyed every moment of it. And it set me wondering why the Ganges, or Ganga, River should be so fascinating for Endō. Why would a Japanese Roman Catholic writer be fixated on Ganga? Endō, presumably, like millions of Hindus and non-Hindus, believes deep down that this river really does wash away human sins and carry the human ashes consigned to its waters to the next world. No other river in the world appears to have this ability. And many contributors to this instructive volume seem to concur.

I want to say "mythical" ability because this power really is in the mind. It doesn't matter if the mind is Hindu, Buddhist, or Catholic. For years I also believed that Ganga is unique because she alone possesses mythological and biochemical properties that no other river contains. Today, I am less certain.[1] Ever since I traveled down the Ganga by country boat in 2004, I have been fascinated by the mythology that Ganga cleanses humans of their sins and cures them of diseases. I wanted to find out why and how, like any good journalist. Was there science that would confirm or deny the mythology? The *constant* in this argument appears to be the powers of Ganga as the Supreme Goddess. But today, I am not so sure that, even in mythology, Ganga is that unique. There are simply too many texts that state that other "sacred" rivers possess most, if not all the same, powers to cleanse humans of their sins to prevent disease.

But first, why and how did this mythology about Ganga's unique powers come into being?[2] In the *Rig Veda*, *Upaniṣads*, and *Purāṇas*, there are copious references to the powers of Ganga as a goddess,[3] just as there are to the other seven sacred rivers.[4] But in all the subsequent references right up to the present day, these powers are almost always referred to as *unique* to Ganga, presumably because she is the Supreme Goddess—not just a shallow and polluted river, although that is another story![5]

The Ganges is a *sacred* river to Hindus along every fragment of its length. Hindus bathe in its waters, paying homage to their ancestors and to their gods by cupping the water in their hands, lifting it and letting it fall back into the river; they offer flowers and rose petals and float shallow clay dishes filled with oil and lit with wicks (*diyas*). On the journey back home from the Ganges, they carry small quantities of river water with them for use in rituals.[6]

There are many myths about how Ganga came down to earth. The most famous myth tells how Ganga came down through the locks of Śiva's hair to restore the bodies of King Sagira's sixty thousand sons burned to ashes by the gaze of the sage Kapil,[7] hence the belief that *Ganga jal*—the waters of Ganga—purifies human souls and cleanses them of sin.[8]

If one is cremated upon the Ganga's banks, and one's ashes are scattered in the river, particularly at Varanasi, this will ensure liberation from further rebirths. If you cannot make it to Ganga or to Varanasi, then a drink of *Ganga jal* will at least ease the pains of dying.[9]

Ganga is therefore more than just a river. She is the archetype of all sacred waters. If a person cannot get to Ganga, any of the seven will do. If they are not available, then any other river will do, because Ganga is literally everywhere. Dig and water will spring forth—it is Ganga. Even in Mumbai there is a famous bathing tank called *Bana Ganga*.[10] Nor is Ganga "depicted ambiguously, like the other gods, with a lotus leaf in one hand and a weapon in the other. She bears the lotus and the Kumbha, the water pot, both symbols of auspicious blessing."[11]

Ganga is present in all rituals in temple or home, either by mixing ordinary water with a few drops of Ganga water or by uttering the name and mantras of Ganga to invoke her presence. "Thus, the Ganga is the quintessence and source of all sacred waters indeed of all waters, everywhere."[12] Ganga abandons no one. "She nourishes the land and all its creatures, living and dying."[13]

What the Ganges River removes, however, is not necessarily physical dirt, but symbolic dirt; it wipes away the sins of the bather, not just of the present but of his or her lifetime.[14] A dip in Ganga is widely believed to bring believers purification and freedom from sins. Nothing is more stirring for a

Hindu than a dip in the actual river, especially at one of the famous *tīrthas* such as Gangotri, Haridwar, Prayag, or Varanasi. The symbolic and religious importance of the Ganges is one of the few things that all of Hindu India, even its skeptics, agreed upon. Jawaharlal Nehru, a religious iconoclast if ever there was one, asked for a handful of his ashes to be thrown into the Ganges. "The Ganga," he wrote in his will, "is the river of India, beloved of her people, round which are intertwined her racial memories, her hopes and fears, her songs of triumph, her victories and her defeats. She has been a symbol of India's age-long culture and civilization, ever-changing, ever-flowing, and yet ever the same Ganga."[15]

Ganga, however, is not unique in this function. Each of the other Seven Sacred Rivers[16] possesses similar powers of purification, albeit with important variations.[17] If Ganga is divinity herself, where does this place the other six sacred rivers? What powers do they possess? Are they similar or subtly different? This is where doubts may begin.

The *Skanda Purāṇa*[18] states that "all rivers are holy"[19] and ranks them: "There are hundreds of rivers. All remove sins. All of them are bestowers of merit. Of all the rivers, those that fall into the sea are the most excellent. Of all those rivers, Ganga, Yamuna, Narmada and Saraswati are the most excellent rivers, O meritorious sages. These four are highly meritorious."[20] Therefore, in Vedic texts, rivers in general and certain named rivers are referred to with great reverence as holy and are deified. Ganga, moreover, was not the first or only river to come down from heaven to earth. The Godavari was brought to earth *before* Ganga and is hence called *Vṛddha*, or "elder," Ganga. But such is the power of the Ganga juggernaut that few in northern India have ever even heard of Godavari or Saraswati. The writer Bill Aitken maintains that the Indus, Saraswati, and Narmada all have greater claims to be considered divine rivers than Ganga.[21] There are important differences. For example, Ganga is a lunar river; Yamuna is a solar river. Yamuna bargains with her brother Yama, the god of death, for her devotee's life. While Yamuna is associated with purification as preparation for death, she is above all associated with the blessings of this life. These things matter to their respective devotees.

Ganga is shorthand for the embodiment of all sacred waters in Hindu mythology. Local rivers are said to be like the Ganges and are sometimes called the "local Ganges" (Ganga). The Kaveri River of Karnataka and Tamil Nadu in southern India is called the "Ganges of the South"; the Godavari is the Ganges that flows through central India.

I have been talking of seven sacred rivers. But where did this idea come from? "When Ganga mythology was elaborated, the notion of the seven divine rivers continued in the popular myth of her descent from heaven, in which the Ganga herself split into seven branches—three flowing east, three flowing west, and one, the Bhagirathi, flowing south into India. There were seven Gangas, watering not only India, but, in this vision of things, the whole inhabited earth."[22]

Each of the seven sacred rivers is linked with a mountain range: Narmada with the Riksha Mountains, Godavari and Kṛṣṇa with the Sahya Mountains, Kaveri with the Malaya Mountains. All seven rivers are also ladders to heaven. They repeat Ganga's divine descent to earth.

Each river displays its own special powers: Yamuna is the sister of Ganga,[23] a river of heaven, the daughter of the Sun,[24] and like Ganga is seen as a liquid goddess. Yamuna is Kṛṣṇa's river, hence her color is referred to as blue. "Like the Ganga, she carries the waters of purification. But the Yamuna carries something else that is quite distinctive: the waters of love. Only after the Ganga merges with Yamuna at Prayaga does Ganga come to enjoy the love of Lord Krishna."[25] How Yamuna came down to earth is similar to Ganga's descent with one vital difference—Bhagirathi brought Ganga down for *mukti*, or the liberation at death, whereas Jayamuni and other sages brought Yamuna down to develop devotional insights, or *bhakti*, of the living. Yamuna's waters are said by the sage Narada to be especially efficacious for washing "the mind of poverty, sins and disease."[26] The sage Narada emphasizes Yamuna's abilities to purify those who bathe in her waters of "all minor and major sins [which] are reduced to ashes."[27]

Yamuna seems a lot more approachable to her devotees than Ganga. But is she superior to Ganga in their eyes? Apparently, yes! "Only after she merges with Yamuna at her confluence in Allahabad does Ganga become a lover of Krishna herself and acquire the ability to love."[28] The poet Krishnadas spells it out: "Ganges obtained Krishna from merging with Yamuna, and she became filled with the power to grant all spiritual powers."[29] Yamuna's devotees therefore regard her as superior to Ganges because Yamuna alone can grant, nurture, and perfect devotional love without the aid of another. For this reason, Yamuna's devotees claim they only worship Ganga downstream of Allabahad, when the river has merged with Yamuna. As a sign in Vrindaban says: "A single sip of Yamuna water here gives one more spiritual freedom than one hundred baths in Ganges."[30]

Eight special qualities of Yamuna are listed in the *Yamunashakatam*. The fifth quality involves the ability to remove all sins that stand as a barrier to the ultimate relationship with God.[31] The *Padma Purāṇa* declares that "all minor and major sins are reduced to ashes by taking a bath in Yamuna."[32] In other *purāṇas* and commentaries one can read that Yamuna "eradicates the evil consequences of former births for the person who touches but a few drops of her water."[33] Similarly, Yamuna removes all physical disease. The second *ashtakam* of Rupa Gosvamin's *Yamunashtakam* praises Yamuna: "You remove all misfortune and disease," and "sickness, poverty and death never comes near your water."[34] Yamuna therefore came into this world to purify it. Her physical form cleanses the body, her spiritual form is the soul, and her divine form prepares the soul for a love affair with the divine.

I have spent some time elaborating on Yamuna's powers because she is perhaps the best documented in sacred texts. And what is documented strongly suggests she possesses the same powers as Ganga. But one finds the same powers with other of the sacred rivers. Śiva, for example, offers Narmada a boon. She replies: "I ask a boon for all creatures: that I may remain immortal to destroy the sins of the world, even in the time when you destroy the earth with your Tandava dance. Give the greatness that Ganga has in the north to me in the south. Let there be no difference between me and Ganga. Thus, whoever bathes in my waters on Makar Sankranti will receive the benefit of bathing in all the tirthas of India. And whoever dies on my banks, having worshipped you, will receive moksha."[35] The *tirthas* of Narmada are extremely well documented, as are the river's powers of removing sins from human beings. "The Ganga is sacred at Kankhala, the Saraswati at Kurukshetra, but the Narmada is sacred all along her banks, in the forests as well as in the places of habitation. The waters of the Saraswati purify one in the course of five days, those of the Yamuna in seven days, of the Ganga instantaneously, and of the Narmada at the mere sight of it."[36]

The origins of Kaveri and Godavari are quite convoluted. And Saraswati is a whole different chapter.[37] But they each possess similar powers to cleanse and prevent disease. In recorded conversations with me in 2014 and 2016, priests and pilgrims at Godavari (Nasik) and Kaveri (Talakaveri) all said the same thing: that these last two rivers have the same powers as Ganga, that Ganga is actually a junior sister to both Godavari and Kaveri.[38] I would expect to hear the same about Yamuna and Narmada! But for devotees, all seven sacred rivers have the power to cleanse men and women of sins. Some are more specific than others. But in some *mahatmya*, one will always find a verse that ascribes to a particular river a particular power to purify humankind.

Bill Aitken has questioned how and why Ganga replaced Indus and then Saraswati in the sacerdotal status of Hinduism.[39] Ganga seems to be placed above the others today because of her heavenly origins. She is a goddess before taking the form of the Milky Way and then coming down to earth. Yamuna also is quite clearly divine and Ganga's sister. Of the others, only Narmada rises to the same level of exalted origin. Many devotees can get to Ganga. But for those who cannot the waters of the other sacred rivers are a more than adequate substitute. As long as human beings have the conviction that their sins will be purified and their souls enter heaven, they will believe in Ganga and *Ganga jal*. Endō's characters are drawn to the Ganga, like iron filings to a magnet, and several believe in its curative and mythological powers. Essayists in this anthology detail the convictions that motivate such pilgrimage making. In life as in fiction, nothing can shake such faith unless the river dries up. Unfortunately, that is not impossible.

The other variable and reason to question Ganga's claims to be unique is the science. It has to be prised out. Trained scientists have spent a huge amount of time and effort in an attempt to show that the presence of bacteriophages and other microorganisms, in combination with water temperature, velocity of the river, all sorts of other wonderful microorganisms, give Ganga alone these unique abilities. Ten years ago, I christened these biochemical properties "the Mysterious Factor X"; the term has been reproduced in articles all over the internet and has even found its way into Wikipedia and the editorial pages of the *Times of India*.[40]

Various studies reveal tantalizing fragments that would support the notion that science confirms the mythology of Ganga's powers. But they are just flashes—never sustained through multiple testing at different times. It is astonishing how little sustained scientific experiment has actually been done on Ganga.

Once again, the word that reoccurs is *unique*. The studies that have been carried out suggest (no more than that) the waters of Ganga—*Ganga jal*—possess special properties. And because Ganga is Ganga, they must be unique. No other river can by definition possess Ganga's unique powers. How could they? None are the Supreme Goddess.

Now fast-forward to 2016: Gokul Rajan and Professor Kiran Kondabagil at the laboratory of Molecular Virology in the Department of Biosciences and Bioengineering at IIT-Bombay analyzed water from Ganga and the Kaveri River in Karnataka (another of the so-called seven sacred rivers). They sampled at Rishikesh, Kanpur, and Varanasi, and at Nimishamba on Kaveri. As test samples they used distilled and Milli-Q water. And what did they conclude? They found that both Kaveri and Ganga have the same antibacterial properties. In fact, Professor Kondabagil wrote to me that "this antibacterial property is probably found, not just in Indian rivers, but in just about any stream of running water you can find—from Russia to Kenya, from Fiji to Chili and what have you!"[41]

In other words: all rivers probably have these antibacterial properties. There is nothing remotely *unique* about Ganga. And why is this? It's because no one (or almost no one) has ever bothered to test the water of any other river. And when they did they didn't realize the significance of their findings. They had been culturally brainwashed over generations to assume Ganga is unique. But the evidence was always there. In 1896, Hankin discovered bacteriophages in Yamuna, not Ganga. He says it in black and white.[42] Why has nobody ever seized on this? Perhaps because in the original French, Yamuna was used interchangeably with Ganga; for a geographer, the former is by definition the tributary of the latter.

Indian scientists have been rather sloppy in allowing culture to dictate the questions they ask. In 2014, I showed the original of Hankin's paper to a well-known hydrologist who has made a career of posing as the champion of Ganga's unique biochemical abilities. He has often cited Hankin as a major source for his research. I suspected he had never read the original. Sure enough, he hadn't. He'd read a four-page summary written by an Indian author in the 1930s. As Yamuna is a tributary of Ganga, this professor assumed Hankin must have meant Ganga. He then spent a lifetime repeating that Ganga alone had the power to cleanse itself. No mention of microorganisms or bacteriophages. Why? In his own words, "I am a hydrologist not a biochemist."

In his PhD thesis, this same professor had compared re-oxygenation rates in Ganga, Yamuna, and a highly polluted tributary—the Kali.[43] And surprise surprise; all three had the same powers to restore their oxygen levels! How could he so blatantly disregard his own findings? Were a generation of papers, accepted the world over, built on intellectual laziness? Similarly, a well-known zoologist believes firmly that *Ganga jal* does not putrefy.[44] Another reputable scientist begins a well-known research paper by stating that for centuries it is accepted that *Ganga jal* does not putrefy.[45] No proof—just a bold statement without apparent foundation. The absence of putrefaction may well be true but it begs an obvious question: Has anyone actually tested other Indian rivers, such as Godavari, Kaveri, or Narmada to see if they also do not putrefy? It appears no one has ever run such a test! Astonishing but true. Did no one ever ask himself or herself the question? Is the power of centuries of cultural hegemony so great that everyone assumes that Ganga is unique?

So where does this myth about Ganga come from? If you put to one side this adjective "unique," which is redundant, one has to start looking at where Ganga gets its reputation? How has the modern mythology of Hinduism been constructed? When and by whom and to whose benefit? And then there is Saraswati, who throws another spanner in the works, because Saraswati was the Supreme Goddess and river *before* Ganga is even mentioned in the *Vedas!*[46] Most people believe Saraswati is a mythical river that probably never existed. Ah, but that's where they're so very wrong! So what happened to her? A combination of natural events—earthquakes closed off the major source of her water, which was Yamuna and runoff from the Shivaliks. And the lack of water meant she started to dry up in summer.[47] Today, remote sensing reveals she still flows underground in Punjab. The myth maintains that the Saraswati flows east in the opposite direction, into the Sangam at Allahabad to form a sacred *Triveni*, or a junction of three rivers. This really is a myth!

Within a few hundred years of her quasi-disappearance, Ganga had taken over her functions as the river. As Hinduism became codified between the eighth and twelfth centuries CE, with bathing *ghāts*, mythologies, rituals, other sacred rivers became subordinated to the Supreme Goddess—Ganga.[48] And that's where we are today. Everyone has been brought up to believe that Ganga alone has these wonderful powers to cleanse and heal, that she is a supreme and unique river and goddess. Tens of millions of rupees have been spent trying to see if science actually confirms or denies this.[49]

Nobody has ever bothered to check whether Ganga's scientific properties are unique or not. The little science available, plus common sense, suggests that *all* rivers in India may have these self-cleansing properties. In which case all that is left is *faith*. Such faith is not to be ridiculed. But faith can splinter and lose its potency, especially if Ganga continues to dry up.

Therefore, it's Ganga's uniqueness that may be the real myth! Not unique in mythology. Not in scientific terms. A secret that dare not say its name!

None of which detracts in any way from the uniqueness of Endō's *Deep River*, which it was my pleasure to read for the first time only recently. And I commend this singular collection of essays, which stands poised to help readers of all kinds navigate the many twists and turns of Endō's final, and perhaps most audacious, novel.

Notes

1. I am flattered to find myself quoted by Mini Chandran in her paper in this volume. But as will become clear, my ideas have shifted and I am doubtful that the *Mysterious Factor X* is unique to Ganga. I suspect it is common to many of India's sacred rivers, for reasons this Foreword tries to demonstrate.

2. Bill Aitken, *Seven Sacred Rivers* (New Delhi: Penguin India, 1992), 190–94, and interviews with the author in Mussoorie, April 30, 2014. See also Alice Albinia, *Empires of the Indus—The Story of a River* (London: John Murray, 2008), xvii, 366.

3. Julian Crandall Hollick, "Ganga and *Ganga jal* in Mythology" (unpublished thesis, Leeds, 2015), chapter 3.

4. Ganga, Yamuna, Saraswati, Sindhu (or Indus), Narmada, Godavari, and Kaveri.

5. See Kelly D. Alley, *On the Banks of the Ganga: When Wastewater meets a Sacred River* (Ann Arbor: University of Michigan Press, 2003), 296. Alley explains the duality of Ganga's identity as both goddess and physical river succinctly and clearly.

6. Diana L. Eck, *Banaras: City of Light* (New York: Knopf, 1982), 212.

7. Most Indians also know the story of how the dead at Kurukshetra are restored to life by bathing in Ganga. After the great battle between the Pandava and Kauravas in the *Mahābhārata*, "then Vyasa entered the *sacred* water of the Ganga, and summoned all the warriors. . . . Immediately there was a deafening roar from within the waters, and the kings . . . with all their armies, arose in their thousands from the waters of the Ganges . . . free from all animosity and pride, anger and jealousy . . . and purged of every sin, the heroes met with each other. All of them were happy of heart. Son met with father or mother, wife with husband, brother with brother, and friend with friend. . . . All the warriors . . . reconciled with each other, renouncing enmity and becoming established in friendship. Thus they passed that night in great happiness. When the day dawned, they embraced each other and took their respective places. Thereupon, Vyasa, the foremost of ascetics, dismissed them. Within the twinkling of an eye, they disappeared in the very sight of all. Plunging into the *sacred* river Ganga, they proceeded to their respective abodes." *Mahābhārata* 15: 41, 15–25.

8. Sharma, Nidhish IBA transcripts 24-02, April 24, 2004, 30–32.

9. Ibid., 33.

10. Diana L. Eck, *India: a Sacred Geography* (New York: Three Rivers Press, 2012), 438 and 159.

11. Ibid., 161.

12. Ibid., 159.

13. Ibid., 163.

14. Ibid., 216–17.

15. Ibid., 214–15.

16. These rivers are Ganga, Yamuna, Saraswati, Sindhu (Indus), Godavari, Narmada and Kaveri (Cauvery). There are, however, many other rivers that possess similar attributes.

17. Other rivers, such as the Shipra in Maharasthra, are also obviously sacred. Ujjain on the Shipra is one of the four sites (the others are Haridwar and Allahabad on the Ganga, Nashik on the Godavari) where drops from the cosmic struggle for possession of the *kumbh* (pot) containing *amrit* (nectar) fell. The *Ardh Kumbha Mela* is held here.

18. *Purāṇas* are important for the study and documentation of the history of Hindu India. They are the transmitters of Hindu thought down through the ages and are therefore indispensable for understanding Hinduism today. Ludo Rocher says, "Every Hindu is influenced by the *Puranas*, and his activities are guided by them." See Ludo Rocher, "The Puranas," in *The History of Indian Literature*, no. 2, ed. Jan Gonda (Wiesbaden: Otto Harrassowitz, 1986). This citation is from the *Padma Purāṇa*, pt. 6, trans. N. A. Deshpande, 1990, 2110.

19. Ibid.

20. *Skanda Purāṇa*, pt. 11, trans. G. V. Tagore, 1997 verses IV.ii.92.3–6, 382.

21. Aitken, *Seven Sacred Rivers*, 179–90.

22. Eck, *Banaras: City of Light*, 167.

23. Yamuna is also known as *Ganga ki Bahan*, or "sister of Ganga." See David L. Haberman, *River of Love in an Age of Pollution: The Yamuna River of Northern India* (Berkeley: University of California Press, 2006), 61.

24. Ibid., 169.

25. Ibid., 170.

26. Ibid., 126.

27. *Padma Purāṇa*, 14443–46.

28. Haberman, *River of Love*, 123.

29. *Yamunashtakam* of Vallabhacharya, quoted in Haberman, 122. See also forty-one Yamuna poems in Appendix 1 of Haberman, 202–15.

30. Haberman, *River of Love*, 123.

31. Ibid., 124.

32. *Padma Purāṇa*, 1445.

33. See Haberman, Appendix 1, 197–222.

34. Ibid., 127.

35. *Skanda Purāṇa*, Reva Kanda V.iii.

36. *Matsya Purāṇa*, 186.8–12.

37. Michel Danino, *The Lost River: On the Trail of the Saraswati* (New Delhi: Penguin India, 2010), 357. Danino's book is a good introduction to readers who believe that the Saraswati is mythical.

38. Recorded conversations at Trimbekashwar Temple April 6, 2014, and Talalkaveri February 16, 2016.

39. Aitken, *Seven Sacred Rivers*, 190.

40. Dipankar Gupta, "Irresistible colonialism: Why some of our leaders seek foreign sanction for Hindu intellectual property," *The Times of India*, August 17, 2013. The writer caricatured me as an unwitting apologist for *Hindutva* and the RSS. Not altogether to my amusement.

41. Email communication with the author, May 20, 2016.

42. M. E. Hankin, "The bacterial action of the waters of the Jamuna and Ganga rivers on Cholera microbes," *Annales de l'Institut Pasteur* 10 (1986): 511–23.

43. D. S. Bhargava, "Water Quality in Three Typical Rivers in UP: Ganga, Yamuna and Kali" (PhD thesis, Civil Engineering, IIT Kanpur, India, 1983), 266.

44. B. D. Joshi interview in Haridwar, April 2, 2013.

45. Chandra Nautiyal, "Self-purificatory Ganga water facilitates death of pathogenic Eschrichia coli O157:H7," *Current Microbiology* 58 (2009): 25–29.

46. *Rig Veda* 6.61.13, 7.95.1, 6.61.8, 7.36.6, and 7.96.2.

47. Danino, *The Lost River*, 357.

48. Steven G. Darian, "Gaṅgā and Sarasvatī: An Incidence of Mythological Projection," *East and West*, vol. 26. 1–2 (1976): 153–65.

49. Cf. the studies conducted under the aegis of NEERI in Nagpur into various properties of *Ganga jal*. As the government funded them, they have never been released to the public.

Introduction

A Novel We Have Loved

MARK W. DENNIS AND DARREN J. N. MIDDLETON

"April is the cruellest month," T. S. Eliot says; yet spring's sweet showers fall in April and people, according to Chaucer, long to go on pilgrimages.² The power of pilgrimage permeates the world's religions, from Canterbury to Vārānasī, and in April 1994, Peter Owen Publishers released Van C. Gessel's English translation of *Deep River* (*Fukai kawa*, 1993), an emotional quest narrative in which four careworn Japanese tourists journey to India's holy Ganga in search of spiritual as well as existential renewal.³ The story's author, Endō Shūsaku (aka Shusaku Endo [1923–1996]), had just marked his seventy-first birthday. That autumn, Stockholm's literary circles were abuzz with speculation that Endō would be awarded the Nobel Prize in Literature. It was not to be. Endō's younger countryman, Ōe Kenzaburō, was the winner. Gessel informs us that journalists were assembled outside Endō's Tokyo home awaiting the Swedish committee's announcement that he had won.⁴ When Ōe's name was broadcast, the reporters pressed Endō to evaluate the decision before they made their way to Ōe's home. Endō's tactful response involved noting that Ōe excelled at writing about a world without God. We think that Endō here describes himself, not simply Ōe, since Endō was, at seventy-one, an award-winning writer who had spent his decades-long career, trying to give words to faith, doubt, love, anxiety, and transcendent mystery.

Born in Tokyo in 1923, Endō spent his childhood in Dalian, part of Japanese-occupied Manchuria. After his parents' divorce, he returned with his mother to Japan in 1933 and lived in Kobe, where he and his mother, through his aunt's influence, converted to Roman Catholicism.[5] Endō was baptized in 1934 at the age of eleven, and his experience as a Japanese Catholic, which he described as clothes that were ill-fitting, deeply influenced his later literary art, as the present volume, *Navigating* Deep River*: New Perspectives on Shūsaku Endō's Final Novel*, shows. Endō eventually studied at Keiō University, an elite private institution founded by Fukuzawa Yukichi in 1858, just ten years before Japan's Meiji Restoration, which focused on *rangaku*, or "Western learning." Indeed, Endō received a bachelor's degree in French Literature in 1949, an interest that led him to travel to France where he studied Catholic fiction at the University of Lyon. His experience as a Japanese living in the West and attempting to assimilate French culture informed his writing, as did his regular bouts of illness, some of them serious. The pain and weariness of the numerous surgeries Endō endured galvanized him, since *Deep River* might be seen as Endō's own *Book of Job*, Gessel (chapter 9) argues in our anthology. In chapter 10, Justyna W. Kasza alludes to Endō's interest in the story of Job while focusing on *Deep River*'s "autobiographical space," arguing that each of its characters, which we describe in the next paragraph, "embodies a trace of the author."

Endō burst onto the Japanese literary scene in 1955 when *White Person* (*Shiroi Hito*; also, *White Man*) won the Akutagawa Prize, one of Japan's most prestigious literary awards given to young and emerging authors. Over the next forty years, Endō published an extensive body of fiction that includes short stories and novels, which feature wayfarers wrestling with issues of belief and unbelief, Christian presence in non-Christian environments, apostasy and betrayal, indigenous discipleship and Western triumphalism, martyrdom as well as theodicy, and religious pluralism. In *Deep River*, the wayfaring theme emerges through five characters, each one of them walking wounded and wandering through India's solemn geographies, motivated by different reasons and equipped with varied hopes. The assassination of Prime Minister Indira Gandhi punctuates the story of the twists and turns of Endō's pilgrims, but all are inexorably drawn to the Ganga, where their spirituality intensifies. Isobe is a salaryman whose wife has died of cancer. Her deathbed wish urged Isobe to look for her in a future reincarnation, and thus Isobe—a believing skeptic on the subject of the transmigration of souls—visits India, cautiously optimistic of finding her somewhere in the country's felicitous, eulogized spaces. A traumatized veteran of the armed conflict in Burma (now Myanmar), Kiguchi treks to India in search of Buddhist rituals he hopes will soothe the souls of fallen friends and deceased enemies. When a foreign Christian displays many kindnesses toward Tsukada, a sick man also dealing with severe anxiety brought on by his remembrance of war's terror, Kiguchi feels inspired. Another pilgrim, Numada, was raised in Manchuria, and his childhood was marked by an ardent love for animals. Numada believes his pet bird has died in India, and so he visits a bird sanctuary there. Fleeing a failed marriage, Mitsuko explores India on a quest to ascertain life's significance, and there she reunites with Ōtsu, a former school friend, whom she once seduced and then abandoned. Ōtsu is a failed Catholic seminarian, his priestly promise cut short by church superiors appalled by his unorthodox theological views. Outside the church, where some might say there is no salvation, Ōtsu makes meaning by caring for the voiceless of Vārānasī, a beloved city through which flows the sacred Ganga; in imitation of Christ, he helps the outcastes carry corpses to be cremated at the burning *ghāts,* after which their ashes are scattered over the holy river. Ōtsu's pastoral ministry is precarious. When Sikh militants assassinate Prime Minister Indira Gandhi, for example, he becomes entangled in anti-Sikh skirmishes and protests. Inspired by two nuns associated with Mother Teresa's Missionaries of Charity, Mitsuko begins to work alongside India's indigent, and her appreciation for Ōtsu's pantheistic or panentheistic model of God unfurls in unexpectedly spacious directions.

Deep River is not alone of its kind. Throughout Endō's writing runs a generous curiosity about women and men, seemingly lonely without God, and this curiosity displays itself through an acclaimed storytelling skill—vivid plots, hauntingly suggestive characters, tender pathos, and serene humor. Although Endō did not secure the Nobel Prize in Literature, he was the recipient of other tributes during his lifetime, including the Tanizaki Prize for Japanese Literature, awarded in 1966 for *Silence* (*Chinmoku*), the novel that Martin Scorsese recently adapted for the cinema. We feature Scorsese's "Afterword" in our *Approaching* Silence*: New Perspectives on Shusaku Endo's Classic Novel*, an anthology of essays that we designed, among other things, as a movie tie-in.[6] Our current volume, *Navigating* Deep River, is a bookend to *Approaching* Silence.[1] One reason for our saying this involves returning, in the mind's eye, to Endō's final two years.

April may be the "cruellest" month. Beleaguered by poor health throughout his life, Endō reentered the hospital in April 1995, one year after Gessel's translation, but was released long enough to see two screenings of Kumai Kei's adaptation of *Deep River*.[7] Endō reportedly wept at seeing the film, observing that some scenes were better realized than in the novel. In September, Endō suffered a cerebral hemorrhage; this stroke left him unable to speak. Just two months later, he received the highest honor Japan bestows on its citizens, the

Bunka Kunshō (Order of Culture). In June 1996, he began hemodialysis, but passed away on September 29 of that year. Several thousand people in attendance at the funeral services at the St. Ignatius Church in Tokyo placed flowers on the altar. Copies of both *Silence* and *Deep River* were placed in the casket.[8]

Bookends and Titles

Whatever else they signify, *Deep River* and *Silence* are novels that Endō loved. And we love them, too, which is why we view *Navigating* Deep River as a bookend to our *Approaching* Silence. In the earlier anthology's title, *Approaching* connotes our collective effort to help our readers draw closer to *Silence*, the novel's single-word title that suggests a state or condition—that is, a lack of sound. The volume's individual chapters reveal the multivalence of this term, including God's *silence* in the face of human suffering but also, writes Gessel, the *silencing* of the protagonist's ego as he witnesses, and ponders his own role in causing, that suffering among Japan's "hidden Christians."[9] And while that word choice was meant to suggest our movement toward a deeper engagement with the novel, we also understood *Approaching* to signify that which was drawing near to us, from a reverse angle, in relation to George Steiner's arresting metaphor of the *pilot fish*. Steiner thinks the role of the literary critic is like the "pilot fish, those strange tiny creatures, which go out in front of the real thing, the great shark or the great whale, warning, saying to the people, 'It's coming.'"[10] Our use of the word *approach* therefore invoked this metaphorical role of these fish that signal something quite substantial is coming this way—in this case, the fiftieth anniversary of the novel's publication in Japanese but also the *arrival* of Scorsese's adaptation of the novel for the silver screen. In *Approaching* Silence's "Introduction," we further probed the meaning of *it* as a pronoun standing in for *the real thing*, concluding that Endō's *Silence*, like any great literary work, opens out to the multiple readings advanced by our contributors.[11]

Interpretive diversity will be evident to readers of the present volume, *Navigating* Deep River, for which we have selected a different word, the verb *to navigate*. We have done so because of the distinct ways in which we conceive of *silence*, a state or condition marked by an absence of sound, and a *river*, a flowing or surging body of water with a distinct semantic range that generates different sorts of figurative associations.

For instance, in Mark Twain's *The Adventures of Huckleberry Finn*, the mighty Mississippi River serves as a metaphor for the freedom that Huck and Jim must navigate to avoid all manner of dangers. Huck says, "So in two seconds away we went a-sliding down the river, and it did seem so good to be free again and all by ourselves on the big river, and nobody to bother us."[12] While Huck seeks freedom from an abusive family, Jim, a slave, seeks the same freedom from bondage as was sought by those who sang the African American spiritual from which Endō's title is drawn; it begins, "Deep river, Lord: I want to cross over into campground."

Or in Hermann Hesse's *Siddhartha*, a creative retelling of the Buddha's story recounted in Mark Dennis's chapter from *Approaching* Silence, the river plays a central role in the novel, serving for most travelers as an obstacle that blocks them from reaching the other shore from which they will continue on their way. But for those who listen intently to the river's sacred sound *Om*, it becomes, instead, a teacher and pathway to attaining a different sort of freedom than that sought by the African American slaves. Here, it is freedom from the ubiquitous and inevitable suffering that human beings experience in *saṃsāra*—the cycle of birth, death, and rebirth—a spiritual paradigm accepted by Hinduism, Sikhism, and Buddhism, each of which plays a prominent role in *Deep River* and will be the subject of the next section.

To navigate the historical and religious context of the novel, we begin with an introduction to the history and key teachings of these South Asian religions. That material includes a discussion of their roles in the Partition of 1947, which divided the subcontinent into the separate modern states of India and Pakistan, and the religious tensions that have bedeviled the subcontinent ever since. Those tensions led to the assassination of Prime Minister Indira Gandhi by her Sikh bodyguards, one of the novel's key plot elements, which is the subject of Ronald Green's chapter (chapter 4).

Hinduism

As Green and others describe in the chapters that follow, rebirth and reincarnation serve as an important plot element in *Deep River*, especially as they pertain to Isobe, who travels to India in search of his wife Keiko's reincarnation. Just before dying from cancer, she tells her husband in a gasping voice, "I . . . I know for sure . . . I'll be reborn somewhere in this world. Look for me . . . find me . . . promise . . . promise!"[13] After his wife's death, he joins the tour to India led by the Japanese tour guide Enami—the subject of P. A. George's chapter (chapter 11)—to look for her reincarnation, having received information on the topic from scholars at the University of Virginia.

The notion of humans and other creatures being born again and again not only serves as background to *Deep River* but also as a key element within a shared South Asian religious paradigm. Trapped in *saṃsāra* ("wandering" and "world"), human beings transmigrate ceaselessly in the world of birth, death, and rebirth. Although interpreting this cycle differently, each of the indigenous South Asian traditions described below accept the proposition that karma, however understood and calculated, helps determine one's rebirth in variously conceived cosmological systems. Within this paradigm, the ultimate goal of religious practice is to attain liberation from the cycle of *saṃsāra*, a state of freedom commonly known as *mokṣa* in Hinduism, *mukti* in Sikhism, and *nirvāṇa* in Buddhism.

Hinduism traces its roots back almost four millennia to the Vedic tradition practiced by Brahmin priests, who memorized and chanted the Vedic texts while performing sacrifices meant to please the gods, such as Agni and Indra, and maintain cosmic balance.[14] Over time, the highly varied group of traditions that constitute modern-day Hinduism produced many other sacred texts, including the *Upaniṣads*, some of which equate the *ātman*, the individual self or soul, to *Brahman*, the ultimate reality. But blinded by *māyā*, or "illusion," we remain ignorant of this ultimate truth. The *Upaniṣads* and later Hindu texts offer pathways to the realization of the liberated state of *mokṣa* noted above. The *Vedas*, *Upaniṣads*, and other early classical Hindu texts are classified as *śruti*, meaning "that which is heard," to distinguish them from texts that are *smṛti*, or "that which is remembered." The former are generally considered to be authorless and unchanging, holding a special position of authority within the six orthodox Hindu *darśanas* ("viewpoint," "philosophy," or "teaching"), although interpretations of their provenance and authority vary.

Since Hindus believe the *smṛti* texts are of human authorship, they are subject to change and reinterpretation; they thus possess, for some, a lower degree of religious authority. These texts include the *Yoga Sūtras of Patañjali*, two epics (the *Rāmāyaṇa* and *Mahābhārata*), the *Dharmasūtra* and *Dharmaśāstra*, the wide-ranging corpus of the *Purāṇas*, and many others. For instance, the *Manusmṛti*, one of the *Dharmaśāstra* texts, detail one's duty, or *dharma*, within the hierarchical caste system that developed over a long period of time and still exists today. In *Deep River*, the Japanese tour guide Enami tells the group in the informational session before their departure:

> In India there is a religious system of social ranking known as the caste system. They call it *varna jati*. It is very complex, and I can't explain it in simple terms. But it would probably be useful for you to know that there is a group of people who do not fit into

even the lowest varna. These people are known as outcasts or as untouchables. Today the untouchables are called Harijans, a perfunctory title that means "children of God," but in reality they are a people who have been subjected to bigotry from early times. As you witness this discrimination on your trip, it may be disturbing to you, but please bear in mind that there is a long religious and historical background to this situation.[15]

While much more complex on the ground as Enami suggests, the system places the Brahmin priests at the top, followed by the warriors (*kśatriya*), merchants and farmers (*vaiśya*), and laborers (*śūdra*). Hindus describe the top three castes as *dvija*, or "twice born," since children of each group go through a caste-specific initiation ceremony in which they undergo spiritual rebirth. But these texts also describe the outcasts, noted by Enami, as occupying a social space beneath even that of the *śūdras*.[16] The *Dharmaśāstra* and other texts addressing this system assert members of this caste are born into this lowly position because of a negative karmic debt carried forward from a previous lifetime; as such, their duty is to perform the polluting jobs shunned by the other castes, such as cleaning latrines, working with leather, and, as we see in *Deep River*, carrying corpses to the burning *ghāts* and cremating them beside the Ganga. Ōtsu, whom several essayists take up, joins them in this activity in imitation of Christ; at the end of the novel, while helping carry a corpse, a mob mistakenly attacks and seriously injures him.

The *Purāṇas*, part of the *smṛti* literature, and other texts put forth *bhakti*, or "devotion," toward a particular deity as a central Hindu religious practice. Hindus can express *bhakti* through *pūjā*, the ritual bathing of statues; *bhajans*, singing hymns dedicated to that deity; and *yātrā*, or pilgrimage, to the temples and other sites associated with a particular deity. In the *bhakti* traditions, many Hindus express devotion to the *deva*, male deities like Śiva and Viṣṇu, and to the latter's *avatars*, or "descents" into the world, such as Kṛṣṇa, an *avatar* of Viṣṇu. Devotees also express devotion to the *devī*, female deities who manifest in multiple forms, both warm and compassionate as well as fierce and wrathful. Possessing *śakti*, or divine feminine energy and power, the *devī* include Kālī and Chāmundā, two goddesses who figure prominently in Endō's novel.

At the informational meeting before the tour to India, Enami advises the tourists-pilgrims as follows:

"Hinduism is very complex, and I can't explain it in simple terms. I think the best way is to have you look at the images of their gods after we actually arrive there. They believe in many different gods, and let me show you a few slides right now."

A peculiar female image was projected on to the screen. With one foot she trampled on the corpse of a man, and her neck was adorned not with a necklace but with severed human heads that she had flung over her shoulder with one of her four arms.

"This is a representation of the goddess Kālī, which often adorns temples and homes in India. The holy mother Mary in Christianity is a symbol of tender maternal love, but the goddesses of India are for the most part called earth-mother goddesses, and while they are gentle deities at times, they are also fearsome beings. There is one goddess in particular, Chāmundā, who has taken upon herself all of the sufferings of the people of India. I want to be sure to take all of you to see her image."

When the lights came on, Mrs Okubo exclaimed, "Whoo, that was scary!," making everyone chuckle.[17]

During the tour, some members of the group become fascinated by images of these deities in the Hindu temples they visit while others find them repulsive. For instance, Mitsuko becomes intrigued by Kālī and Chāmundā and, in the final scene, immerses herself in the deep waters of the Ganga, which is the subject of Mini Chandran's chapter (chapter 2). Chandran mentions a scene, which Mark Dennis returns to in his chapter (chapter 1), in which Mitsuko says to herself:

> *What I can believe in now is the sight of all these people, each carrying his or her own individual burdens, praying at this deep river.* At some point, the words Mitsuko muttered to herself were transmuted into the words of a prayer. *I believe that the river embraces these people and carries them away. A river of humanity. The sorrows of this deep river of humanity. And I am a part of it.*[18]

As Chandran explains, the river is also known as Ganga Devi, the goddess whose sacred waters are the destination of one of the most popular Hindu pilgrimages, a key form of *bhakti*. Indeed, India's landscape is dotted with sacred sites that serve as pilgrimage destinations (*tīrtha*), including the Dakshineshwar temple dedicated to Kālī and the many Kṛṣṇa temples of Vrindavan in the north and the Ayyappan pilgrimage in the south.[19]

In anticipation of death, many Hindus hope to make their final pilgrimage to the Ganga, where it flows through Vārānasī (also known as Benares and Kashi), believing that to die in the city and have one's ashes sprinkled on the river's waters guarantees liberation, or *mokṣa*. Mini Chandran observes, "The Ganga is not just a river to the Hindus of India. She is a goddess to be worshipped, the deliverer from the mortal coil of birth and rebirth, and a presence in the mind of each believer even if far removed from her physically."

Sikhism

Sikhism, another South Asian religious tradition, plays a key role in *Deep River*. As Ronald Green discusses in his chapter, Indira Gandhi's 1984 assassination precipitates the novel's climactic events, in which a mob attacks Ōtsu, who had been carrying corpses with the Harijans to the burning *ghāts*.[20] Gandhi's assassination unleashed an orgy of religiously inspired violence against the Sikh community, which traces its origins to Guru Nanak (1469–1539).

Born near the modern Pakistani city of Lahore into the merchant caste of a Hindu family, Nanak and his friend Mardana, a Muslim, first gained notice by playing music to express their devotion to God. One day, Nanak disappeared into the River Bein, only to surface some three days later, having experienced a spiritual transformation. For the rest of his life, he traveled in the northwestern part of the Indian subcontinent to teach the oneness of God, which served as the central tenet of Sikhism, a word derived from the Punjabi *sikh*, which means "disciple" or "student."

Guru Nanak and his successors viewed the one God as eternal, existing beyond the cycle of birth, death, and rebirth described above, thereby offering a fascinating mix of beliefs in both monotheism and transmigration within *saṃsāra*. Some observers also describe Sikhism as a panentheistic religion,[21] which Darren J. N. Middleton (chapter 13) defines as "the participating of everything in God." Sikhs refer to the oneness of God as *Waheguru*, the "Wonderful Lord," but also as *Satnām*, "True Name," and *Akal Purakh*, "Immortal, Timeless Being," among others. Sikh teachings appear in the *Guru Granth Sahib* (also known as the *Adi Granth*), the tradition's central text, written in the Punjabi language using the Gurmukhī ("[from the] mouth of the guru") script. Central Sikh practices articulated in the *Guru Granth Sahib* include *nām japō*, the repetition of God's name; *kirtan*, the recitation of sacred hymns; *simran*, meditation on passages from the text; and the pursuit of selfless service and social justice.

Guru Nanak and the other nine human gurus of Sikhism lived during the Mughal era (1526–40 and 1555–1857), a period of Muslim rule that begins with Emperor Babur (1483–1530), who defeated the last ruler of the

Delhi Sultanate in 1526 in the First Battle of Panipat. The Mughal Empire survived for more than three hundred years with shifting borders and varying degrees of power. At its zenith, the empire controlled almost the entire Indian subcontinent, except for a small section in the very south and parts of modern-day Afghanistan. Building capitals in Agra, Lahore, Delhi, and other cities, the Mughal emperors varied greatly in their degree of religious tolerance.

For instance, Akbar (1542–1605) and his son Jahangir (1569–1627), the third and fourth emperors, respectively, expressed deep interest in other religions, and the former may have even started a new ecumenical religious movement known as the Din-i-Ilahi, or the "Religion of God." But other Mughal emperors were less tolerant and, in some cases, persecuted the Sikhs. For example, Guru Tegh Bahadur, the ninth Sikh guru, was executed by Aurangzeb (1618–1707) for refusing to convert to Islam. In response, Bahadur's son, Guru Gobind Singh (1666–1708), the tenth and final human guru, founded the Sikh warrior community known as the Khalsa in 1699 and introduced the Five Ks traditionally worn by Sikhs initiated into that community: uncut hair (*kesh*), a wooden comb (*khanga*), a cotton undergarment (*kachera*), an iron bracelet (*kara*), and a dagger (*kirpan*). The *kirpan* serves as both a weapon and a symbol of defending the faith against external threats. Indeed, over time, the Sikhs developed a strong martial tradition and gained wide recognition as effective soldiers, serving in various roles in the armies of the British East India Company and, after the establishment of direct rule in 1858, the British government, as described below.

Before his death, Guru Gobindh Singh bestowed guruship onto the *Guru Granth Sahib*, which contains 1,430 pages divided into thirty-one sections. Sikhs refer to its words and content as *gurbāni*, or "the speech of wisdom," pointing toward the religious insights of the six Sikh gurus whose hymns the text includes. Although the bulk of the text comes from these six teachers, it also contains hymns from Hindu *bhakti* saints and one Muslim Sufi saint. The *Guru Granth Sahib* is installed in a *gurdwara*, or temple, with the Harmandir Sahib (Temple of God)—known as the Golden Temple in English—serving as the tradition's central temple. Guru Amar Das, the third Sikh guru, conceived of the temple, located in Amritsar, a city in the Punjab region of northwest India and eastern Pakistan; its construction began, however, under the supervision of his successor Guru Ram Das.

The temple was the location of a violent encounter between Sikh militants and the Indian military that preceded Prime Minister Indira Gandhi's assassination on October 31, 1984. As Ronald Green elaborates in his chapter, the Sikh militants were led by Jarnail Singh Bhindranwale, who sought to purify the tradition by emphasizing traditional Sikh practices, eschewing alcohol and other mind-altering substances, and supporting the implementation of the 1974 Anandpur Sahib Resolution. Created by the Akali Dal, a Sikh political party, the resolution called for free expression of Sikh identity and greater autonomy. The Sikhs intended the resolution to address numerous religious and political grievances, but it did not go so far as to call for the creation of Khalistan (Land of the Pure), a separate homeland for the Sikhs that had been an issue at the time of Partition. In response to Bhindranwale's stockpiling weapons in the Golden Temple, Prime Minister Indira Gandhi authorized the use of force as part of Operation Blue Star. Many Sikh militants, including Bhindranwale, and Indian soldiers died in the attack, which destroyed large sections of Sikhism's holiest site. In retaliation, two Sikh bodyguards shot her at close range as she walked through the garden of the prime minister's residence to an interview with the English actor Peter Ustinov. This attack unleashed the ferocious anti-Sikh violence that is a central event in the last section of *Deep River*.

Partition 1947

As Sikhism was growing during the early part of the Mughal period, so, too, were Britain's ever-greater commercial ties to the subcontinent. Over time, the British East India Company established a strong commercial presence in Mughal India,[22] slowly building up an army comprised mainly of Indian soldiers, known as *sepoys*, who came from various religious and ethnic groups. Eventually, as the power of the Mughals waned, so did the power of their emperors, reduced to the status of pensioners of the company with little actual power.

In 1857, Hindu and Muslim *sepoys* became incensed by a rumor that the new cartridge of the Enfield rifle was being coated with the fat of cows and pigs. Since soldiers had to bite into the greased end of the cartridge to release the gunpowder, which they then poured into the rifle's muzzle, *sepoys* of both religions felt deeply offended by being put in the position of performing a sacrilegious act. For this and other reasons, large numbers rebelled against the company in the north, a momentous event of South Asian history remembered by many in India as the First War of Liberation but by the British as the Sepoy Rebellion.[23] The company eventually crushed this uprising, in part with the help of Sikh soldiers who had remained loyal to it.

In the aftermath, the British government passed the 1858 Government of India Act that placed India under direct governmental rule. It would remain so for a period of almost ninety years that is described as the Raj, or "rule," in which India served as the crown jewel of the British Empire. During this period, protests against British rule intensified under the leadership of Mahatma Gandhi, who had spent some twenty years advocating on behalf of Indians living in South Africa, Jawaharlal Nehru (Indira Gandhi's father), Muhammad Ali Jinnah (leader of the Muslim League), B. R. Ambedkar (leader of the Dalits), Master Tara Singh (a Sikh leader), and many other deeply fascinating figures from the Indian independence movement.

Moreover, once it became clear that the British were leaving, the many factions who had fought for independence sought to secure their own, generally contradictory, visions of an independent country. For instance, Gandhi, Nehru, and the leadership of the Congress Party pushed hard for a unified India, recognizing that Hindus, possessing a vast majority, could shape independent India's development to their own liking. Many, but not all, Muslims sought an independent Muslim state, which their leader Jinnah called Pakistan (Land of the Pure). But different Hindu and Muslim groups engaged in impassioned disagreements, and many other voices advocated alternative visions of postindependence India, including the Sikhs, Dalits, communists, the so-called Princely States, and others.

Finally, on August 15, 1947, when the British "quit" India, the country was divided in two: the Dominion of India and the Dominion of Pakistan. Nehru, the leader of independent India, famously described this moment in his "Tryst with Destiny" speech that reads, in part:

> Long years ago we made a tryst with destiny, and now the time comes when we shall redeem our pledge, not wholly or in full measure, but very substantially. At the stroke of the midnight hour, when the world sleeps, India will awake to life and freedom. A moment comes, which comes but rarely in history, when we step out from the old to the new, when an age ends, and when the soul of a nation, long suppressed, finds utterance.[24]

As noted above, this division, commonly referred to as "Partition," was a cataclysmic event in modern South Asian history that convulsed the region and whose effects still resonate in the present day. It would be difficult to overstate the trauma that accompanied the immense violence and human suffering that Partition unleashed on the Indian subcontinent, with estimates of six million Indians displaced and at least one million more—Hindus, Sikhs, Muslims, and others—losing their lives in a tidal wave of attacks and reprisals. Many critical events from South Asian history that followed, including the assassination of Indira Gandhi, have antecedents in the poisoned soil of Partition.

Those events include the 1948 assassination of Mahatma Gandhi by Nathuram Godse, a member of a Hindu nationalist organization who, in his final address to the court titled "Why I killed Gandhi," explained that he believed Gandhi was giving too much away to the Muslims. Unfortunately, Gandhi's murder was just one in a long history of politically and religiously motivated assassinations on the subcontinent, a seemingly insatiable demon who stretched its ugly fingers forward into the 1980s, when Indira Gandhi, a Hindu, was gunned down in her garden. Afterward, her son Rajiv scattered her ashes over the Himalayas from an Indian transport plane flown at twenty-five thousand feet "between Gangotri, the source of the holy Ganges River, to Amarnath, a traditional shrine for Hindu pilgrims."[25] In 1991, just seven years later, Rajiv Gandhi would also become the victim of assassination, killed by a suicide bomber from the Liberation Tigers of Tamil Eelam (LTTE) in retaliation for his sending to Sri Lanka the Indian Peace Keeping Force (IPKF), which, claimed Sri Lankan Tamils, committed atrocities against their community.

Buddhism

The climax of *Deep River*, which occurs soon after Indira Gandhi's assassination, takes place in Vārāṇasī along the banks of the Ganga, which flows through the city and offers a fascinating and cacophonic mix of sacred and secular activities. Mark Williams (chapter 5) and other contributors note that it serves as the novel's locus for the main characters' spiritual reflection and insight. For instance, while Mitsuko immerses herself in its holy waters as described above, Kiguchi, a soldier who survived the Japanese army's retreat during World War II through the Burmese jungles, stands beside the river and chants from Pure Land Buddhist texts. At the information session before the trip, he tells Enami and the others, "I lost a lot of friends during the war in the fighting in Burma, and I fought against some Indian soldiers myself, so I thought maybe I could request a memorial service on behalf of comrade and foe alike."[26] Williams interprets this scene as follows:

> But it is only as he himself stands beside the river that he senses that he can now "understand for the first time why Shakyamuni appeared in this land." Here, for the first time, his journey assumes

a spiritual dimension, enabling him to intone the *Amida Sūtra*. This may be a passage that he had "committed to memory"; at this point, however, it comes to assume a new meaning for him, as the esoteric text comes to assume a more personal significance. More specifically, he is now in a position, for the first time in his life, to make sense of the scripture, so familiar and yet somehow so foreign to him, that "Good and Evil are as one"—to acknowledge the presence of the "seeds of salvation buried in every act of evil." Only now do the words and actions of Gaston, the hospital volunteer with whom he had shared some fleeting exchanges as the two cared for the dying Tsukada, begin to take root in his heart; only now does the narrative hint at a newfound inner peace that will remain with him as he returns home.

The *Amida Sūtra* mentioned by Williams is a central text in the Japanese Pure Land Buddhist tradition, which is one of many Buddhist schools that trace their origins, in distinct ways, to Śākyamuni, the "Sage of the Śākya" clan, whose appearance in the world Kiguchi has understood, having approached the deep river and chanted the sūtra's sacred words. Better known as the Buddha (the "Awakened One"), Śākyamuni lived in the Ganga region and would have crossed that same deep river a number of times, including on his last journey from Pāṭaliputra (modern-day Patna) to Vaiśālī (now an archaeological site in Bihar state), passing into final *nirvāṇa* at Kuśīnagara, not far from Vārāṇasī, some 2,500 years ago. Before his death, he put forth a distinct vision of the path to liberation from what Mini Chandran describes as "the mortal coil of birth and rebirth."

Śākyamuni was born in Lumbinī, located in modern-day Nepal, one of the Buddhist pilgrimage sites that the tour visits in the novel that also include Bodh Gayā, the site of the Buddha's enlightenment, Sarnath, where he delivered his first lecture, and Kuśīnagara, noted above, where he died, entering *parinirvāṇa*, the final *nirvāṇa*. Given the name Siddhārtha ("One who Attains the Goal"), he belonged to Hinduism's warrior caste and grew up leading a sheltered life of luxury and sensual indulgence inside his father's palace. Venturing outside the cloistered palace walls, however, he witnessed "four passing sights": a sick man, an aged man, a dead man, and a wandering ascetic who was "dead to the world." The first three, which represent common sorts of human suffering, agitated his mind, while the fourth planted the seed that would lead him to abandon his life of luxury and seek out the cause and cure for the suffering he had witnessed.

Having left the palace in pursuit of such understanding, he studied with several teachers but was unable to discover the spiritual insights he sought; he then joined a group of five ascetics and practiced severe spiritual austerities. But he eventually abandoned that lifestyle too, taking up a "middle path" that moderated these extremes between sensual indulgence and asceticism. He then sat in meditation beneath the *bodhi* (wisdom) tree, seeking answers to his questions about the cause of human suffering and the nature of reality. Buddhist texts describe Siddhārtha being subjected to ferocious attacks by Māra (Death) and his minions; a central figure in Buddhism, one can understand Māra to represent our negative mental states—especially the three poisons of greed, anger, and ignorance—that lead to actions that generate bad karma. But Siddhārtha remained steadfast in his meditative state and experienced a spiritual awakening wherein he understood the cause of and the cure for human suffering.

This epiphany marked his transformation from Prince Siddhārtha to Buddha, the teacher who would, over the next forty-five years, travel in the region near Vārānasī and the Ganga, teaching all who would listen.[27] Soon after his enlightenment, he found his former ascetic companions in the deer park of Sarnath, located not far to the northeast of Vārānasī; he taught them about the nature of reality encapsulated in the so-called Four Noble Truths whose promulgation is remembered by Buddhists as the "First Turning of the Wheel of Dharma." The truths he expounded describe the cause of human suffering in *saṃsāra* and the path to freedom from it—the state of *nirvāṇa*. Before addressing those teachings, which Mark Dennis will use to interpret several themes taken up by our essayists, we will first examine the transmission of Buddhism outside of the subcontinent where its many schools, including Pure Land, took root.

Although Buddhism would thrive outside of India, it lost much of its vitality in the land of its birth. At the informational meeting before the trip, Enami explains this development to the group: "The caste system has, in any case, been a pillar that has supported Hinduism and supported Indian society, and as a result Buddhism has weakened there."[28] He cites the figure of just some 3 million Indian Buddhists at a time when the population would have been about 750 million, surprising some of those going on the trip, whose "main purpose in traveling to India was to visit famous locales associated with Buddhism, and the impression was strong in their minds that India was the land of the Buddha, the land of Sakyamuni."[29]

From the Buddha's initial teaching offered to his five ascetic companions, distinct schools developed as teachers and practitioners traveled south from the northern part of the subcontinent to Sri Lanka and then eastward to the area occupied by the modern southeast Asian countries of Burma, Thailand, Laos, and Vietnam. In contrast to these schools, commonly referred to as the Theravāda (School of the Elders), a distinct tradition moved north and east through Central Asia into China, and from China on to the Korean peninsula, and then to the Japanese archipelago. This latter tradition proclaimed itself the Mahāyāna, or "Great Vehicle," ramifying into distinct schools and sub-schools, mostly in East Asia, including the Japanese Zen and Pure Land schools from the Kamakura era (1185–1333).

The Mahāyāna schools put forth the *bodhisattva* (wisdom being) as their ideal in contrast to the *arhat*, or "worthy one," of the Theravāda traditions. The Mahāyāna schools imagined buddhas in addition to Śākyamuni, including the Buddha Lokeśvararāja, the teacher of the Bodhisattva Dharmākara, taken up below. Buddhists have used this multivalent term *bodhisattva* to describe the Buddha in his previous lives, kings and emperors who patronize the Dharma, and those who, having generated the mind of enlightenment (*bodhicitta*), vow to postpone final liberation until all sentient beings have attained freedom from suffering. Among this third group, some embody key Buddhist principles, such as the compassion of Avalokiteśvara and the wisdom of Mahāsthāmaprāpta. Indeed, these two *bodhisattvas* often appear in Buddhist iconography seated on either side of the Buddha Amitābha, the central figure of Pure Land Buddhism, which provides the lens through which Dennis Hirota (chapter 14) reads *Deep River* but is also touched upon by Mark Williams, Zhange Ni (chapter 3), and other essayists.

Pure Land Buddhism

Hirota's chapter draws from the work of Shinran (1173–1263), the founding figure of Jōdo Shinshū, one of the two main forms of Japanese Pure Land Buddhism.[30] Particularly popular in East Asia, the Pure Land schools trace their origins to a set of forty-eight vows made by the bodhisattva Dharmākara predicated on his attaining buddhahood. Those vows include the eighteenth vow, which guarantees that if he were to attain buddhahood, then all sentient beings who call out his name with sincerity just ten times would be reborn in his land. Upon making these vows, Dharmākara's teacher, the Buddha Lokeśvararāja, prophesied that his student would eventually rule over a pure land called Sukhāvatī, the Pure Land of the West (literally, "Land Filled with Bliss") as the Buddha Amitābha (Buddha of Infinite Light).

Indeed, having practiced the "perfections" of the *bodhisattva* for a very long time, Dharmākara realized his teacher's prediction and, through that arduous practice, created a huge store of merit from which sentient beings can benefit simply by calling out his name. This practice, known in Japanese Pure Land traditions as the *nembutsu* (remembering the Buddha), involves reciting the simple mantra, *namu Amida Butsu* (I pay homage to the Buddha Amitābha). The goal of this and other Pure Land practices is to be reborn in Amitābha's Pure Land of Sukhāvatī. Another such practice is to chant, as Kiguchi does near the Ganga, passages from the *Amida Sūtra* or one of the tradition's other key texts.[31] Since Pure Land practitioners rely on the stored pool of merit and salvific power of the Buddha Amitābha in these and other ways, their practice is oriented toward *tariki*, or "other power." In contrast, scholars describe *jiriki*, or "self power," as the central orientation of Zen Buddhism and other Japanese Buddhist schools since liberation is attained through the self-effort associated with seated meditation, following the ethical teachings, and so on. Despite such differences, these and other schools of Buddhism share a core set of ideas, touched upon above, about the nature of reality expressed in the Four Noble Truths and the other doctrines that Mark Dennis takes up in his (the anthology's first) chapter.

Catholic Sensibilities

Faith in the Word made flesh in Jesus Christ represents the basic, energizing impulse behind the many as well as varied Roman Catholic contributions to culture, including literary art, Robert Barron declares:

> Essential to the Catholic mind is what I would characterize as a keen sense of the prolongation of the Incarnation throughout space and time, an extension that is made possible through the mystery of the church. Catholics see God's continued enfleshment in the oil, water, bread, imposed hands, wine, and salt of the sacraments; they appreciate it in the gestures, movements, incensations, and songs of the Liturgy; they savor it in the texts, arguments, and debates of the theologians; they sense it in the graced governance of popes and bishops; they love it in the struggles and missions of the saints; *they know it in the writings of Catholic poets* and in the cathedrals crafted by Catholic architects, artists, and workers. In short, all this discloses to the Catholic eye and mind the ongoing presence of the Word made flesh, namely Christ.[32]

For our purposes, Barron's observations may be summarized thusly: Catholic aesthetics flow from belief in the Incarnation as a perpetual reality. Mary R. Reichardt concurs. In her view, Catholic artists find God everywhere:

> The vital Catholic sense of Jesus dwelling with us on earth, animating and transforming everything that exists, and the consequent sacramentality of all creation, permeates Catholic literature. All things, events, and experiences "tell" of God and can lead us to God if we have the eyes to see and the ears to hear. By grounding their work in the concrete, material world, literary artists in the Catholic tradition can reveal the supernatural and convey spiritual truths. Thus literature, too, can serve as a sacramental, a vehicle of grace for those disposed to receive it.[33]

If Catholic writers like Flannery O'Connor grasp literature in this way, and Elizabeth Cameron Galbraith (chapter 7) compares O'Connor and Endō in her chapter, then it is because they open their eyes wide and describe how life is awash with signs and wonders of God's graces and goodness.

Navigating Deep River accentuates how Endō models such incarnational aesthetics. We see it in the longing and loss at the heart of the five main characters in *Deep River*, for instance, and how every gesture they make is an outward sign or, better put, a sacramental, of their inner disposition. We witness it in the novel's imagery of the servant-God, taken from Isaiah 53, which recurs throughout Endō's novel, beginning with Mitsuko's chance discovery of the biblical text in a chapel and ending with the *alter Christus* Ōtsu struggling to empty himself by attending to the sick and the dying at the river of cleansing and rebirth. Furthermore, the divine sacrament is in the wider world, careening and then releasing itself through mountains, trees, and those rivers, like the Ganga, which are an extension of God and repeat the divine glory, disclosing the holy in the common. Catholicism's pansacramentalism floods *Deep River*, and our essayists appraise as well as probe the part that this particular overlay plays in Endō's lifelong artistic and spiritual quest to craft a version of Christianity that made most sense to him.

Mark Bosco and Christopher Wachal (chapter 6) note that the stress on sacramentalism that revitalized the Second Vatican Council (aka: Vatican II [1962–65]), which inspired Catholicism's wider sense of divine mercy as well as a fresh openness to non-Christian faith traditions, was not lost on Endō. *Deep River* denotes a convergence of Endō's long-standing theological challenges, they argue, and certainly the challenge of religious diversity or pluralism, metaphorically situated in the confluence of the Ganga. Mark Williams and Darren J. N. Middleton also touch on Endō's Vatican II–inspired Christian inclusivism. Middleton contextualizes Endō's belief in God's ubiquitous grace within the context of post–Vatican II thought, for example, and he notes that such thinking displays pansacramental or, as he puts it, panentheistic considerations. If we speak of the Incarnation as a perpetual reality, realized through the mystery of the church across the ages, then the church may best be grasped as a pilgrim people; and, the church's evolution is the evolution of its parishioners, and it is a part of God's evolution, but the church does not and need not monopolize divine grace. Ōtsu's panentheistic God dwells in all things, all people, and in all religions.

Endō's Catholic sensibilities were never fixed; rather, they flowed like a river. Maeri Megumi (chapter 8) announces, for example, that in the autumn of his life, Endō seemed to be "catholic" with a small "c," which is to say: Endō welcomed and incorporated a wide variety of ideas. Emi Mase-Hasegawa agrees (chapter 12). She reveals that Endō read and admired Protestant, as well as Catholic, writers, including the British theologian John Hick, who identified with Great Britain's United Reformed Church[34] until he joined the Quakers shortly before he passed in 2012. Hick's often-controversial belief that God has many names influenced Endō's imagination, as we discover, even if we also learn that our essayists agree to disagree on the theological appropriateness of Hick's theocentric model of global faiths.

Megumi sympathizes with theocentrism, though it must be said that her focus involves showing how Endō's small-c catholicism helped him succeed in pushing beyond his lifelong fascination with religious and national identity formation. *Deep River* delineates universal or basic human problems, she maintains, and in ways that seem meticulous and exigent and true, using India as a microcosm of our world. Put differently: Catholicism always appeared to have a hand at Endō's elbow, as it were, yet toward the end of his life it was a gentle touch rather than a firm push.

With Endō at his elbow, S. Brent Plate's writerly imagination also appears to move from Catholicism to small-c catholicism. In our volume's Afterword, for example, he reflects on his experiences walking the Camino de Santiago, a traditionally "Catholic" pilgrimage route in Spain that today attracts hundreds of thousands of Buddhists, atheists, secularists, Jews, and Christians from around the world. Plate reads *Deep River* through this lens, finding a deeply human quest for fulfillment in the act of traveling. This quest, he finds, has very little to do with doctrines, dogmas, or even beliefs. Instead, the cross-cultural activity of today's spiritual travels, whether to Santiago or the Ganga, reaffirms the physicality of human bodies moving across landscapes—wayfarers sensing the sacred in the everyday. In the deep regions where human bodies, with their sore feet and blisters, meet the earth, sky, and waters of landscapes, a sacramental interreligious activity can be found.

Faith, Hope, Love, and Reading

"Faith and fiction alike deal with a greater mystery than either fully appreciates," Paul Lakeland says, "and each has much more in common with the other than it suspects."[35] Essayists in our volume agree. And we love *Deep River* for its attractively wide and compellingly varied approach to telling a tale that blends human meaning-seeking and divine transcendence in a way that avoids crude conflicts or reductionistic hostilities between the two. We hope that this novel, crafted in the seclusion born of Endō's infirmity will, through our anthology, reach new readers, achieving communion and, of course, love.

We have divided the collection's essays into two categories: historical and comparative approaches (chapters 1–5) and literary and theological approaches (chapters 6–14). As is evident from the material above, we have not offered a synopsis of each chapter, a common and useful technique we employed in the Introduction of *Approaching* Silence. Here, we have decided instead to cast the work as an imagined literary pilgrimage to but also within the deep river Ganga, wherein each essayist helps our readers *navigate* a portion of the novel. As such, the tidiness and linearity of our previous approach seemed incongruent with the fascinating intermingling of clamor and solemnity, raucousness and reverence the novel's characters experience at the river's sacred banks, described eloquently by Julian Crandall Hollick in his Foreword. To honor that strategy, we have briefly mentioned each contributor's chapter above as a signpost pointing forward to a particular piece of the journey. Mark W. Dennis's first chapter offers additional context by discussing those chapters using a Buddhist reading of the novel.

The volume is meant to serve not only as a bookend to our previous *Silence* anthology, but also as a testament to the enduring significance of this beautiful novel beloved by each of the contributors. While *Navigating* Deep River offers a wide range of interpretive approaches, it naturally is not exhaustive, including but a few contributions from Japan where scholarly interest remains robust. Indeed, recent Japanese-language scholarship addresses a wide range of topics, including the broader significance of the novel within Endō's literary art.[36] These studies investigate how *Deep River* represents the "closing of the loop" in Endō's theological journey, a topic taken up in the present volume, while others address particular Christian or theological elements, such as the novel's connection to Isaiah 53. Others read *Deep River* as a declaration of the author's mature Christian faith, which embraces the religious pluralism that is central to the novel.

Another group of Japanese language studies examines the novel through the lens of its Indian cultural and religious elements. For instance, scholars investigate the significant role played by the Hindu goddess Chāmundā—a role addressed by several of our contributors—with some offering comparisons to Mary. These India-centered studies include investigations of how the Ganga embraces lost souls within its healing waters as well as the search for the *anima* in the sacred landscape of India.

Several Japanese language studies focus on the novel's other major themes, such as suffering, reincarnation, and the search for an authentic sense of self and a meaningful life. They take up, for instance, the suffering experienced in sickness and old age in the context of modern life and the related concern of searching for authenticity and meaning amid the suffering that pervades the cycle of *saṃsāra*. But reincarnation is addressed in other ways. For example, one study compares it to the process of resurrection.

Japanese language studies also address a wide range of other topics that include love in Asia's natural environment, a companion in the wilderness, and the role of the novel's narrator as Companion. Another addresses the meaning of cannibalism, which is a key element in the story of the Japanese soldier Kiguchi and is addressed by Zhange Ni.

Finally, Japanese scholars continue to be fascinated by comparisons of Endō's literary art to that of Graham Greene, an issue taken up by several essayists in *Approaching* Silence. Darren J. N. Middleton, for instance, considered "how the relationship between Endo and Greene influenced the other's literary work by examining letters, publicity blurbs, and other sorts of materials that illuminate this crucial relationship." He investigated three points of theological agreement between the two novelists: their desire to probe the mystery of sin, affirm the breadth of God's mercy, and to "emphasize faith as troubled commitment." Despite our two volumes dedicated to Endō's work and the other English-language studies listed in the bibliography, Middleton maintains that Endō has not been given his due as a twentieth-century Catholic novelist, equal in stature to Greene, O'Connor, and Evelyn Waugh.

Despite this wide range of scholarly approaches, there is still much depth to be plumbed; as such, we offer just a few suggestions for future research. As readers will see in the pages that follow, *Deep River* is an instructive example of comparative religion and literature, opening itself up to all manner of hermeneutical approaches.[37] These approaches include comparisons to other Catholic novelists like that made by Elizabeth Cameron Galbraith in this volume, but also pilgrimage novels, such as Graham Swift's *Last Orders*, set in England and published in 1996, the year of Endō's death, and Lee Smith's *The Last Girls* (2002), which takes place along the Mississippi River, the setting for Mark Twain's *The Adventures of Huckleberry Finn* mentioned above.

Finally, we have permitted variation in the use of spellings and diacritic markings. For instance, the quotation from the tour guide Enami above includes the phrase *varna jati*, which could also be rendered with diacritic markings as *varṇa jāti*, as we have done in an endnote. Readers will also see both "Ganges" and "Ganga" to refer to the deep river, as well as variation in Japanese names, which are generally written, surname first, in *kanji*. For example, the author's name is written in *kanji* as 遠藤 (Endō) 周作 (Shūsaku). Long vowel sounds, which appear in both his names, are indicated in transliterations with a macron over the vowel, although these diacritical markings are omitted in some renderings in this work. We have, however, left them in them in the title, giving us "Shūsaku Endō." We respect both renderings in our anthology, leaving individual essayists to adopt their own style.

Notes

1. Copies of *Silence* and *Deep River* were placed in Endō's casket in 1996, as we explain later, and clearly he loved both novels—perhaps as summaries of his life and work. Additionally, we note that Endō's fondness for François Mauriac's *Thérèse Desqueyroux* appears in his book-length essay, *Watashi no ai shita shōsetsu* [A Novel I Have Loved] (Tokyo: Shinchōsha, 1985). Like our 2015 anthology on Endō's *Silence*, the present volume represents our token of affection for a novel we have loved.

2. See T. S. Eliot, *The Wasteland and Other Poems* (New York: Harcourt Brace Jovanovich, 1979), 29. Also see Geoffrey Chaucer, *The Canterbury Tales* (London and New York: Penguin Classics, 2003), 3.

3. For the Japanese version, see Endō Shūsaku, *Fukai kawa* (Tokyo: Kōdansha, 1993). And for the English translation, see Shusaku Endo, *Deep River*, trans. Van C. Gessel (New York: New Directions, 1994). We should clarify the use of texts: When citing from Endō's work, the present volume's essayists use editions to hand, and each chapter provides full bibliographical information. For additional details regarding Endō's literary art and secondary or critical sources, see the section entitled "For Further Reading," which is located at the anthology's close.

4. Personal e-mail to the editors, July 10, 2017.

5. For additional biographical details, see: Mark B. Williams, *Endō Shūsaku: A Literature of Reconciliation* (London and New York: Routledge, 1999), 225–27.

6. Martin Scorsese, "Afterword," in Mark W. Dennis and Darren J. N. Middleton, eds., *Approaching* Silence*: New Perspectives on Shusaku Endo's Classic Novel* (London and New York: Bloomsbury, 2015), 397–98.

7. In the decade or so leading up to the 1993 publication of *Fukai kawa*, Japanese society was convulsed by political, economic, and religious crises that occasioned national soul-searching. These include the rise of the Aum Shinrikyō cult, led by Asahara Shōkō who was executed in July 2018. The cult manufactured and then released sarin gas in the Tokyo subway system, killing twelve people. Members of the group were also found guilty of kidnapping and murdering a Japanese lawyer and his family who was working on behalf of former cult members, as well as the murder of other Japanese citizens inside and outside the group.

The late 1980s also included several attacks by the Japanese Red Army, which sought to foment a Marxist revolution that would lead to the overthrow of the Japanese state. This period also witnessed the 1988 Recruit (a Japanese human resources company) scandal, involving insider trading and corruption charges leveled against prominent politicians and business leaders. Although politicians from several parties were implicated, the ruling LDP (Liberal Democratic Party) was hurt quite badly by the scandal, forcing the dissolution of the cabinet of LDP prime minister Noboru Takeshita. The scandal led to the short-lived prime ministership of Morihiro Hosokawa, the first non-LDP government since 1955.

The period also included the bursting of the Japanese economic bubble, which had been preceded by the rapid appreciation of real estate prices and stock values from the mid-1980s until late 1991, when prices began falling. The aftermath of this catastrophic economic reversal was the so-called lost decade wherein the Japanese economy remained stagnant for the rest of the 1990s with significant losses in GDP, wages, land values, and so on.

But there were other highly charged events including the death of Emperor Hirohito in 1989 and the unsolved 1991 murder of Hitoshi Igarashi, a professor at the University of Tsukuba who translated Salman Rushdie's *Satanic Verses* into Japanese.

8. The editors deeply appreciate the assistance of Van C. Gessel for details regarding the last three years of Endo's life.

9. Van C. Gessel, "*Silence* on Opposite Shores: Critical Reactions to the Novel in Japan and the West," in Dennis and Middleton, eds., *Approaching* Silence, 25–41.

10. Darren J. N. Middleton, "Endo and Greene's Literary Theology," in Dennis and Middleton, eds., *Approaching* Silence, 71–72.

11. Mark W. Dennis and Darren J. N. Middleton, "Introduction: *Silence* in the World," in Dennis and Middleton, eds., *Approaching* Silence, xi–xxiv.

12. Mark Twain, *The Project Gutenberg EBook of Adventures of Huckleberry Finn, Complete* (Salt Lake City: Project Gutenberg Literary Archive Foundation, 2004), 611.

13. Endo, *Deep River*, 17.

14. The term "Hindu" first appeared as a geographic and cultural identifier in Greek and Persian references, pointing to the peoples living near or beyond the Indus River. Over time, it also took on religious connotations meant to distinguish religions that arose on the Indian subcontinent from those of the others, especially the Muslims.

15. Endo, *Deep River*, 29.

16. Unlike Enami, scholars generally distinguish *varṇa* and *jāti*: the former, which means "color, class, order," and so on, refers to these four groups but excludes the outcasts who are described as *avarṇa*, or "without a *varṇa*." The latter term, which means "birth," refers to hundreds of different groups whose identity can reflect multiple factors that include community, clan, language, and so on.

17. Endo, *Deep River*, 31.

18. Ibid., 211.

19. Dennis lived in the south Indian state of Tamil Nadu from 1992 to 1995 and twice went on the Ayyappan pilgrimage, which takes place in the neighboring state of Kerala. The pilgrimage is dedicated to Ayyappan, believed to be the son of Śiva and Mohinī, the female avatar of Viṣṇu.

20. Although sharing the name Gandhi with Mahatma Gandhi, Indira Gandhi married a man who was not directly related to the Mahatma. Even so, she was born into a political family: her father, Jawaharlal Nehru, served as one of the key leaders in the Indian independence movement and became the first prime minister of India.

21. For an extended discussion of this term in Endō's work, see Middleton's chapter in the present volume.

22. The company established a foothold in the northeastern part of the country with its victory over the Nawab of Bengal—nominally subordinate to the Mughal Empire—and French allies in the Battle of Plassey in 1757, which led to the company's annexation of the Bengal region of the subcontinent.

23. See for instance, the work of Vinayak Damodar Savarkar, a leader of the Hindu Mahasabha, who wrote *The Indian War of Independence, 1857* (Bombay: Phoenix Publications, 1909). The other names for this event include the Sepoy Mutiny, the Indian Rebellion of 1857, the Revolt of 1857 in India, the Great Rebellion, the Revolt of 1857, and the Indian Insurrection.

24. See https://www.theguardian.com/theguardian/2007/may/01/greatspeeches, accessed November 22, 2017.

25. William Claiborne, "Gandhi's Ashes Strewn to Snows," *The Washington Post*, November 12, 1984. See http://tinyurl.com/yakgk76w accessed November 22, 2017.

26. Endo, *Deep River*, 30.

27. The Buddha moved in a rich spiritual world wherein diverse religious teachers and their schools debated the true nature of reality, including the constituent elements of the self and consciousness. Scholars often distinguish between the Vedic tradition practiced by the Brahmin priests and the *śramaṇa*, or "striver," traditions—a varied group of religious practitioners that include the Buddhists, Jains, Ājīvikas, and others. Despite their diverse teachings, the latter group was united by their rejection of the religious

authority of the Vedic tradition and the Brahmins as its chief arbiters. But there were other critiques: Buddhism, for instance, rejected the ordering of society based on the caste system described above and the early community attracted a number of converts from those of high and low social stations. Although the vitality of Buddhism in India has decreased significantly over time, it still exists in pockets, including members of the Dalit Buddhist movement created, in part, through the efforts of Bhimrao Ramji Ambedkar, a Dalit himself who earned a PhD in economics at Columbia University and became a key voice representing the depressed classes of India.

28. Endo, *Deep River*, 30.

29. Ibid., 30–31.

30. Although Pure Land teachings appeared in Japan before the Kamakura era (1185–1333), distinct Pure Land schools were established in this period. The two main schools of Japanese Pure Land are the Jōdoshū, founded by Hōnen (1133–1212), and the Jōdo Shinshū, founded by his disciple Shinran (1173–1263).

31. In addition to the *Amida Sūtra*, also known as the *Shorter Sukhāvatīvyūha Sūtra*, the other key texts of the tradition are the *Longer Sukhāvatīvyūha Sūtra* (Infinite Life Sutra) and the *Amitayurdhyana Sūtra* (*Contemplation Sūtra*).

32. Robert Barron, *Catholicism: A Journey to the Heart of the Faith* (New York: Image Books, 2011), 3; emphasis is ours.

33. Mary R. Reichardt, *Exploring Catholic Literature: A Companion and Resource Guide* (Lanham, MD: Roman & Littlefield Publishers, 2003), 6.

34. In Great Britain, the United Reformed Church came into existence in 1972, the union of the Presbyterian Church of England and the Congregational Church in England and Wales.

35. Paul Lakeland, *The Wounded Angel: Fiction and the Religious Imagination* (Collegeville, MN: Liturgical Press, 2017), ix. We owe much to Lakeland's integrative approach to faith and fiction, which he explores throughout his book, in Part One especially (3–68).

36. We are grateful to Van C. Gessel for helping us put together this information on the current state of Japanese-language *Deep River* scholarship.

37. It is important to note, however, that religion and literature has generally focused on Christianity, leaving out Buddhism, Hinduism, and other religions with rich literary traditions. For details, see Darren J. N. Middleton, "Religion and Literature's Unfinished Story," *Religion and Literature* 41, no. 2 (Summer 2009): 149–57.

PART ONE
HISTORICAL AND COMPARATIVE APPROACHES

Chapter One

Navigating *Deep River* through the Lens of Buddhist Thought

MARK W. DENNIS

The world of dew
Is the world of dew
And yet, and yet . . .[1]

—Taitetsu Unno, *River of Fire, River of Water:
An Introduction to the Pure Land Tradition of Shin Buddhism*

Introduction

This poem about the world of dew was written by the Pure Land Buddhist priest-poet Issa (1763–1828) about the evanescence of our shared world. I came upon it in Taitesu Unno's wonderful book about the Japanese Shin sect of Pure Land Buddhism titled *River of Fire, River of Water*. Unno tells us that Issa was married, as were many priests from his tradition, and had three children, each of whom died before living even a single year. The poem, in just thirteen English words, powerfully expresses an inherent tension on the Buddhist path between its core teachings about the nature of reality and human behavior. That is, our shared world, ephemeral like morning dew, is in constant flux. Thus, no matter how tightly we hold on to wealth or fame, or to a little daughter, change is, paradoxically, the only constant in the world of dew. But even if we intellectually understand this tension—and Issa would surely have imbibed this core Buddhist teaching—it still seems all but impossible for each of us not to hold on tightly to these fleeting appearances. And so, "And yet, and yet . . ."

The Buddhist tradition from which Pure Land developed represents just one of the religions of South Asia discussed in the introduction that are crucial to navigating the historical context of *Deep River*. In this first chapter, I draw from the Buddhist teachings that inform Issa's poem to consider several of the novel's themes—including suffering and impermanence; the self, rebirth, and interdependence; and metaphor—taken up by the volume's other essayists. I note the chapter number for the first appearance of each of the other essayists. In this way, my chapter will serve as a guide to the anthology's other chapters as we collectively navigate the deep waters of the Ganga.

Suffering and Impermanence

By now the morning light had begun to trickle into the city, as if to suggest that God had finally noticed the sufferings of man. Shops opened their doors, and flocks of cows and sheep, the bells around their necks tingling, crossed the streets. Unlike Japan, here no one gave Ōtsu a strange look as he passed by with the old woman on his back.

How many people, how much human agony had he taken on his shoulders and brought to the River Ganges? Ōtsu wiped away the sweat with a soiled cloth and tried to steady his breathing. Having only a fleeting connection with these people, Ōtsu could have no idea what their past lives had been like. All he knew about them was that each was an outcast in this land, a member of an abandoned caste of humanity.

He could tell how high the sun had climbed from the intensity of the light that struck his neck and back.

O Lord, Ōtsu offered up a prayer. *You carried the cross upon your back and climbed the hill to Golgotha. I now imitate that act.* A single thread of smoke already was rising from the funeral pyres at the Manikarnikā Ghāt. *You carried the sorrows of all men on your back and climbed the hill to Golgotha. I now imitate that act.*[2]

The first of Buddhism's Four Noble Truths proclaims that our lives, in this world of *saṃsāra*, are permeated by *duḥkha*, often translated into English as "suffering"—a term that appears in the quotation above and regularly throughout the novel. But *duḥkha* also connotes a wide range of negative feelings and emotions, including other words that appear in that quotation and flow throughout the novel: "agony," "anxiety," "burden," "concern," "difficulty," "disease," "dissatisfaction," "distress," "uneasy," "misfortune," "pain," "problem," "sorrow," "torment," "trouble," and "worry." We read again and again about the suffering and pain, the burdens and sorrows of individual characters whose experience of *duḥkha* brings them, as part of the tour group, to Vārāṇasī and the Ganga, where each gains some sort of spiritual insight.

Van C. Gessel (chapter 9) and other essayists take up the pain and suffering of these characters but also that of their creator, Shūsaku Endō himself. Gessel, for instance, engages the Book of Job to explore the possible resonance between the suffering of the author and his characters, using language that resonates with my description above of *duḥkha*. He writes of Endō:

> Nor do I want to get into the business of probing his psyche to see whether some unconscious motivation led him to weave bits and pieces of his own lifetime of physical, emotional, and spiritual sufferings into the lives of the novel's main characters. What *is* clear from the text is that each character carries burdens of pain, loss, betrayal, loneliness, and disillusionment in the baggage they bring on their pilgrimage to India. Even if Endō did not set out to write *Deep River* as a commentary or meditation on the Book of Job, I hope to demonstrate that he most certainly lived a Job-like life (as do many of his fictional characters), and that, in a way not dissimilar to the struggles that Fr. Rodrigues faces in *Silence*, *Deep River* is a meditative response to the dilemmas of human suffering in the face of a frequently *silent* God who could easily be regarded as uncaring.

Among these characters from *Deep River*, Kiguchi experienced the grotesque horrors of the Highway of Death and then witnessed his comrade Tsukada, who had saved his life in the jungle, drink himself to death having been tormented by recurring visions of the face of PFC Minamikawa, a Japanese soldier whose flesh he had eaten to survive that retreat. Mitsuko remains dissatisfied with her empty life, searching desperately for meaning in the depths of the sacred river. And Isobe suffers from the loss of his wife who had experienced physical pain during her illness, while Numada, like Endō himself, had experienced prolonged bouts of pain from the physical ailments discussed in our introduction. And just like Endō, Numada had spent time in Japanese-occupied Manchuria, where he had a dog named Blackie. The novel's narrator describes Numada, a writer of children's stories populated by animals, recalling:

> Blackie was the first dog to teach him that animals can converse with humans. Not just conversing—he had also learned they can be companions who understand your sorrows. . . . He took great pleasure writing in his books about dogs and goats and ponies, and, yes, birds too, who understood the sorrows of children—because the various sorrows associated with human life have already been generated in childhood.[3]

Sorrow and suffering are central to Elizabeth Cameron Galbraith's chapter (chapter 7), comparing *Deep River* to Endō's *The Girl I Left Behind*, which tells the story of Mitsu, whom doctors falsely diagnose with leprosy, but who chooses to return and work with a group of nuns at the leprosarium where she had been sent for quarantine. Galbraith observes that the

> catalytic thread between suffering and Christ-like love is the wider import of suffering, known in Endō's novel to Sister Yamagata and the leprosarium's nuns, who believe "when human beings suffer, Our Lord suffers alongside us." According to Sister Yamagata, Mitsu, who had once prayed by the bed of a child dying in agony that she would "willingly take his leprosy" upon herself, and wondered if the God in whom she apparently did not believe would "hear" her prayer, clearly "experienced this solidarity with suffering in her own life."

Galbraith offers the following description of suffering in a story she relates of Nathaniel Hawthorne's recollection of an "'unlovely and unwholesome' little imp with a humor in its eye" who had followed him in a Liverpool workhouse. She writes, "The point of the Hawthorne story is that suffering, and especially the suffering of children, is grotesque. Yet, as both Hawthorne and [Flannery] O'Connor knew, and as Paul Elie eloquently states in his account of O'Connor, 'in human suffering the believer sees the grounds of our common humanity.' Moreover, it is 'through suffering, above all, that human beings are stirred to the love of one another, and to the love of God, who showed his love for humanity through his willingness to suffer as one of us.'"

Several of the characters' suffering can be understood against the backdrop of the redemptive suffering borne by Jesus and his symbolic representations, including the river itself, Ōtsu, the Onion, Pierrot, and, argues Zhange Ni (chapter 3), animals. Ronald Green (chapter 4) argues that the Pierrot and the Onion serve Endō as "artistic symbols of the universal principle of suffering."

But vast human suffering is also borne by the goddess Chāmundā and, ultimately, the Ganga herself. Before leaving for India, Enami tells the tour group that Chāmundā takes on the suffering of all the Indian people, and later, in a scene with Numada and Mitsuko at the Ganga, the following exchange occurs:

> "It's the body of an old woman, isn't it?" Numada mumbled as he looked at the gaunt legs and ankles. He could not see the face for the flames. Mitsuko compared this old woman's life with that of the goddess Chāmundā. Like the goddess, she had suffered and persevered in this life, and after suckling her children with her withered breasts she had died. And Ōtsu lifted such people on to his back as though shouldering a cross and brought them here to the river . . .[4]

Described as the "reincarnation" of Mitsu from *The Girl I Left Behind*, Ōtsu is a bumbling and failed seminarian who grieves at the loss of his mother, whose warmth and faith in Jesus Christ had sustained him in life. His superiors at the seminary repeatedly berate him for his "heretical," pantheistic beliefs, having argued before them that God has many faces that one can find among the Jews, Buddhists, Hindus, and others. But it was his seduction and callous abandonment by Mitsuko that helped him better understand "just a little the sufferings of that man who was rejected by all men."[5] Mark Bosco, S.J., and Christopher Wachal write, "Once she has seduced Ōtsu into her bed, she thinks, 'the pleasure she took from Ōtsu derived not from anything even remotely carnal, but from Ōtsu's rejection of that man.' Believing her battle won, Mitsuko harshly rebukes and rejects Ōtsu's affections, setting both characters on journeys of suffering and discovery." Ōtsu's journey leads him to India where, in imitation of "that man," he joins the outcast Doms, discussed by Mini Chandran (chapter 2), to carry dead bodies to the burning *ghāts*, intoning the passage from the quotation at the beginning of this section. Darren J. N. Middleton (chapter 13) also takes up this fascinating character, writing:

> A trace of Thomism in Ōtsu's allegedly heretical soul thus inspires him to ruminate analogically when thinking theologically. Later, he moves in his mind's eye from his mother to "my Onion," then from God to Jesus, "the warmth of life," and finally, from Jesus to Christians across time, the followers who have found themselves energized by their Master's example to serve others, by the banks of the Ganga or, indeed, anywhere where suffering holds people in thrall.

The Six Realms of Rebirth

Although Buddhism teaches that *duḥkha* is part of the human condition and that our shared experiences of it can help us see our interconnectedness with other human beings and other forms of sentient life, the tradition understands its genesis and elimination differently from the Christian traditions. The second truth put forth by the Buddha states that *duḥkha* results mainly from *tṛṣhṇā*, or "thirst," which one can understand as craving, desire, and even greed. However understood, the term refers to a range of negative feelings and emotions that ensnare us in Māra's web. The third truth asserts that by removing craving, *duḥkha* will dissipate, eventually leading to a state of liberation from suffering—the ineffable state of *nirvāṇa* often described in Buddhist texts as the far shore of a river. To reach that state of freedom, one follows the eightfold path—the fourth truth—often divided into ethical principles, mental discipline, and spiritual insight.

In propounding this view about the nature of reality and the causes of human suffering, the Buddha accepted the *saṃsāra* paradigm described above but reinterpreted some of its core elements. He devised a code of ethics based on karma, much like the Hindus, Sikhs, Jains, and others, but argued that it was the intention of a particular act that serves as the key determinant of its karmic consequences. An ethically positive action was based on a wholesome mental intention, motivated by compassion, loving kindness, and so on; these sorts of actions naturally help reduce the suffering of others, a central goal of Buddhist practice. Such acts will also eventually bring about a sweet tasting karmic fruit, just as negative actions, those motivated by greed, anger, and other such emotions, will eventually bring about a bitter tasting fruit. Based on the karma accumulated over a lifetime, one is reborn in one of the three positive realms (humans, demigods, and gods) and three negative realms (hells, hungry ghosts, and animals) that constitute *saṃsāra* in Buddhist cosmology.[6]

And while many Buddhists conceive the six realms to truly exist, others interpret them as metaphors for psychological states. For instance, when our minds become consumed by an insatiable craving for alcohol or food, sex or fame—whatever it may be—we psychologically inhabit, even if for an instant, the negative realm of the hungry ghosts whose long pencil-thin necks prevent them from satiating immense appetites symbolized by huge bellies. We can imagine, for instance, Mitsuko's string of lovers meant to ease her unrelenting feelings of emptiness and meaninglessness, or Kiguchi's comrade and friend Tsukada, who, writes Zhange Ni, "believing that he will fall into the evil realm of 'hungry ghosts' . . . literally drinks himself to death."

This process of rebirth is depicted in Buddhist texts and art, including paintings that show a series of concentric wheels called the *bhavacakra*, or "wheel of life." The *bhavacakra* depicts not only the process of rebirth in *saṃsāra* but also suggests there is a way out—the path to freedom described above. The center of the *bhavacakra* depicts the three poisons—greed, anger, and ignorance—the most toxic of the negative emotions, with images of a bird, snake, and pig, which represent the base human impulses that dominate the animal realm. Buddhists believe ignorance, the last poison, sets in motion actions that keep us bound in *saṃsāra*; indeed, Māra, the demon of death and impermanence, holds the entire wheel of *saṃsāra* clenched in its mouth.

From this simple foundation of four truths, Buddhism developed other key doctrines like impermanence, represented by Māra and poignantly expressed in Issa's poem about his little daughter's death in the world of dew. The manifestations of impermanence, represented in the constant flow of the Ganga, appear throughout the novel, especially in the loss of life, both anonymous and named.[7] The former includes the many unnamed Japanese and Allied soldiers who perished along the Highway of Death as well as the throngs of Hindu pilgrims who travel to Vārāṇasī to die and the large number of the city's impoverished who perish on its streets and are cremated, together with the pilgrims, at the burning *ghāts* along the Ganga. The latter include the deaths of Isobe's wife Keiko and Kiguchi's comrade Tsukada, but also the murder of Indira Gandhi, and, possibly, Ōtsu along the river's banks.

The Self

Other core Buddhist doctrines include emptiness and interdependence: the former asserts that all things appearing in *saṃsāra*—whether solid like a rock or a book, or fluid and ephemeral like a river or the morning dew—lack a substantial, unchanging foundation. This absence includes what we may perceive to be a substantial and enduring self, the subject of the self-referential "I" that we, as English speakers, repeat constantly in our minds and articulate in our speech. Although the Buddha accepted the pan-Indian *saṃsāra* paradigm described above, he rejected the existence of the *ātman* as understood by the Hindus and other South Asian co-religionists, positing instead *anātman*, or "selflessness." In this view, what we mistakenly take to be the self represents, instead, a temporary and constantly changing combination of five elements, the *skandhas*, which include the physical body, feelings, perceptions, mental formations, and consciousness. This view of self and the ultimate path to freedom differ not only with the Hindu and Sikh positions described above, but also with some Christian notions of self, as discussed by several essayists, although it clearly resonates with the language Darren J. N. Middleton uses to describe the self in his chapter on Endō's process panentheism: "We are not inflexible entities that trek unchanged through time. Rather, we are the many experiences and changes we have had; thus, we are relational and processive."

Such a broad questioning of self and its *relationality* appears in other essayists' interpretations of the novel and in comparison to Endō's other works. For example, Justyna Weronika Kasza (chapter 10) contributes an extended meditation on the relationship between Endō and the characters he has created, focusing on Mitsuko. She writes, "While working on this final novel, struggling with anxieties and with the topic that haunted him since his very first encounter with François Mauriac, Endō notes in his diary: 'I have no confidence whether the novel will ever become my masterpiece. Nevertheless, it is certain that this work contains most of myself.'" She adds, "*Deep River* reconstructs the hermeneutical circle, the circle of understanding, and explanation of the self. The *self* is not stable or confident; it is the 'I' in the making and is being recreated through the stories that 'demand to be told.'"

And drawing on Philippe Lejeune's notion of the "autobiographical space," she argues, "Like Ricoeur, Lejeune perceives selfhood to be unstable, constantly being remade. Autobiographical space shows that the autobiography is, therefore, dispersed and always incomplete." And while this description of the instability of the self pertains to a literary genre, she reminds us that we can discover it when we make cross-cultural comparisons. For example, Kasza notes Akiyama Shun's observation that the Japanese often avoid the first-person pronoun *watashi* in speech and writing, which introduces a particular form of ambiguity into the language, and she quotes the work of Katsumata Hiroshi, who argues, "There is nothing more misleading than thinking that the Japanese *watashi* equals the English *I*, French *je*, or German *ich*. . . . *Watashi* is not the *I*. Western individuals and the societies they create are made up of *I*'s. The problem consists in the fact that the Japanese *watashi* and the Western *I* are structurally and fundamentally different."

If we compare *Deep River* to *Silence*, the novel that thrust Endō onto the international literary stage, we discover fascinating reflections on the relation between self and other. For instance, Van C. Gessel argues in *Approaching Silence* that the narrative's shift from the first to the third person represents the taming of the ego of the novel's protagonist Fr. Rodrigues, a Portuguese Jesuit priest who travels to Japan in search of his mentor, knowing he would likely die because of a brutal crackdown on Christians. As the story progresses, the beautiful, blue-eyed Jesus of his imagination transforms into the broken-down, exhausted, and suffering Christ upon whose image he must step to eliminate the horrible pain and suffering of a group of Japanese Christians. Having been forced to confront the essential teachings of "that man," whose face he calls to mind again and again, he subjugates the demands of his ego for a glorious martyrdom and exalted position within the church and, in so doing, reimagines martyrdom itself. In *Approaching* Silence, I wrote,

> Rodrigues must confront what William Cavanaugh describes as the "paradox of the cross": to love the poor and dispossessed, even the despicable and evil. By witnessing the suffering in the face of the beautiful and transcendent made ugly and low, moreover, Rodrigues reimagines the meaning of martyrdom itself. Cavanaugh argues,
>
>> "In effect, *Silence* asks if there is only one kind of martyrdom. Could one sacrifice not only one's body, but one's very moral integrity for the sake of others? . . . But Endo suggests that a deeper martyrdom may await Rodrigues—the death of his very self as a Christian and as a moral person. This suggests that the standard concept of heroic virtue is radically effaced by the logic of God's kenosis, by God's self-emptying to take the form of a slave, as Paul puts it in Philippians. In *Silence*, Endo provocatively pushes basic Christian logic, already paradoxical, to a more extreme conclusion. If it is true, as many Christian martyrs have affirmed, that for the Christian, the body is as nothing when compared to the eternity of the soul, then is the crucifixion of the soul a martyrdom which makes other martyrdoms pale in comparison?"
>
> These descriptions—"the death of his very self," "kenosis," and "self-emptying"—resonate with the Buddhist teaching of selflessness. . . . [Fr. Rodrigues] thereby shifts the locus of activity from a self-seeking martyrdom to this utter abandonment of self. [In Buddhist thought, freedom ultimately comes], paradoxically, in precisely this radical effacing of the self and privileging the suffering of the "other."[8]

Unlike *Silence*, which focuses on the transformation of self mainly through the lens of Fr. Rodrigues, *Deep River* lacks a central character as Maeri Megumi (chapter 8) and others note. Rather, the novel begins with introductions to the five main characters, whose individual chapters are, she notes, titled "The Case of ~": for instance, "The Case of Kiguchi." The novel moves on to reveal how these characters reflect on their own experiences of *duḥkha* and how their sense of self and other evolves as their lives intersect while traveling in India and visiting the Ganga.

And while Megumi argues that this structure prevents Endō from adding depth to the characters, Mark Williams (chapter 5) suggests one possible reading of this novelistic device. In considering Carl Jung and John Hick's influence on Endō, Williams notes Hick's description of the transformation from self-centeredness to "Reality-centeredness," a process in which one moves away from the narrow concerns of the self to find meaning, as each character attempts to do, in a personal transformation in which there is "a new and limitlessly better quality of existence." Williams adds:

> There have been those who have questioned the group tour structure—and the lack of a single identifiable focus figure—in *Deep River*. Reviewed in the light of Endō's avowed interest in Jung, I would suggest, such a format represents an ideal backdrop for a literary exploration of a series of characters each engaged in what Jung would have described as very personal "journeys of individuation."

William continues:

> Again, with the benefit of hindsight, Endō's literature, traced right back to "Saul," can be identified as populated by a series of protagonists engaged on just such a journey from self-centeredness to "Reality-centeredness." But it is in *Deep River* that this notion receives its most nuanced literary treatment—in the portrayal of a series of tourists, specifically identified as lacking a "firm understanding of why [they] had decided to come to India" and yet vaguely aware that they had "come here in search of something." On several occasions, the various characters are depicted as ending a day of searching in despair, convinced, on one occasion for example, that they have been "chasing phantoms." And it is only at the conclusion of the novel, as each stands alone beside the Ganges, that, one by one, they find themselves confronted by previously ignored aspects of their inner being. Each interprets the experience of epiphany differently. But, in each case, the result is the emergence of a greater self-awareness, a shift toward what Hick would describe as Reality-centeredness.

Interdependence

In the present volume, Dennis Hirota (chapter 14) makes the following observation about relationality within Shinran's view of reality in Pure Land thought:

> There are various facets of the embeddedness in nature or the cosmos. For example, Shinran states: "All sentient beings, without exception, have been our parents and brothers and sisters in the course of countless lives in the many states of existence. On attaining Buddhahood after this present life, we will be able to save every one of them." Each person has personal bonds with all other life forms going back into the unknowable past. Endō evokes this intuition in Isobe's search for his wife's reincarnation, during which he comes to grasp the nature of "the bond uniting a husband and wife. The connection that brought two people together to become lifelong companions from amidst the countless men and women in the world. . . . Isobe now had the feeling that those ties had existed even before birth."

Whether a novel or a river, whether the "I" or *watashi* that gestures toward the self, all phenomena are described in Buddhist thought, as interdependent, *pratītyasamutpāda*, or "dependently co-arisen," suggesting that anything we experience in *saṃsāra* emerges from an interrelated set of causes and conditions. In this way, each of these things depends upon other similarly dependently co-arisen things for its existence, abiding, and subsequent disappearance. Buddhist texts often describe this tenet using the sort of language appearing in the quotation above from Hirota's chapter: "embeddedness," "bonds," "connections," and "ties." The modern Vietnamese Zen Buddhist monk Thich Nhat Hanh describes this tenet as "interbeing,"[9] suggesting that to gain insight into the nature of reality and to truly live—language that resonates with Hick's notion of Reality-centeredness—we must remain mindful and deeply appreciative of the interconnectedness of our own lives with all the sentient beings and other things that appear in the world of dew, whether a little daughter or a pet dog, a sweet tangerine or a deep river.[10]

This sort of interconnectedness appears in the novel in ways both beautiful and gruesome: in the deep feeling of connection and gratitude that Isobe's wife Keiko feels for all of nature, speaking openly and lovingly to flowers and trees, in Ōtsu's pantheistic view of the interconnectedness of all the people of the world's religions with the divine, but also in the soldier Tsukada's consumption of the flesh of his comrade PVC Minamikawa to survive the death march in the jungles of Burma. It also appears as nostalgic absence in the comments of Kiguchi and Numada who, having witnessed Indian villagers living side by side with cows and other animals, lament modern Japan's sterile distance from the animal realm. Having seen such sights from the tour bus in a passing Indian village, Numada states, "'This is wonderful. I haven't seen anything like this for a long time.' From his seat directly behind Enami, Numada muttered to himself, struck to the depths of his heart. 'In Japan in the old days you could see animals and human beings living side by side.'"¹¹

Zhange Ni addresses Endō's complication of the self's relationship with the other by examining the interdependence of the human and animal realms through the stories of Kiguchi and Numada. She writes:

> To wrestle with this aporia, Endō turned to dismantle the "anthropological machine" that elevated little Numada above the Chinese boy and Blackie and turned Kiguchi's co-combatants into cannibals and lizard meat. Given the tripartite world geography (West-Japan-Rest) of *Deep River*, the problem of animality has a particularly charged valence. The setting of Endō's animal stories overlaps with the novel's portrayal of non-Japanese Asia during the war. The acknowledgement that the human-animal distinction has always been a site of contestation where "relations of power operate in their exemplary purity (that is, operate with the fewest moral and material obstacles)" suggests the reverse as well: When power relations operate, lose control, and become unhindered (e.g., at the time of war), we arrive at a moment when the always already-indecisive human-animal distinction dissolves, as in Dalian and Burma.
>
> By focusing on these animal stories, we retrieve not only the overlooked non-Japanese, non-Western Rest from the all-too-familiar binary of East (Japan) and West, but also the equally overlooked dimension of animality in Endō's pluralist theology. The West-Japan-Asia tripartite in the novel corresponds to Endō's attentiveness toward the interlinked issues of divinity, humanity, and animality. With regard to the last, another set of signifying practices in which Endō's narrative intervenes is the view of animals and human-animal relations in Christianity and Buddhism. These traditions, neither of which is static or homogeneous, are loaded with anthropocentricism as well as resources for posthumanism. Steering between the Scylla of Christian universalism and the Charybdis of Japanese nationalism (which once appropriated Buddhism), Endō again turned to ani-

mals, their sacrificiality, and their salvation. He creatively deployed traditional and unconventional resources to push the limits of religious orthodoxy in his alignment of animals with Jesus Christ and Amida Buddha. By doing so, he inserted theology into the posthumanist discussion of the human-animal relation to make it postsecular and, vice versa, he revitalized comparative theology by further complicating and destabilizing the self-other relation.

But notions of the interdependence of self and other appear in the chapters that follow in other ways. Justyna Weronika Kasza, for example, argues that we can gain a deeper understanding of the novel by considering its "relation and interdependence" with Endō's other works, which requires acknowledging that the "life of the writing persona is dispersed among other narratives and the author's selfhood becomes" the "storied self." She adds, "I am convinced that the methodology proposed by [Philippe] Lejeune offers insight into what I term 'the inner workings of Endō's novel,' and the extent to which the novel remains in strong interdependence and dialogue with his other works, particularly his nonfiction texts." That sort of interdependence is also evident in the ways in which characters reappear across those works, and thus experience one sort of rebirth, a key topic in *Deep River*.

Scholars know much about Endō's creative process in writing *Deep River* because he penned the Fukai kawa *sōsaku nikki* (*Deep River* composition diary), mentioned by a number of essayists, which records his reflections on how the characters and plot developed. In preparation to write the novel, Endō visited India and read widely about the country: P. A. George (chapter 11) notes that the novelist read whatever materials on India were available in Japanese and that he was particularly influenced by Hotta Yoshie's *Thoughts from India* and Yukio Mishima's *The Temple of Dawn* from his tetralogy *The Sea of Fertility*, which, George writes,

> deals mainly with the concepts of karma and reincarnation, though Mishima himself did not believe in these Buddhist notions. Endō is said to have been greatly moved by Mishima's description of the cremation of dead bodies in Vārāṇasī at the *ghāts* on the banks of the Ganga and by the concepts of karmic retribution and reincarnation. He writes, "Faith in transmigration, or the karmic-rebirth, is a commonly held notion among Indians; this is truly enviable from the Japanese point of view. This notion differs from the Japanese way of thinking where each individual thinks only about "his own death" or "thinks only about one's own life after death."

Those Buddhist notions of rebirth were, as noted above, based on karma and selflessness, wherein what we take as a self is unstable and dispersed, constantly being remade in a single lifetime until death brings about the process of rebirth in one of the six realms. But this position led Hindu and other sorts of critics to ask: If there is no self, then who or what is reborn? How can the process work without a stable, identifiable *ātman*, or self? To explain this apparent conundrum, Buddhaghoṣa and other Buddhist philosophers liken the process of rebirth in *saṃsāra* to the flame of one candle lighting another candle. Thus, while we can identify continuity by tracing the first flame to the second, they are not precisely the same flame because each is, as it flickers, in constant flux. Likewise, a person who has died, like Isobe's wife Keiko, takes on a new birth in one of the six realms that is distinct from, yet can be traced back to, that previous life, just as the flame of the second candle can be traced to the first.

Indeed, the most explicit example of rebirth in *Deep River* relates to Keiko who dies early in the novel from cancer. Although Isobe disavows a belief in the concept, he travels with the group to India in search of his wife's reincarnation, and had, upon arriving in India, "sensed that he had at last entered into the land of rebirth."[12] He had set out in search of Rajini Puniral, a young Indian girl from the village of Kamloji near Vārāṇasī, who seems to remember a past life as a Japanese. During Isobe's visits to see his wife in the hospital, we learn that she had had seemingly mystical visions and experiences. Ronald Green writes, "Keiko's near-death vision of reincarnation in the opening chapter of *Deep River* sets up the novel's motifs of destruction and rebirth." We also learn that Keiko had a dream in which she sees her husband had left a pot with water boiling on the gas stove. She struggles to yell out to him to turn it off but he cannot hear her. While she recognizes it had been just a dream, her husband had, in fact, left a pot on the stove. Green adds, "That Keiko's vision corresponds to an actual event reinforces the notion that her insight into reincarnation may also be reliable." Moreover, Mitsuko's appearance in Keiko's hospital room as a volunteer where Isobe meets her for the first time and their meeting at the organizational meeting for the India tour, suggests a relationship that is "more karmic than coincidental." Despite Isobe's efforts, he fails to locate the young girl in Kamloji; even so, Mitsuko seeks to buoy his spirits, reassuring him that at "the very least, I'm sure your wife has come back to life inside your heart."[13]

Although Endō had read the material about Buddhist notions of rebirth, he does not make clear whether the Japanese tourists-pilgrims, who had come from a country steeped in Buddhist history and ideas, understood this concept purely in Buddhist terms, or whether he meant the story's recurring references to rebirth, reincarnation, and transmigration—the twelfth chapter is titled "Rebirth"—to reflect a more general understanding of it since those references range from the clearly Buddhist notions of the soldier Kiguchi, who chants from the *Amida Sūtra* at the Ganga, to new age, popular beliefs. In a scene after his wife's death, Isobe, having discussed the topic with his niece and her husband, purchases copies of Shirley MacLaine's 1986 *Out on a Limb* and Ian Stevenson's 1987 *Children Who Remember Previous Lives: A Question of Reincarnation* at the airport.[14] And Emi Mase-Hasegawa (chapter 12) argues, "It is worth noting that Endō has Isobe's dying wife use the word '*umarekawari*' (reincarnation or rebirth), which means she eschews the technical Buddhist word '*saṃsāra*' as well as the Christian word 'resurrection.' This word choice hints at Endō's sense of a universal soteriology."

Indeed, Endō's "universal soteriology," or religious pluralism, naturally helps explain the novel's wide-ranging religious beliefs as they pertain to notions of self and other, freedom and salvation, but also toward rebirth and reincarnation, all of which flow together in the deep river. For instance, I have already described rebirth in the pan-Indian *saṃsāra* paradigm, noting that in the Hindu caste system it refers to the first three castes as *dvija*—those who are "twice born" since they experience a physical birth and a spiritual rebirth through their caste specific initiation ceremonies. Mini Chandran adds that for Hindus "Kashi is the hoped for destination as it is the gateway to *mokṣa*, or salvation, from the cycle of birth and rebirth. Kashi *yātrā* is a pilgrimage, a journey of no return for you either never come back, or, if you do, you do so not as the same person after you have been to the Ganga."

We can readily multiply examples of that sort of religious or spiritual rebirth that does not entail physical death, including those Christians who are "born again," a form of rebirth mentioned in the New Testament in the Gospel of John wherein Jesus tells Nicodemus, "Very truly I tell you, no one can see the kingdom of God unless they are born again" (John 3:3). And Mitsuko describes Christ's rebirth in the lives of the Christian characters in the novel, concluding, as in the quotation above, that although Christ had died a long time ago, he had been reborn in the nuns of the Missionaries of Charity and in her friend and former lover Ōtsu. In discussing Ōtsu's time in Indian society, P. A. George focuses on Ōtsu's rebirth as a Christian, drawing from the following passage, "The Onion had died many long years ago, but he had been reborn in the lives of other people. Even after nearly two thousand years had passed, he had been reborn in these nuns, and had been reborn in Ōtsu. And just as Ōtsu had been taken off to a hospital on a litter, the nuns likewise disappeared into the river of people."[49] P. A. George adds:

Ōtsu never did anything which would have disturbed the peace, tranquility and equanimity of society. Rather, he discovered the true meaning of the teachings of Christ after coming to Vārānasī, equating the Ganga with Christ. He says, "Every time I look at the River Ganges, I think of my Onion. The Ganges swallows up the ashes of every person as it flows along, rejecting neither the beggar woman who stretches out her fingerless hands nor the murdered prime minister, Gandhi. The river of love that is my Onion flows past, accepting all, rejecting neither the ugliest of men nor the filthiest." Ōtsu did not feel awkward in juxtaposing the Ganga with Christ, as he realized that both Christ and the Ganga treat everything and everybody equally, accepting all human suffering and pathos without any discrimination of high or low, rich or poor, Brahmin or outcast. Ōtsu's realization of this truth not only helped him discover the uniqueness of India's spiritual greatness but also helped him to be reborn as a true Christian.

Rebirth of Individual Characters

But we encounter rebirth in other ways: for instance, several essayists detail how Endō himself appears, and is thus "reborn," in the characters of his novels and short stories. In a short reflection on Martin Scorsese's filmic adaptation of *Silence*, Van C. Gessel recalls how Endō had declared, "Kichijiro is me,"[15] a reference to the drunken, conniving Japanese apostate who serves as the guide for Fr. Rodrigues and a fellow priest, who sneak into the closed country to find their mentor and minister to the Japanese "hidden Christians." Likewise, Justyna Weronika Kasza observes in the present volume, "We can effortlessly prove that each character—whether Ōtsu, Mitsuko, Isobe, Numada, or Kiguchi—embodies a trace of the author." So, too, individual characters are "reborn" across Endō's works—his novels, short stories, and plays—both with the same and different names. For instance, Gaston, who tends to Tsukada in the hospital in *Deep River*, appears in *Wonderful Fool*, while Elizabeth Cameron Galbraith quotes Endō's own description of Mitsu's "rebirth" from *The Girl I Left Behind* to *Deep River*:

> Through the medium of this novel I sought to portray the drama of "the Jesus I Left Behind." Mitsu can be seen as modeled on Jesus, abandoned by his own disciples; she is modeled on the Jesus whom all Christians are guilty of abandoning on a daily basis in

their everyday lives. Mitsu has continued to live within me ever since and can be seen reincarnated in my most recent novel, *Deep River*, in the person of the protagonist, Ōtsu. It is my profound wish that my readers will acknowledge the connection between these two novels.

And Kasza elaborates on Mitsuko's connection to her creator, writing,

The focal point of my investigation is the female character Naruse Mitsuko, whom I treat as the axis of the entire narrative; she binds together the plot and is tied to the other characters and to Endō himself. Through her, we can immerse ourselves again into the author's experience of reading the novel he loved: *Thérèse Desqueyroux* by François Mauriac. In Mitsuko, Endō included an essential part of his own personal experience. That is, like Endō, she studies French literature at university and then travels to France. Though *Deep River* depicts the journey to India, Mitsuko continuously recalls the moments when she was wandering around the forests of Bordeaux.

But Mitsuko represents other forms of "rebirth." Kasza argues that "Mitsuko does not instantly become *Thérèse*; rather, she evolves with Endō's process of rereading the novels of Western writers; her attitude toward Ōtsu reminds us first of Sarah (Miles) from *The End of the Affair*, then of Julien Green's *Moïra*. Finally, she becomes Thérèse." Thus, not only is she "reborn" from a character in Endō's previous works, but her life in the novel comes to embody a fictional character in another novelist's work. As noted above, Mitsuko finally immerses herself in the deep waters of the Ganga and, in describing the experience, concludes that it "embraces these people and carries them away. A river of humanity. The sorrows of this deep river of humanity. And I am a part of it."[16] This statement, which several essayists cite, suggests that she, too, has been spiritually "reborn," whether we understand this rebirth as a move toward Reality-centeredness as suggested by Mark Williams, as a nascent expression of Hindu goddess devotion, or in any number of other possible ways.

Metaphor

As such, the deep river serves as both the locus of spiritual transformation and as the novel's central metaphor that is, in the chapters that follow, interpreted variously by our contributors. Metaphors use that which is familiar to convey the meaning of something that may be difficult to grasp; that difficulty often arises from the abstract nature of a particular subject: time or love, God or *nirvāṇa*. When I ask my students in a discussion about language and metaphors, "Time is *what?*," they have no difficulty identifying the metaphor "time is money." That is, in contemporary American society, we conceive of time in terms of our ideas about money, serving as a "root metaphor."[17] Root metaphors may become so deeply ingrained in our thinking that we often fail to recognize them as metaphors, nor do we question how they can limit our field of critical vision since they create a semantic range from which we can generate all sorts of seemingly natural, even inevitable, associations. For instance, because we conceive time in terms of money, we can "spend" and "waste," "invest" and "economize" time because each verb relates in some way to our understanding of money.

Christian texts are replete with metaphors deployed to express the abstract and ineffable: for instance, God is described metaphorically as a "rock," "shepherd," and "father," which naturally help the faithful approach and understand, while also, perhaps, limiting their imaginative horizon. We also find common metaphors for Jesus and those faithful: the New Testament depicts the former as the "bread" of life and the "vine," while the latter appear as "salt" and "clay." But in *Deep River*, and in Endō's literary art more broadly, the author deploys the other metaphors noted above, including the "river," "Onion," "Pierrot," "animals," and others, each of which creates a distinct and richly evocative semantic range that expresses his pluralistic, process panentheistic view of the many compelling, equally legitimate, faces of Christ that can fully engage our imagination.

Zhange Ni identifies a connection between one of Numada's birds and Jesus Christ, writing, "Numada's bird not only has a voice but also a real face, that is, the face of Jesus Christ: 'It is a strange metaphor, to compare such a bird with Jesus, but Numada had his reasons for doing so. Numada had taken a liking to Rouault's paintings, and there was something about the many Pierrot faces he portrayed in his works that resembled this hornbill. He knew that for Rouault clowns were a symbol of Christ.'" Ronald Green adds, "When Numada becomes deathly ill with tuberculosis, his myna bird, named Pierrot, is likened to Jesus. In this, the novel references the painting by that name by the French artist Georges Henri Rouault. For Rouault, the clown serves as a metaphor for humanity and Jesus; the clown has a somber face and appears as if praying. This is seen as concern with the human condition of perpetual suffering."

In a similar way, several essayists in this volume and *Approaching* Silence examine Endō's reimagining of the Eurocentric father metaphor, recasting both God and Christ as a warm and kind-hearted mother, an image that resonates with Japanese religious sensibilities. Van C. Gessel discusses the translation of a crucial scene in *Silence* wherein the voice of Christ speaks to Fr. Rodrigues, the novel's protagonist described above. Gessel and others note that the voice of Christ in the English translation of that scene tells him, "Trample! Trample! I more than anyone know of the pain in your foot. Trample! It was to be trampled on by men that I was born into this world. It was to share men's pain that I carried my cross."[18] Gessel observes, "Much has already been written about the misinterpretation of Christ's words from the *fumie* because of William Johnston's incorrect rendition in his English translation; *Fumu ga ii* does *not* mean 'Trample!' It is a tender expression of Christ's empathy for the priest's pain, a loving admonition that 'It is all right to trample.'"[19] This rendering is considerably softer than the imperative construction "Trample!," which we can easily imagine coming from the mouth of a stern father. Gessel's reworking as "It is all right to trample" is a linguistic choice reflected in Martin Scorsese's filmic adaptation of the novel, for which Gessel served as a script consultant.

And that wording more accurately reflects the "motherly" face of God and Christ that resonates with the Japanese religious sensibilities taken up in *Approaching* Silence and the current volume by Dennis Hirota, who mentions Enami's depiction of the Ganga, representing Christ, as the "maternal waters" and "a holy, motherly river," where "holy means to embrace all without differentiation." Mark Bosco, and Christopher Wachal (chapter 6) argue, "Similarly, the river itself becomes Christic: 'The Ganges swallows up the ashes of every person as it flows along, rejecting neither the beggar woman who stretches out her fingerless hands nor the murdered prime minister, Gandhi. *The river of love that is my Onion flows past*, accepting all, rejecting neither the ugliest of men nor the filthiest.' This analogical amplification—the Ganga as Christ—articulates the similarity-in-difference of the two faces of God, and orders the religious forms appropriate to each expression of the divine." And Darren J. N. Middleton observes, "The God of *Deep River* is a benevolent energy event, fructifying, as well as surrounding, life's changeability. 'God is not so much an existence as a force,' Ōtsu states. Likewise: 'I don't think God is someone to be looked up to as a being separate from man, the way you [Mitsuko] regard him. I think he is within man, and that he is a great life force that envelops man, envelops the trees, envelops the flowers and grasses.'"

As these and other essayists observe, much of Endō's literary art has sought to reimagine the Christian tradition through the lens of those sensibilities, as the author famously described the Catholicism he had received from his mother as ill-fitting clothing. For example, Hirota mentions the author's goal, expressed in *Deep River* through Ōtsu, "to contemplate a Christianity that accords with the minds of the Japanese." Hirota also quotes the following observation of S. N. Eisenstadt: "This capacity of the Japanese to absorb . . . has been vividly described by Endō Shūsaku, in his novel *Silence*, in the powerful metaphor of the Japanese swamp. This 'swamping' capacity can be identified in . . . the transformation of Christian beliefs." Hirota adds, "The swamp image is of course a recurring motif throughout Endō's works (in *Deep River*, the name of the author of children's literature—the character who shares Endō's childhood and medical experience—includes the word 'swamp' or 'marsh,' *numa*)."

In *Approaching* Silence, Hirota examines *Silence*'s swamp metaphor that comes from the Japanese *numachi*,[20] which he and others also translate as "mudswamp," "swampland," and "marshland." He writes,

> In *Silence*, the metaphor of the swamp is first employed by Ferreira, the accomplished theologian who has become unable to accept either the rift in the understanding of the Japanese, who have bent Christian symbols to their own predilections—"twisted and changed our God"—or the challenge presented by God's "silence" amidst the excruciating suffering and fervent prayers of those very Christians. It has, however, also been adopted by Inoue, and perhaps even has its origins with the notorious persecutor. The order of appearance in the novel is significant. For Ferreira, the image of Japan as mudswamp forms part of the argument for apostasy that he makes to Rodrigues; for Inoue, it encapsulates an attempt to come to terms with his own success in defeating the missionaries. In *The Golden Country*, the play produced the same year as the publication of *Silence*, Endō depicts Ferreira's own prior apostasy. There, it is Inoue who remains torn, wounded by the temperament of his countrymen and the power of the "swampland" of Japan to alter the faith of the Christians.

Indeed, Ferreira's criticism of the "mudswamp" of Japan, which kills off the healthy roots of authentic—that is, European and white—Christianity, echoes the attitude of the French seminarians who use different language to accuse Ōtsu of "twisting and changing our God" through his "heretical," pantheistic beliefs. Ōtsu imitates Christ's slow, painful climb to crucifixion, intoning the passage quoted above: "O Lord. . . . You carried the cross upon your back and climbed the hill to Golgotha. I now imitate that act. . . . You carried the sorrows of all men on your back and climbed the hill to Golgotha. I now imitate that act."[21]

Hirota also interprets passages from Endō himself reflecting on the Onion, writing:

> "Rather than an existence, God is a working. The Onion is simply the congealment of love performing its work." The Onion is, of course, Ōtsu's symbol for the nonsubstantialist divine, the God compatible with Japanese perceptions and aspirations. From a newspaper column published during the period of the composition of *Deep River*, it is clear that these thoughts given to Ōtsu are Endō's own. There Endō states: "God is not an existence, but a working. Moreover, I have been able to experience this working in various ways in my own life."

Ronald Green compares Ōtsu's Onion to the parable of the onion in Dostoevsky's *The Brothers Karamazov*, investigating the connection between Jesus Christ and Ōtsu. He argues that the Onion is also "a metaphor for Ōtsu, who is often covered in filth and who appears to be humble and lowly; it points, moreover, to the quotation about comeliness, which Endō uses several times as a biblical description of Jesus: '[He] hath no form nor comeliness; and when we shall see him, there is no beauty that we should desire him.' An onion is earthy, not heavenly, growing in the ground." Green concludes that readers can understand the Onion and pierrot as artistic symbols deployed by Endō to depict the "universal principle of suffering," addressed above through the lens of *duḥkha*. And in *Christ in Japanese Culture: Theological Themes in Shusaku Endo's Literary Works*, Emi Mase-Hasegawa writes, "Endo explained that Onion is a metaphor for love. . . . If Japanese do not prefer using the term ['Christ'], it can be called 'Onion,' or 'X.' However, the 'X' took the form as Christ for me. For others, it may appear as Buddha."[22]

River Metaphor

All of these metaphors coalesce and churn in the Ganga that is the inspiration for the novel's title and serves as its central metaphor. As discussed in the introduction, the novel begins with the African American spiritual: "Deep river, Lord: I want to cross over into campground." Emi Mase-Hasegawa observes,

It is important to mention that the title of the novel was *kawa* [River] in the beginning. The river is the presiding symbol for Christians, helping them to understand rebirth through the ritual of baptism. Endō changed the title to *Fukai kawa* [Deep River] after the first galley proofs were finished and in the final stage of printing when he heard and was moved by the faith encapsulated in the African-American spiritual of the same name: "*River* is the river of Love, and the river of Spirituality," he later wrote in his diary. Through the metaphor of rivers leading to the ocean, Endō sought to situate Christianity within the soteriological framework of Hick's Religious Pluralism.

Mark Bosco, S. J., and Christopher Wachal emphasize the metaphor's fluidity, writing, "Their final destination is the Ganga, the deep river of the book's title, in the town of Vārānasī, the spiritual heart of Hinduism, but also where the Buddha is believed to have taught. The river serves as a fluid metaphor that provokes a revelatory moment for many of the Japanese tourists, unmasking their personal afflictions hidden deeply beneath the surface of their lives." S. Brent Plate (Afterword) offers another interpretation, reminding us of how the river metaphor and "deep," its qualifier, can foreclose interpretive possibilities. He writes,

> The river is deep, as Mitsuko says, "so deep I feel as though it's not just for the Hindus but for everyone." The metaphor is profusely pluralistic, providing a place of learning for Japanese Buddhists, nonbelievers, and devout Christians alike. Readers may want, as Endo does, to find the river sufficiently deep.
>
> Yet I wonder: Can it be wide as well? So wide that it rolls out beyond its banks to create pools of knee-deep water? That is, can it include those who don't want or can't take the full immersion, but instead want to wade around in the shallows? The tourist? The infirm? The doubter? The one with no pious intentions? The "*river of humanity*" includes Christians, Buddhists, and Hindus, but it also includes tourists and pilgrims, blending the sacred and profane. Pious or party-hardy, out for devotion or diversion, the tourist and the pilgrim walk side by side, regardless of interior intent. The river is deep and wide.

He adds,

To understand the spiritual journey we need to understand the importance of the shallows. The journey's dynamic hinges on the fact that it is a skin deep, "superficial" experience, as much as it occasionally promotes deep thoughts. External actions often mean more than contrite hearts, which is also to say the journey, undertaken by pilgrim *or* tourist, is thoroughly and unfailingly a physical process that our linguistic narratives and metaphors often only serve to cover over. Once the journey is captured in words, put into forms of rational knowledge (as I'm doing here), the body is left behind, the sensual engagements cut off. Uncovering the deeper meaning of the superficial lets us learn in the face of things, like a poetic physiognomy.

Metaphors in Buddhist Thought

Plate's suggestion that linguistic narratives and metaphors can obscure what we see and understand resonates with common Buddhist views of language. That is, the tradition's understanding of the nature of reality articulated above naturally led to a distrust of language because of an inevitable disjuncture between a word, as a signifier, and its referent, as the signified, whether the former is "river," "Ganga," "Chāmundā," "Ōtsu," or "God."[23] Since language fixes the identities of things that are inherently unstable, words can best serve us as "skillful means" for describing the many things that appear in the world of *saṃsāra* and for teaching the Dharma that leads to release from it.

Even so, Buddhist texts are replete with words that fill up a massive canonical and noncanonical body of literature, often deploying metaphors to express ineffable notions like *nirvāṇa* or emptiness, or to describe the Buddha himself. Linda Covill details how the Buddha is often depicted as a guide who can lead us to the other shore of enlightenment,[24] but he also appears as a physician who helps heal the suffering of the world. Buddhist texts frequently refer to the Buddha-dharma as a wheel or a raft, often in conjunction with rivers like the Ganga—a massive amount of something is compared to the sands in the Ganga—serving as one of Buddhism's deepest and most fruitful metaphors.

Flowing continuously, rivers symbolize the constant change that characterizes *saṃsāra* in Buddhist cosmology and the tradition's texts often depict the near side of the river as *saṃsāra*, the world of dew, while the far shore represents the state of *nirvāṇa*. Due to an ambiguity in Sanskrit grammar, *Tathāgata*, one of the Buddha's epithets, has the double meaning of the one who has "thus" (*tathā*) "gone" (*gata*) to the other shore of enlightenment, but has also "thus" (*tathā*) "returned" (*agata*) to the near shore to save sentient beings through his teachings. Those teachings, in turn, serve as a raft to ford that river to get to the freedom from *duḥkha* that lies waiting at the other shore.

The river also serves as a key metaphor in the Pure Land Buddhist tradition of Issa and Kiguchi, of Dennis Hirota and Taitetsu Unno. Unno writes movingly about how he had come to a deeper understanding of Pure Land teachings after confronting immense suffering as he tried to comfort the grieving mother of his close friend, who had just taken his own life, with empty words from the sūtras he had learned in his academic studies. Like Kiguchi in *Deep River*, he struggled to make sense of these teachings about the evanescence of our shared world of dew captured beautifully and excruciatingly in Issa's simple poem. By deeply engaging those teachings, Unno, like Kiguchi, finally came to a deeper understanding of the Pure Land path that is, as in Buddhism more broadly, depicted through the metaphor of the river—a word appearing twice in Unno's title, *River of Fire, River of Water*.[25]

He explains that the title comes from the Pure Land patriarch Shantao's "The Parable of the White Path," which describes a traveler—in some accounts a pilgrim—trying to escape bandits and wild beasts intent on killing him. He arrives at a river divided in two: to the south rages a river of fire, and to the north, a wild river of water. Between the two lies a narrow white path crossing to the other shore, thus representing the only path of escape. But the flames from the left and the waves from the right whip across it, confronting him with the prospect of multiple sorts of death. As bandits and beasts draw closer, he hears a voice on the near shore telling him to cross over to the other shore and a second voice coming from the far shore telling him to cross over, that all will be well.

Metaphorically, the river of fire represents anger and the river of water represents greed—two of the three poisons—while the voice from the near shore is Śākyamuni, the historical Buddha, and the voice calling out from the other shore is the Buddha Amitābha, the Buddha of Infinite Life and Light, who beckons the traveler to Sukhāvatī, a land of bliss where *duḥkha* is quiescent. Toward the end of the novel, we find the passage discussed by Dennis Hirota and Mark Williams:

> Staring into the river, Kiguchi began to intone a passage from the Amida Sutra that he had committed to memory.
> The river flowed by. The River Ganges moved from north to south, describing a gentle curve as it went along. Before his eyes Kiguchi saw the faces of the dead soldiers on the Highway

of Death, those lying prone on the ground, and those with their faces turned to the sky.

> In the land of the Buddha may always be found
> Rare and multicoloured birds of all varieties:
> White swans, peacocks, parrots, kalavinkas and curlews.
> Three times each day and three times each night
> These myriad varieties of birds join together in songs
>   of harmony.

Standing beside Kiguchi as he chanted the Amida Sutra, the young girl kept her large black eyes fixed on him and did not move a muscle. Each time he intoned this passage from the Amida Sutra, Kiguchi thought of the countless birds he had heard singing in the jungles of Burma.

> In that land of the Buddha
> A gentle breeze stirs
> Through the rows of palm trees and strings of bells
> And a sweet, enrapturing sound proceeds from them.[26]

But here on this shore, where dew evaporates, the Pure Land and other Buddhist traditions maintain the inevitability of our individual suffering, whether experienced in the excruciating pain of a Japanese mother losing her son in the twentieth century, of a Pure Land monk losing his little daughter centuries earlier, or in the fictions of Ōtsu, Mitsuko, and the other "hauntingly suggestive" characters created by Endō in the "tender pathos" of his compelling prose. As such, *duḥkha* serves as the positional star by which we can navigate Endō's wonderful novel in which these characters' lives represent, in distinct ways, something of their creator's own suffering.

The chapters that follow are meant, then, to serve as guides, like the pilot fish of the introduction, helping readers navigate an imagined journey to a river that contains in its waters all of the binaries and contradictions that we use to make sense of the world of dew, including the Mother Ganga who is deep as she is shallow, sacred as she is profane, filthy as she is pure. Whether in our minds we immerse ourselves in its depths or its shallows, whether we perceive the other shore to be a pure land or a blessed campground of freedom, the creator of this imagined journey has told us that it flowed from the depths of his mind as a spiritual river of love.

Notes

1. Taitetsu Unno, *River of Fire, River of Water: An Introduction to the Pure Land Tradition of Shin Buddhism* (New York: Doubleday, 1998), 165.

2. Shusaku Endo, *Deep River*, trans. Van C. Gessel (New York: New Directions, 1994), 193.

3. Ibid., 74.

4. Ibid., 162.

5. Ibid., 62.

6. Even though the *deva*, or "god," realm was conceived as being higher than that of the human realm, human birth was seen in Buddhist thought to be auspicious since liberation from *saṃsāra* was possible only from the human realm.

7. See Darren J. N. Middleton's chapter describing Endō's process panentheism. He writes, "Process panentheism promotes the idea that change brands everything. We do not occupy a static milieu. From elementary particles like bosons to complex organisms like ourselves, all reality discloses itself to us as lively. Rivers flow, stars burn, gravity bends light, space curves, and our universe expands."

8. See Mark W. Dennis, "A Buddhist Reading of the Blue Eyes of Jesus in *Silence*," in Mark W. Dennis and Darren J. N. Middleton, eds., *Approaching* Silence: *New Perspectives on Shusaku Endo's Classic Novel* (New York: Bloomsbury, 2015), 165–66.

9. See, for instance, http://orderofinterbeing.org. See also Helen Tworkov, "Interbeing with Thich Nhat Hanh: An Interview," *Tricycle*, Summer 1995, http://tinyurl.com/yd5kktgw, accessed November 7, 2017.

10. See Van C. Gessel's chapter in the present volume; he quotes Endō's lament, which appeared in a short article he published just two months after *Deep River* came out: "I think many Japanese people in former times were able to discover at the end of their lives a place where they could finally come to rest in the midst of nature, whether beside the sea or in the mountains. But all such places have disappeared now. We have become victors in our daily lives, but losers at truly living."

11. Endo, *Deep River*, 106.

12. Ibid., 108.

13. Ibid., 214.

14. See Shirley MacLaine, *Out on a Limb* (New York: Bantam Books, 1986), and Ian Stevenson, *Children Who Remember Previous Lives: A Question of Reincarnation* (Charlottesville: University Press of Virginia, 1987).

15. Gessel addresses the following question in his essay titled "The Long Road to Silence": "How significant is Kichijiro, the repeated fallen one through this whole story? Mr. Endo said, 'Kichijiro is me.' Kichijiro by the end of the film is also [Father] Rodrigues. Kichijiro is also Martin Scorsese. And we'll just leave open the possibility that Kichijiro is also me." See http://tinyurl.com/ydctmpbn, accessed November 7, 2017.

16. Endo, *Deep River*, 211.

17. Sallie McFague writes: "As Paul Ricoeur says, 'Root metaphors assemble and scatter. They assemble subordinate images together and they scatter concepts at a higher level. They are the dominant metaphors capable of both engendering and organizing a network.' The content of a religious tradition, then, is known through its root-metaphor and the subordinate models which support and enrich it." See *Metaphorical Theology: Models of God in Religious Language* (Minneapolis, MN: Fortress Press, 1982), 110.

18. Shusaku Endo, *Silence*, trans. William Johnston (New York: Taplinger Publishing Company, 1980), 171.

19. See Van C. Gessel, "Silence on Opposite Shores: Critical Reactions to the Novel in Japan and the West," in Mark W. Dennis and Darren J. N. Middleton, eds., *Approaching* Silence*: New Perspectives on Shusaku Endo's Classic Novel* (New York: Bloomsbury, 2015), 38n10.

20. Ibid., 140–41. In a discussion of these issues, Hirota observes, "Endō appears to have employed some name symbolism in the novel. Although not apparent in translation, the Japanese reader will note that Ōtsu (great harbor) and Mitsuko (beauty-harbor) share a Chinese character. Their surnames in early versions were Fukatsu (deep-harbor) and Yoshikawa (good-river). There are a number of names with words related to bodies of water: Mitsuko's surname becomes Naruse (become-rapids); Isobe (seashore-surroundings); Enami (inlet-wave). Kiguchi's name (tree-mouth) also resonates with the narrative." At a roundtable discussion addressing this anthology at the 2017 conference of the Association of Asian Studies in Toronto, Canada, Van C. Gessel offered a similar observation that most of the characters' names contained a water-related *kanji*.

21. Endo, *Deep River*, 193.

22. Emi Mase-Hasegawa, *Christ in Japanese Culture: Theological Themes in Shusaku Endo's Literary Works* (Leiden and Boston: Brill, 2008), 148n22.

23. For an introduction to the "valuation" and "devaluation" of language in religion and philosophy, see Ben-Ami Scharfstein, *Ineffability: The Failure of Words in Philosophy and Religion* (New York: State University of New York Publishing, 1993).

24. Linda Covill, *A Metaphorical Study of Saundarananda* (Delhi: Motilal Banarsidass Publishers, 2013).

25. Dennis Hirota notes Shinran's preference for the image of the ocean, quoting the following passage: "The Buddha's nondiscriminating, unobstructed, and nonexclusive guidance of all sentient beings is likened to the all-embracing waters of the great ocean."

26. Endo, *Deep River*, 201.

Chapter Two

A Gaze Turned Inward

Perspectives from the Orient

MINI CHANDRAN

Introduction

The globalized world today acknowledges and celebrates pluralism in cultures and communities, with cultural diversity being considered the hallmark of a democratic liberal society. Nevertheless, Homi Bhabha makes a distinction between cultural diversity and cultural difference, arguing that a "containment of cultural difference" is embedded within the apparently liberalist concept of cultural diversity.[1] He contends that there is "incommensurability" in the differences between cultures, which makes it difficult for them to co-exist; what often happens in a so-called culturally diverse community is that the dominant culture evolves a transparent norm that understands and accepts alterity only on its own terms. This chapter argues that the religious and philosophical quest documented by Shūsaku Endō in his *Deep River* comes close to a worldview that accepts cultural difference without ignoring or attempting to flatten out awkward corners in its negotiation of alterity. I juxtapose it with Indian texts like M. T. Vasudevan Nair's Malayalam novel *Varanasi* and Hindu religious hymns, as well as Julian Crandall Hollick's *Ganga*.

M. T. Vasudevan Nair, popularly known by his acronym MT, is one of the greatest living writers in Malayalam, the language of the south Indian state of Kerala. He has a prolific output with hundreds of short stories, six novels, numerous screenplays, and one drama, with the novel *Varanasi* published in 2002 being the latest creative work he has produced. The novel centers on

Sudhakaran, whose return to Varanasi is also a remembering and *re-membering* of the past, as it sets him out on an introspective journey into himself, wrenching out the half-buried sins (mostly of the flesh) of his youth. Varanasi and the Ganga provide a heterotopic space of death and desire with the river providing a hope of spiritual salvation.[2] The novel unfolds in nonlinear time: starting with the present, it zigzags through his life and his encounters with various women in numerous cities until it culminates in Varanasi.

Julian Crandall Hollick's *Ganga* is a 2007 nonfiction work, an account of a journalist's attempt to answer the questions he poses at the very beginning: "How can Indians pollute Ganga yet at the same time worship her as a goddess? How can so many millions take a 'holy dip' every morning to wash away their sins in a river that is polluted by so much waste, both human and industrial? How does one explain this paradox?"[3] He journeys with the river, and occasionally on her, from her birthplace Gaumukh to Farakka, where she flows into the Bay of Bengal. Although he uses the name "Ganga," which Indians use for the river instead of the Anglicized "Ganges," he is mainly addressing the non-Indian reader through his objective approach, which tries to distinguish between the goddess and the river. Read in juxtaposition with the fictional texts, Hollick's text becomes a contrapuntal nonfictional narrative that, like the two novels, eventually validates the mystique of the river.

The River

The Ganga is not just a river to India's Hindus. She is a goddess to be worshipped, the deliverer from the mortal coil of birth and rebirth, and a presence in the mind of each believer even if far removed from her physically. However, today the Ganga is one of the most polluted rivers in India and a symbol of the environmental damage that Indians are callously capable of inflicting. Rising from the Himalayas in the north and flowing for about 2,500 miles through the states of Uttarakhand, Uttar Pradesh, Bihar, and West Bengal before flowing into the Bay of Bengal, the Ganga is facing a slow death because of pollution and indiscriminate use of her water. This is why an Indian court had to step in to protect the river and, along with the Yamuna, grant her legal status as a person: "The Rivers Ganga and Yamuna, all their tributaries, streams, every natural water flowing continuously or intermittently of these rivers, are declared as juristic/legal persons/living entities having the status of a legal person with all corresponding rights, duties and liabilities of a living person in order to preserve and conserve river Ganga and Yamuna"—states the judgment delivered on March 20, 2017, by the Division Bench of the High Court of the Indian state of Uttarakhand.[4]

Ganga is thus both person and goddess, but she primarily remains a religious symbol. Varanasi (earlier known as Kashi or Benares), situated on the banks of the Ganga, is attributed with the same spiritual and sacral qualities as the river. A trip to Varanasi and the Ganga is never for worldly aspirations or sightseeing. According to Hindu belief, Kashi is the hoped for destination as it is the gateway to *mokṣa*, or salvation, from the cycle of birth and rebirth. Kashi *yātrā* is a pilgrimage, a journey of no return for you either never come back, or, if you do, you do so not as the same person after you have been to the Ganga.

One of the earliest mentions of the Ganga is in the *Nadī sūktam* (hymn to the rivers) in the *Rig Veda*. The belief is that Ganga, who dwelt in the heavens, was persuaded to descend to earth by Bhagīratha, who wanted her to grant salvation to his dead ancestors. The matted locks of Śiva broke the force of the mighty Ganga before it crashed down to earth. Ganga thus became the ultimate *tīrtha*, or place of pilgrimage, where the Hindus go to immerse the ashes of the dead. A dip in the Ganga washes you of your sins; for those who are unable to travel to the river, a drop of the river water (*gangājal*) at the time of death is supposed to liberate you from the bonds of material life.

The Ganga has taken myriad forms in Hindu mythology. She is the willful and perverse wife of King Shantanu who, because of a curse, threw her first seven newborn sons into the river. Shantanu begged her not to do the same with Bhīṣma, the eighth and last son, who grew up to become the patriarch of the Kuru family and a towering presence in the *Mahābhārata*. She is the love interest in Śiva's life, the mistress he hides in his locks to the eternal jealousy of his consort Pārvatī. She is Jāhnavī, daughter to Jahnu and Ganga ma, the mother who receives all and refuses none.

Ādi Śaṅkarācārya's *Ganga Stotram* and Jagannātha Paṇḍita's *Ganga Lahari* are two famous hymns to the Ganga. The death-defying and liberating powers of the river are praised by Śaṅkarācārya as follows:

> *Tava jalam amalaṃ yena nipītaṃ* (Those who drink your pure water);
> *Parama padaṃ khalu tena gṛhītam* (They attain the ultimate stage of life);
> *Mātar gaṅge tvayi yo bhaktaḥ* (O Mother Ganga, those who are your worshippers);
> *Kila taṃ draṣṭum na yamaḥ śaktaḥ* (Death is powerless to even look at them).[5]

Even Hollick, who states, "When I first became fascinated by Ganga, I used to discount the mythology that surrounded her,"[6] admits that there is some inexplicable factor in the water of the Ganga, which he terms as "the mysterious factor X."[7] Based on inputs from scientists in the United States and India, Hollick's speculation is that the presence of bacteriophages in the water could explain why there are no pandemics caused by the Ganga, despite millions bathing in it during times of special festivals like the Kumbh Mela.[8] But he hastens to add that the mysterious factor X is not the bacteriophage but a quality that "Ganga possesses that no other river does, [which] is perhaps its extraordinary rate of re-oxygenation," before asserting, "The river does have some extraordinary rejuvenating powers."[9]

Hollick tackles the East-West difference when he argues that the term "pollution" must be understood in a different way in the context of the Ganga. "While the scientific method is universal, what a scientist chooses to examine may be determined by his or her culture. The danger is that the dominance of Western science within India has caused a corresponding loss of knowledge of and confidence in India's own scientific values and heritage."[10] He points out how Indians make a distinction between "polluted" and "dirty" when it comes to the river: "For millions of Hindus, Ganga can therefore never be dirty in the Western sense of pollution. For them physical pollution and spiritual pollution are two entirely different creatures. Only the most intellectually sophisticated attempt to make a possible connection; to argue that severe physical pollution might affect the spiritual purity of the goddess."[11]

Pilgrimage to Kashi and Ganga

Nevertheless, MT's *Varanasi* shows that this East-West difference is not an easy binary. Sudhakaran initially comes to Varanasi to escape the adulterous liaison with Shanta, his boss's wife. The avuncular affection that his boss Moorthy bestows on him adds to the guilt and he sees no other recourse but to flee the city of Bangalore and go to Varanasi on the pretext of doing a PhD in the Benares Hindu University. Varanasi opens up a different cultural vista to the South Indian Sudhakaran. By virtue of being an Indian and a Hindu, he should be able to relate to the mystical aura of the city and the river. However, like most non-Indians, he is simultaneously fascinated and repelled by the Ganga, which carries along dead bodies and flower offerings alike in its currents. His first encounter with the river is far from pleasant or spiritual. He jumps back in revulsion from the sight of what he thinks to be the carcass of a cow in the waters, only to realize later that it was alive. The reputation of the river precedes this misunderstanding: "He had heard that half-burnt bodies were dumped in the river. Apparently the bodies of those who had died of small pox would be taken by boat to the middle and drowned with stones tied to them. That was later banned. Would dead cows also be thrown into the Ganga?"[12]

The new relationships he forges with Om Prakash, Ramlal, Gangaprasad, and, most of all, Sumita Nagpal are also introductions to ways of life with which he is unfamiliar. Sumita Nagpal, the Indian lecturer at the School of Oriental and African Studies, University of London, shares the insider-outsider space with Sudhakaran. Literally and figuratively the camera eye which looks upon everything disinterestedly and records faithfully, she is the hybrid who occupies the interstitial third space. However, the latent possibility of the third space to generate "something different, something new and unrecognizable, a new area of negotiation of meaning and representation" is left unrealized in Sumita.[13] She leaves Benares only to write an account of the city much later, dismissed contemptuously by one of her friends as "something on the exotic east," and locating her very much in the neo-imperialist Orientalist genealogy.[14]

Shūsaku Endō's *Deep River* also recounts a pilgrimage to the exotic, although, given the geographic location of Japan, the "East" should be read figuratively here. The set of Japanese people who come to India see it as a Buddhist destination: "Their main purpose in travelling to India was to visit famous locales associated with Buddhism, and the impression was strong in their minds that India was the land of the Buddha, the land of Sakyamuni."[15] It comes as a surprise to them that India was predominantly Hindu and Buddhism was a barely perceptible presence. The notion of difference is evident in the question of one of the group: "What is it then that the Hindus believe?"[16] As an answer to this, Enami, their Japanese tour guide, projects the picture of the ferocious Kālī onto the screen, which underscores the stereotypical Orientalist perception of Hinduism as barbaric and irrational, expressed through Mrs. Okubo's rather flippant "Whoo, that was scary!" response.[17] It is also ironic that Enami equates Chāmundā as the mother, "the goddess who has taken upon herself all of the sufferings of the people of India," thus becoming the *other* to the gentle mother Mary in Christianity.[18] It is noteworthy that this image of Chāmundā is contradictory to the popular iconic depiction of Mother India, which is usually as Durgā, the benign goddess, as opposed to the demonic Kālī-Chāmundā.

The motley group of pilgrims represents varying shades of responses ranging from bewilderment to disgust when confronted by the chaotic difference of India. This orientalist attitude, generally understood as a Eurocentric bias, appears incongruous when manifested in an all-Asian context. This is sharply etched in Sanjō, who reacts to the swarm of child-beggars with "What a wretched country."[19] Kiguchi has no patience for this conceited and pretentious disavowal of the ugliness of life, which he sees as a consequence of not being rooted in their history, of not knowing anything about a defeated Japan. Kiguchi has memories which are humbling: "Even in Japan right after the defeat, everywhere you looked similarly starving children had surrounded the American soldiers and begged for chewing-gum and chocolate."[20] According to Kiguchi, the newly wed couple's uninhibited public display of affection is very un-Japanese behavior, unthinkable in his generation. Numada points out that they are prosperous "globalized" newly weds: "In my day too, a honeymoon overseas was beyond all possibility. But now Japan has prospered, and these young people are no different from the foreigners."[21] For Kiguchi, the problem with the Sanjōs appears to be that they are Westernized-Orientalized in their outlook on poverty and squalor; Kiguchi's perspective, on the other hand, is tainted with "Occidentalism."

Defined by Buruma and Margalit as the "cluster of prejudices" that the non-Western world has to the West, Occidentalism is best exemplified in the perception of America as a "rootless, cosmopolitan, superficial, trivial, materialistic, racially mixed, fashion-addicted civilization."[22] Most of these adjectives can be attributed to the Sanjōs who seem to be (willfully?) unaware of a shared Asian heritage that India and Japan have, making Enami rebuke them: "Please make the effort to enter into this unique world, a realm utterly removed from Europe or Japan. . . . We're about to enter into a unique world that we once knew but have now forgotten."[23] The Sanjōs are urbanized representatives of the modern Occidental city "given to commerce and pleasure instead of religious worship."[24] Benares, with its timeless spirituality and unrelenting squalor, is the *other* to this occidental city, disturbing the Sanjōs with its cultural alterity.

The cultural difference is unsettling for all members of the group, including Enami, and each one's way of negotiation with it reflects his or her deeply buried insecurity or hope. Mitsuko's identification with the images of Kālī in her gentle and bloodthirsty forms, feeling that "both images were herself,"[25] indicates the profound disquiet in her soul, a disquiet that she refuses to articulate even to herself. Kālī makes her aware of the duality in her—the libertine who sucks her lovers dry and the nurturer who tends to the dying—and helps her compromise with these seemingly irreconcilable differences.

Likewise, India tends to tease out and accentuate the irrational in the rational mind. This is brought out starkly when Enami takes them to the Nakshar Bhagavatī temple: "The stifling air. The dark subterranean interior. The eerie sculptures floated before their eyes. The hideousness of the images were reminiscent of the feelings of loathing that people experience when they have an unobstructed view of the writhing elements concealed beneath the level of their own conscious minds."[26] The idea of rebirth that is nagging Isobe makes him search in vain for an image that resembles his wife; he finds nothing compassionate about the images on the temple walls. Numada's telepathic communication with the birds is shaken by the images he confronts in India: "The Nature he had taken up in his children's stories over the years had been nothing so turbulent and fearful. To him Nature had been a force that gently embraced mankind."[27] To Kiguchi who has traversed the Highway of Death, the images represent the reality of war and destruction. Enami's understanding of Chāmundā is premised on binaries: gentle Eurocentric Mother Mary–gaunt, skeletal, disease-ridden Chāmundā; pure and refined-ugly and worn; smiling-old and drooping.[28] This simplistic Manichean reductionism, which apparently seeks to legitimize the squalor of India, is actually reinforcing the Orientalist stereotype of India as the land of death and disease.

Hollick undermines this Orientalist as well as "Occidentalist" stereotype of the city. He seeks to deflate the mythos of Benares as the "world's oldest continuously inhabited city,"[29] citing a local historian, Rana B. Singh, who claims that the *ghāts* of Varanasi date only from the seventeenth century. Varanasi, and by extension India, is a self-perpetuating myth, according to Hollick, determined by "television and video"; he again quotes from Singh to suggest that "the images the world sees of Varanasi (and that Varanasi itself probably now believes in) are therefore quite recent and reinforced and narrowed down by modern technology."[30] Nevertheless, Hollick attests to the fact that the very public cremation *ghāts* along the riverside could be unsettling to European and American visitors who are unused to the sight and smell of death in public places, thereby highlighting the Bhabhaian incommensurability of cultural difference.

Ōtsu and Vedānta

Mitsuko's search for Ōtsu is simultaneously an inward pilgrimage, a quest for the spiritual center that sustains and uplifts, as well as a physical search for a friend-lover whom she loves and hates. The corporeal and sexual power that Mitsuko wields over him is a direct challenge to the noncorporeal, spiritual power of his religious belief, and the cat-and-mouse game of seduction she plays with him is really a reflection of the vast spiritual emptiness she discovers in the heart of her glamorous body. While she spirals down into the abyss of total spiritual emptiness, the bumbling and foolish Ōtsu slowly but surely claws his way up the cliff-face of a secure philosophical acceptance of God and the world.

Nonetheless, Ōtsu's refusal to confine himself within the bounds of sectarian dogma places him outside the pale of established religion, a liminal "third space" in between theism and humanism. The nebulousness of Ōtsu's God-Onion concept frays the sharply defined edges of European belief and perhaps this is why the distinction that he draws between the Asian and the European minds is refuted by the seminarians who admonish him, saying, "the truth knows no distinction between Europe and Asia," and attributing the chaos of his thoughts to his "neurosis or . . . complex or whatever."[31] Ōtsu's complex, all-encompassing notion of God, with its failure to distinguish neatly between good and evil, is inherently heterodox and threatens to fracture the unidimensional, homogenizing tendency of Eurocentric Christianity. He flounders in the amoral/immoral/moral world of his own making through his confession: "I can't make the clear distinction that these people make between good and evil. I think that evil lurks within good, and that good things can lie hidden within evil as well. That's the very reason God can wield his magic. He made use even of my sins and turned me towards salvation."[32]

This theologizing is closer to the Hindu concept of God, which can reconcile antithetical and seemingly irreconcilable entities. For instance, Śiva is both destroyer and preserver; or, in the *Lalitāsahasranāma*, some of the thousand attributes of the Devi include *sṛishṭi kartṛi* (the Creator), *goptṛī* (the Protector), *samhāriṇi* (the Destroyer), and *thirodhānakari* (the One Who Causes the Disappearance of Things).[33] The *Bhagavad Gītā* states: "I am the origin and the dissolution, the existence, the treasury and the imperishable seed."[34] This could also explain why Hinduism does not have a Satan-like figure that is pure evil. A god like Indra is fallible and guilty of sins arising out of jealousy and covetousness. On the other hand is the story of an *asura* (demon) like Prahlāda who was punished by his father for being a steadfast devotee of Viṣṇu. The sufferings of Prahlāda for the sake of his beliefs motivate Viṣṇu to appear on earth as an *avatār* in the form of Narasiṃha to rescue him from his travails. The lines between good and evil are fuzzy at best in Hindu religious belief, and Ōtsu's superiors at the seminary are quite right in inferring the pantheistic roots of his outlook.

Ōtsu yet again becomes the site for articulating the difference between European and Asian minds with respect to belief: "In the final analysis, the faith of the Europeans is conscious and rational, and these people reject anything they cannot slice into categories with their rationality and their conscious minds."³⁵ Ōtsu's statement that the seminary at Lyon was unhappy with what they perceive to be a "pantheistic sentiment lurking in my unconscious mind" evokes the Orientalist binary of the West as rational, logical, and conscious and the East (Asia) as irrational, illogical, and unconscious.³⁶

Nevertheless, eventually Ōtsu manages to reach the formidably unattainable heights of spirituality that transcend the mundane and the narrow confines of man-made religiosity, a state which comes close to the Hindu Vedāntic philosophy, as is evident in his declaration: "God has many different faces. I don't think God exists exclusively in the churches and chapels of Europe. I think he is also among the Jews and the Buddhists and the Hindus."³⁷ Vedānta, according to V. Subrahmanya Iyer, "is knowledge that has for its aim the solution of the mystery of all existence."³⁸ It is a school of thought that consists of multiple streams, all of which are considered equally valid. As Iyer elucidates:

> While every religion and every school of mysticism vouchsafes its joys or satisfactions only to the individual or individuals entering its fold, Vedānta seeks, without stooping to proselytization, the good of all men, nay, of all beings, and that in the highest degree, though at first sight such an objective appears too ambitious to be within actual human reach. Further, whereas every religion promises the highest good or bliss after death, Vedānta aims at realizing such good in this world.³⁹

The state of mind that Vedānta engenders is brought out through an image in the novel *Varanasi*. Sudhakaran, who is accompanying Sumita on her photographic journey through the city, sees a child flying a kite on a *ghāt*:

> It was a ghat where five pyres were burning. There was nobody else. Standing close to the low wall facing the river, a six- or seven-year-old boy was flying a kite. He was paying no attention to the burning pyres behind him. He did not pay any attention to the people who had come there either. He was intent on moving the strings so that the kite could reach further heights in the sky.⁴⁰

This is the ideal Vedāntic mind, which can concentrate on achieving greater heights even as it knows that it is standing on ground which is, potentially, a funeral pyre; in other words, it is aware of, but supremely indifferent to, its mortality even as it immerses itself in the mundane activities of worldly life.

The aim is to arrive at a state of disinterestedness, even while you are involved in all the affairs of worldly life; according to the *Bhagavad Gītā*, this is the state of *niṣkāma* karma, where you work without worrying about the consequences of your actions.[41] This is what Ōtsu achieves finally when he is working among the deprived poor, carrying dead bodies to the cremation *ghāt*, which is work delegated to the lowest of India's low castes.

The Doms of Benares are the caste traditionally assigned to burning the bodies on the Manikarnikā Ghat, and legend has it that they are the descendants of the puranic king Harischandra. It is believed that a piece of coal from the fire (believed to have been burning since the time of Harischandra) has to be handed over by a Dom to light the funeral pyre even today. The Doms are paid handsomely for this action; death is their business and livelihood. Ramlal in *Varanasi* is a Dom who tries to break free of the calling of his caste, but to no avail. Sudhakaran's friendship with Ramlal transgresses caste restrictions when he, along with his friends, visits his house (palace, to be precise, because Ramlal belongs to the family of Doms who are considered the rulers); however, all of them are reluctant to eat or drink anything that is offered to them at his house since that would mean violating caste restrictions. Ōtsu is not guided by any such caste rules by virtue of being an outsider but more because he is beyond such man-made restrictions and encompasses cultural differences with an unprejudiced mind.

Moreover, although all those who come to Benares are seekers in one way or the other, it is only Ōtsu who "qualifies" to be the true seeker. Iyer explains that all are not competent to seek Vedāntic truth: "He who is satisfied with any particular kind or degree of truth other than the highest, and is not eager to get at the latter, is not qualified to make the Vedāntic inquiry."[42] Ōtsu's restlessness and frustration in Europe are indicative of his thirst for knowledge beyond the ordinary. His questions are seen as heretical doubts by the authorities but "to those who possess the strength and capacity to think acutely, doubt is a stimulus to further inquiry. As the *Nasadīya-sūkta* or the *Uddhava-Gīta* indicates, doubt is the mother of knowledge."[43] Ōtsu is impelled to search for truths to attain a state of peaceful acceptance that is denied to all the others who come to the Ganga for deliverance.

As Ōtsu explains to Mitsuko, he is finally part of a group of *sādhus* who are itinerant mendicants on a journey of spiritual training. Mitsuko can only understand them as "abandoned dogs," but for Ōtsu it is a life that comes closest to the Onion's life and message.[44] Ōtsu feels that, had Christ been in Benares, he would have been working likewise among the lowest of the low, carrying the dead bodies of outcasts and prostitutes. Ōtsu says: "Every time I look at the River Ganges, I think of my Onion. The Ganges swallows up the ashes of every person as it flows along, rejecting neither the beggar woman who stretches out her fingerless hands nor the murdered prime minister, Gandhi. The river of love that is my Onion flows past, accepting all, rejecting neither the ugliest of men nor the filthiest."[45]

This state of mind is denied even to the Hindu Sudhakaran, whose journey becomes a penance when he decides to do the *tarpaṇa*, the rites for his dead ancestors and friends. The rite for the dead is usually performed by the living that remain after them, but it takes an unusual turn when Sudhakaran performs it for himself. He is supposedly liberated from the bonds of life and death, the ultimate salvation that believers aspire to reach in their pilgrimage to Kashi and the Ganga. As the officiating priest blesses him and wishes him the fruitful realization of his desires, he ruminates: "Desires? What are the remaining desires? When he looked into himself, he found nothing. A mind as empty as a broken begging bowl. Nothing to give. Nothing will hold even if it is taken."[46] This sensibility can be construed as the true state of *nirvāṇa*, completely detached and disinterested, but it is empty of hope or love. There is no feeling of fulfillment here. In contrast to Ōtsu's dying words, "My life . . . this is how it should be,"[47] Sudhakaran leaves Varanasi with a blank mind bereft of emotions, and with the realization that even this city of deliverance was but a temporary way station for him: "This city which is at the same time a pleasure garden and a great cremation ground became yet another way station. Tomorrow I begin my journey. To another way station."[48]

It is also not surprising that Mitsuko feels that Ōtsu was completely foolish and had thrown away his life for nothing. She feels that he was powerless to change this world "full of hatred and egotism."[49] Nevertheless, the sight of Mother Teresa's Missionaries of Charity tending the dying woman on the Calcutta street evokes memories of Ōtsu and motivates her to ask them why they were doing this work. Their answer is: "Because, except for this . . . there is nothing in the world we can believe in."[50] Mitsuko is made aware of the cyclicality of life and death, and that what appears to be failure in worldly terms could be construed differently in another realm: "The Onion had died many long years ago, but he had been reborn in the lives of other people. Even after nearly two thousand years had passed, he had been reborn in these nuns, and had been reborn in Ōtsu. And just as Ōtsu had been taken off to a hospital on a litter, the nuns likewise disappeared into the river of people."[51]

Negotiating Differences

The synthesis that Endō arrives at through the character of Ōtsu could be attributed to his outsider-insider position by virtue of being non-Indian but belonging to a shared pan-Asian heritage. In his analysis of xenophobia, Tabish Khair points to the emotional nature of the encounter between the self and the *other*:

> Moments of heightened emotion coincide with confrontations between the self and the other, or a recollection or evaluation of such a confrontation. The capacity for emotion can also be seen as a recognition, however subconscious, of that (a body/life with another consciousness) which is shared by the self and the other, that which exceeds the consciousness or language employed by the self to capture, describe, conscribe or deny the other.[52]

It is an uneasy awareness of this shared consciousness with the *other* that seems to impel Endō's characters, making them use a language which accentuates not "difference," but, to borrow Khair's term, "non-sameness"; this is perhaps why the confrontation with the *other* never escalates to the feeling of terror that lies at the base of xenophobia.[53] Even Sanjō is moved to disgust but not terror and consequent hatred.

Ōtsu bridges the self and the *other*, forging a language that negotiates and understands the differences without condescension. Even as he grapples with the paradox of the Indian mind that does not believe in either-or when it comes to the belief in Ganga as a goddess and a river, Hollick reflects the bafflement of the outsider. As A. K. Ramanujan has pointed out, this is what Orientalist critics of India termed "inconsistency" in the Indian character.[54] However, he attributes this not to a lack of education or logical rigor, but to a "different 'logic' altogether."[55] He foregrounds the unwillingness of the Indian mind to accept absolute or universalized values: "Indian philosophers do not seem to make synoptic 'systems' like Hegel's or Kant's. Sheryl Daniel (1983) speaks of a 'tool-box' of ideas that Indians carry about, and from which they use one or another without much show of logic; anything goes into their 'bricolage.'"[56]

This is what helps Sudhakaran in his encounter with the apparent *other* in Varanasi. His initial recoil from the difference of Varanasi soon balances on the fundamental recognition of the self in the *other*, or the "sameness" of the *other*. He is what Diana Brydon would term an "insider by virtue of experience" as distinct from an "insider by virtue of method"; however, she questions the radical difference between the two positions of "imaginatively entering the experience of another to write as the *other* and presuming to speak *for* the *other* if both work to silence the *other*."[57] Endō's novel is conspicuous by its lack of Indian voices and can be accused of writing as the *other* but what redeems it is its lack of silencing the *other*. It openly accepts cultural difference without attempting to downplay it and becomes a "river of humanity," leaving us like Mitsuko with the realization: "I believe that the river embraces these people and carries them away. A river of humanity. The sorrows of this deep river of humanity. And I am a part of it."[58]

Notes

1. Jonathan Rutherford, "The Third Space: Interview with Homi Bhabha," in *Identity: Community, Culture, Difference*, ed. Jonathan Rutherford (London: Lawrence and Wishart, 1990), 209.

2. Borrowed from Foucault's concept of heterotopia, which becomes a space that has many layers. Varanasi becomes a heterotopic space for Sudhakaran, because the city of death and salvation also offers him the prospect of love and life with Sumita.

3. Julian Crandall Hollick, *Ganga* (New Delhi: Random House India, 2007), 1.

4. http://www.livelaw.in/first-india-uttarakhand-hc-declares-ganga-yamuna-rivers-living-legal-entities/, accessed September 17, 2017.

5. http://greenmesg.org/mantras_slokas/devi_ganga-ganga_stotram.php, accessed September 17, 2017.

6. Hollick, 15.

7. Ibid., 131.

8. The Kumbh Mela is a festival held once every twelve years in four cities—Haridwar, Allahabad, Nasik, and Ujjain. The Kumbh Mela at Haridwar and Allahabad is on the banks of the Ganga. Millions of pilgrims gather at these places during two months and take a dip in the Ganga, which is believed to be very auspicious. Despite the huge crowds that gather at one spot to bathe in the river, the Kumbh Mela has never been marked by violence or outbreak of diseases.

9. Hollick, 148.

10. Ibid., 9.

11. Ibid., 115.

12. M. T. Vasudevan Nair, *Varanasi* (Thrissur: Current Books, 2005), 28. This and all subsequent translations are mine.

13. Rutherford, 211.

14. MT, 31.

15. Shusaku Endo, *Deep River*, trans. Van C. Gessel (New York: New Directions, 1994), 30–31.

16. Ibid.
17. Ibid.
18. Ibid.
19. Ibid., 105.
20. Ibid.
21. Ibid., 134.
22. Ian Buruma and Avishai Margalit, *Occidentalism: The West in the Eyes of its Enemies* (New York: Penguin, 2004), 8.
23. Endo, 108.
24. Buruma and Margalit, 16.
25. Endo, 115.
26. Ibid., 138.
27. Ibid., 139.
28. Ibid., 139–40.
29. Hollick, 116.
30. Ibid., 120.
31. Endo, 65.
32. Ibid.
33. http://slokas4all.blogspot.in/2015/01/lalitha-sahasranamam.html, accessed September 17, 2017.
34. Boris Marjanovic, *Translation of Abhinavagupta's Commentary of the Bhagavad Gita* (Varanasi: Indica Books, 2004), 215.
35. Endo, 117–18.
36. Ibid., 118.
37. Ibid., 121.
38. V. Subrahmanya Iyer, "Essentials of Vedānta," in *The Cultural Heritage of India*, vol. III: *The Philosophies*, ed. Haridas Bhattacharya (Calcutta: The Ramakrishna Mission Institute of Culture, 2000), 211.
39. Ibid., 212.
40. MT, 48.
41. Marjanovic, 93.
42. Iyer, 212.
43. Ibid., 213.
44. Endo, 183.
45. Ibid., 185.
46. MT, 175.
47. Endo, 212.
48. MT, 177.
49. Endo, 212.
50. Ibid., 215.
51. Ibid.

52. Tabish Khair, "Capital and the New Xenophobia," *Economic & Political Weekly*, 46–47 (November 21, 2015): 45.
53. Ibid.
54. A. K. Ramanujan, "Is there an Indian Way of Thinking?" in *The Collected Essays of Ramanujan*, ed. Vinay Dharwadker (New Delhi: Oxford University Press, 2004), 38.
55. Ibid.
56. Ibid., 40.
57. Diana Brydon, "New Approaches to the New Literatures in English: Are we in Danger of Incorporating Disparity?" in *A Shaping of Connections: Commonwealth Literature Series, Then and Now*, ed. Hena Maes-Jelinek, Kirsten Holst Petersen, and Anna Rutherford (New South Wales: Dangaroo Press, 1989), 96.
58. Endo, 211.

Chapter Three

Japan's Orient and Animal Theology in Endō Shūsaku's *Deep River*

ZHANGE NI

Introduction

Endō Shūsaku's *Deep River* portrays the diverse life experiences of a group of Japanese tourists and their shared spiritual journey in India.[1] The focus on the Ganges in India fascinated and puzzled his readers, who found *Deep River* particularly "intriguing in that the author chose India (the Ganges) as the novel's central locale, which suggests that the terminal place of Endō's lifelong journeys, both spiritual and physical, is neither Japan nor Jerusalem, but India."[2] Most likely, this turn to India was conditioned by a new Christian interest in its Others and Japan's quest for its cultural location in the postwar world.[3] Little attempt, however, has been made to approach *Deep River* with reference to the literary accounts of "pilgrimages to India" that flourished in Europe in the nineteenth and twentieth centuries.[4] Among the various factors that contributed to this Indophilia are the intertwined discourses of Orientalism and Romanticism. The Japanese variant of Orientalism and Romanticism that made *Deep River* Endō's "Passage to India" both reiterated the rhetoric of its Western predecessors and strenuously disconnected India from modern Europe, positing instead a cultural continuum between Japan and South Asia.

For the Japanese tourists-pilgrims who followed the Europeans and Americans, India is a "realm utterly removed from Europe or Japan . . . and a unique world that [they] once knew but have now forgotten."[5] India was no longer the ancient anchorage or spiritual alternative for the modern West, but was claimed by the Japanese in their pan-Asian vision. Adrian Pinnington observes that, in contrast to "European arrogance and ethnocentrism," Endō espoused a "Japanese discovery of tolerance and ecumenicity, deriving from an Asian background."[6] The polarity between Asia and Europe is best encapsulated in the contrast of the Asian mother *Chāmundā* and the Holy Mother of Europe:

> It was . . . the image of the goddess Chāmundā . . . festering with leprosy, encoiled by poisonous vipers, gaunt, yet nursing children from her drooping breasts . . . the Asian mother who groans beneath the weight of the torments of this life . . . utterly different from the lofty, dignified Holy Mother of Europe.[7]

Translated as "Asian mother," the original expression Endō used, *tōyō no haha*, alerts us to Japan's tradition of *tōyō-gaku* (Oriental studies). Japan's Oriental studies invented the geopolitical and cultural category of *tōyō*—Japan's orient (China and inner Asia in particular and the whole of Asia in general)—after the model of, and in competition with, Western Orientalism. Stephen Tanaka comments that "the notion of *tōyō* bears several key similarities to changes occurring in Europe during the eighteenth and nineteenth centuries, in particular the emergence of Romantic historiography and the European (especially German) discovery of the Orient. . . . Whereas Romantic historians looked to the Orient for their origins; Japanese historians found them in *tōyō*."[8]

The irony of the myopic modern perspective implicit in the discourse of *tōyō* (literally, "the Eastern Ocean") cannot be more poignant: Since Japan itself is part of the "Eastern Ocean," Japanese scholars expanded this category to Asia in general; but the non-Japanese regions (that is, Japan's Orient) were a continent that lay west of Japan (that is, properly "East" only from a Eurocentric, Orientalist perspective). This problematic rejiggering of *tōyō* lurks in and behind *Deep River*, and so the rich insights of Endō's literature and theology are by no means exhausted by a simple juxtaposition of the East (reduced to Japan) and West. Relatedly, Endō's sense of animality that destabilizes the binary of humanity and divinity arises precisely from this complication.

Endō's last novel presents India, which lacked the prosperity of either Europe or Japan, as a land of grotesque suffering and "ghastly vulgarity."[9] This enactment of an Indian primitivism is typical of Orientalist writing, whether European or Japanese. According to Endō's diary, he consulted the dialogues of Uehara Kazu (1924–2017) and Hirayama Ikuo (1930–2009), two scholars of Japan's Oriental studies, over Indian art while working on his last novel.[10] Equally discernible is the influence of Watsuji Tetsurō (1889–1960), a cultural particularist and Japanese nativist who contrasted the Asian and Western cultural climates and on this basis promoted a non-Western, pan-Asian culture. Endō borrowed his mudswamp metaphor to describe Japanese culture in both *Silence* and *Deep River*, turning the disparity between India and Japan into a temporal scheme that links India (the past) to Japan (the present), whereas Western schemes set up a categorical difference between India's chaos and an orderly Europe.[11]

From the Irony of Japan's Orient to the Aporia of "Overcoming Modernity"

Watsuji's cultural particularism was one of the prevailing intellectual trends of the 1930s and 1940s. In that same period, the Japan Romantic School (*Nihon Romanha*) also emerged, and its scholars promoted an aesthetic nationalism on the basis of ethnic/cultural particularity in relation to Japan's Asian others. Countering Westernization and modernization, they reasserted the primacy of "tradition" in "Asia" and posited Japan as its righteous guardian.[12] Kamei Katsuichirō (1907–1966), a leading member of the Japan Romantic School, has been credited with organizing the "Kindai no Chōkoku" (*Overcoming Modernity*) symposium held in 1942. The connection between Kamei and Endō, who revered the former as a spiritual mentor, has yet to be properly studied. A no-less-important yet equally neglected mentor of Endō's circle is Yoshimitsu Yoshihiko (1904–1945), a Japanese Catholic theologian who presented at the symposium and critiqued the secular modernity of the West. It is these two figures, with whom Endō maintained close personal contact,[13] who lay the blueprint for *Deep River*. However, given Endō's postwar disillusionment, there is both continuity and disparity between Endō's Asian vision and the pan-Asianism of his mentors.

Endō's emphasis on suffering rather than the glories of Asia embodies his ambivalence toward the controversial heritage of Japanese Orientalism, especially its sinister intertwining of an aesthetic/spiritual pan-Asianism and Japan's history of military expansion and colonial conquest. Having spent his adolescence surrounded by war's devastation and narrowly escaped conscription thanks to his poor health, Endō distinguished himself as a talented young writer in the 1950s. He was perhaps more familiar with postwar critiques of "Overcoming Modernity" than the symposium itself.[14] The traumas of saturation bombing and the nuclear assaults turned the Japanese against their "Holy War." Embracing defeat, they began to question, if not outright condemn, their broken dreams. Moreover, it is worth mentioning that Hara Tamiki (1905–1951), a renowned poet and close friend of Kamei, Yoshimitsu, and Endō, narrowly survived the atomic bombing of Hiroshima, only to commit suicide in 1951. Anguished over his death and devoted to the commemoration of war victims, Endō developed into an antiwar writer and never hesitated to revisit war memories in order to combat wishful forgetting.[15] No wonder his India (and all Asia by extension) is the site of dreadful suffering, encapsulated in the "inhuman" figure of *Chāmundā*, the mother of *tōyō*. While Japanese tourists-pilgrims sought an abstract "Japanese past" in India, some brought with them memories of wartime experience in other parts of Asia (that is, China and Burma).

To seek the salvation of the sacrificed—that is, those sacrificed by the symbolic and actual violence unleashed in the triangular entanglement of Japan, the West, and the Rest—is the primary theological agenda of Endō's last novel. Among the central images of the novel, paralleling *Chāmundā* the Asian mother, is "the bloated corpse of a grey dog" carried and caressed by the waves of the holy river.[16] The overlap of war memories and human-animal stories, coupled with the conflation of meaningless sacrifice and unconditional salvation, directed Endō's literary and religious career to its climax, the significance of which has yet to be unpacked. Key here is the vexed relationship between Endō and his mentors.

Endō's essay "Shūkyō to Bungaku" (Religion and literature)[17] synthesizes the theses proclaimed by Yoshimitsu and Kamei at the "Overcoming Modernity" symposium.[18] In the summer of 1942, seven months after the Pacific War broke out in December 1941, members of the Japan Romantic School, the Kyoto School of Philosophy, and the journal *Bungakkai* (Literary world) met at the "Overcoming Modernity" symposium to discuss how to throw off the Western form of modernity and to create and then preserve a distinct cultural identity for modern Japan. Although no consensus was reached about just what constituted modernity or how to overcome its then-current forms, the symposium was unmistakably an outcome of the intertwined development of Japanese nationalism, Orientalism, and pan-Asianism. On a smaller scale, the intellectual resonance between Kamei and Yoshimitsu, who both questioned the modern discourse of secularism, attracted young Endō's attention.

What Endō's essay "Shūkyō to Bungaku" brings to light is the postsecular dimension of that "infamous" symposium, which, at least for Kamei and Yoshimitsu, had to overcome secularism in particular. This is particularly useful for understanding Endō's attempts to revive Asianism. Yoshimitsu, an antimodern Catholic theologian (and a former Protestant) who studied Neo-Thomism with Jacques Maritain in the 1930s, never openly opposed Japanese militarism but remained aloof from wartime politics.[19] Kamei, once an impassioned proclaimer of the "Holy War," eventually recanted publicly his wartime collaboration. However, the crucial transition in his career was not his postwar repentance, but his conversion from Marxist materialism to the spiritual sustenance of Pure Land Buddhism. The former Protestant and former Marxist shared a suspicion of modern, Western secularism.

At the symposium, Yoshimitsu critiqued the Protestant form of modernity and looked back to the Catholic medieval West as an alternative that modern Japan could model. In a similar light, Kamei, in his search for a non-Western norm for an alternative modernity, idealized the premodern history of Buddhism in Japan and envisioned an Asianist world order. Since Yoshimitsu passed away in 1945, Kamei clearly exerted more influence on Endō. While Japan was waging war, Kamei was studying Japanese classics, visiting Buddhist temples, and promoting the spiritual deliverance of Japanese and Asian people out of the grip of secular Western modernity.[20] His version of spiritual salvation is offered by the "motherly" religion of Asia, represented by *Chāmundā* the Asian mother, which was later popularized by Endō among his Japanese and Western audiences.

Kamei's 1957 book *Religion and Literature* begins by acknowledging the split of religion and literature described by Uchimura Kanzō (1861–1930). According to Uchimura, a Japanese Protestant thinker with whom Yoshimitsu studied before his conversion to Catholicism, religion claimed the author had a moral obligation to shun a world rampant with evil and avoid corrupting her readers by soliciting them to commit sins; by contrast, literature claimed autonomy from any external determination and endeavored to confront the complications, ambiguities, and sinfulness of our world.[21] But for Kamei, religion was not synonymous with Christianity. Studying Japanese Buddhist figures such as Prince Shōtoku (573–621) and the Pure Land monk Shinran (1173–1263), Kamei proclaimed Pure Land Buddhism to be a "motherly religion," in contrast to Uchimura's Protestant "fatherly" religion of prohibition and punishment. The Buddhist "motherly" religion faced up to and forgave human vulnerability and depravity. In the world of this motherly religion, the seemingly unbridgeable gap between religion and literature gave way to their confluence in overcoming the modern secular alienation from God. Only by plumbing the depth and darkness of human existence can people recover their lost *seishin kyōdōtai* (spiritual commonality).

In his essay "Religion and Literature," Endō argues that the conflict between religion and literature was a consequence of the progression of modernization that dissolved the "spiritual commonality" found in medieval Catholic France and in premodern Buddhist Japan. Tracing the line of the Catholic tradition,

Endō studied the revival of Catholic literature in modern Europe and focused on François Mauriac's *Thérèse Desqueyroux* and Julien Green's *Moïra*, both literary explorations into the realm of human depravity. He, like Kamei, turned to Pure Land Buddhism as a model of "motherly" compassionate religion. In *Deep River*, Mitsuko and Ōtsu, the dual protagonists, play out Endō's engagement with the literature of evil and the religion of forgiveness, respectively. Mitsuko was a reader of literature and imitated Thérèse and Moïra in her own life, whereas Ōtsu pursued a motherly religion that transcended the boundaries of Catholicism and Buddhism.

Endō believed that the false dichotomy of religion and literature was symptomatic of modern fragmentation and alienation; hence, overcoming this dichotomy depended on the recovery of *spiritual commonalities*. Most interestingly, it is to India—rather than France or Japan—that his characters travel in their search. I trace Endō's idealist, if not essentialist, vision of premodern Catholic Europe and Buddhist Japan back to Yoshimitsu and Kamei. Moreover, the fictional geography of Asia in *Deep River*, with India as the definitive "Asian" destination, attests to Endō's efforts to salvage Japanese pan-Asianism from the grip of wartime ideologies and propaganda.

Asian War, Sacrificial Animal, and Animal Salvation

Published in the early 1990s and premised on the Japanese economic and cultural vitality of the 1980s, Endō's *Deep River* is shot through with a sense of national pride as well as nostalgia for a forgotten Asian past. However, this is a past that has been tainted by Japan's Asian war. *Deep River* came out at the same time incisive critiques of Japanese militarism, colonialism, and imperialism were being leveled across Japanese and Western academia. The novel's enactment of war-related experiences in particular points to Endō's ambivalence regarding the failed and/or still unfinished projects of his mentors. Most relevant to our investigation here are the stories of Numada and Kiguchi.[22] These two stories share their setting in the midst of Japan's military aggression in other parts of Asia and their theme, the human-animal relation. Numada is a writer of children's stories who spent his childhood in Dalian, a Japanese colonial city in China's northeast, while Kiguchi is a veteran who survived the "Highway of Death" in the Burmese jungles. Numada's childhood friendship with a Chinese boy and a Manchu dog turned him into a writer of fantasy stories that dissolved the human-animal distinction. Kiguchi witnessed the rise of a secret trade in the heart of Burma's dark forests, that is, a trade in human flesh peddled as "lizard meat," which heralds another kind of dissolution of human-animal boundaries.

When the Japanese tourists-pilgrims first arrive in Delhi, they are greeted by a tepid wind filled with "the smell of the earth and the vibrant aroma of trees that cities even in the provinces of Japan had lost."[23] Numada in particular is struck by the sight of animals wandering the streets and mutters to himself: "In Japan in the old days you could see animals and human beings living side by side."[24] Although this nostalgia for a "Japanese" past rediscovered in today's India smacks of Orientalism, still another layer of the past is carried by Numada and Kiguchi; that is, the inescapable past of Japan's Asian war. "The moment he inhaled that air, Kiguchi remembered a small town in Burma where he had been stationed during the war."[25] And the first animal Numada befriends is a stray dog in Dalian, China. Kiguchi has traveled to India hoping to offer a Buddhist ceremony to commemorate the deaths of his fellow and enemy soldiers alike; whereas Numada goes there to visit a wild bird sanctuary where he can release a caged bird (another Buddhist ceremony) to pay tribute to his animal friends.[26]

Endō's peculiar focus on the human-animal relation in his Asian war stories must be factored into his engagement with the immediate and inescapable past of Japanese colonialism, militarism, and imperialism. Numada's story is based on Endō's own childhood experiences in Dalian. At the age of three, Endō moved to the city of Dalian with his parents. He returned to Japan in 1933 when his parents divorced, shortly after the Japanese-controlled puppet state of Manshū-koku (1932–45) was established in Northeast China. He wrote about the Chinese boy Li and the stray dog Blackie in a series of short stories and essays before invoking them one last time in *Deep River*.[27] Suffering from his parents' deteriorating relationship, Endō (Numada) the lonely boy had the Chinese servant boy Li as his only friend. Out of sympathy for his young master, Li helped him adopt a dog, Blackie. But the Endō (Numada) family fired Li for a theft he never committed; whereas Blackie, who followed little Endō (Numada) everywhere and always listened to his complaints, was abandoned when his master was sent back to Japan.

Historical contextualization is in order. Japan established colonial rule in Dalian in 1905, right after the Russo-Japanese War (1904–5). In the novel, the city was "filled with the smells of the Russians who had occupied the land before Japan . . . and the Japanese, brimming with the vulgarity and high-handedness of the parvenu, [strolled] these streets disdainful of the Chinese who had lived here for countless years. Even to the eyes of a child like Numada, the district where the Chinese lived seemed squalid and pitiful."[28] Li, the Chinese boy, was suspected of having stolen coal and summarily kicked out of the Numada house because "there were any number of houseboys or amahs to be found in Dalian to take his place."[29] Numada first lost Li and then had to abandon Blackie when he left Dalian. "It was thanks to Li and to this dog that he had first come to know the meaning of separation."[30]

The affinity of Li and Blackie, who both looked up to Numada as their "master," destroyed for good the rosy vision of a children's story. The "meaning of separation" in the story refers to the distinction of the Japanese from the animal realm of their colonies. The Chinese marketplace in Dalian reeked of garlic and was a wild exhibition of "pigs' heads and plucked chickens."[31] The dehumanization of the colonized is a mechanism of the "anthropological machine" of Japanese colonialism and imperialism, to borrow a term from Giorgio Agamben, who compares the history of Western science and philosophy to an anthropological machine: "In the machine of the moderns, the outside is produced through the exclusion of an inside and the inhuman produced by animalizing the human."[32]

In the Burmese jungles, another animal (or, colonized) world, one dominated by downpours, trees, and reptiles, the Japanese anthropological machine backfired. In Kiguchi's story, imperial soldiers struggling for survival discarded weapons "presented to them on behalf of the Emperor as objects more precious than their own lives"[33] and cursed their commanding officer, who ordered every one of them "to believe firmly in inevitable victory . . . and to attack the enemy with all [their] might."[34] Kiguchi and his fellow soldiers were reduced to walking skeletons carrying on their bodies squirming maggots and swarms of flies. His friend Tsukada purchased some lizard meat and devoured it, but Kiguchi was too weak to swallow. It turns out that the "lizard meat" was human flesh, the remains of PFC Mimamikawa, whom both Kiguchi and Tsukada knew. The reversed status of the Japanese in these two episodes exposes the ultimate irony of the anthropological machine. In Dalian, the non-Japanese are made less human (i.e., animalized), while in Burma, this happened to the Japanese themselves.

The target of Endō's critique is not just Japanese colonialism per se (Numada's experience in Dalian), but also Japan's reinscription of the power structure of Western modernity in its resistance against it—Japan's military confrontation with British-Indian allies in Burma. His novel is a fascinating mixture of Japanese Orientalism (whose rhetoric he could not entirely escape) and a strong undercurrent that questions the legitimacy of Japan's historical quest for cultural specificity and an alternative modernity, without disclaiming that quest itself. Endō's ultimate dilemma centered on what had gone wrong not only in the Western form of modernity but also in the counter invention of its opposite, an aesthetic, spiritual, and traditional Asia, at the hands of Japanese intellectuals.

To wrestle with this aporia, Endō turned to dismantle the anthropological machine that elevated little Numada above the Chinese boy and Blackie and turned Kiguchi's co-combatants into cannibals and "lizard meat." Given the tripartite world geography (West-Japan-Rest) of *Deep River*, the problem of animality has a particularly charged valence. The setting of Endō's animal stories overlaps with the novel's portrayal of non-Japanese Asia during the war. The acknowledgement that the human-animal distinction has always been a site of contestation where "relations of power operate in their exemplary purity (that is, operate with the fewest moral and material obstacles)"[35] suggests the reverse as well: When power relations operate, lose control, and become unhindered (e.g., at the time of war), we arrive at a moment when the always already-indecisive human-animal distinction dissolves, as in Dalian and Burma.

By focusing on these animal stories, we retrieve not only the overlooked non-Japanese, non-Western Rest from the all-too-familiar binary of East (Japan) and West, but also the equally overlooked dimension of animality in Endō's pluralist theology. The West-Japan-Asia tripartite in the novel corresponds to Endō's attentiveness toward the interlinked issues of divinity, humanity, and animality.[36] With regard to the last, another set of signifying practices in which Endō's narrative intervenes is the view of animals and human-animal relations in Christianity and Buddhism. These traditions, neither of which is static or homogeneous, are loaded with anthropocentrism, as well as resources for posthumanism. Steering between the Scylla of Christian universalism and the Charybdis of Japanese nationalism (which once appropriated Buddhism), Endō again turned to animals, their sacrificiality, and their salvation. He creatively deployed traditional and unconventional resources to push the limits of religious orthodoxy in his alignment of animals with Jesus Christ and Amida Buddha. By doing so, he inserted theology into the posthumanist discussion of the human-animal relation to make it postsecular and, vice versa, he revitalized comparative theology by further complicating and destabilizing the self-other relation.

By the Ganges, Kiguchi shares with Mitsuko his fellow soldiers' cannibalism story. Trying to console the old man, Mitsuko says, "To one degree or other, we all live by eating others."[37] Kiguchi shakes his head, realizing that Mitsuko (the postwar generation) has reduced the reality of human/animal sacrifice to a mere metaphor. Kiguchi and his fellow soldiers were first sacrificed by the anthropological machine of Japanese militarism and then, even more devastatingly, through postwar democratization and the peace movement. These unknown soldiers—canon fodder who had to bear the branding of war criminals—suffered discrimination and abandonment in Japanese society. They are modern reincarnations of Rokuemon Hasekura, the protagonist in Endō's novel *Samurai* (1980). Ambitious European missionaries and local political warlords manipulate Rokuemon, a low-level samurai, to travel to South America and then to the Vatican, in pursuit of favorable trade relations. He compares himself with a snail snatched out of its shell and flung away from its mudswamp to the land of the unknown. However, when this human-snail returns to Japan, a new political regime has taken power and orders his execution.

Another sense of sacrifice, Christ's on Golgotha, is also suggested by Endō's fiction. The sacrificed human-snail Rokuemon finds that Jesus Christ, the crucified god, is his only companion at the end of his life. When this human-snail has transformed into the human-lizard in *Deep River*, where then can it find salvation? When Derrida theorized the sacrificial structure that forms the human subject in relation to the animal other, he emphasized that "the subject does not want just to master and possess nature actively. In our cultures, he accepts sacrifice and eats flesh."[38] In the story of Kiguchi and his fellow soldiers, the Japanese consuming themselves embodies this sacrificial animality, and they suffer the crumbling of their already problematic humanity. Can they still be saved?

Salvation comes from the sacrificial and sacrificed animal. Once caught naked in the gaze of his cat, Derrida realized that "it has its point of view regarding me,"[39] and he critiqued Heidegger and Levinas for having presented animals as mute and faceless. In a very similar light, Endō's theology adopts an animal point of view. Separated from his childhood friends, Numada grew into a writer of children's stories. He kept a pet bird (a hornbill) by the name of Pierrot. The hornbill and the myna (Numada's second bird) both died while Numada was hospitalized for a dangerous operation from which he survived. Thinking that they had died in his place—in other words, that they had sacrificed themselves for him—Numada decides to travel to India to visit the birds there. There is this conversation between Numada and Pierrot the hornbill about the former's writing:

> [PIERROT:] "Boring. Those are just dreams made up to please yourself, aren't they? Take a look at me. I've been brought from the distant forests where my friends reside to this alien land so that I can be a source of comfort to you."

[NUMADA:] "Maybe that's true. But you have no idea how much comfort birds like you and dogs have brought me since I was a child. Even tonight . . . having you here in the room with me . . . it helps."[40]

Numada's bird not only has a voice but also a real face, that is, the face of Jesus Christ: "It is a strange metaphor, to compare such a bird with Jesus, but Numada had his reasons for doing so. Numada had taken a liking to Rouault's paintings, and there was something about the many Pierrot faces he portrayed in his works that resembled this hornbill. He knew that for Rouault clowns were a symbol of Christ."[41] Pierrot's face is not just the face of Jesus Christ, but also his trampled face. In a short story titled "The Hornbill," Endō depicts the intimate relationship between a novelist and his hornbill.[42] The writer, apparently a self-projection of Endō, constantly talks to his hornbill and even writes the bird into his fiction. He is actually researching and writing about a certain Father F., whose story immediately reminds us of Fr. Ferreira, the Portuguese missionary who appears in *Silence* and *The Golden Country*. In that writer's imagination, Father F. identifies with a hornbill and talks to the bird, since both of them travel across the oceans from the sunny south to the mud-swamp of Japan where they are trapped.

Ferreira (or Father F.), having trampled the face of Jesus to renounce Christianity, starts his new life in Japan and invents *fumie*, the practice of forcing Japanese Christians to trample on portraits of Jesus and Mary. Kitamori Kazō (1916–1998), a Japanese Protestant theologian and author of *The Theology of the Pain of God*, once remarked that Endō wrote a "theology of pain in the foot."[43] By this he refers to the foot that steps upon the face of Jesus and reads Endō's theology as deviating from the traditional Christian notion of sin to a new focus on vulnerability.[44] As an apostate who has abandoned God, Father F. can only pray to his hornbill, his substitute God, who alone listens to his pleas for forgiveness. The bird is not merely a symbol of Christ; it is God. In *Deep River*, we read that although Numada "doesn't know anything about God," he loves his Blackie and birds as God, in that "God is someone humans can talk to from the heart."[45]

The sacrificed are both saved and salvific. This same message comes across in the story of Kiguchi as well. In the postwar section of Kiguchi's story, believing that he will fall into the evil realm of "hungry ghosts," Tsukada, Kiguchi's comrade, literally drinks himself to death. At his deathbed, a strange foreigner who does volunteer work at the hospital (a protagonist in

Endō's earlier novel, *Wonderful Fool*) tells him a Eucharist story: When a plane crashed in the Andes Mountains, someone critically injured offered his own flesh to his fellow travelers and helped to sustain them until the rescue team arrived. (Here Endō rewrote his short story "Last Supper.") This alternative meaning of sacrifice brought peace to the afflicted Tsukada. After Tsukada's funeral, Kiguchi flew to India, the home of their wartime enemies, and chanted by the Ganges passages about "songs of harmony" by "white swans, peacocks, parrots, kalavinkas and curlews" from the *Amida Sūtra*, one of the founding scriptures of Pure Land Buddhism.[46]

Birdsong in the Buddhist paradise echoes the birds' chirping in the Burmese jungle. "In spite of the grisly scene [of the dying and dead soldiers], when the rains stopped, the birds chirped happily away."[47] The birds' chirping may be read as signifying the indifference of nature or the working of blind necessity. However, the conflation of the hellish jungle and the Pure Land paradise suggests the salvation of the sacrificed. The unconditional compassion of Pure Land Buddhism (the "motherly" religion of Kamei and Endō) derived from the notion of universal salvation in the *Amida Sūtra*. Within Buddhist cosmology, animals (birds included), hungry ghosts, and the denizens of hell constitute the three evil realms. But Pure Land Buddhists believe that even beings occupying these evil realms will be saved eventually. Endō's theology of the animal Christ challenges the anthropocentric monotheism of Christianity, whereas his vision of the animal Buddha, though not so radical, is again peripheral to much of the Buddhist tradition.[48]

Having considered Endō's posthumanist synthesis of Christianity and Buddhism, I stress that *Deep River* embraces animal theology, creaturely poetics, and posthumanist Asianism. On reading Simone Weil's statement that "the vulnerability of precious things is beautiful because vulnerability is a mark of existence," Anat Pick proposed that the inherently ethical conception of beauty in fragility and finitude "implies a sort of sacred recognition of life's value as material and temporal."[49] This vision of a creaturely aesthetics/ethics is based on Weil's reflections on gravity (blind material necessity) and grace (perfect love in the absence of God), a paradox by no means absent from Endō's fiction.

Weil regards the pure necessity of our material and mortal bodies (best exemplified by the sacrificed animals, as Pick points out) as the abandoned and forsaken state we suffer. Bare life—abandoned, forsaken, stripped of any illusions of humanity—is the affliction or ultimate thing-ness to which we are reduced by the blind law of necessity. However, it is in this abandonment or separation from God, Weil writes, that we encounter the grace of the absent

God: "Compassion for every creature, because it is far from Good. Infinitely far. Abandoned. God abandons our whole entire being-flesh, blood, sensibility, intelligence, love—to the pitiless necessity of matter."[50]

This "compassion for every creature" in Endō's stories is the saving grace of Jesus Christ and Amida Buddha, which turns the sacrifice of animals into the very site of salvation. According to Weil, reality is where the blind necessity of matter and the loving grace of God meet. One particularly vivid illustration of this reality in Endō's novel is the embrace of the body of a dead dog (our materiality and mortality) by the sacred river (the boundless compassion of God). There are more moments of the "sacred recognition" and redemption of our vulnerability and mortality, as represented by the overlapping of the face of the animal and that of the Christ, or the resonance of birdsong in both the Burmese hell and the Buddhist paradise.

In light of Weil's "attentiveness to reality," I return to *Chāmundā*, the Asian mother. This image is a palimpsest. From under the thick layers of Japanese nationalism, Orientalism, and Asianism, Endō's new vision of a postsecular/posthumanist Asianism and Christian-Buddhist synthesis shines through. The Japanese tourists, who search for some lost "spiritual commonality," experience a revelation: the body of this Asian mother who sinks down into the realm of nonhuman creatures and becomes entangled with the phantoms of war victims. The lightness of our being is unbearable because we are unbearably vulnerable, suffering the gravity of violence and trauma. However, to invoke Weil one last time, grace makes and fills fissures and voids. Endō's achievement has been to cut through the ideational boundaries imposed by Western and non-Western powers, which once blocked the flow of grace into those empty spaces. He has made a new channel instead, which welcomes the deep river of divine love that embraces the lightness of our being.

Notes

1. Shusaku Endo, *Deep River*, trans. Van C. Gessel (New York: New Directions, 1994).

2. Takao Hagiwara, "Return to Japan: The Case of Endō Shūsaku," *Comparative Literature Studies* 37, no. 2 (2000): 125–54, 145.

3. For the influences of John Hick and Ninian Smart on Endō, see Mark Williams, "Crossing the Deep River: Endō Shūsaku and the Problem of Religious Pluralism," in *Xavier's Legacies: Catholicism in Modern Japanese Culture*, ed. Kevin M. Doak (Vancouver: UBC Press, 2011), 115–33. For postwar Japan, where shame was

replaced by pride during the economic boom of the 1980s, see Emi Mase-Hasegawa, *Christ in Japanese Culture: Theological Themes in Shūsaku Endō's Literary Works* (Leiden; Boston: Brill, 2008), 139–80.

4. Theodore Ziolkowski, "Pilgrimages to India," in *Modes of Faith: Secular Surrogates for Lost Religious Belief* (Chicago: University of Chicago Press, 2007), 83–118.

5. Ibid., 108.

6. Adrian Pinnington, "Yoshimitsu, Benedict, Endō: Guilt, Shame and the Post-War Idea of Japan," *Japan Forum* 13, no. 1 (2001): 91–105, 101.

7. Endo, *Deep River*, 175.

8. Stephen Tanaka, *Japan's Orient: Rendering Pasts into History* (Berkeley: University of California Press, 1993), 13–14.

9. Endo, *Deep River*, 132.

10. Endō Shūsaku, Fukai kawa *sōsaku nikki* [*Deep River* composition diary] (Tōkyō: Kōdansha, 1997), 106–7.

11. Watsuji Tetsurō, *Fūdo: ningengakuteki kōsatsu* [Climate: studying the science of humanity] (Tōkyō: Iwanami Shoten, 1940); For Watsuji's influence on Endō's novel *Silence*, see J. Netland, "From Cultural Alterity to the Habitations of Grace: The Evolving Moral Topography of Endō's Mudswamp Trope," *Christianity & Literature* 59, no. 1 (2009): 27–48.

12. Kevin Michael Doak, *Dreams of Difference: the Japan Romantic School and the Crisis of Modernity* (Berkeley: University of California Press, 1994).

13. See "Yoshimitsu sensei no koto" [About Mr. Yoshimitsu] in *Endō Shūsaku bungaku zenshū* [Complete literary works of Endō Shūsaku], vol. 12 (Tokyo: Shinchosha, 1975), 207–9. Endō wrote about Kamei in two essays, "The Split between Beauty and Faith: Katsuichirō Kamei" and "Something about Mr. Kamei," *Zenshū*, vol. 13, 56–58, 226–29.

14. For a critique (and retrieval) of Japanese nationalism and Asianism, see Takeuchi Yoshimi, "Overcoming Modernity," in *What Is Modernity? Writings of Takeuchi Yoshimi*, ed. and trans. Richard F. Calichman (New York: Columbia University Press, 2005), 103–48; Harry D. Harootunian, *Overcome by Modernity: History, Culture, and Community in Interwar Japan* (Princeton: Princeton University Press, 2000).

15. For a historical survey and analysis of the catastrophic psychic and political consequences of Japan's defeat in World War II, see Robert Jay Lifton, *Death in Life: Survivors of Hiroshima* (Chapel Hill: University of North Carolina Press, 1991); John W. Dower, *Ways of Forgetting, Ways of Remembering: Japan in the Modern World* (New York: New Press, 2012).

16. Endo, *Deep River*, 144.

17. Endō, "Shūkyō to Bungaku" [Religion and literature], *Zenshū*, vol. 12, 310–18.

18. Yoshimitsu, "The Theological Grounds of Overcoming Modernity: How Can Modern Man Find God?" in *Overcoming Modernity: Cultural Identity in Wartime Japan*, trans. and ed. Richard Calichman (New York: Columbia University Press, 2008), 77–91; Kamei Katsuichirō, "A Note on Contemporary Spirit," in *Overcoming Modernity*, 42–50.

19. Pinnington, "Yoshimitsu, Benedict, Endō"; Akira Takahashi, "Understanding Yoshimitsu Yoshihiko's Mysticism," *Comparative Literature Studies* 39, no. 4 (2002): 272–81; Kevin Doak, "Time, Culture and Faith: *Yoshimitsu Yoshihiko*'s Critique of Modernity," *University of Tokyo Center of Philosophy Bulletin* I (2003): 85–95.

20. *On Faith* was published in 1942. See *Dreams of Difference*, 104.

21. Kamei Katsuichirō, "Watashi no Shūkyō Kan" [My view on religion], in *Shūkyō to Bungaku* [Religion and literature] (Tōkyō: Dainihon'yūbenkaikōdansha, 1957), 266–67. For Kamei's comments on Uchimura, see Katsuichirō, *Nihonjin no bi to shinkō* [Beauty and faith of the Japanese people] (Tōkyō: Daiwa Shobō, 1969).

22. According to Endō's diary, the original storyline of *Deep River* evolved around a war veteran (Kiguchi), a writer (Numada), and Mitsuko, with Ōtsu being a character later inserted into the novel. For a concise chart illustrating the character developments during Endō's composition of *Deep River*, see Yamane Michihiro, *Endō Shūsaku Dīpu ribā o yomu: Mazā Teresa, Miyazawa Kenji to hibikiau sekai* [Reading Endō Shūsaku's *Deep River*: a world that resonates with Mother Theresa and Miyazawa Kenji] (Tōkyō: Chōbunsha, 2010), 259–66.

23. Endo, *Deep River*, 104.

24. Ibid., 106.

25. Ibid., 104.

26. "Animal liberation" is a popular Buddhist practice in East Asia. See Duncan Williams, "Animal Liberation, Death, and the State: Rites to Release Animals in Medieval Japan," in *Buddhism and Ecology: The Interconnection of Dharma and Deeds*, ed. Mary Evelyn Tucker and Duncan Williams (Cambridge: Harvard University Press, 1997).

27. Yamane, *Reading Endō Shūsaku's* Deep River, 129–30.

28. Endo, *Deep River*, 70.

29. Ibid., 72.

30. Ibid., 74.

31. Ibid., 70.

32. Giorgio Agamben, *The Open: Man and Animal*, trans. Kevin Attell (Stanford: Stanford University Press, 2004), 37.

33. Endo, *Deep River*, 86.

34. Ibid., 87.

35. Anat Pick, *Creaturely Poetics: Animality and Vulnerability in Literature and Film* (New York: Columbia University Press, 2011), 1.

36. For a reading that stresses the humanity side of Endō's Christology, see Leith Morton, *The Image of Christ in the Fiction of Endō Shūsaku* ([Clayton, Vic.]: Japanese Studies Centre, 1994).

37. Endo, *Deep River*, 198.

38. Jacques Derrida, *The Animal That Therefore I Am*, ed. Marie-Louise Mallet and trans. David Wills (New York: Fordham University Press, 2008), 114.

39. Ibid., 380.

40. Endo, *Deep River*, 75–76.

41. Ibid., 77.
42. Yamane, 135–39.
43. Ibid.
44. Ibid.
45. Endo, *Deep River*, 81.
46. Ibid., 201.
47. Ibid., 87.
48. See Paul Waldau, *The Specter of Speciesism: Buddhist and Christian Views of Animals* (New York: Oxford University Press, 2001).
49. Pick, *Creaturely Poetics*, 3.
50. Simone Weil, *Gravity and Grace*, trans. Emma Crawford and Mario von der Ruhr (London: Routledge, 2004), 142.

Chapter Four

Religion and Violence in *Deep River*

RONALD GREEN

Introduction

The 1995 Japanese movie version of *Deep River*, directed by Kei Kumai, remains faithful to Endō Shūsaku's manuscript, with the exception of two crucial omissions: it leaves out the assassination of Indira Gandhi, and other major incidents involving Sikhs that play a part in Endō's overall scheme. This chapter reveals these events' narrative significance for the novel by examining how Endō blends destructive and violent experiences and personality traits with violence on a larger sociopolitical scale, ultimately presenting violence as universal and even redemptive through the metaphor of the Onion. Leaving aside nature, which could be considered a fourth element completing the circle of his narration, the chapter examines these destructive and violent elements in three sections. It begins by considering the place of religion and violence in the lives of individual characters, focusing on the novel's first half. It then provides a narrative history of the 1984 anti-Sikh riots, also known as the 1984 genocide of Sikhs, which is one example of Endō's taking violence from the individual to the sociopolitical sphere. It concludes by examining Endō's presentation of religion and violence as a universal phenomenon, which relates to his use of artistic religious imagery such as the destructive goddess Chāmundā, the suffering pierrot, and the Onion. To understand these issues, it will be helpful to consider the correspondence between Ōtsu's Onion and the parable of the onion in *The Brothers Karamazov* by Dostoevsky. Following this pattern, religion and violence are presented in Endō's novel as layers of the Onion.[1]

Religion and Violence in Individual Lives: The Drive to Destroy Herself

Keiko's near-death vision of reincarnation in the opening chapter of *Deep River* sets up the novel's motifs of destruction and rebirth playing out at the individual level. As an integral part of his storytelling, Endō relies on the Hindu conception of human life, or *saṃsāra*, as having three aspects that make up an ongoing and eternal process. These are creation, maintenance, and destruction, often conceived through the so-called Trimūrti represented by the male Hindu deities Brahmā (creation), Viṣṇu (maintenance), and Śiva (destruction). Endō gives us evidence that at least in the fictional universe of his novel, some people who are near death truly attain special insights into aspects of reality that are ordinarily considered matters of faith. Proof can be found, for instance, in another vision Keiko has of her husband, Isobe, leaving a pot on their gas stove. In her vision, she repeatedly calls out to Isobe to go and turn off the gas. Isobe admits that in fact, outside of the vision, he had gone to sleep with a pot on the gas burning just as Keiko had described. He woke up, as if because she was calling from her vision, and hurried to turn off the gas. That Keiko's vision corresponds to an actual event reinforces the notion that her insight into reincarnation may also be reliable. Although it is possibly a coincidence, the implication is that it might well be more, both inside and outside the novel; even if it is not so, the belief in this possibility still drives Isobe's subsequent actions. In light of the extraordinary events transpiring around Keiko at this time in her life, we may take the appearance of Mitsuko in her hospital room and Mitsuko's meeting with Isobe as more karmic than coincidental, particularly because they will come together again at the informational meeting for a pilgrimage tour to India described in chapter 2. Endō does not seem to be implying that the same extraordinary insights occur to Ōtsu when he is on the bamboo litter, although he does tell Mitsuko that his life is how it should be.[2]

Chapter 2 begins with a description of the Ganges River given by Enami, the Japanese tour guide; it is this river, sacred to Hindus and other Indian religionists, that must, in part, contribute to the novel's title. In some sense, the title combines the idea of the sacred river with the deep and troubled history of humanity, like Bashō's "old pond" or Father Zosima's all-encompassing ocean in *The Brothers Karamazov*.[3] Although short, chapter 2 introduces themes crucial to our analysis of religion and violence in *Deep River*. After explaining the significance of the Ganges and briefly mentioning other important religious sites their tour will visit, Enami describes the Hindu caste system, based on the belief in reincarnation noted above. In this description he speaks of untouchability and the lowly position of the so-called Harijans, explaining that while the name means "children of God," other Hindus above them in the caste hierarchy have subjected the group to long-standing bigotry and discrimination. Such contradictions between uplifting religious euphemism and human cruelty repeat as the novel explores the relationship between individual and social violence.

When asked by one of the pilgrims what Hindus believe, Enami shows the group a slide depicting the fierce goddess Kālī. In this way, Endō begins to connect individual and social suffering and destruction. Kālī is the consort of Śiva, the god of destruction, but is also seen to be the destroyer herself. She is described in the novel as trampling on a human corpse and wearing a necklace of severed heads. And yet Enami rightly relates the image of Kālī, who is also called the divine mother, to that of the Holy Mother Mary in Christianity. In this context, he next mentions Chāmundā, a frightening manifestation of Hinduism's divine mother. Again, Endō is building the backdrop for his own tale of the relationship between destruction and redemption, as recurring at the individual, social, and universal levels in the deep river of humanity.

While Kālī has divine knowledge about the role of her destructive power in the eternal scheme of creation, maintenance, and destruction, Mitsuko, who also plays the role of the destroyer, does so not out of compassion but from a natural urge. After mentioning Eve's seduction of Adam, the narrator states, "Within each woman lurked the impulsive drive to destroy herself."[4] As we will see, however, the Onion can transform evil, which cannot be clearly distinguished from good, into a tool of salvation.

In some ways, Ōtsu serves as the "impact character" for Mitsuko, just as she does for him. An impact or "influence character," as Melanie Anne Phillips and Chris Huntley call it, causes doubt in another character's approach to life by being diametrically opposed to it.[5] This tension with Ōtsu eventually leads to Mitsuko's transformation, bringing about an end to her own destructiveness and the birth of her compassion. But Ōtsu's character serves as much more than just a foil for Mitsuko. He resembles, states Mitsuko, Joseph from Julien Green's *Moïra*, who is seduced by, but then kills, the titular character. But Ōtsu also resembles Alyosha Karamazov from Dostoyevsky's *The Brothers Karamazov* in some ways and even, perhaps, Dostoyevsky's *The Idiot*, especially when we consider Endō's frequent mention of pierrot in relation to Ōtsu, Jesus, and others. "The Idiot" in the title of Dostoyevsky's novel refers to its main character, Prince Myshkin, whose simple goodness, like that of Ōtsu, is mistaken for a lack of intelligence. Endō may be making another connection between Ōtsu and Alyosha in the repeated reference to God as the Onion in the context of destruction, a point to which we return in the third section. Like Alyosha, Ōtsu serves as a counterbalance to the strongly expressed atheist views of some characters and is summarily abused as a result, even if willingly, for the naïveté others assume of him. But more than serving to counter Mitsuko on this point, Ōtsu's doubt mirrors Mitsuko's own self-doubt and reveals many things about her internal conflict; Endō smoothly connects this conflict to recurring external conflicts in society, leading to the assassination of Indira Gandhi and the 1984 anti-Sikh riots.

Endō represents Mitsuko's destructive urge, which is evident in her first sleeping with Ōtsu, as a natural part of all women. This characterization, which must be objectionable to many readers, also brings Kālī back to mind. The author reinforces this idea with numerous statements from the narrator and with the thoughts of Mitsuko, who questions herself saying internally, *"What the hell am I searching for, doing these ridiculous things? Letting these men goad me on, making fun of Ōtsu—is this what my life is all about?"*[6] The narrator further explains that Mitsuko's anger was directed toward her own hollowness. Endō also refers to the Japanese Christians of the Middle Ages, who were forced to trample on the sacred face of Christ—the so-called *fumie*—to prove they were not "hidden Christians." The *fumie* was, of course, important in his novel *Silence*, released in 1966, twenty-seven years before *Deep River*.

While waiting to see if Ōtsu will come to the Kultur Heim, Mitsuko casually reads a passage from the Bible, stating, "[He] hath no form nor comeliness; and when we shall see him, there is no beauty that we should desire him."[7] This passage, which serves as the title of chapter 13, is drawn from Isaiah 53:2 and refers to the servant of God who believes His message and to whom God's arms have been outstretched. The next passage in Isaiah tells us that such a person suffers much. For Endō, this description encapsulates not only the characteristics of Ōtsu, but also the nondescript universality of the variously faithful around the world. Finding a book by Nakamura Hajime, a famous Japanese scholar of Hinduism and Buddhism, among Ōtsu's possessions, Mitsuko becomes ever more scornful. Nakamura is known for having written books that talk about the similarities and universal themes found across religions. She wonders about Ōtsu, whom she hopes to destroy, "Why were all men the same in the end?"[8]

Endō skillfully ties the suffering experienced by most characters in the book to the destruction that occurs on a larger scale among social groups. The culmination of this large-scale violence occurs while the Japanese tourists are in India, with the assassination of Indira Gandhi and the subsequent 1984 anti-Sikh riots, which also lead to Ōtsu's possibly fatal injuries.

The 1984 Anti-Sikh Riots: More by Enmity than Love

The 1984 Hindu-Sikh riots punctuate *Deep River*'s last section, tying the characters' experience of violence and destruction to socio-historical incidents of the same. Ultimately, Endō links these violent conflicts to nature itself and to universal truths expressed in religious art and literature. This section summarizes the events alluded to in the novel that interrupt the Japanese pilgrims' journey and lead to Ōtsu's possibly mortal injuries.

Many consider the central *gurdwara* (meaning "gateway to the guru") of Sikhism, the Golden Temple, to be one of the most beautiful buildings on earth. Located in Amritsar, a city in in the northeastern Indian state of Punjab, it is the most sacred place in a holy city for millions of Sikhs. It is where the hallowed scripture of Sikhism, the *Adi Granth* (also known as the *Guru Granth Sahib*), considered a living guru, is installed. But in 1984, tanks rolled into the temple to capture the controversial figure Jarnail Singh Bhindranwale (1947–1984); some called him a great saint, while others reviled him as a terrorist. In June 1984, Indira Gandhi, India's prime minister, issued the order to capture Bhindranwale in order to gain control of the Golden Temple. This order set off a chain of events that led to thousands of deaths, many of them Sikh, including her own. Since thousands of Sikhs were killed in retribution for her assassination by her Sikh bodyguards, one common description for this religiously inspired violence is the 1984 genocide of Sikhs.

As background, Sikhism is one of the youngest large religions of the world. Originating in the Punjab with Guru Nanak in the fifteenth century, today it is the ninth-largest religion in the world with an estimated twenty-five to twenty-eight million adherents worldwide. India naturally has the largest number of Sikh followers, just over twenty million. Even so, at the time of the 2011 Indian census, Sikhs made up only 1.72 percent of India's population, around the same percentage as in 1984; the census also showed that Hindus comprised about 80 percent of the population with over 827 million adherents.[9] The fact that Hindus so greatly outnumber Sikhs plays into the events of the massacre.

The fundamental beliefs of Sikhism are expressed in its sacred scripture the *Adi Granth*, including the belief in only one God who lacks form and gender but who can be accessed by all. So, too, Sikhs believe that all are equal before God, that empty religious rituals and superstitions have no value, and that all should live honestly and should care for others. Like the character Ōtsu, Sikhism holds that no one religion has exclusive access to ultimate truth. Indeed, the Golden Temple has a doorway on each side symbolizing its openness to all, even those of other faiths. Also like Ōtsu, Sikhs believe that doing good deeds is more important than practicing symbolic rituals.

The leading Sikh party in 1984 was the Akali Dal, which campaigned for greater autonomy for the Punjab. Similar to organizations with that name today, the Akali Dal was a Sikh centrist party that believed religion and state should not be separated. Some of its political stances opposed those of India's Congress Party, dominated by Indira Gandhi and her son Sanjay, which argued for a secular and united India. Prime Minister Gandhi feared that the call for greater autonomy by the Akali Dal in fact meant the creation of a separate Sikh religious state, which some Sikhs had envisioned in 1947, when India was partitioned into India and Pakistan.

In 1977, Indira Gandhi asked Sanjay to find a way to break the influence of the Akali Dal in the Punjab. As a result, Sanjay came up with a list of twenty people who could be potential rivals. The strongest among these was Jarnail Singh Bhindranwale, the new leader of the Sikh educational group Taksal, and a young devout Sikh, who was told by the Congress Party that if he would fall in line with their political agenda, they would make him the ruler of the Punjab. As Congress and Taksal were negotiating, Bhindranwale's popularity surged; that popularity sprung from his back-to-Sikh-basics campaign that pressed Sikhs to refrain from drinking, taking drugs, and cutting their hair. This program attracted hundreds of young men and women, whom he baptized. Known as the Amrit ceremony, baptism is the Sikh's initiation rite for both men and women in which one confirms full commitment to the religion. During the ceremony, which takes place in a *gurdwara* in the company of five Sikhs, the initiate drinks and then is sprinkled with a mixture of sugar and water stirred with a ceremonial sword, and sacred passages are recited.

Bhindranwale and his group believed they were fighting heresies and sought to create a Sikh state known as Khalistān, the "Land of the Pure."[10] However, in the early eighties, they were regularly accused of intimidating and murdering their opponents. For instance, in September 1981, Bhindranwale was arrested for masterminding the murder of a well-known owner of a newspaper chain critical of him, but was released for lack of evidence after the trial had begun. It may be that the government believed that Bhindranwale was of more use to them out of prison campaigning against the Akali Dal party. For this reason, the Akali Dal at first considered Bhindranwale to be an agent of the Congress Party, but later began to see common ground with him. Bhindranwale came to be seen as a hero by many in the Sikh community who had stood up to the government. To bolster this image, he took a victory drive around Delhi.

In June 1982, Bhindranwale and a group of his followers moved into a section of the Golden Temple complex called the Guru Nanak Niwas (Guesthouse). His critics claimed he sought sanctuary to avoid another arrest while supporters believed he wished to be close to the spiritual center of their faith. Fanned by Bhindranwale and other factions, tensions escalated over the next year as Sikhs and Hindus attacked and desecrated each other's temples. There were numerous incidents in which local police, while searching for militants, killed Sikhs. These incidents only strengthened Bhindranwale's cause and pilgrims began leaving alms to him rather than the Golden Temple. In September 1983, Bhindranwale advocated taking revenge on those who had killed or humiliated Sikhs.[11] He went as far as to demand that all Hindus leave the Punjab.[12] It was clear to journalists that Bhindranwale was gearing up for a fight. In December, he moved into the Akal Takht, "the Throne of the Timeless One," one of the five centers of Sikh political power.[13] In response, Rajiv Gandhi, Sanjay's brother and a rising star of the Congress Party, recommended that he be expelled from the Golden Temple. To this demand, Bhindranwale retorted derisively, "*Tell him to come* and *try* . . . I am not afraid of *him* or his mother."[14]

On June 1, 1984, a Sikh officer named Lieutenant General Kuldip Singh Brar arrived in Amritsar to coordinate the army plans to capture Bhindranwale. Still hopeful that some sort of settlement could be reached, Indira Gandhi made an appeal the next day to the people of the Punjab on All India Radio, saying, "Don't shed blood, shed hatred."[15] Her appeal failed and the army received orders to proceed. As tanks and troops surrounded the complex, Brar instructed his soldiers not to fire on the Akal Takht or the Golden Temple without direct orders. A curfew was ordered and a news blackout was imposed as all journalists were ejected from the city. Under the operation code name "Blue Star," General Brar sent his troops descending the steps of the temple. But Sikh gunmen hiding on both sides of the walls opened fire, repulsing the attack. Brar then sent a second wave of soldiers who succeeded in getting down the stairs. Having done so, however, they came under machine-gun fire from the surrounding buildings and from militants hiding in manholes. The military had undoubtedly miscalculated the strength of its adversary.

After being surprised by having an army truck hit by a rocket-propelled grenade, General Brar decided on a dramatic new plan and sent tanks into the temple complex. The gunfire and shelling from the tanks nearly destroyed the

Akal Takht, and Bhindranwale was likely shot as he and others retreated from the building. The government estimated that about one hundred soldiers and some two hundred of Bhindranwale's men died during Operation Blue Star. Bhindranwale's body was photographed then hastily cremated. General Brar needed constant police protection for decades afterward.

A few weeks after Operation Blue Star, one of Indira Gandhi's personal bodyguards, a Sikh named Beant Singh, brought his family to the Golden Temple. Being deeply moved by the devastation he saw there, he began to plan the prime minister's assassination. Although others around the prime minister insisted that all Sikhs be removed from her close team, she refused.

On the morning of October 31, 1984, as Indira Gandhi walked from her home in Delhi to do a television interview, she saw Beant Singh and smiled at him. He drew a .38-caliber revolver and shot her in the abdomen several times at close range. His accomplice, Satwant Singh, also opened fire, emptying thirty rounds from his submachine gun. Mrs. Gandhi was spun by the impact and fell dead on the ground. Beant Singh was killed on the spot. Satwant Singh, his accomplice, was wounded; he was later tried and executed for the assassination.

Anti-Sikh riots followed Mrs. Gandhi's assassination and Hindu mobs, which included members of the Congress Party, killed Sikhs across India. While estimates vary, some eight thousand Sikhs may be have been killed in the subsequent orgy of religiously inspired violence. Three thousand Sikhs were killed in Delhi alone and some fifty thousand fled the city. The effects of this conflict, which can be traced to 1947's Partition, still reverberate in the present. For example, the Al Jazeera news agency reports that the fact that many Sikhs live in poverty today can be traced back to the 1984 anti-Sikh riots and that "beneath the veneer of normalcy lie hidden collective scars of a carnage that bled parts of the nation about 30 years ago."[16]

Endō's narrator sums up the individual and universal implications of the anti-Sikh riots in the novel as follows:

> Antagonism and hatred characterized not just the relationship between one nation and another; they persisted between one religion and another as well. A difference in religion had yesterday resulted in the death of the woman who had been prime minister of India. People were linked together more by enmity than by love. It was not love but the formation of mutual enemies that made a bonding between human beings possible. By such means had every nation

and every religion survived over the long span of years. In the midst of all that strife, a pierrot like Ōtsu had aped the behaviour of his Onion and in the end been discarded.[17]

The significance of the pierrot and the Onion for Endō as artistic symbols of the universal principle of suffering is explored below.

Religion and Violence as Universal Phenomena: The Love and Wrath of the Onion

It is clear that Endō was interested in Dostoevsky and his views on human consciousness and religion outside the boundaries of existing institutions. He references Dostoevsky's novel *The Double* in his own 1986 work *Scandal*. Dostoevsky's novel is about the psychology of a man who meets his doppelgänger in appearance, but has the opposite personality. In Endō's novel, a Christian writer discovers that there is a man impersonating him who is involved in masochism and prostitution. In the end the writer comes to realize that the impersonator is a reflection of his own obscure characteristics.

Endō published *Deep River* seven years later and we have to wonder about the extent to which Ōtsu's Onion is related to the famous onion story Dostoevsky has Grushenka tell in *The Brothers Karamazov*. The doppelgänger, or impersonator, characters in *The Double* and *Scandal* bring to light the necessary existence of what appears to be the dark or disgraceful side of an otherwise upright personality, or the interrelationship between conformity and transgression. Likewise, the Onion reveals the overlapping layers of individuals, societies, and religions, but also of the ongoing process of death and rebirth, creation and destruction. Comparing these *onions* will help us understand how destruction is depicted in their respective worlds. When Grushenka is first introduced, she is unpredictable and malicious. She was deserted by a former lover and becomes a financially independent "free-spirit." However, she begins to change due to her interactions with the Karamazov family.

For our analysis, it is significant that Grushenka is the character that relates the parable of the onion in *The Brothers Karamazov*. She plans to destroy Alyosha and asks Rakitin to lay a trap to lure him into her room, just as Mitsuko does with Ōtsu and other college acquaintances. Like Rakitin, Mitsuko's associates embrace fashionable ideas, including atheism. In the case of both women, the motive in attempting to bring down their target is contempt for piousness and, at least we are told in the case of Mitsuko, a perverse desire to cause suffering harbored by a seductive woman. This impulse springs from the feeling of being judged by the standards of the man in question, even though, in both cases, that man is not judging the woman. Once Grushenka has Alyosha in her room, she begins to toy with him. Grushenka sits in Alyosha's lap, takes his hand, and flirts, again much like Mitsuko. Like Ōtsu, Alyosha is ready to give in even if it means giving up his devotion. But when Grushenka learns that Father Zosima has died and sees that Alyosha is in a vulnerable position, to his surprise, she suddenly becomes compassionate. It takes longer for Mitsuko to do the same for Ōtsu. Grushenka gets off of Alyosha's lap, stops toying with him, and soberly recounts the following story she heard as a child about God, hell, and an onion.

> Once upon a time there was a peasant woman and a very wicked woman she was. And she died and did not leave a single good deed behind. The devils caught her and plunged her into the lake of fire. So her guardian angel stood and wondered what good deed of hers he could remember to tell to God; "She once pulled up an onion in her garden," said he, "and gave it to a beggar woman." And God answered: "You take that onion then, hold it out to her in the lake, and let her take hold and be pulled out. And if you can pull her out of the lake, let her come to Paradise, but if the onion breaks, then the woman must stay where she is." The angel ran to the woman and held out the onion to her. "Come," said he, "catch hold and I'll pull you out." He began cautiously pulling her out. He had just pulled her right out, when the other sinners in the lake, seeing how she was being drawn out, began catching hold of her so as to be pulled out with her. But she was a very wicked woman and she began kicking them. "I'm to be pulled out, not you. It's my onion, not yours." As soon as she said that, the onion broke. And the woman fell into the lake and she is burning there to this day.[18]

In considering the likenesses between the onion in Dostoevsky and Endō's stories, we should first note that an onion is a rather plain vegetable. In Dostoevsky's novel, it represents an exceedingly modest offering; likewise, Endō chooses it because it is such a lowly plant. It smells pungent, which points to the "stinking saint," Father Zosima, whose corpse is naturally decaying. It is also a metaphor for Ōtsu, who is often covered in filth and who appears to be humble and lowly; it points, moreover, to the quotation about comeliness, which Endō uses several times as a Biblical description of Jesus: "[He] hath no form nor comeliness; and when we shall see him, there is no beauty that we should desire him."[19] An onion is earthy, not heavenly, growing in the ground. Father Zosima kisses the earth and wants to forgive everyone. Like Ōtsu, his earthiness is related to nature's cycles, which seems at odds with the beliefs of the adherents of the institutional religion, who think saints' bodies should not decay. As mentioned, nature itself and the deep-seated love of nature among the Japanese inform Endō's narrative trajectory, as do individual, social, and universal suffering. This focus on nature begins with Keiko's talk with the Gingko tree and ends with the Ganges where Ōtsu carries the dead and dying.

In both stories, God is active in the world as universal love rather than cloistered in temples and available only to the ordained; as such, what is required to enter heaven is compassion for all beings. Ōtsu tells Mitsuko that the Onion is inside her and all beings. "I don't think God exists exclusively in the churches and chapels of Europe," he says, "I think he is also among the Jews and the Buddhists and the Hindus."[20] In this and other ways throughout the novel, Ōtsu metaphorically offers Mitsuko an onion, often in the form of his own actions. But as does the wicked woman in Dostoevsky's story, she kicks even as she's being pulled out of hell. The comeliness quotation is repeated four times in the novel and appears, in part, in the title of chapter 13. If we consider the passage that precedes this Bible verse, also in Isaiah 53:2, we get another clue to Endō's use of the onion. It reads, "For he shall grow up before him as a tender plant, and as a root out of a dry ground: he hath no form nor comeliness; and when we shall see him, *there is* no beauty that we should desire him."[21]

It would be easy to see the moral in Dostoevsky's story as being it only takes one good deed in life to save a person from hell fire; in *Deep River*, one such deed could be Mitsuko's short-term volunteering at the hospital. However, this is clearly not the case in either context. Nor does it fit the earlier theme in *The Brothers Karamazov* that salvation is not a matter of mathematics. Instead, the one good deed affords the opportunity to experience true change. Nor does the woman begin kicking because she thinks the onion will not hold the weight of everyone. In fact, it will. Instead, she says, "I'm to be pulled out, not you. It's my onion, not yours." It is not the one act of giving that might save countless others, but the change within from greediness to selflessness that could do so; that is, love and an unequivocal commitment to help all beings is the mark of spiritual awakening and the necessary element for salvation. At the same time, it means that we can only save ourselves by saving others, or, as referenced earlier in *The Brothers Karamazov*, by being one's brother's keeper. This is also Father Zosima's view, which is present in the onion metaphor. After his death, Zosima's reputation is besmirched, even by those he had tirelessly served. Ōtsu too is like this at the end of the novel, not only in the case of the Sanjōs, but also in terms of the Indian community with whom he resided and attended. The Onion does not break because of the physical weight of souls, but due to divine retribution, the wrath of God.

Like the layers of an onion, each comprised of an identical substance, the various characters in the story blend together as a part of Endō's idea of a universal interconnectedness. Deep connections can be found among Isobe, Keiko, Tsukada, Mitsuko, Numada, Kiguchi, Enami, the Sanjōs, and Ōtsu. Most of these characters have suffered from a life-changing event, experienced as violence or destruction. These stories show that such traumas are a universal part of the human condition and serve, therefore, to unite not just the novel's characters but all people and religions. The suffering and eventual death of Isobe's wife brings the two together for the first time. Before this, he had always considered her "as air" without taking time to get to know neither her feelings nor his own. The promise she extracts from him, to search for her reincarnation, is only made under duress. Even so, it sets him on a quest for spiritual truth that is beyond human knowing. Just as in *The Brothers Karamazov*, such uncertainty plays a central role in *Deep River*, most clearly in Ōtsu's faith but also in Mitsuko's growing ambiguity about him and herself.

As mentioned, Endō portrays Keiko's end-of-life revelations as possibly valid. There may also be a karma-like connection established at the time between Isobe and Mitsuko through Keiko. Otherwise, their chance meeting on the trip becomes even more unlikely. So, too, Mitsuko reunites with Ōtsu, first in France and then in India, as if due to karma rather than chance. Just in these few examples, we see that Keiko and Isobe are connected to Mitsuko, and she is connected to Ōtsu. Karmic or not, these connections point to the interdependence of the characters and all of humanity, which is important to Endō's overarching theme that includes violence, destruction, and rebirth. In some ways Mitsuko serves as the doppelgänger, or impersonator, for Ōtsu and vice versa as characters in *The Double* and *Scandal*. But in *Deep River*, Endō takes this interconnectivity a step further. In this novel, opposites are presented as necessary for one another's existence. Ōtsu realizes what Endō offers as religious truth vis-à-vis Dostoyevsky, that each person is responsible for all others. But Endō innovates by bringing into this formula the concrete examples of death and destruction. This is particularly apparent in the eradication of boundaries between Mitsuko, the goddess Chāmundā, and the goddess Kālī. Not only do Mitsuko and Ōtsu realize the necessity of violence and destruction, which could be subjective, but also the narrator confirms that this view is correct.

Once Ōtsu realizes that he is responsible for all people, just as everyone is, he no longer needs the sanction of the church. Instead, he directly imitates Christ, who had come to the same realization. To this end, Ōtsu carries bodies of the dead and dying in imitation of Jesus, praying, "You carried the cross upon your back and climbed the hill to Golgotha. I now imitate that act."[22] He then sacrifices his life to save the Sanjōs, even though they are oblivious both to his intervention and, apparently, to the deplorable nature of their behavior. He is put on a bamboo litter used for corpses and taken away, just as the body of Jesus was taken from the cross to the tomb.

Earlier, Ōtsu said that he had become tired of the mistaken self-assuredness of European theists. He tells Mitsuko, "I can't make the clear distinction that these people make between good and evil. I think that evil lurks within good, and that good things can lie hidden within evil as well. That's the very reason God can wield his magic. He made use even of my sins and turned me toward salvation."[23] We come to learn that this applies to those who denied Jesus at the time of his crucifixion and to those who have promoted violence throughout history. So, too, it applies in the novel to those who assassinated Indira Gandhi and massacred Sikhs, to the senseless violence of the Indians who attacked the innocent Ōtsu, to the Sanjōs, who ridiculed him and India itself, and to Mitsuko in her cruel treatment of Ōtsu. Endō describes Mrs. Gandhi's demise as like that of Jesus and Ōtsu: she is put on a gun carriage and the narrator says, "She tried to bring some kind of harmony to it all, but in the end she failed."[24]

Early on, Ōtsu tells Mitsuko that God can transform any situation, but later expands on this notion, arguing that "God makes use not only of our good acts, but even of our sins in order to save us."[25] This idea recurs elsewhere in the novel and seems to drive the multiple threads interwoven among the characters' lives.

When Kiguchi sees the image of Chāmundā, he says, "On the battlefields in Burma, I always felt as though death was close at hand, and when I look at this gaunt statue now, I remember all the soldiers who died in the rain. The war was . . . horrible. And all those soldiers . . . they looked just like this."[26] Enami explains the suffering goddess; as he spoke of the goddess, he always thought of his own mother, who had been abandoned by her husband. On the next page, Enami calls the Ganges the "great mother" and then visits the sacred river, and the narrator says that this reminds the group of Chāmundā, "the mother of India."²⁷ The title of "Mother of India" links Chāmundā to Indira Gandhi, who is referred to as such at several points later in the novel. The connection further extends to Mitsuko, who is attracted to both Chāmundā and Kālī. Her fascination with these goddesses of destruction is linked to her own tendency to want to destroy Ōtsu and herself, even if this drive is beyond her comprehension. It will also serve as her redemptive wellspring, pointing to the interrelationship of good and evil and God's ability to transform both. In this, Ōtsu's Onion differs from the one in Grushenka's story, even if Dostoevsky might have agreed with Ōtsu. The evil kicking by Dostoevsky's woman could be redemptive for Endō, for whom good things can lie hidden within that which is evil or wicked. This reference to Indira Gandhi completes a circle comprised of the human impulse toward religiosity captured in the image of Chāmundā and the holy waters of the Ganges representing nature itself; this circle includes, moreover, the recurring historical events happening around the characters, including the assassination of Gandhi, but also the individual destructive goddess in Mitsuko. This is the circle that Endō follows throughout. In terms of Mitsuko as a mother figure, Ōtsu buries his head between her breasts, she nurses Isobe's wife Keiko, nurses Kiguchi, and sees herself in Chāmundā-mātā, "Mother Chāmundā."

To understand Endō's view that human nature contains an impulse for destruction and the potentiality for salvific transformation, we can examine the recurring appearance of the pierrot in *Deep River*. For example, when Numada becomes deathly ill with tuberculosis, his myna bird, named Pierrot, is likened to Jesus.²⁸ In this, the novel references the painting by that name by the French artist Georges Henri Rouault. For Rouault, the clown serves as a metaphor for humanity and Jesus; the clown has a somber face and appears as if he is praying. This is seen as concern with the human condition of perpetual suffering. Rouault was a keen enthusiast of the eighteenth-century Catholic movement to revive the use of Christian images in art and literature, a goal Endō seems to meet in his work. The myna bird, which kept Numada's spirits up, dies from neglect, but immediately afterward, Numada experiences a recovery that is "nearly miraculous."²⁹ It is clear that Endō is drawing a parallel with Jesus's sacrifice. In the next chapter, Gaston, a foreign Christian nurse, is likened to a praying monk with a "stern look on his comical horse face."³⁰ This connects Gaston, who compassionately cares for Tsukada and tells him that God forgives sins, to the pierrot and to Jesus. Like Jesus, Ōtsu, and others, Gaston suffers from the ridicule of those he tries to help. However, when read through Endō's view articulated above, their malicious behavior may be redemptive. Furthermore, Tsukada had taken suffering on himself to save Kiguchi, by feeding him human flesh he had taken. Kiguchi commented on how alike Tsukada and Gaston were, which is also, naturally, like Ōtsu and Jesus.

References to the sad clown in the novel significantly include Ōtsu, whose bloody face makes him look like a pierrot.[31] Perhaps the most telling lines to indicate Endō's all-encompassing circle or onion's layers relate to Jesus having no comeliness or beauty. Having once again seen this biblical passage, Mitsuko has the following experience related to the figure of Jesus:

> The image of the goddess Chāmundā was superimposed upon that of this man, and the wretched figure of Ōtsu as she had seen him in Lyon overlapped them both. As she thought about it now, it seemed as though she had unconsciously been following in Ōtsu's wake, chasing after something she could not define. This fellow they had nicknamed Pierrot, who had "no form nor comeliness," whom she had despised and rejected. Though she had made him a plaything of her pride, he had deeply wounded that same pride.[32]

Corresponding to the merging of all of these seemingly diverse elements, Ōtsu and others find unity in what he comes to see as superficially different religions and cultures. Specifically, while all give rise to violence and hatred, love is hidden within each of the overlapping layers of a tradition. *Deep River* suggests that the Passion Play recurs in the lives of individuals and also in political and religious spheres, as exemplified by the Sikh incident. Indeed, resurrection through the deep river of human suffering, implying both baptism and reincarnation, is the central motif of the novel.

Notes

1. Definitions of "religion" vary widely among scholars; In this chapter, I use the term to mean organizations—here, "Sikhism" and "Hinduism"—that are legally defined or societally understood as such, recognizing that this is a broad definition. For an excellent discussion of key theoretical issues related to the relationship between "religion" and "violence," see William T. Cavanaugh's *The Myth of Religious Violence: Secular Ideology and the Roots of Modern Conflict* (Oxford: Oxford University Press, 2009). Cavaugh argues that any *ideology* can, under certain conditions, resort to violence; he also offers useful critiques of key theorists of religious violence.

2. Shusaku Endo, *Deep River*, trans. Van C. Gessel (New York: New Directions, 1994), 212.

3. Critics have noted that the old pond in Matsuo Bashō's most famous haiku, "old pond; frog leaps in; sound of water," refers to both a physical pond and the long span of human history. Father Zosima says, "All is like an ocean, all is flowing and blending; a touch in one place sets up movement at the other end of the earth." Fyodor Dostoyevsky, *The Brothers Karamazov: A Novel in Four Parts and an Epilogue*, trans. Constance Garnett (New York: Macmillan, 1922), 340.

4. Ibid., 41.

5. Melanie Anne Phillips and Chris Huntley, *Dramatica: A New Theory of Story*, tenth-anniversary edition (Glendale, CA: Write Brothers, 2004), 14.

6. Endo, 40–41.

7. Ibid., 44.

8. Ibid., 47.

9. James M. Markham, "Violence Makes Sikhs Fear for their Future in India," *New York Times*, November 11, 1984, http://www.nytimes.com/1984/11/11/weekinreview/violence-makes-sikhs-fear-for-their-future-in-india.html, accessed June 23, 2017.

10. For example, Bhindranwale opposed heresy as the Sikh Nirankaris' reverence for a twentieth-century guru and the Ahmadis' reverence for a nineteenth-century prophet. See John Keay, *Midnight's Descendants: A History of South Asia Since Partition* (New York: Basic Books, 2014), 257.

11. Ranbir Singh Sandhu, *Struggle for Justice: Speeches and Conversations of Sant Jarnail Singh Khalsa Bhindranwale* (Dublin, OH: Sikh Educational & Religious Foundation, 1999), 286. See also http://www.sikhtimes.com/bios_060604a.html, accessed April 25, 2017.

12. Chand Joshi, *Bhindranwale: Myth and Reality* (New Delhi: Vikas Publishing House, 1984), 148–49.

13. The Akal Takht, one of five *takhts* of Sikhism, is located in part of the Golden Temple, with *takht* meaning seat or throne of authority. The four other Takhts are Takht Shri Keshgarh in the Punjabi city of Anandpur Sahib, Takht Sri Damdama in the village of Talwandi Sabo in the southern part of the Punjab state, Takht Sri Patna in Patna city, the capital of Bihar state, and Takht Sri Hazur in the Marathwada region of the state of Maharashtra.

14. Pranay Gupte, *Mother India: A Political Biography of Indira Gandhi* (London: Penguin Books, 2011), 319.

15. V. D. Chopra, R. K. Mishra, and Nirmal Singh, *Agony of Punjab* (New Delhi: Patriot Publishers, 1984), 189.

16. "In Pictures: Delhi's 'Widow Colony': Residents of neighbourhood in India's capital are back in focus, as anti-Sikh riots of 1984 become political fodder," Al Jazeera Showkat Shafi, 04 Feb 2014 08:46 GMT, http://www.aljazeera.com/indepth/inpictures/2014/02/pictures-delhi-widow-colony-20142381643420910.html, accessed July 23, 2017.

17. Endo, 195.
18. Dostoyevsky, 375. Akutagawa Ryūnosuke tells a very similar story in his 1918 *Kumo no Ito* [The spider's thread], likely based, at least in part, on this one.
19. Endo, 44.
20. Ibid., 121.
21. Isaiah 53:2, King James Version of the Bible.
22. Endo, 193.
23. Ibid., 65.
24. Ibid., 213.
25. Ibid., 118.
26. Ibid., 140.
27. Ibid., 141.
28. Ibid., 77.
29. Ibid., 82.
30. Ibid., 102.
31. Ibid., 212.
32. Ibid., 175.

Chapter Five

Endō Shūsaku

The Long Road to the Deep River

MARK WILLIAMS

> "The work with which an author marks his or her debut on the literary stage determines the direction of all their subsequent literary oeuvre."[1]
>
> —Iwanami Gō, "Gojūnen-me no 'kiseki'"
> (A Fiftieth Year Miracle)

Introduction

When Endō Shūsaku made the above epigraph toward the outset of his career, he had yet to make much of a mark on the literary establishment. Indeed, the contribution that he had made was believed to be confined exclusively to the works of literary criticism that he had penned since his days as a university student—with *Aden made* (To Aden), a work not written until 1954 and born of his three-year sojourn in France in the early 1950s, usually cited as his first work of fiction. The literary career that ensued, culminating with publication of *Deep River* in 1993, would, however, provide plenty of material against which to judge the accuracy of this assessment in the case of Endō himself. But it was not until after the author's death—and the chance discovery of the previously unpublished, and virtually unknown, manuscript of the three-act drama "Saolo" (Saul)—that critics had cause to reassess the true identity of Endō's "debut work."

The discovery itself owed everything to chance. During the course of a 1998 lecture at her alma mater, Obayashi seishin joshi gakuin, the haiku poet, Inabata Teiko, happened to mention that her abiding memory of her school days was of watching a performance of a play "Saul" written by Endō (whose mother, Ikuko, was a music teacher at the school at the time). Given Endō's reputation as one of the most prominent Japanese authors of the postwar era, the remark inspired a flurry of activity among students and staff at the school—and, within hours, a musty, handwritten manuscript had been produced. The sheets were heavily annotated and Endō's widow, Junko, was quick to authenticate the handwriting as that of her husband.

Junko was as surprised as the literary critics by the discovery. Not only had there been no mention of the work in any of the open forum discussions in which Endō had participated during the course of his lengthy career, but there was no reference to "Saul" in any of the biographical sketches of Endō's oeuvre that had appeared over the years. Of even greater interest, however, was the fact that—calculating from the dates during which Inabata attended the school and the subsequent discovery of a school review of the event in which "the author, Endō Shūsaku," is described as attending the event "wearing his student uniform"—the work can be dated to no later than 1948, the year in which Endō graduated from Keiō University.

The discovery inspired a minor flurry of activity among Endō aficionados in Japan,[2] and efforts were made to ensure that this newfound piece did find its way into the definitive collection of Endō's work,[3] planning for which, by this stage, was already well advanced. Less well considered, however, was the extent to which the author's assessment concerning the significance of an author's debut work required recalibration in light of this unexpected discovery. And of particular significance in this regard was the question of the debt that can be identified, even in Endō's final work of fiction, *Deep River*, to his earliest forays into the literary world. It is this lacuna that this chapter will seek to address. More specifically, I shall be placing "Saul," Endō's first attempt at fictional writing, alongside the two critical essays, "Kamigami to kami to" (The gods and God) and "Katorikku sakka no mondai" (The issues confronting the Catholic author), penned at roughly the same time (late 1947) and traditionally cited as his debut pieces—and assessing the extent to which these can indeed be viewed as harbingers of developments in *Deep River*.

The task of finding parallels between these works, separated by almost half a century, seems apt—particularly in light of the plethora of critics who hurried to characterize *Deep River* as Endō's *sōkessan* (overall reckoning on his oeuvre),[4] or his *shūtaisei* (definitive work).[5] Others have gone further: in his consideration of Endō as literary mediator, Tsuji Mitsuhiko portrays *Deep River* as "Endō's interpretation of Christianity and a mediology of his entire theology";⁶ in a similar vein, in her book-length study of the theological import of Endō's oeuvre, Emi Mase-Hasegawa describes *Deep River* as "a conclusion of Endō's theological journey."⁷ But it was left to Satō Yasumasa to venture the claim that *Deep River* is "a work that encapsulates Endō's entire oeuvre since *Silence*—no, since his first essay 'The gods and God' and his first novel *To Aden*."⁸ And, in a more considered response, penned some years after Endō's death, Satō was to conclude that *Deep River* represents Endō's "return to his original archetype."⁹ Indeed, Endō himself appeared to concur with such assessments, and in his diary entry for July 30, 1992, he admitted, "I can't help feeling that this story [*Deep River*] encapsulates the form of all my novels over the years."¹⁰ The question informing all these analyses is the nature of the tropes discernible in Endō's earliest works that continue to resonate, even in Endō's final work.

Writ large, the answer to this question may best be encapsulated in the single notion of epiphany, that sense of sudden awakening epitomized in the biblical story, depicted in Acts 9, of Saul/Paul's experience of "seeing the light" as he traveled the road to Damascus. Inspired by this experience to abandon his plans to intensify the persecution of the Christians in the city, within days, Paul would convert into the most vociferous advocate of the fledgling faith. The notion of each of the various characters engaged on the tour of Indian holy sites in *Deep River* as experiencing their own respective moment of epiphany toward the end of the novel as they stand on the banks of the Ganges is compelling. And we shall return to a closer examination of the form these moments of awakening assume for the various characters later in this chapter.

At this stage, however, it is of interest to note that this story of sudden conversion equally forms the backdrop for Endō's initial work, "Saul," a drama in which Saul finds himself increasingly threatened by a crowd intractably opposed to his attacks on the political and religious status quo in Damascus. At the heart of Endō's drama is Cornelius, a young man whose antipathy toward Saul gradually diminishes (largely as a result of the entreaties of his fiancée, Dorothea, who has been captivated by Saul's inspirational teaching), but who is too weak to resist the taunts of his "friends" who have determined that he should be the one to cast the first stone at Saul. The drama ends in a manner reminiscent of so much in Endō's subsequent oeuvre—with the hapless Cornelius throwing a stone at Saul in spite of himself, but hitting instead his fiancée. As the curtain falls, Dorothea's life hangs in the balance.

Echoes with *Deep River*—of Mitsuko playing with Ōtsu during their university days in spite of herself, and of the drama ending with the pivotal character, in this case Ōtsu, fighting for his life—are readily apparent. Before moving to a closer examination of these similarities, however, let us briefly consider the nonfictional works, penned by Endō as he was working on "Saul" in the immediate aftermath of the Asia-Pacific War, as offering further signposts with regard to Endō's literary direction.

Endō as Literary Critic

The two works with which Endō made his first tentative steps as a literary critic, "The gods and God" and "The Issues Confronting the Catholic Author," were initially published as discrete pieces in separate journals in December 1947 (in *Shiki* and *Mita bungaku*, respectively). They were subsequently reprinted as part of a longer critical study in 1954—and they are included as such in *Endō Shūsaku bungaku zenshū* (*The Complete Literary Works of Endō Shūsaku*, or *ESBZ*). The overall tenor of this work is to posit a clear distinction between the "monotheistic" West and the "pantheistic" East—with Endō arguing passionately that "it is impossible to journey to the 'realm of God' without being lured toward the 'realm of the gods.'"[11] To Endō, the latter represents a "passive" world, one that stands in sharp contradistinction to the "monotheistic" West in which the individual is charged with "affirming their state of existence as neither God nor angel and waging constant battle against death, sin and the Devil."[12] Deducing from this that "those of us who are not raised in the [Western] Christian tradition are in danger of mis-reading, not just Western Catholic authors, but even non-Christian Western authors—or at least of distorting them to our own devices"[13]—Endō concludes with an assertion of his belief that his role, as author, was to "scrutinize individual human beings." This role was unlike that of the "saints and poets whose primary aim is to focus on God and sing His praises," and, more specifically, to emulate the more recent French Catholic writers in "investigating the godless individual as individual in the first instance."[14]

To this end, Endō here offers two pieces of advice to himself and other would-be artists, both of which will, as we shall see, continue to reverberate throughout his fictional oeuvre and find clear echoes in *Deep River*. The first of these is encapsulated in his reference to the "light that shines in front of the author's anxious eyes, a light that purifies and sanctifies sin. The author should bear witness to this light."[15] Drawing on his years of consideration of Mauriac's art, Endō describes this as "the light of grace, a twilight glow reminiscent of Rembrandt's art that shines upon Mauriac's dark characters"[16]: he cites the task of the author as the discovery of "the hidden vestiges of God" that lurk within the psyche of all their creations.[17]

The second conclusion that Endō derived from his study of French Catholic literature is that "no matter how much the author prays that the light of grace will [save] . . . his characters, this is something he is not allowed to project onto the surface of his novel. It just happens. As he writes, there are occasions when the author waits for his character to be saved; but he is powerless to distort the free will of his creations."[18]

The sense of himself as author seeking to shine a spotlight on the potential for salvation latent even within the weakest of his characters—and, at the same time, of finding himself unable to lead his characters away from the mire in which they all too frequently find themselves immersed—is one to which Endō continued to allude throughout his career. Indeed, it reappeared with increasing frequency in his personal musings on the nature of his art written toward the end of his life. The *Sōsaku nikki* (Composition diary) that Endō kept as he was writing *Deep River*, for example, is full of references to his desire to home in on what can, in retrospect, be seen as "the hidden vestiges of God" present, yet initially largely hidden, in all the tour participants. And, with particular regard to the second conclusion cited above, as he wrote *Deep River*, Endō was at pains to acknowledge how his initial desire to take the template he had already established for Mitsuko in the figure of Madame Naruse in his earlier novel, *Scandal*, and to establish her as the protagonist of *Deep River* was ultimately thwarted by his growing realization that his literary creations were not susceptible to authorial manipulation in this way.[19]

The developments are significant as we consider the overall tenor of Endō's art. And, viewed through the retrospective prism of *Deep River*, one can discern clear parallels between both the search for the "hidden vestiges of God" and the author's concomitant acknowledgement of his inability to manipulate the evolution of his various creations and the depiction of the various characters who populate both his first drama and his final novel. In short, the overwhelming focus in both works—and indeed a defining aspect of Endō's art—is on the portrayal of individual characters engaged in their own individual journeys of self-discovery. To a large extent, these various journeys prove inconclusive, the purported aim of the journey ultimately remaining largely unfulfilled. But, for so many, there is that moment of epiphany—that instant of self-realization, whereby the lives of individual characters are transformed and they end up looking back at their earlier lives as lacking in clear direction, particularly of a spiritual dimension.

In "Saul," depiction of this journey of self-discovery remains relatively bland. In the case of Dorothea it is initially depicted as the epitome of meek subservience: awareness of inner strength and resources to which she had hitherto remained oblivious is directly attributed to her meeting with Paul. Inspired by his teaching and example, she emerges as a figure of strength, those very qualities that had earlier been seen as signs of weakness now recast as integral to her courage and constancy. A similar process of reevaluation takes place in the figure of Cornelius. Cast at the outset as the successful and confident figure of strength, it is only when confronted by the conflicting pulls of his friends and of Dorothea that he finds himself troubled by his conscience. And it is only in succumbing to the taunts of his friends to prove his "strength" that Cornelius comes to respond to the promptings of his inner being, and to acknowledge his own abject powerlessness in the face of Dorothea's inner strength. In a fascinating portent of Endō's more mature works, the wheel has come full circle, the roles clearly reversed. At the same time, Cornelius has come to acknowledge the indelible marks that Saul, his erstwhile object of derision, has left on him—and, in this, he embodies a classic Endō prototype evident in a whole range of Endō protagonists throughout his oeuvre, but most memorably encapsulated in the portrayal, in *Deep River*, of Ōtsu. For it is here, in Ōtsu, the forlorn figure who nevertheless leaves indelible marks, not just on Mitsuko, but, in choosing to risk his own life to protect the cameraman Sanjō at the very end of the novel, on all of the tour members, that Endō offers his most concerted consideration of the indelible marks that result from each and every human interaction. This view is most memorably encapsulated in his explanation to Mitsuko that, even though Christ may have died, "He continued to live in the hearts of his disciples."[20]

During the course of his career, Endō committed himself to the portrayal of a host of characters engaged in a similar journey of self-discovery. From Suguro in *The Sea and Poison*, through the haunting portrayal of Rodrigues in *Silence*, acknowledging an increased sense of self-awareness following his decision to trample on the *fumie*, to Hasekura in *Samurai*, the lower-ranking samurai who is ultimately imbued with the strength and moral fiber to die for the faith he had only adopted out of expediency, Endō's oeuvre is marked off by its relentless focus on such journeys. By the time of composition of *Deep River*, however, Endō's exploration of this trope had been augmented by the time spent, in the late 1970s and the 1980s, in consideration of the works of two critics, Carl Jung and John Hick, who, by his own admission, had led him to a more nuanced understanding of human psychology and spirituality.

In the case of the former, Endō's fascination with Jungian psychology reached its zenith in the late 1970s and the 1980s as he studied various key texts voraciously.[21] The fruits of this research may be most in evidence in Endō's subsequent novels; but, as suggested above, there is evidence of an approach to his creations that bears clear Jungian hallmarks in the portrayal of multifarious characters, even in his works that predate this formal period of study. Indeed, recalibration of the journey of self-discovery upon which so many of these protagonists are engaged throws up sharp parallels with the process as outlined by Jung: "What comes to us from outside and, for that matter, everything that rises up from within, can only be made our own if we are capable of an inner amplitude equal to that of the incoming content. *Real increase of personality means consciousness of an enlargement that flows from inner sources.*"[22]

Significantly, however, by the time of composition of *Deep River*, Endō appears to have embedded this process even more deeply in a Jungian context—in the decision to have his various individual tour participants (and, with the exception of Mitsuko and Isobe's brief encounters in the hospital at the latter's dying wife's bedside, they do all embark on the tour as complete strangers) come increasingly to identify with other tour members. For Jung, such group identification was cited as one of several transformations of personality accessible to psychological investigation and, in a variety of fora, he argued strongly for the propensity for individuals to identify with a number of people who, as a group, attain a collective experience of transformation. Extrapolating from this, Jung continued by arguing that "this takes place on a lower level of consciousness than the experience of an individual" and is therefore "much easier to achieve because the presence of so many people together exerts great suggestive force."[23] There have been those who have questioned the group tour structure—and the lack of a single identifiable focus figure—in *Deep River*. Reviewed in the light of Endō's avowed interest in Jung, I would suggest, such a format represents an ideal backdrop for a literary exploration of a series of characters each engaged in what Jung would have described as very personal "journeys of individuation."[24]

Turning next to John Hick, the second significant influence on Endō's evolving understanding of the nature of the individual's journey toward greater self-awareness, again the author was at pains to stress the extent to which his reading of the various works in which Hick expanded on his vision of religious pluralism had influenced his deployment of this trope in his final novel.[25] At the heart of Hick's vision was his discernment of "something of vital religious significance taking different forms all over the world within the contexts of different religious traditions"[26] and his belief that the search for this "something" involved a "transformation of human existence from self-centeredness to Reality-centeredness."[27] Salvation, for Hick, was to be found in this transformation—as it was this that enabled the individual to experience "a new and limitlessly better quality of existence."[28] Of greater significance in terms of Endō's emerging religiosity was Hick's assessment that "what is important is not the conventional religious organisations and their official formulations—but the religious way of experiencing and participating in human existence and the forms of life in which this is expressed."[29]

Again, with the benefit of hindsight, Endō's literature, traced right back to "Saul," can be identified as populated by a series of protagonists engaged on just such a journey from self-centeredness to "Reality-centeredness." But it is in *Deep River* that this notion receives its most nuanced literary treatment—in the portrayal of a series of tourists, specifically identified as lacking a "firm understanding of why [they] had decided to come to India" and yet vaguely aware that they had "come here in search of something."[30] On several occasions, the various characters are depicted as ending a day of searching in despair, convinced, on one occasion for example, that they have been "chasing phantoms."[31] And it is only at the conclusion of the novel, as each stands alone beside the Ganges, that, one by one, they find themselves confronted by previously ignored aspects of their inner being. Each interprets the experience of epiphany differently. But, in each case, the result is the emergence of a greater self-awareness, a shift toward what Hick would describe as Reality-centeredness.

Before moving to a more detailed consideration of these respective moments of self-awakening, however, let us briefly return to our overall consideration of similarities between Endō's opening and concluding salvos on the literary stage—with a consideration of the often-uncanny echoes that can be discerned between the characters in "Saul" and in *Deep River*. As already noted, both works are marked by a preponderance of characters whose lives are empty and devoid of hopes and dreams—until they experience their moment of epiphany. In the figures of Paul in "Saul" and Ōtsu in *Deep River*, however, we have examples of two characters whose transformation is effected early enough in the narrative for the Reality-centered, post-epiphany self to be in a position to exercise a profound influence on the narrative flow of the respective stories. Not only does the *Deep River* narrative echo "Saul" in its frequent references to Ōtsu's attachment to Acts 9, but also, just as the early drama focuses on Paul's decision to heed Christ's call to live as a faithful disciple, so, too, does Ōtsu attribute his eventual decision to serve the dying beside the Ganges to a mind-set based on that of Paul.

The scenarios in each case are similar. Initially depicted as "weak" and easily manipulated, both characters emerge as men resolute in their commitment to the call of the gospel—and prepared, if necessary, to accept death as a martyr at the hands of an angry mob. "We must leave all to God's providence,"[32] Saul reassures the concerned Dorothea—in a manner echoed in the various lifestyle decisions adopted by Ōtsu. Significantly, though, both narratives begin by emphasizing the status of both men as passive, even reluctant, converts (in a manner heavily reminiscent of Endō's own spiritual awakening), with considerable emphasis on their ability—their determination—to endure the barbs and insults of those around them for a faith that they had never consciously adopted.

Both men treat these barbs as crosses they have to bear, and both take it upon themselves to encourage the women with whom their lives become entwined to acknowledge their own crosses. And it is only gradually, through the narrative emphasis on their humanity, that each comes to be seen as possessed of an initially unconscionable strength and inner vigor. Significantly, in so doing, such characters are not suddenly endowed with qualities that they did not formerly possess. Rather, in casting increasing doubts upon the initial categorization of such characters as "weaklings," Endō seeks to hint at the potential within these characters to influence, not only their own destinies, but also the lives of those with whom they come into contact.

Endō himself came increasingly to describe this construct as the *dōhansha*, the "constant companion" figure who populates so many of his novels; the quiet yet reassuring presence who comes alongside those in greatest need and encourages those around him on their respective journeys. The upshot for such selflessness may not always be encouraging—and here we should note that, in their respective dramas, the lives of Paul and Ōtsu are left at the end of the respective works quite literally in limbo, with both confronted by a baying mob intent on their elimination. There is, nevertheless, a charisma that surrounds them both, a moral fiber that touches all whom they encounter.

The parallels are not, however, restricted to these two figures. Indeed, in the figure of Dorothea, the young woman whose meek and unassuming manner belies a determination to stand by her convictions that is only gradually evidenced, we have the template for a raft of Endō protagonists, yet mirrored most memorably in Ōtsu in *Deep River*. At this point, therefore, let us turn to a closer consideration of the manner in which Endō can be seen as extrapolating on the journeys toward self-awareness, only vaguely sketched in "Saul," yet offering, at the denouement of his final novel, his most concerted explanation of this as a process of epiphany.

The Journeys

Taken in narrative order, the first to experience the sense of release and salvation beside the Ganges in *Deep River* is Isobe. Introduced at the outset of the novel as a typical "salaryman," he is only induced to meditate on some higher meaning to his hitherto mundane existence by the promise, offered him by his wife from her deathbed, that she would be "reborn somewhere in this world" and her plea that her husband "look for" her.[33] Unable to conceive of the notion of rebirth as anything but a physical phenomenon, Isobe finds himself signing up for the tour in the hope of making contact with a certain young girl, Rajini, who claims to be the reincarnation of a Japanese lady. As with so many of his fellow tourists, however, at the conclusion of the drama, the purported aim of Isobe's trip remains unaccomplished: he fails to establish contact with Rajini and ends up drowning his sorrows in an attempt to forget his "failed" mission. And yet, as he then proceeds to the banks of the Ganges, a light is switched on—as he "finally comes to understand that there is a fundamental difference between being alive and truly living."[34] It is at this point that Isobe feels "a power of some kind in that silvery silence."[35] And, as he stands there, he comes to appreciate that, in addition to simply being alive, with its surfeit of egoism, there is the need for true living. It is only memories of his dead wife that can awaken him to this realization: only now can he appreciate that his wife has indeed been reborn—within his heart.

Next to experience the sense of epiphany is Kiguchi. Having suffered for decades from traumatic memories of his experience of the ignominious retreat that he and his fellow soldiers had been obliged to effect along the infamous Burma Road at the end of the Asia-Pacific War, and troubled, in particular, by the recent revelation from his dying comrade, Tsukada, that the meat that the two men had shared at one of the most harrowing moments of the march had been cut from the corpse of a dead colleague, Kiguchi had come to view the tour of India as an "itinerant pilgrimage."[36] Determined to take advantage of this opportunity to hold a memorial service for those who had lost their lives during that march, he comes to juxtapose, shortly after arrival in Varanasi, the image of the Hindus attempting a final journey to the holy river with recollections of the scene in the Burmese jungle.

In both cases, humanity was on the move "in order to die."[37] But it is only as he himself stands beside the river that he senses that he can now "understand for the first time why Shakyamuni appeared in this land."[38] Here, for the first time, his journey assumes a spiritual dimension, enabling him to intone the *Amida Sūtra*. This may be a passage that he had "committed to memory"[39]; at this point, however, it comes to assume a new meaning for him, as the esoteric text comes to assume a more personal significance. More specifically, he is now in a position, for the first time in his life, to make sense of the scripture, so familiar and yet somehow so foreign to him that "Good and Evil are as one"—to acknowledge the presence of the "seeds of salvation buried in every act of evil."[40] Only now do the words and actions of Gaston, the hospital volunteer with whom he had shared some fleeting exchanges as the two cared for the dying Tsukada, begin to take root in his heart; only now does the narrative hint at a newfound inner peace that will remain with him as he returns home.

In the case of Numada, the moment of epiphany comes as he succeeds in procuring a myna bird and releasing it into the wild in memory of the bird that had died, years earlier, in the Tokyo hospital as Numada's own life had hung in the balance during the course of major surgery. Numada had recovered, but the perception of the bird dying "as though in his stead" had remained with him.[41] Only now, as he enables another bird to find sanctuary in the wild, does he experience a sense of resolution—of expiation. The feelings he experiences at that moment may be "of no marketable value in the world of human affairs."[42] They do, however, act as a catalyst in his search for peace, the implication being that he will now be able to return to Japan and write his children's books about birds and animals again.

The above three cases are fundamental to the establishment of *Deep River* as a narrative of evolving self-awareness. At the very heart of this narrative design, however, are the figures of Mitsuko and Ōtsu. Their respective journeys of self-discovery may converge at crucial moments; the processes do, nevertheless, differ markedly. In the case of Mitsuko, Endō's narrative appears intent from the outset on establishing her as a woman acutely aware of "the whim of some other invisible power" playing out in her life and which accounts for her predilection for impulsive action.[43] At the same time, Mitsuko herself feels as though her life had been spent "unconsciously chasing after something she could not define."[44] Succumbing to such emotions, she comes to persuade herself that it is Ōtsu—the very man she had ridiculed during their student days—who represents the focus of her search; it is Ōtsu who draws her to Varanasi.

Mitsuko's approach toward—and ultimate entry into—the holy waters of the Ganges is, however, delineated as if in slow motion. Her very arrival in the town and viewing of the river from a distance are sufficient to bring her to a sudden realization that "everything in her life had been meaningless and futile" and a concomitant appreciation that "she yearned for . . . something that would provide her with a sense of fulfilment."⁴⁵ Her search for Ōtsu's physical presence nevertheless continues: she remains blissfully unaware of the quest for salvation of her parched soul to which she will only awaken following closer communion with the river.

The following day sees Mitsuko at the water's edge. And, as she gazes at the waters and the sea of humanity all around her, she is drawn to acknowledge "the individual dramas of the soul to be found in every one of the people cupping their hands and praying down by the river. And in the corpses. . . ."⁴⁶ She remains hesitant, however, and it is only as she submerges her entire body into the water that "the unpleasant feeling disappeared" and she comes to feel comfortable in joining the other bathers.⁴⁷ As she does so, as she recognizes that "life and death coexist in harmony in this river,"⁴⁸ she finds herself—in spite of herself—drawn to prayer. She may dismiss this as a "manufactured prayer,"⁴⁹ and may have no idea to whom this prayer is directed. Her gaze, however, is now firmly set on "the light sparkl[ing on the river], as though it were eternity itself."⁵⁰ And, in keeping with the spiritual uplifting she derives from her circumstances, she begins to understand, not only "what [she] was yearning for through all the many mistakes of [her] past,"⁵¹ but also that she was "a part of . . . the sorrows of this deep river of humanity."⁵² The transformation is now complete—and, as exemplified in the brief concluding section as the tourists embark on their return journey, she is now in a position to look outward—to share the journeys of her fellow travelers, rather than continuing to gaze inward, at herself.

Of all the journeys, however, it is the one pursued by Ōtsu that is most painstakingly developed by Endō's narrator. From the outset, Ōtsu is troubled, not so much by the tenets of the faith he readily admits to having naïvely adopted from his parents, but by the institution of the church that had been developed ostensibly to propagate a gospel of universal hope. He expresses his growing conviction in a letter to Mitsuko, writing that he had been admonished by the spiritual director at the seminary for arguing that "God has many different faces. I don't think God exists exclusively in the churches and chapels of Europe. I think He is also among the Jews and the Buddhists and the Hindus."⁵³ This statement appears, at one level, as an unadorned echo of the pantheistic vision developed by Endō himself in his earliest essays. Indeed, for much of the narrative, Ōtsu's decision to refrain from using specifically Christian vocabulary—to refer to God as his "Onion" or some "great life force"—ostensibly to aid Mitsuko in her understanding of his message actually appears designed more for his own consumption than for his skeptical companion. The more he devotes himself to his daily routine helping the weak and dying to reach the holy river, however, the more he comes to see his God, not as the omnipotent, distant being existing outside of himself toward whom his attention had been directed during his days at theological seminary, more as an all-pervasive force living within him, instigating his every act of humanity.

For Ōtsu, as for Isobe, Numada, and the other tourists, the concept of rebirth represents a long-standing conundrum. Aware of the unshakeable conviction of all those he helped to reach the holy waters that this alone represented the path to salvation, he nevertheless struggles to reconcile this with the specifically Christian belief in resurrection that had been inculcated in him during his years of study. It takes the innocent questioning of Mitsuko—and his recognition of the power of what he comes to acknowledge as "the river of love"—for him to come to a clearer acceptance, an understanding that represents a significant step in his journey of reconciliation.[54] Confronted by the spectacle of the sea of humanity seeking salvation in the holy waters, Ōtsu is now able to acknowledge that, following his death, Christ continued not only "to live in the hearts of his disciples," but also that "he's alive even inside a man like me."[55] The realization represents a profound moment of insight for Ōtsu; for if he can now accept Christ as alive within himself, then he is equally obliged to acknowledge his presence within all humanity. As he now tells Mitsuko, "my Onion flows past, accepting all, rejecting neither the ugliest of men nor the filthiest."[56] Buoyed by this newly found appreciation, Ōtsu is now able to see, as if for the first time, that his daily acts of charity represent no more, nor less, than "imitations" of Christ's act in "carry[ing] the sorrows of all men on [his] back."[57] More significantly, however, Ōtsu is now in a position to acknowledge a newfound relationship with his "Onion." And, in a manner that builds upon the depictions of a growing appreciation of a more personal relationship with God following their moments of greatest doubt in so many earlier Endō protagonists—Rodrigues in *Silence* and the Tecali monk in *The Samurai* spring most readily to mind—Ōtsu is now in a position to recognize that "this is how [my life] should be."[58] At the end of the novel, Ōtsu is left, quite literally, in limbo. Significantly, however, the question of whether he will live or die is no longer relevant: his journey of self-realization has been run and his understanding of rebirth now occupies a spiritual dimension divorced from more mundane concerns with physical reincarnation.

Conclusion

In a discussion with fellow novelist, Kaga Otohiko, shortly after publication of *Deep River*, Endō admitted that his original aim for this novel had been to produce a "case study of pure evil."[59] The attempt came as no surprise to

Endō aficionados who instinctively traced such fascination back to the author's earliest writings introduced at the beginning of this study. The narrative of "Saul," for example, revolves around the plot of the angry mob intending to kill the innocent Saul simply because they took exception to his public pronouncements. And, in an attempt to fathom the human propensity for such hatred, in "The gods and God," Endō posited a carefully constructed and seemingly irreconcilable opposition between what he presents as the "monotheistic" Western and "pantheistic" Eastern worldviews.

The distinction may be only crudely sketched in the early works. A reading of Endō's final novel with the benefit of such hindsight does, however, allow for a more nuanced reading of the experiences of rebirth—of epiphany—enjoyed by various characters in *Deep River*. Significant in this regard is the fact that none of those involved in the tour of India achieves their original goal for the journey: they had traveled to India alone—and, at the end, they appear destined to return home equally alone. The narrative emphasis has, however, focused on an inner growth in each character: for each, the experience of awakening beside the Ganges has involved confrontation with hitherto ignored aspects of their inner being. Each individual interprets this experience differently. But in each case, there is a sense of spiritual awakening embodied in the shift from self-centeredness to Reality-centeredness, the implication thereby engendered being that none of their lives will ever be the same again. Seen thus, the rebirth for which all the tourists are ostensibly searching clearly involves release from the shackles of the past. At the same time, however, one by one they come to appreciate that it entails, not so much being born again, but living on in the heart and soul of another/others.

The critic Kawamura Minato has encapsulated this progression as a realization, experienced by each of the tourists at the end, that they had lived their lives to date "without the help of the anima."[60] As each comes to acknowledge the centrality of the human spirit, so each comes to see the various deities to which their attention had been drawn during the course of their tour—the "Onion," Chāmundā, Kālī, and others—as serving the same purpose—that of "guiding the anima and of bringing salvation to the individual."[61] Central to this narrative design is the symbolic force of the Ganges, the "deep river" that, as with the African American spiritual to which the title alludes, leads to the "promised land where all is peace." To Mitsuko, the experience of self-awakening is accompanied by an appreciation that this "river embraces everything about mankind."[62] And, in a manner echoed in the moments of epiphany experienced by the other tourists, it is as she comes to recognize, in those holy waters, a fusion of life and death, of beauty and ugliness, of hope and despair, that Mitsuko is enabled to move beyond traditional binaries and to better appreciate the significance of the symbiotic relationship engendered in each of these oppositions.

Deep River concludes not just with the depiction of Ōtsu working in harmony with a group of Hindu ascetics committed to selfless support of the sick and dying, but with the portrayal of two young nuns from Mother Theresa's "Home for the Dying"—a white woman and an Indian woman—engaged in similarly altruistic acts of love. Totally absent from this scenario is the opposition between God and the gods that had represented Endō's starting point. In its stead, we are left with the author's most explicit delineation in his entire oeuvre of what he would describe in several of his nonfictional writings of the time as a "third way of religion," one that transcends traditional boundaries. The issue is a recurrent theme in the diary that Endō wrote in conjunction with *Deep River*[63]; it also dominated the discussion the author held with William Johnston as he wrote the novel, a conversation in which he delineated his vision of the "third way of religion" in the following terms: "The third way is not a systematized religion in the sense that Christianity, Buddhism and Islam have been set up. It's a religion that transcends denominationalism—or rather, it's an experience of religiosity."[64]

Parallels with Hick's advocacy of the centrality of the religious *way of experiencing*, introduced earlier, are readily apparent in this definition. In its focus on the coexistence and synchronicity evident in so much contemporary Asian religiosity, moreover, this comment—and the *Deep River* narrative that encapsulates this same ideology—can be cited as the author's final attempt to consider the implications contained within some of the seemingly intractable issues raised in "Saul" and the early essays. Whether this qualifies *Deep River* as an "overall reckoning of [Endō's] oeuvre" is a question open to debate. In its ability to pick up on the issues that had pervaded the author's work since those first tentative steps while, at the same time, opening up a plethora of new interpretations, however, the novel *Deep River* serves as a fitting culmination to almost half a century of theological questioning.

Notes

1. Iwanami Gō, "Gojūnen-me no 'kiseki'" [A fiftieth year miracle], *Shinchō* (June 2000): 193.

2. Much of this is documented in Iwanami, "Gojūnen-me."

3. Endō Shūsaku, *Endō Shūsaku bungaku zenshū* [Complete literary works of Endō Shūsaku], 15 vols. (Tokyo: Shinchōsha, 2000) (cited below as *ESBZ*).

4. See Endō Shūsaku, Inoue Yōji, and Yasuoka Shōtarō, "'Shin' to 'katachi': *Fukai kawa* o tegakari ni" ["Faith" and "form": a reading of *Deep River*], *Gunzō* (September 1993): 209.

5. See Kawamura Minato, "Indo ni anima o motomete: *Fukai kawa*-ron" [To India in search of the soul: a reading of *Deep River*], *Kokubungaku* (September 1993): 66.

6. Tsuji Mitsuhiko, "Iesu no mediorojī: mediētā toshite no Endō Shūsaku" [The mediology of Jesus: Endō Shūsaku as mediator], *Kokugo to kokubungaku* (April 1998): 5.

7. Emi Mase-Hasegawa, *Christ in Japanese Culture: Theological Themes in Endō Shūsaku's Literary Works* (Boston and Leiden: Brill, 2008), 141.

8. Satō Yasumasa, "Sukyandaru o tōtte, *Fukai kawa* e" [Via *Scandal* to *Deep River*], *Kokubungaku* (September 1993): 48.

9. Satō Yasumasa, "*Fukai kawa* saidoku" [On re-reading *Deep River*], *Kirisutokyō bungaku kenkyū* 16 (1999): 49.

10. Endō Shūsaku, *Fukai kawa: sōsaku nikki* [*Deep River* composition diary] (Tokyo: Kōdansha, 1997), 112.

11. Endō, *ESBZ*, vol. 12, 17.

12. Ibid., 24.

13. Ibid., 18.

14. Ibid., 24–25 (emphasis in original).

15. Ibid., 27.

16. Ibid.

17. Ibid.

18. Ibid.

19. Endō discusses his ultimately aborted desire to establish Mitsuko as the main protagonist of *Deep River* at several points in Shūsaku Endō and Otohiko Kaga, "Saishinsaku[,] Fukai kawa: tamashī no mondai" [New publication, *Deep River*: the question of the soul], *Kokubungaku* (September 1993): 7ff.

20. Shusaku Endo, *Deep River*, trans. Van Gessel (London: Peter Owen, 1994), 185.

21. For Endō's own portrayal of the extent to which he devoted this period of his life to study of Jungian psychology, cf. *Watashi no aishita shōsetsu* [A novel I have loved] (Tokyo: Shinchōsha, 1985). For an analysis of the Jungian influences on Endō's mature fiction, especially *Scandal*, see Mark Williams, *Endō Shūsaku: A Literature of Reconciliation* (London: Routledge, 1999).

22. Carl Jung (1953–1977), *Collected Works of C. J. Jung*, vol. 9–Part One (London: Routledge, 1953), 120 (my emphasis).

23. Ibid., 125–26.

24. Ibid., 275.

25. Cross-reference, for example, his discussion of Hickian theology in Shūsaku Endō, *Fukai kawa o saguru* [In search of the *Deep River*] (Tokyo: Bungei shunjū, 1994)

and Shūsaku Endō and Yasumasa Satō, *Jinsei no dōhansha* [The constant companion in life] (Tokyo: Shunjūsha, 1991).

26. John Hick, *Problems of Religious Pluralism* (Basingstoke: Macmillan, 1985), 329.
27. Ibid., 28ff.
28. Ibid., 69.
29. Ibid., 18.
30. Endo, *Deep River*, 113–14. "Something" is a translation of "X" in the original Japanese.
31. Ibid., 170.
32. Endō, *ESBZ*, vol. 14, 450.
33. Endo, *Deep River*, 17.
34. Ibid., 189.
35. Ibid.
36. Ibid., 197.
37. Ibid., 142.
38. Ibid., 141.
39. Ibid., 201.
40. Ibid., 200.
41. Ibid., 203.
42. Ibid., 204.
43. Ibid., 113.
44. Ibid., 175.
45. Ibid., 180.
46. Ibid., 200.
47. Ibid., 210.
48. Ibid.
49. Ibid., 211.
50. Ibid., 210.
51. Ibid.
52. Ibid., 211.
53. Ibid., 121.
54. Ibid., 185.
55. Ibid.
56. Ibid.
57. Ibid., 193.
58. Ibid., 212.
59. Endō and Kaga, "Saishinsaku, Fukai kawa," 7.
60. Kawamura, "Indo ni anima," 67.
61. Ibid., 69.
62. Endo, *Deep River*, 199.
63. Endō, *Fukai kawa: sōsaku nikki,*
64. Endō, *Fukai kawa o saguru*, 181.

PART TWO
LITERARY AND THEOLOGICAL APPROACHES

Chapter Six

Catholic Convergences in *Deep River*

MARK BOSCO AND CHRISTOPHER WACHAL

> It seems possible, then, to speak, after Pierre Teilhard de Chardin, of a 'marvelous convergence' which is to take place in the *eschaton*, of all things and all religious traditions, in the Reign of God and in the Christ-*omega*; of a 'mysticism of unification' towards which Christianity and the religious traditions of the East tend together.[1]
>
> —Jacques Dupuis, "Renewal of Christianity through Interreligious Dialogue"

> Little by little the dialogue is getting under way. A while ago in Sophia University I heard Buddhist monks chanting the sutras during Mass instead of Gregorian chant.[2]
>
> —Shusaku Endo interview with William Johnston, translated from the Japanese by Johnston, from the Japanese publisher, *Bungei Shunjusha*

Introduction

Shūsaku Endō's best-known literary works deal with issues of Christianity's fitful inculturation into Japanese soil. His novels and short stories mine the theological themes of the twentieth-century Roman Catholic Revival but set them in the context of Japanese history and religious faith. Such early works as *Wonderful Fool*, *The Girl I Left Behind*, and his most famous work, *Silence*, show Endō's full engagement with the literary aesthetics that he so admired.

Through his appreciation and deep affinity for the work of Catholic novelists François Mauriac and Georges Bernanos in France, and Graham Greene in Great Britain, Endō drew upon these exemplars of a Catholic literary imagination to dramatize the existential questions of faith and belief. This genealogy of Catholic literary form—from its European roots to its appropriation in Endō's acclaimed novel, *Silence*—has been well documented.[3] *Silence* explores Japan's seventeenth-century Catholic martyrs through the complex spiritual struggle of a missionary priest, distraught at the silence of God, as he discerns whether to trample on the image of Christ and face the shame of apostasy, or refuse to do so and accept martyrdom for his faith. The torment the priest undergoes in his spiritual life is situated in the larger question of the very possibility of religious inculturation: how can the Christian ideas that arise from Western culture—good and evil, sin and redemption—not sink within the "mud swamp" of Japanese culture?

Written early in his career, *Silence* illustrates Endō's commitment to employing many of the dramatic elements found in European Catholic literature: the sinner—the weak, the apostate—at the heart of the Christian story; the existential, spiritual hounding of characters to accept their own darkness and imperfection; the clash between the bourgeois formalities of faith and belief's countercultural commitments; and the kenotic, self-emptying gestures that reveal a character's spiritual selflessness, drawn from the Suffering Servant image of the Jewish and Christian traditions (Isa. 53). These theological themes in various expressions came to embody what was often called the "Catholic novel" of the early and mid-twentieth century. Through immersing himself in this genre and making it his own, Endō found a way to wrestle with Christianity in a Japanese context.

From his early success with *Silence* through *Deep River*, Endō continued to explore themes of suffering, sacrifice, and redemption. However, in this his final novel, he offers a spiritual contrast to Japan by situating the novel in India. Set in 1984, at the time of Indira Gandhi's assassination, *Deep River* tells the story of a modern pilgrimage of Japanese tourists on a journey to Buddhist holy sites in India. Their final destination is the Ganga, the deep river of the book's title, in the town of Vārānasī, the spiritual heart of Hinduism, but also where the Buddha is believed to have taught. The river serves as a fluid metaphor that provokes a revelatory moment for many of the Japanese tourists, unmasking their personal afflictions hidden deeply beneath the surface of their lives. Endō brings a cast of Japanese characters—Isobe, who seeks the reincarnation of his wife; Numada, who seeks a deeper connection with the natural world; Kiguchi, who seeks to quiet the trauma of war; and Mitsuko, who seeks meaningful relationships to fill an inexplicable emptiness—to the river's shores where the rituals of Hindu spirituality shock each to some revelation. Awaiting the tourists in Vārānasī is Ōtsu: a Japanese, an outcast Catholic priest, Mitsuko's one-time classmate and paramour, and Endō's chief spokesman in the novel. Ōtsu ministers to the dying, transporting untouchables to the funeral pyres along the Ganga. As the characters encounter the strangeness of Indian culture and spirituality, and especially in the interaction between Mitsuko and Ōtsu, Endō covers a wide spectrum of religious thought and practice, from Buddhism through Hinduism to Christianity. Ultimately, the novel suggests a fundamental convergence between Christianity and other faiths, a way to imagine the relationship between Christian, Buddhist, and Hindu paths to the divine.

Early reception of *Deep River* was positive and it won critical acclaim both in Japan and abroad as a summation of Endō's lifelong struggle with his "borrowed" religion. Yet many commentators interested in the polemics of Christian doctrine in the novel have focused on what seems Endō's unorthodox acceptance of religious pantheism over the Christian doctrine of the sovereignty of Christ. Harold Netland, an otherwise astute reader of Endō, suggests that Endō rejected "orthodox Christianity in favor of pluralistic interpretations of Jesus."[4] Joan Frawley Desmond wonders, "perhaps [Ōtsu] mirrored the author's apparent difficulties with Catholicism . . . Endō's crusade—part literary, part theological, part personal—slowly drove a wedge between his life and his faith."[5] Still others focus on Endō's explicit influence by the Protestant theologian John Hick, whose pluralist philosophy of religions that Endō was reading at the time. Hick's *Problems of Religious Pluralism* argues that the great religions (in this book, Christianity, Buddhism, and Islam) all describe different aspects of the same reality, giving philosophical credence to claims for a pantheistic faith. He argues that pluralism calls for religious traditions to give up their assertions of difference.[6] Endō wrote of his discovery of Hick's book in his personal journal, dated September 5, 1991, reflecting on Hick's provocative thesis: "[Hick] criticizes Christianity for maintaining the tendency of subsuming the other religions within itself while at the same time claiming to dialogue with them following Vatican II." Endō further reflects what Hick dares to suggest, "true religious pluralism has no place for a theology that proclaims Jesus as the Christ. In other words, the problems of Jesus' incarnation and the Trinity should be subject to the surgeon's knife."[7]

Though we know of Hick's influence on Endō in writing *Deep River*, we would argue that Endō was ready to receive Hick's thesis in a critical and only partial way. From *Silence* to *Deep River*, Endō's religious imagination continued to be informed by the theological developments and intellectual currents of his Catholic faith. Roman Catholicism's attitude toward and serious engagement with modernity at the Second Vatican Council (1962–65) opened up new ways to understand religious pluralism, the universalism implicit in the experience of Christian mysticism, and a reevaluation of the evangelization of peoples in a globalized context. *Deep River* builds upon a theology of deep interpersonal dialogue with other religious traditions, but it does so in light of the last sixty years of Catholic thought and practice, profoundly animated by French Catholic intellectuals of the twentieth century. They played a part in paving the way for the Church's—and Endō's—understanding of religious pluralism, one that varies greatly from Hick's philosophical argument. We would like to provide a brief overview of what is known of Endō's reading in Catholic intellectual life during his last decades, discuss some of the developments around Catholic thought on religious pluralism that seem to resonate with *Deep River*, and suggest that Endō's novel, contrary to its seeming unorthodoxy, dramatizes an encounter with religious pluralism shaped by the analogical tendencies of his Catholic imagination in dialogue with new Catholic approaches to interfaith work.

Endō and the French Catholic Intellectual Heritage

Endō's literary and theological reading was substantial throughout his life. In his critical essays and personal diaries, he frequently refers to the intellectual movements in Catholic contemporary thought in France. His personal library—now mostly held in museums in Nagasaki and Tokyo—is filled with French titles and European authors translated into Japanese. Tokyo's Machida Museum of Literature, in particular, contains an extensive bibliography of titles translated into Japanese from various languages, including works of both English and French. While Endō was in Lyon, France, in 1950 studying and writing his thesis on French Catholic writers, he became a regular reader of the influential literary magazine *Esprit*. Published in Lyon and founded by the philosopher-theologian Emmanuel Mounier, the magazine championed what might be called the French Catholic left of the 1930s through the 1960s. Mounier was a guiding figure of the personalist movement in theistic philosophy, which argued that the dignity and respect of human persons flows from the biblical claim to be "made in the image and likeness of God," and thus carries with it responsibilities for safe-guarding all persons. As a philosophical movement, personalism denounced both the exploitation of capitalism and the excesses of individualism, at the same time that it deplored the collectivist tendencies of Fascism and Marxism.[8] As early as May 1935, *Esprit* published essays on religious pluralism, including Mounier's own, entitled "La Religion et le Monde: Pluralism Chrétien" (Religion and the World: Christian Pluralism). Endō was quite familiar with Mounier and the broader desire among Catholic intellectuals to foster a response to the modern world.[9]

Other intellectual voices that Endō encountered during his time in France included two French Jesuits, the paleontologist Pierre Teilhard de Chardin and the theologian Henri de Lubac. Essays about them in *Esprit* are found in issues of the magazine as far back as 1946. Both Jesuit thinkers were considered progressive for their time and were in constant tension with their religious superiors. De Lubac's research in the patristic sources of Catholic theology was at variance with the rather dry and cerebral scholastic Thomism that reigned in most centers of Catholic theology before Vatican II. Because of this, de Lubac was removed from his post in Lyon and the Vatican's Holy Office censored his books for a period of six years during the 1950s, though he still continued to study, write, and publish during that time. Interestingly, de Lubac was deeply attentive to Buddhism throughout his life. He researched and lectured on Buddhism while in Lyon, bringing out three well-regarded volumes on Buddhist thought between 1951 and 1955, a forerunner of interreligious dialogue in the Catholic Church. He saw in Buddhism a new resource, like the early Greco-Roman philosophies of early Christianity, for ways of thinking about contemporary Christian faith.[10] De Lubac was ultimately allowed to return to teaching and his books were exonerated. His research and theological positions were vindicated in a public way when authorities in Rome invited him to serve as a theological expert at the Second Vatican Council. Historians note that he contributed much to the style and substance of many of its documents.[11]

Teilhard, on the other hand, was a noted priest-scientist fascinated with Buddhist and Hindu traditions. Teilhard first went to China in 1923 and worked there as a geologist and paleontologist, part of an archeological team that discovered the fossils of "Peking Man" in 1929. He would stay in the East until 1946, traveling to many other countries including India, Indonesia, Sri Lanka, and Japan. In his personal writing, he sought to reconcile his Catholic spirituality with his scientific research, producing a vision of the human family in evolutionary movement toward the divine. Teilhard came to see the religions of Asia as a complementary and active belief system in the evolutionary process of spirit upon matter. Yet because his theological positions and scientific speculations were considered unorthodox, he was forbidden to give public lectures on religious topics, nor to publish any of his writings. While in Paris between 1948 and 1950, Teilhard contributed texts for the French branch of the World Congress of Faiths, a group that included not only prominent Catholic intellectuals of the era—Etienne Gilson, Gabriel Marcel, and Eduard Le Roy—but also Sufi, Confucian, and Hindu scholars. In his preliminary text shared and read by members at the congress, Teilhard assumes the diversity and complementarity of religious faiths:

> There can be no doubt that in each of the great religious branches that cover the world at this moment, a certain spiritual attitude and vision which have been produced by centuries of experience are preserved and continued; these are as indispensable and irreplaceable for the integrity of a total terrestrial religious consciousness. . . . What is carried along by the various currents of faith that are still active on the earth, working in their incommunicable core, is no longer only the irreplaceable elements of a certain complete image of the universe. Very much more even than fragments of vision, it is experiences of contact with a supreme Ineffable which they preserve and pass on.[12]

Teilhard's sense of a sacred respect and awareness in all religious traditions, coupled with his insistence that one could encounter personally the "fragments of vision" in these traditions, echoed throughout Catholic theology in the preparations for the Second Vatican Council.

Upon Teilhard's death in 1955, de Lubac, his lifelong friend and fellow Jesuit, took it upon himself to write and publish books and articles in defense of Teilhard's work; he helped secure, with the blessing of his Jesuit superiors, that the manuscripts were finally published, as well. Indeed, *The Phenomenon of Man* became a bestseller when it was posthumously published in France in 1955. Endō's diaries from the early 1950s suggest that he was reading Teilhard, and the bibliography from the Machida Museum mentions that Endō owned one book by Teilhard in Japanese translation (English version, *Man's Place in Nature*) and many more books about his thought, written in French. Though it is not certain the extent to which Endō's admiration of these two figures continued into the later years of his life, his unique experiences as a Japanese Catholic educated in France would likely have made him receptive to de Lubac and Teilhard's engagement in interreligious dialogue. The scholarly research of both Jesuits was intricately bound up in the spiritual and the practical considerations between Eastern and Western religious thought.[13]

Vatican II and Catholic Development on Religious Pluralism

Building upon the progressive theological movements that were being felt in the Catholic Church before and directly after World War II, the Second Vatican Council began an effort to enter into a new relationship with contemporary cultures. Pivotal Council documents were well known to Endō, as he experienced the changes in Catholic life and worship firsthand.[14] The council's emphasis on an inner renewal of the Church centered on, among other things, the effort at interreligious dialogue, the clear affirmation of religious freedom to worship according to one's conscience, and the emphasis on human rights as fundamental to religious faith. Contemporary theologians such as Hans Küng and David Tracy argue that a paradigm shift occurred in Catholicism during the Council, a shift seen most markedly in its use of language.[15] The rhetoric of reproach that echoes through previous Church councils was replaced with the rhetoric of affirmation and invitation. "Dialogue" became the subject of many of the documents. As the Church historian John W. O'Malley suggests, "dialogue is horizontal not vertical."[16] If Catholicism had in the past stressed a vertical relationship between God and the human person, the new impetus of the Council was to imagine Catholicism in horizontal relationships that saw religious faith as affecting the social, political, intellectual, and scientific discourses of the times. Known in English as "The Pastoral Constitution on the Church in the Modern World," *Gaudium et Spes* encouraged believers and unbelievers alike to engage in a "sincere and prudent dialogue" in order to build a better world. The document echoes Teilhard's evolutionary notion of the "Cosmic Christ" in which human participation in the effects of the Incarnation (humans made in God's image) is ultimately an ongoing extension of Christ into the whole universe, a gradual consummation of all creation: "All progress, whether in organic life or in scientific knowledge, in aesthetic faculties or in social consciousness, can therefore be made Christian . . . the Christ who animates and gathers up all the biological and spiritual energies developed by the universe . . . Christ the evolver."[17] Dialogue with the world—and the faith traditions of the world—is part of this evolution, this "gradual consummation" of all Creation.

The importance of dialogue is chiefly embodied in two other Vatican Council documents that had a significant impact in shaping Endō's Catholicism within the context of a multi-faith world: the "Declaration on the Relation of the Church to Non-Christian Religions" (*Nostra Aetate*) and "The Decree on the Church's Missionary Activity" (*Ad Gentes*). The former recognizes for the first time that holiness and truth can be found in other religions and this can lead to a "ray of that truth that illuminates all [human]kind"; the latter focuses on the evangelical, missionary nature of the church in light of postcolonial concerns formed after World War II. *Nostra Aetate* recognizes the faith heritage of Hinduism and Buddhism, exhorting the Church to enter into "dialogue and collaboration with the followers of other religions, carried out with prudence and love and in witness to the Christian faith and life."[18]

In *Ad Gentes*, the Council acknowledges the presence of "seeds of the word" and "the riches which a generous God has planted among the nations."[19] It confirms that "without doubt, the Holy Spirit was already at work in the world before Christ was glorified," and exhorts Christians that "while witnessing to their own faith and way of life, acknowledge, preserve and encourage the spiritual and moral good found among non-Christians, as well as their social and cultural values."[20] The document goes on to spell out the implications of this affirmation and the need for dialogue:

> In order to be able to witness to Christ fruitfully, Christians must be united to those people in esteem and love [for] just as Christ searched the hearts of people and led them to the divine by truly human contacts, so his disciples, deeply imbued with the Spirit of Christ, should know the human persons among whom they live and associate. In this way, through sincere and patient dialogue, they will learn what treasures the bountiful God has distributed among the nations.[21]

The emphasis on dialogue, encounter, and engagement, became the leitmotif of the council documents.

This shift in language is a far cry from the rigid missiology of the pre–Vatican II Church that Endō first confronted as a young convert. Based on the traditional conviction *extra ecclesiam nulla salus* (outside the church there is no salvation), the primary focus of missionary work was the conversion of "pagans" and the establishment of a fully organized, Western-style Church. Though preservation of positive customs and observances of pagan peoples were often affirmed, the general tenor was for the propagation of the faith via conversion in order to save souls.[22] This is the context of—and source of tension for—Endō's *Silence*. Endō claims that the Catholicism he learned early in life "was under the shadow of the end of the nineteenth century and the beginning of the twentieth [century]," a time that "seemed to indicate that

God was outside man. We felt as if we did not look within to find God, but looked out of ourselves up to God."²³ This vertical approach to Catholic faith—looking up to God—is tempered and repositioned by Vatican II as a horizontal engagement with the spirit of God at work in the lives of one another by the time Endō is writing *Deep River*.

The Catholic Church continued to explore religious pluralism in many of the documents of Pope John Paul II, himself a participant at the Vatican Council in his role as archbishop of Krakow, Poland. During his tenure as pope, John Paul II deepened the Church's theological commitment to interfaith dialogue through a focus on the universal action of the Holy Spirit in world religions. His many papal encyclicals illustrate this affirmation. In *Redemptor Hominis*, he sounds the note that would characterize a new Catholic approach—namely, respect for the presence and activity of the Holy Spirit among non-Christians, a presence and activity discernible even in their religious life, in their practice of virtue, their spirituality, and their prayers. John Paul II thinks of such fruit as being "an effect of the Spirit of truth, operating outside the visible confines of the mystical body of Christ."²⁴ Indeed, he credits everything good that has been brought about in non-Christians to the Spirit. In *Dominum et Vivifacantem*, he notes that the Spirit is always and everywhere active in God's world-embracing plan of redemption. Since Christ died for all, he says, "We ought to believe that the Holy Spirit, in a manner known only to God, offers to every human person the possibility of being associated with the paschal mystery."²⁵ In *Redemptoris Missio*, after insisting on the unique role of Jesus Christ in salvation, he echoes the phrases from Vatican II, claiming, "It is the Spirit who sows 'seeds of the word' which are present in various customs and cultures."²⁶ John Paul II developed a promising logic for Catholic theology, for it argued that the reality of the Holy Spirit, alive and active in world history both before and after Christ, inspires the spiritual quests of humankind: while there are many religions in the world, there is one (Holy) Spirit seeking to bear fruit in them all.²⁷

Discernment on how best to understand interreligious dialogue moved from (without abandoning) its focus on the centrality of Christ to the ongoing work of the Holy Spirit. The Belgian Jesuit Jacques Dupuis, who spent over three decades in India working on Hindu-Catholic dialogue, took up the charge of Pope John Paul II, exhorting the Church to move beyond the "fulfillment model" of Christian theology (i.e., that whatever good is found in other religions has to be shown to be fulfilled in Christianity) because the model places too much of a limitation on the Spirit. If the Spirit is active in history, Dupuis suggests, then what the Spirit is doing could be different from God's word in Jesus—not contradictory to it, but different from it. Dupuis proposes that there is more truth in the history of God's dealings with humanity than is available to the Church at any given moment.[28]

In this regard, Catholic theology asserted that interreligious dialogue is not a one-sided phenomenon of Christianity subsuming other cultures and faith traditions. Dialogue offers mutual enrichment and transformation. This, then, is the status of Catholic thought on interreligious dialogue during the last half of Endō's life. Inspired by the ideas of French thinkers like Pierre Teilhard de Chardin and Henri de Lubac, and the ongoing development of the papal teaching of John Paul II, Endō inherited a rich discourse on religious pluralism. His lifelong journey to explore what he calls the "confrontation of my Catholic self with the self that lies underneath,"[29] comes to fruition in his final novel. Rather than looking for a philosophical stance that transcends the East and the West, Endō's novel suggests how the encounter with each tradition penetrates the mystery of the other, deepening the spiritual analogies that make faith humbler and more meaningful. Endō does not jettison a Catholic imagination in favor of something syncretic but offers a very orthodox theological drama of faith.

The Deep River of Catholic Interfaith Work

Within the narrative of *Deep River*, Endō's vision of engagement between Catholicism and other religious faiths finds voice in Ōtsu, the Japanese ordained priest who studies theology in Europe before coming to live the life of a Hindu *sādhu* on the shores of the deep Ganga. Endō unfolds Ōtsu's story across a vast geography, bringing the novel's only named Catholic into contact with a range of cultural and religious convictions distinct from the ones that formed him. These confrontations are often tense affairs that cause Ōtsu a good deal of suffering. At numerous turns he is challenged on the authenticity of his Christian faith and Japanese identity. Indeed, one of the novel's precipitating events is Mitsuko's cruel seduction and rejection of Ōtsu while at university together—treatment she justifies by insisting on the incompatibility of Japanese culture and European Christianity. She says the Catholic priests who run their college "talk like they know everything there is to know about Buddhism and Shinto, but in their hearts they think that European Christianity is the only true religion."[30] She posits, "Western Christianity plundered many lands and killed many people in the name of spreading their gospel."[31] Mitsuko sets out to "win" Ōtsu's soul from the God she claims, as a Japanese, not to believe in. "What would you think if I stole this fellow away from you?" she asks a crucifix at the front of the school's chapel.[32] Once she has seduced Ōtsu into her bed, she thinks, "The pleasure she took from Ōtsu derived not from anything even remotely carnal, but from Ōtsu's rejection of that man."[33] Believing her battle won, Mitsuko harshly rebukes and rejects Ōtsu's affections, setting both characters on journeys of suffering and discovery.

Endō crafts these two narratives such that they repeatedly intersect: Ōtsu's faith journey continually confounds the premises of the questions that Mitsuko imagines herself trying to answer. Mitsuko is haunted by Ōtsu's faith. While in Lyon on her honeymoon, she tracks Ōtsu down at a Catholic seminary. She tells him, "It makes my teeth stand on edge just to think of you as a Japanese believing in this European Christianity nonsense."[34] Mitsuko also claims credit for Ōtsu's entering religious orders after he recalls the day after her rejection:

After you broke up with me, I fell to pieces. . . . I didn't know where to go or what to do. I couldn't think of anything else, so I went back to the Kultur Heim again, and as I was kneeling there, I heard it.

Heard it? Heard what?

A voice saying, "Come to me. Come. I was rejected as you have been. So I will never abandon you." That's what the voice said.

Who was it?

I don't know. But I do know for certain that the voice told me to come.

And what did you do?

I answered "I come."[35]

This relationship between rejection and revelation is one Endō returns to throughout Ōtsu's narrative. Ōtsu is everywhere an outcast. Mitsuko's rejection is merely the first of many that punctuate Ōtsu's faith development. Organizing Ōtsu's evolving religious sentiment around episodes of rejection and suffering places Endō's *Deep River* squarely within the Catholic literary tradition and its preoccupation with the drama of kenosis. John T. Netland argues that

Endō figures this kenosis—this self-emptying gesture—in cultural terms, that suffering empties the self of cultural attachments in favor of a syncretic, hybrid faith formed (at least in Ōtsu's case) in the liminal space between Eastern and Western faith traditions.[36] Yet this reading is incomplete. Ōtsu certainly suffers as a consequence of the tensions between his faith and European theology, not to mention the myriad personal rejections that structure his narrative. However, he does not abandon his culture or his faith in favor of an abstract religious sentiment. By the novel's end, Ōtsu comes to a way of religious practice tied to a personal Christ encountered in particular analogical expressions rooted in cultural and historical situations. It is Endō's fullest expression of the novel's most famous and theologically challenging proclamation: "God has many faces."[37]

In their first conversation in Europe and in a series of letters over the novel's middle chapters, Ōtsu attempts to explain to Mitsuko the growing tension between his faith and the teaching of his European superiors. "I've tired of the way people here think," he says after three years in Lyon. "I can't make the clear distinction that these people make between good and evil. I think that evil lurks within good, and that good things can lie hidden within evil as well . . ."[38] In a later letter, he says, "After nearly five years of living in a foreign country, I can't help but be struck by the clarity and logic of the way Europeans think, but it seems to me as an Asian that there's something they have lost sight of with their excessive clarity and the overabundance of logic, and I just can't go along with it."[39] When his European superiors challenge these sentiments as pantheistic, Ōtsu replies with words that echo the vision of Teilhard de Chardin: "I don't think God is someone to be looked up to as a being separate from man, the way you regard him. I think he is within man, and that he is a great life force that envelops man, envelops the trees, envelops the flowers and grasses."[40] What is noteworthy here is that Endō figures Ōtsu's tensions with Christianity in cultural terms. It is European religious logic that Ōtsu, "as an Asian," struggles to integrate with his experience of the divine call. He "just can't go along with" the rigorous delineations and taxonomies that define scholastic Catholicism in Europe. He retains Japanese habits of mind that imagine the divine differently. His growth in faith does not entail the abandonment—or annihilation—of Asian cultural approaches to religious meaning.

Indeed, as Ōtsu questions the clarity of European Christian dogma, he nonetheless keeps his faith focused on an encounter with the person of Christ, recalling the theological personalism of French thought in the magazine *Esprit*. Ōtsu shares with Mitsuko that it was his mother's love for him that taught him about the person of Christ, remarking that what he has sought is God's personal love, "not any of the other innumerable doctrines mouthed by the various churches."[41] Significantly, Ōtsu connects his faith with the love of particular persons—the love of his Japanese mother analogically representing the love of God in the person of the suffering Christ. This encounter with the divine in particular persons renders problematic any assertion that Endō empties Ōtsu of his cultural associations or has him participate in what John T. Netland refers to as "cultural relinquishment."[42] Attachment to particular persons is, for Ōtsu, the basis of the acts of love by which the divine is manifested.[43] That these attachments and their subsequent acts occur across national, cultural, and religious boundaries is one of Endō's most trenchant assertions concerning interfaith encounter.

The terms of such encounters are of great concern to Ōtsu. His letters with Mitsuko document his repeated confrontations with the impermeable demarcations of European Christianity, the defense of which Ōtsu contends distract from the acts of love performed by and on behalf of the personal Christ he loves. Invoking his and Mitsuko's agreed-upon metaphor for God ("Onion"), Ōtsu writes:

> My trust is in the life of the Onion, who endured torment for the sake of love, who exhibited love on our behalf. As time passes, I feel that trust strengthening within me. I haven't been able to adapt myself to the thinking and theology of Europe, but when I suffer all alone, I can feel the smiling presence of my Onion, who knows all my trials. And just as he told the travelers on the road to Emmaus when he walked beside them, he has said to me, "Come, follow me."[44]

Here, Ōtsu identifies his suffering with Christ's and, perhaps more importantly, roots his own suffering in the intractability of European logic. Such logic leads, Ōtsu asserts, to arrogance that makes interfaith dialogue hopeless. He writes to Mitsuko that "a European scholar once remarked that the noble people of other faiths were actually Christians driving without a license, but you can hardly call this a dialogue among equals."[45] Ōtsu is not interested in the "fulfillment" missiology prevalent before Vatican II. This model makes it impossible for others on the road to Emmaus to hear the call to follow.

In contrast with the chauvinism of European Christianity, Ōtsu develops a theology of interfaith encounter evocative of the work of John Paul II and Jacque Dupuis (not to mention the current Pope Francis). He writes, "I think the real dialogue takes place when you believe that God has many faces, and that he exists in all religions."⁴⁶ "I don't think God exists exclusively in the churches and chapels of Europe," he tells his superiors. "I think he is also among the Jews and the Buddhists and the Hindus."⁴⁷ Predictably, Ōtsu is accused of harboring "pantheistic delusions" and reprimanded for failing to "draw the line between orthodoxy and heresy."⁴⁸ For his errors, Ōtsu is denied ordination and sent to study at a novitiate in the Holy Land where he shares meals with Jews, Christians, and Muslims. "I have found my Onion dwelling amongst them," he writes to Mitsuko. "So why is it that my brethren have to look down on the followers of other religions and feel a subtle sense of superiority in their hearts?"⁴⁹

This pattern of rejection and denial continues as Ōtsu's correspondence with Mitsuko comes to a close, his suffering figured in his absence from the narrative for some sixty pages. If Ōtsu does not speak, he nonetheless haunts Mitsuko. Her seduction and rejection had precipitated both Ōtsu's journey into the depths of his faith and the suffering that accompanied it. By the close of their correspondence, Mitsuko has married and divorced a man she did not love, failed to find comfort in the French literature she consumed as a young woman, and tried and failed to find fulfillment as a hospital volunteer caregiver. This last episode of her life Mitsuko associates with various "imitations of love"—a caring smile, holding a patient's hand, wiping away tears of pain—that appeared sincere to observers but were in fact performed with no affection or depth of feeling.⁵⁰ Endō subtly contrasts Ōtsu's repeated rejections with Mitsuko's apparent inability to feel for or love another person—not Ōtsu, her husband, her patients, or Ōtsu's "Onion." She identifies with the words she reads in a novel by Fukuda Tsuneari: "I cannot truly love another person. I have never once loved anything."⁵¹ Mitsuko suffers with this knowledge, and Endō reveals in the various episodes where she fails to love that Mitsuko experiences this as an acute absence. If Ōtsu loves with all his being the particular person of the suffering Christ despite the criticism he receives from others, Mitsuko can only perform the outward rituals of love, their emptiness only amplifying the sense of her own insufficiency. He suffers for love. She suffers because she's disingenuous. Mitsuko cannot help but feel that Ōtsu has something she does not: "Ōtsu wrote that God has many faces," Mitsuko reflects, "And so do I."⁵²

By the time rumors of Ōtsu's life in India bring Mitsuko to the banks of the Ganga, both characters have suffered. Both have had many of their ties to their previous lives severed. In India, both are brought into contact with a world, a culture, and a faith radically different from their own. Their distinct responses are telling. Confronted by the poverty and disease of those who live near the river, Mitsuko is overwhelmed by powerlessness. She wonders, "What

Catholic Convergences in *Deep River*

is it we tourists can do for them?" In that moment, she is irritated by the cheap sympathies of her fellow travelers. Virtually simultaneously, however, Mitsuko feels another desire: "She no longer wanted imitations of love. She wanted real love and nothing less."[53] Here Endō hints at the transformation Ōtsu will embody in the novel's final chapters. Mitsuko, who is aware that she has never loved another person, comes to desire love when brought face to face with the suffering of a radically distinct other. For the first time in her life, she feels compelled to seek out someone or something to love—some acts of love that might replace her previous imitations.

Unlike Ōtsu, of course, Mitsuko has no form into which she can pour this desire, no person to whom she can attach this newfound impetus to love. Through suffering various rejections, Ōtsu has developed a new way of life rooted in acts of love for fellow outcasts who demand to be loved. The European missionaries have ostracized him. When Mitsuko seeks Ōtsu at the Catholic parish in Vārānasī, the priest says, "We take no responsibility for him."[54] Unable to find a home in Japan, France, or the Holy Land, Ōtsu has made a life as a priest on the Ganga; however, it is not within the walls of the Catholic Church. "The Hindu sadhus have welcomed me warmly," he tells Mitsuko.[55] Ōtsu has come to live the life of the itinerant outcast Hindu, carrying the dead and dying from the streets of Vārānasī to the banks of the holy river, where bodies are cremated and their ashes spread. This work brings him into contact with the old and forgotten, with the terminally ill, with prostitutes and criminals—in short, with the entire outcast class of India. His rejections have prepared Ōtsu to suffer with and serve these fellow suffering outcasts. In contrast with Mitsuko out of whom the encounter with outcasts draws a sense of powerlessness and a desire to be loved, Ōtsu responds to the faces of outcasts by performing acts of love for and with them.

Yet Ōtsu is quite clear that the motivation for his work in Vārānasī lies within his Christian faith. "If the Onion came to this city," Ōtsu tells Mitsuko, "he of all people would carry the fallen on his back and take them to the cremation grounds."[56] "Every time I look at the River Ganges, I think of my Onion," he says.[57] The acts of love that define Ōtsu's response to the outcasts of Vārānasī emerge from his attachment to a personal Christ. As he repeatedly tells Mitsuko, he has not abandoned Christianity for Hinduism. "I'm just like I've always been. Even what you see here now is a Christian priest," he insists.[58] His work transgresses cultural borders and the rigid delineations of orthodoxy and heresy promulgated in European Christian teaching, but Ōtsu is convinced his love for the person of Christ demands he perform these acts of love. They are intensifications of his Christian attachments not an abandonment of them.

While Ōtsu repeatedly insists his faith has not changed, what has changed is the depth of his commitment to his analogical understanding of religious faith. "I've decided that my Onion doesn't live only within European Christianity," he tells Mitsuko. "This is no longer just an idea in my head, it's a way of life I've chosen for myself."[59] Endō reveals this new way of life in Ōtsu's domestic space. Inside the ashram where he lives, Ōtsu rises each morning at four o'clock and performs "a private mass." His living area is framed by a handful of books he has collected: "A prayer-book; the Upanishad; a book by Mother Teresa . . . a book of sayings by Mahatma Gandhi."[60] Endō's intermixing of diverse religious elements is telling. He places a Catholic mass in a Hindu ashram. He places Christian texts alongside Hindu ones. He has a Catholic priest facilitating Hindu death rituals. Ōtsu's chosen "way of life" is the novel's fullest expression of Endō's call to a more contemporary, more globalized understanding of faith than what he finds in pre–Vatican II Catholic thought. What emerges here is a model of interfaith dialogue and encounter built not on the premises of Hick's theodicy but on a vision of religious pluralism that respects difference while insisting on a more fundamental analogical similarity between faith traditions.

Endō's model does not render diverse religious forms as deviations from a single truth (as in earlier Christian thought) or as partial revelations of a denatured, pantheistic divine force (as in Hick). With Ōtsu, Endō asserts the fundamental truth of all faiths. Ōtsu's God actually presents many faces, not one face seen from multiple perspectives with varying degrees of clarity. This is a more radical theological response to the Eurocentric orthodoxies of Ōtsu's superiors. Sleeping on the floor of the ashram, Ōtsu dreams of being back at the French seminary with his new understanding:

"God was fostered in this world of ours. In this Europe you detest so."

"I don't believe that. After he was crucified in Jerusalem, he began to wander through many lands. Even today he roams through various countries. Through India and Vietnam, through China, Korea, Taiwan."

"Enough! If our teachers knew you were such a heretic . . . !"

"Am I . . . am I really a heretic? Was any religion truly heretical to him? He accepted and loved the Samaritan."[61]

Notably, Ōtsu connects his commitment to the truth of all faiths with his commitment to the person of Christ. The two commitments are not separable, as literary critics intuit from Endō's reading of Hick. At no point does Ōtsu disavow his Christianity. He remains a priest. He celebrates mass. He loves Christ. In the person of Christ, Ōtsu finds a face of God suited to his life and situation, a face he can love as completely as he loved his mother. This particularity is key to Endō's theology of encounter. Ōtsu loves a particular face of God, a commitment that necessarily entails honoring and engaging the many other particular faces, loved in many other particular ways. For Endō, to love Christ—to be a Christian—requires seeing God at work in other forms in other places. Acknowledging this multiplicity intensifies one's love of Christ rather than diminishing it.

Ōtsu's new way of life in Vārānasī reveals the depths of his faith in this truth. He superimposes the Christic narrative on his acts of love:

> *O Lord*, Ōtsu offered up a prayer. *You carried the cross upon your back and climbed the hill to Golgotha. I now imitate that act.* A single thread of smoke already was rising from the funeral pyres at the Manikarnikā Ghāt. *You carried the sorrows of all men on your back and climbed the hill to Golgotha. I now imitate that act.*[62]

The practice neither diminishes Ōtsu's Christian attachments nor dissolves the differences between Christianity and Hinduism. Rather, Ōtsu believes his participation in the Christic narrative is bound to the particularities of Vārānasī, just as the person of Christ was bound to the hill of Golgotha. This situatedness—this particularity—is key to the analogical understanding on which Endō's theology of encounter is built. Ōtsu loves the face of Christ because it was the face of God first presented to him as a child. He does not lose his attachment to this face when confronted with others. "It seems perfectly natural to me that many people select the god in whom they place their faith on the basis of the culture and traditions and climate of the land of their birth," he tells his superiors at the seminary.[63] For Endō (as for Ōtsu), God's many faces are culturally expressed. The face of God presented at the Ganga demands different forms and different acts of love than does the face of God presented in the Christic dramas of European culture. However, key for Endō is the fundamental analogical similarity between the various forms. Ōtsu understands his carrying bodies to the cremation grounds as a re-performance of Christ carrying the cross. Similarly, the river itself becomes Christic: "The Ganges swallows up the ashes of every person as it flows along, rejecting neither the beggar woman who stretches out her fingerless hands nor the murdered prime minister, Gandhi. *The river of love that is my Onion flows past,* accepting all, rejecting neither the ugliest of men nor the filthiest."[64] This analogical amplification—the Ganga as Christ—articulates the similarity-in-difference of two faces of God, and orders the religious forms appropriate to each expression of the divine.[65]

If Ōtsu interprets his participation in Hindu rituals as participation in Christian faith, it is also significant that he interprets the outcasts he serves as part of a larger suffering body. "How many people, how much human agony had he taken on his shoulders and brought to the River Ganges?" Ōtsu wonders. "Having only a fleeting connection with these people, Ōtsu could have no idea what their past lives had been like. All he knew about them was that each was an outcast in this land, a member of an abandoned caste of humanity."[66] Each outcast is rejected by a particular land or culture for particular reasons, but all outcasts constitute a united abandoned caste that crosses religious, cultural, and political borders. For Ōtsu, it is Christ as the Suffering Servant that holds together in his mind the variety of such outcasts. Ōtsu participates in the redemption of this collective human suffering by ameliorating the particular sufferings of a particular body of outcasts.

Endō gives us a model of interfaith encounter that takes seriously the generative—not merely the self-emptying—power of kenotic suffering. This is a theology of encounter that is both deeply Christian and deeply committed to the truth as revealed in God's non-Christian faces. Indeed, with Ōtsu's narrative Endō asserts the Catholic's responsibility to find the work of the Spirit behind other sets of eyes. He echoes the vision of another Catholic writer, Gerard Manley Hopkins, also misunderstood and marginalized for his Catholic aesthetic. Hopkins, like Endō, like de Lubac, like Teilhard, like John Paul II, would profess "the just man justices" acts "in God's eye what in God's eye he is—Christ." Endō's understanding of interfaith engagement assumes that "Christ plays in ten thousand places/ Lovely in limbs, and lovely in eyes not his/ To the Father through the features of men's faces."[67] In *Deep River*, he dramatizes the challenges of encountering the divine behind unfamiliar faces and demands the Catholic response be one of suffering, service, and acts of love.

Notes

1. Jacques Dupuis, S.J., "Renewal of Christianity through Interreligious Dialogue," *Bijdragen International Journal for Philosophy and Theology* 65, no. 2 (2004): 143.

2. Shusaku Endo interview with William Johnston, S.J., translated from the Japanese by Johnston, from the Japanese publisher *Bungei Shunjusha*, 1990.

3. Mark Bosco, S.J., "Charting Endō's Catholic Literary Aesthetic," in *Approaching Silence: New Perspectives on Shusaku Endo's Classic Novel*, ed. Mark W. Dennis and Darren J. N. Middleton (New York: Bloomsbury Academic, 2015), 77–92.

4. Harold A. Netland, *Christianity and Religious Diversity: Clarifying Christian Commitments in a Globablizing Age* (Grand Rapids, MI: Baker Academic, 2015).

5. Joan Frawley Desmond, "Shusaku Endō's Borrowed Faith." For details on this online article, see: http://www.crisismagazine.com/2011/shusako-endos-borrowed-faith, accessed September 16, 2017.

6. We disagree with critics who suggest Hick's version of religious pluralism frames *Deep River*'s theology. Hick's argument reduces all faiths to a flat, syncretic sameness, an erasure of difference Endō criticized in other contexts during his conversation with Johnston (note 2): "But in the West . . . people are fascinated by Oriental thought. They are interested in Zen, in esoteric Buddhism and in the Buddhist description of the Great Source of Life. When I read their books, I see little commitment to Christ. They are creating sects that have little in common with Buddhism or Christianity or Islam . . . something that transcends the traditional religions" (19).

7. Endō's journal entry, quoted in Netland, *Christianity and Religious Diversity*, 132–33.

8. Emmanuel Mounier's personalist movement in philosophy and theology played a large part in shaping many Catholic intellectuals throughout the twentieth century, from Jacques Maritain to Pope John Paul II. Based in part on a revival of Thomist thought, personalism regards personhood as the fundamental notion that gives meaning to all reality and constitutes its supreme value. It reacts against the depersonalization and material determinism of the Enlightenment.

9. Other twentieth-century Catholic intellectuals with whom Endō was familiar would include the following: the philosopher Jacques Maritain, mentioned in the previous note; the Thomist philosopher Etienne Gilson; the existential philosopher Gabriel Marcel; and the mathematician and philosopher Eduard Le Roy.

10. See, for example, the English translation of the work, Henri de Lubac, *Aspects of Buddhism* (London: Sheed & Ward, 1954).

11. John W. O'Malley, *Vatican II: Did Anything Happen?* (New York: Continuum, 2008), 75.

12. Teilhard de Chardin, *Activation of Energy* (London: Collins, 1970), 241.

13. We are grateful for conversations with the following Endō scholars and translators for providing us this information: Justyna Kasza, Elizabeth Galbraith, Mark Williams, and Van Gessel.

14. Indeed, Endō discussed these changes with the Jesuit scholars that he befriended at Sophia University, Tokyo, over many years. The late Jesuit literary scholar Peter Milward, a professor for over forty years at Sophia University, relayed in a personal exchange that Endō knew well the documents of Vatican Council II. Milward

noted that fellow Jesuit William Johnston, a lifelong friend of Endō and a professor of Religious Studies at Sophia, spent many hours together talking about the Church's approach to interreligious dialogue, especially as the foundation of building bridges between Catholic and Buddhist spirituality.

15. See, for example, Hans Küng, *Theology for the Third Millennium* (New York: Anchor Doubleday, 1988) 132, 143. See also the collection of articles in Hans Küng and David Tracy, eds, *Paradigm Change in Theology: A Symposium for the Future* (New York: Crossroad, 1989), 182–203.

16. O'Malley, *Vatican II*, 27–28.

17. Pierre Teilhard de Chardin, *Science and Christ* (New York: Harper & Row, 1968), 17, 167.

18. *Nostra Aetate*, 2. The document praises Hindus as those who "contemplate the divine mystery and express it through an inexhaustible abundance of myths and through searching philosophical inquiry. They seek freedom from the anguish of our human condition either through ascetical practices or profound meditation or a flight to God with love and trust." The Church also appreciates that Buddhism, "in its various forms, realizes the radical insufficiency of this changeable world; it teaches a way by which men, in a devout and confident spirit, may be able either to acquire the state of perfect liberation, or attain, by their own efforts or through higher help, supreme illumination." http://www.vatican.va/archive/hist_councils/ii_vatican_council/documents/vat-ii_decl_19651028_nostra-aetate_en.html, accessed September 16, 2017.

19. *Ad Gentes*, 11, http://www.vatican.va/archive/hist_councils/ii_vatican_council/documents/vat-ii_decree_19651207_ad-gentes_en.html, accessed September 16, 2017.

20. Ibid., 4, 2.

21. Ibid., 11.

22. For a scholarly history on Catholic missiology before Vatican II, see *A Century of Catholic Mission: Roman Catholic Missiology 1910 to Present*, ed. Stephen B. Bevans (Oxford: Regnum Books, 2013), 93–101.

23. Quoted in Kazumi Yamagata, "Mr. Shusaku Endo Talks About His Life and Works as a Catholic Writer," *The Chesterton Review* 12, no. 4 (November 1986): 503–4.

24. *Redemptor Hominis*, 6, 12, http://w2.vatican.va/content/john-paul-ii/en/encyclicals/documents/hf_jp-ii_enc_04031979_redemptor-hominis.html, accessed September 16, 2017.

25. *Dominum et Vivificantem*, 25, http://w2.vatican.va/content/john-paul-ii/en/encyclicals/documents/hf_jp-ii_enc_18051986_dominum-et-vivificantem.html, accessed September 16, 2017.

26. *Redemptoris Mission*, 2, http://w2.vatican.va/content/john-paul-ii/en/encyclicals/documents/hf_jp-ii_enc_07121990_redemptoris-missio.html, accessed September 16, 2017.

27. As for the question of whether it would be theologically sound to attribute to non-Christian religions a role of mediation in salvation, John Paul II left it for others. Joseph Ratzinger, later Pope Benedict XVI, called for Catholics to retreat from theories

inspired by religious pluralism. In the Declaration, *Dominus Iesus*, a document issued at an inferior level than an encyclical, Ratzinger sees the mission of the Church endangered by theological relativism and religious pluralism in the ecumenical movement. He offers six fundamental corrections or limits on what he thinks are abuses by Catholic theologians. Though arguably a document that clarifies Catholic identity, it was universally understood as an expression of disrespect toward other religions. For a succinct survey of these so-called abuses in the interfaith movement, and the Declarations correctives, see Julia Savi, "The Declaration *Dominus Iesus*: A Brake on Ecumenism and Interfaith Dialogue?" *World Order* 32, no. 2 (Winter 2000–2001): 7–24.

28. See note 27 above, which illustrated the difficulties Fr. Dupuis had in relationship to then Cardinal Ratzinger when still prefect for the Congregation for the Doctrine of the Faith. In 1998, Ratzinger deemed that Dupuis's book *Toward a Christian Theology of Religious Pluralism* contained ambiguities that were detrimental to Christian faith. Though the Church never disciplined him, future editions of his book had to include the Congregation's notification. After being exonerated two years later, which was seven years after his death, his work was celebrated in Rome in an academic ceremony, one that included the bishops of Asia and Vatican officials.

29. Francis Mathy, "Shusaku Endo: Japanese Catholic Novelist," *Thought* 42, no. 4 (Winter 1967): 592.

30. Shusaku Endo, *Deep River*, trans. Van C. Gessel (New York: New Directions, 1994), 46.

31. Ibid., 43.

32. Ibid., 48.

33. Ibid.

34. Ibid., 64.

35. Ibid., 62.

36. John T. Netland, "From Resistance to Kenosis: Reconciling Cultural Difference in the Fiction of Endo Shusaku," *Christianity and Literature* 48, no. 2 (Winter 1999): 181.

37. *Deep River*, 122.

38. Ibid., 65.

39. Ibid., 117.

40. Ibid., 118.

41. Ibid., 119.

42. Netland, "From Resistance to Kenosis," 193.

43. It is worth noting here that Endō himself contrasted Christianity's insistence on the value of such attachments with Buddhist ideas of disconnection. In his conversation with Johnston (see note 2), Endō claims, "There are vast differences between Buddhism and Christianity. Buddhism talks about abandoning the self. It talks about getting rid of all attachments and it even claims that love is a form of attachment. We can never say that."

44. *Deep River*, 119.

45. Ibid., 122.
46. Ibid.
47. Ibid., 121.
48. Ibid., 122.
49. Ibid., 124.
50. Ibid., 150.
51. Ibid., 117.
52. Ibid., 125.
53. Ibid., 161.
54. Ibid., 163.
55. Ibid., 181.
56. Ibid., 184.
57. Ibid., 185.
58. Ibid., 180–81.
59. Ibid., 184.
60. Ibid., 190.
61. Ibid., 191.
62. Ibid., 193.
63. Ibid., 121.
64. Ibid., 185 (emphasis ours).

65. This religious function of analogy is most fully explored in David Tracy, *The Analogical Imagination: Christian Theology and the Culture of Pluralism* (New York: Crossroad, 1981). Tracy argues that distinct iterations of the divine are best understood as linked and ordered, structured according to an ineffable, inaccessible other (408). Thus each form of divine disclosure must be interpreted both in vertical (toward God) and horizontal (in and through history) orientations. Here, Endō holds two faces of God (Christ and the Ganga) in dynamic tension, their differences attributable to the cultural contexts in which they are expressed but their similarities gesturing toward a more fundamental order.

66. *Deep River*, 193.

67. Gerard Manley Hopkins, "As Kingfishers Catch Fire." https://www.poetryfoundation.org/poems/44389/as-kingfishers-catch-fire, accessed September 16, 2017.

Chapter Seven

Shūsaku Endō and Flannery O'Connor on the Grotesque

ELIZABETH CAMERON GALBRAITH

Introduction

In the afterword to the 1994 English translation of *The Girl I Left Behind*, Shūsaku Endō claims:

> Through the medium of this novel I sought to portray the drama of "the Jesus I Left Behind." Mitsu can be seen as modeled on Jesus, abandoned by his own disciples; she is modeled on the Jesus whom all Christians are guilty of abandoning on a daily basis in their everyday lives. Mitsu has continued to live within me ever since and can be seen reincarnated in my most recent novel, *Deep River*, in the person of the protagonist, Ōtsu. It is my profound wish that my readers will acknowledge the connection between these two novels.[1]

This chapter has as its source a desire to respect Endō's wishes, by delving deeply into the connection between Mitsu from the novel *The Girl I Left Behind* and Ōtsu. In doing so, we shall encounter Endō's conception of *imitatio Christi* (the imitation of Christ), together with that which binds and ultimately transforms even those who abandon his Christic figures. Moreover, enveloping Christic figures and those who abandon them alike, will be the literary vocation Endō shared with Flannery O'Connor for the grotesque, as well as his abiding commitment to the Catholic doctrine of the Communion of Saints.

Suffering and Christ-like Love

The Girl I Left Behind is one of Endō's most loved works.[2] In it he offers us an unattractively innocent and gullible "country bumpkin," factory-working female protagonist Mitsu, whose advertisement in a magazine was responded to by the self-absorbed villain of this novel, a young man named Yoshioka.[3] From the outset, the novel is overladen with impending doom, as a palmist at the bar on Mitsu and Yoshioka's first date predicts Mitsu will bring about her own downfall "as a result of excessive consideration for others."[4] When Mitsu earnestly offers her own money to pay for a room at a seedy "by the hour" hotel, her voice reminds Yoshioka of his mother, who had given him food from her lunch box during serious food shortages during the war. Yoshioka intends to take emotional and sexual advantage of Mitsu by eliciting sympathy for his feigned unpopularity with girls due to a polio limp, and his lies strike "a chord in Mitsu's heart."[5] However, Mitsu has the "frightened expression of a child about to receive an injection" and her "overwhelming concern" invoked in him "feelings of compassion and remorse that were totally out of character."[6] Instead of the inn, Yoshioka turns toward the station and home, en route to which Mitsu enthusiastically purchases four crucifixes from a Salvation Army practitioner, after which Yoshioka casts the one she offers him into the ditch.

Mitsu is both child- and puppy-like, qualities that stall Yoshioka's deceitful intent, at least until their second date. On that occasion, Mitsu is wearing one of her crucifixes, which Yoshioka rips from her neck before he duplicitously coaxes Mitsu into sex, all the while telling her he's lonely, but knowing that he intends to jilt her afterward. Furthermore, it is in that seedy room in the inn that Yoshioka remarks upon the unseemly dark spot about the size of a coin near Mitsu's wrist, which will contribute to her, as well, possibly, to his undoing.

For Mitsu, the time in the inn had represented a "few minutes of wretched endurance" to spare Yoshioka "a degree of sadness."[7] Yoshioka had realized she "had this habit of empathizing with anyone who appeared wretched or bitter. Forgetting herself completely, she would do her utmost to comfort the person in need,"[8] and he had taken complete advantage. This same habit, as well as a "voice" reminding her that "to link your sadness to the sadness of others" is the significance of the cross,[9] enables Mitsu, albeit reluctantly,[10] to give up her hard won earnings to the mother and children of the scoundrel Taguchi. She herself seems forgotten, like a "fool" as she later seeks out Yoshioka at his residence, only to discover he has moved.

Much as he might like to, Yoshioka cannot entirely cast off Mitsu, who has a piece of his apparently heartless heart within her grasp, as the "Dick Minee oldie" he had earlier heard and pondered implies:

> That girl I left behind that day
> I wonder where she's living now.
> I wonder what she's doing now.
> There's no way of knowing.
> But, from time to time, my heart throbs.
> As I recall the girl I left behind that day.[11]

When he does track Mitsu down later in the novel, with no less duplicitously self-absorbed motives than when he first met her,[12] Yoshioka discovers she had moved on from work at the factory to a pachinko parlor, where she had selflessly taken responsibility for another's theft. Thus, as with the palmist's prediction, she had, according to Yoshioka, "taken the sins of others upon herself and deliberately wreaked havoc on her own destiny."[13] The owner of the pachinko parlor had then required Mitsu to work in a seedy bar to pay back the stolen funds. When he waits for her at the café at which they have agreed to meet, Yoshioka contemplates offering Mitsu something warm to eat or some pocket money, and realizes that he seeks by so doing to "assuage his guilty conscience" toward her.[14] When Mitsu does appear she reminds him of an abandoned cat, and it is upon that meeting Yoshioka discovers that, due to the unseemly spot near her wrist, Mitsu is being sent to a leprosarium.

The Hansen's disease diagnosis, though it will ultimately prove mistaken, directs us not only to a shift in the novel's focus toward Mitsu herself, but also to the novel's theological preoccupation with suffering. We learn from Mitsu that her mother had viewed leprosy as a punishment from God for naughty behavior;[15] whereas Mitsu herself, feeling more forsaken than a suffering puppy, questions "why, if God truly exists," then God should "inflict such meaningless suffering upon such a girl as herself."[16]

Mitsu has her first encounter with Catholic nuns, and in particular with Sister Yamagata, when she enters the leprosarium, a world in which patients initially feel wholly abandoned by those who had loved them. As Mitsu's roommate acknowledges, the "really hard bit is not the physical pain . . . the really hard bit . . . is to accept not being loved by anyone,"[17] and Sister Yamagata talks of patients feeling "abandoned . . . and left entirely alone."[18] Mitsu, who cries like a child at her own diagnosis, and who, in spite of herself, finds the bloated face of her roommate at the leprosarium off-putting, asks Sister

Yamagata about the other patients, "if they are such good people—why do they have to suffer . . . such agony?"[19] In response, Sister Yamagata sidesteps the God who "insists on testing His people" in the conviction that such agony carries some wider import.[20]

Mitsu's own agony turns to joy upon discovering that her diagnosis had been mistaken and she is free to leave the leprosarium, upon which she promptly departs, only to return. Sister Yamagata initially mistakes Mitsu's motives for returning for sentimentality, and Mitsu certainly is naïve. But Mitsu, who herself had always wanted "a companion who would give her warmth—a mother like figure who would support her head when she arrived home exhausted and lonely,"[21] returns to the leprosarium, becoming precisely that kind of companion to the other patients. Mitsu thus provides early evidence of Endō's proclivity for the "maternal," or "sacred feminine," and for what will develop into his motif of Christ as an "eternal companion" by the time he writes *A Life of Jesus*.[22]

In the Afterword to *The Girl I Left Behind*, Endō claims,

> there is a model for my female protagonist, Mitsu . . . there was a leprosarium run by the Catholic mission at the foot of Mount Fuji, which as students, my friends and I often visited as volunteers. During the course of one of these visits, I was told about one of the women who was working there. The daughter of a well-to-do family in Tokyo, she was tested for leprosy as a young girl at the university hospital. This young woman was sent to the Catholic leprosarium—only to be pronounced clear of all traces of the disease. Just like Mitsu in the novel, the woman was instinctively overcome with feelings of relief and joy and left the hospital for the station planning to catch a train back to Kyoto. It was at the station she made a life changing decision. Returning to the leprosarium she devoted the rest of her life to the care of lepers.[23]

This young woman's life choice clearly had a profound impact upon Endō and upon his conception of what it means to lead a Christ-like life. In the novel, Sister Yamagata suggests that Mitsu never showed signs of accepting God, not wanting to "believe in someone who can toy with little children."[24] In this way, Mitsu shared what Flannery O'Connor calls "one of the tendencies of our age," which is "to use the suffering of children to discredit the goodness of God," and once you have discredited God's goodness, you are, according to O'Connor, "done with him."[25] Mitsu is not unlike Ivan Karamazov, who, as O'Connor suggests, "cannot believe, as long as one child is in torment."[26]

Such rebellious tendencies are, in O'Connor's view, unrealistic, for it is the believer, not the unbeliever, who is the realist.[27] She makes this argument in her introduction to "A Memoir of Mary Ann."[28] The memoir itself is composed by nuns who had cared for Mary Ann, a child facially deformed by cancer who had spent six of her nine years of life in their home for incurable cancer patients. In her introduction, O'Connor tells the story of how the novelist and short story writer Nathaniel Hawthorne, whose daughter Rose went on to found the home that was to become Mary Ann's sanctuary, had once in a Liverpool workhouse been followed by an "unlovely and unwholesome" little imp with a humor in its eye.[29] "I never saw," notes Hawthorne, "a child that I should feel less inclined to fondle." The child, however, had other plans, and planted itself in front of Hawthorne to be lifted up, whereupon Hawthorne felt as if "God had promised the child this favor on my behalf," and that he "must needs fulfill the contract," concluding afterward that "I should never have forgiven myself had I repelled its advances."[30]

The point of the Hawthorne story is that suffering, especially the suffering of children, is grotesque. Yet, as both Hawthorne and O'Connor knew, and as Paul Elie eloquently states in his account of O'Connor, "in human suffering the believer sees the grounds of our common humanity." Moreover, it is "through suffering, above all, that human beings are stirred to the love of one another, and to the love of God, who showed his love for humanity through his willingness to suffer as one of us."[31]

This catalytic thread between suffering and Christ-like love is the wider import of suffering, known in Endō's novel to Sister Yamagata and the leprosarium's nuns, who believe "when human beings suffer, Our Lord suffers alongside us."[32] According to Sister Yamagata, Mitsu, who had once prayed by the bed of a child dying in agony that she would "willingly take his leprosy" upon herself, and wondered if the God in whom she apparently did not believe would "hear" her prayer,[33] clearly "experienced this solidarity with suffering in her own life."[34] Moreover, in Sister Yamagata's view, Mitsu lived out the biblical command to become "like the smallest of children"[35] through her simple, uncomplicated acts of love,[36] which is perhaps why Sister Yamagata has a priest privately baptize Mitsu[37] when she does die after performing a characteristically altruistic act. A lorry in the town close to the leprosarium hits Mitsu. She was there to sell the eggs raised by the leprosarium's patients in order to garner Christmas funds for the patients. Mitsu might have avoided the oncoming lorry that backed into her, had she not sought to protect the patients' eggs.

O'Connor speaks of the "action by which charity grows invisibly among us, entwining the living and the dead,"[38] and Yoshioka is indeed entwined to the Christ-like Mitsu, whom he has abandoned but can never entirely leave behind. Upon learning that Mitsu had spoken his name in farewell as she died, Yoshioka considers the possibility that "every person with whom we cross paths leaves an indelible mark on us" and wonders, does God "speak to us through these marks?"[39] The reader secures a sense of a charitable stirring in Yoshioka's otherwise hardened heart, as he comes, in retrospect, to view his encounter with Mitsu as key to "understanding the meaning of life," and to recognize the girl he had discarded "like a puppy" as, in fact, "a saint."[40]

Mitsuko in *Deep River*

An even-more-hardened heart, in which "the spark of love had never been kindled,"[41] is possessed by Mitsuko Naruse, who serves as Yoshioka's counterpoint and alter ego to Mitsu, the protagonist in *The Girl I Left Behind*.[42] She is one of several leading characters about to undertake a travel tour to India in Endō's *Deep River*. The purported purpose of the tour is to visit famous locales associated with Buddhism, but for Mitsuko the India tour is a pilgrimage into the murky depths of her own heart as well as a quest for the fellow student, Ōtsu, whom she had seduced and then abandoned in her youth.

As a young college student, Mitsuko had always felt "hollowness in her heart" as well as "anger or desolation directed towards herself"[43]; she felt, in fact, a "bone-chilling sense of emptiness."[44] Her so-called friends,[45] who named Mitsuko "Moïra," after the heroine in Julien Green's novel of that name,[46] suggested to Mitsuko that she should seduce the timid and chubby "sweat-hog," Christian bumpkin Ōtsu, who had been made fun of "ever since he was a child."[47] Initially reluctant, Mitsuko comes to feel a "childish desire to make fun not of Ōtsu,"[48] whose face was the picture of virtue, "but of the God in whom he believed,"[49] for she felt revulsion toward the Christian world in which Ōtsu resided.[50]

Ōtsu, like Mitsu before him, is inexperienced, vulnerable, and gullible. Despite proficiency with the flute, he is "docile" and confesses to not having "much experience at having a good time."[51] He is a practicing Christian, and apologetic for it, acknowledging that, despite his doubts, he continues to pray out of attachment to his dead mother;[52] this maternal feeling is an echo perhaps of the loyalty Endō felt to the mother who had first introduced him to Christianity. This infuriates Mitsuko, who takes great pleasure in inducing him to betray his God—in the process Ōtsu also, presumably, abandons his dead mother—with liquor.[53] As she does so, she recalls the times of persecution in Japan when Christians were forced to trample the *fumie*, thus referencing themes of apostasy central to Endō's earlier novel, *Silence*.[54] Later, Mitsuko has Ōtsu abandon his God through physical intimacy,[55] a plot on the surface successful, since Ōtsu no longer prays at the Kultur Heim and agrees not to attend church.[56] But it is a plot doomed, ultimately, to fail, because as Ōtsu knows, "even if I try to abandon God, God won't abandon me."[57] Try as she might to "escape the hollowness she feels" through the "pleasure of deforming a man's life"[58] and then casting him off, Mitsuko's hardened heart is pricked by contrition for the poor mongrel Ōtsu. Moreover, there is an "invisible" and "inexplicable thread"[59] that will bind Mitsuko to Ōtsu, as is intimated not through a "Dick Minee oldie," but rather through Mitsuko's Augustine evoking[60] biblical encounter with one of the Suffering Servant passages from the prophet Isaiah at the Kultur Heim where Ōtsu used to pray daily:

> He hath no form nor comeliness; and when we shall see him, there is no beauty that we should desire him.
> He is despised and rejected of men; a man of sorrows, and acquainted with grief; and we hid as it were our faces from him. . . . Surely he hath borne our griefs, and carried our sorrows.[61]

Rejection by Mitsuko is what enables Ōtsu to understand, "just a little the sufferings of that man who was rejected by all men," and in his experience of romantic abandonment he is able to discover the one who will "never abandon" him.[62] Ōtsu recounts all of this to Mitsuko when they later meet in France, where he is studying at a seminary to become a priest and where she has chosen to honeymoon with her husband. The meeting takes place in Lyon, the location of the seminary Ōtsu attends, shortly after Mitsuko has made a solitary tour of sites associated with Mauriac's *Thérèse Desqueyroux*, a character in the novel of that name who, perhaps through ennui,[63] poisons her husband and with whom Mitsuko now identifies. Still struggling with the "darkness in the depths of the human heart,"[64] and her inability to love another person, Mitsuko comes across the words, "I cannot truly love another person. I have never once loved anyone. How can such a person assert their own existence in the world?" in Fukuda Tsuneari's *Horatio Diary*, and concludes that they "capture exactly what I am."[65] She could not be a more appropriate candidate for Ōtsu's burgeoning theological convictions.

Ōtsu feels "transformed by the conjurings of God,"[66] who, "like a magician, can turn any situation to the best advantage. Even our weakness and our sins,"[67] and Mitsuko notices that Ōtsu is somewhat transformed. He is more confident and more determined, albeit still apologetic. Though she remains unwilling to credit the God in whom she does not believe, Mitsuko does find this more decisive Ōtsu "different from the somehow ineffectual fellow she had known, whose only redeeming feature was his goodness."[68] Mitsuko even wonders if she would have been happy being married to Ōtsu.[69]

In *The Girl I Left Behind*, Mitsu had struggled with God's relationship to suffering, both her own and especially the suffering of innocent children, as though clenching her fist in "defiance at a God who inflicts leprosy on innocent little children and who ultimately confronts them with nothing but death."[70] Ōtsu's theological struggles as a seminarian revolve around precisely the dualistic conceptions that underlay Mitsu's dilemma, conceptions that abound in European theodicies. "I can't make the clear distinction these people make between good and evil. I think that evil lurks within good and that good things can lie hidden within evil as well. That's the very reason God can wield his magic. He made use even of my sins and turned me towards salvation."[71]

Ōtsu's view is comparable to that of Gaston, another of Endō's Christlike figures from the novel *Wonderful Fool*, who reappears in *Deep River* to soak up "all the anguish"[72] in the heart of Tsukada, a dying soldier who had committed cannibalism in Burma during World War II. Convinced that one can "find the love of God even in the midst of such an awful hell,"[73] Gaston gives solace not only to Tsukada's grieving heart, but also to Tsukada's friend Kiguchi, for whom "the seeds of salvation are buried in every act of evil."[74]

This inability to view good and evil as distinct and mutually incompatible is inseparable from Ōtsu's reluctance to consider God "a being separate from" humankind,[75] along the lines of traditional Christian theism. Rather, for Ōtsu, God is within humans, a great pantheistic life force that envelops them,[76] and all of nature. In a letter to Mitsuko from a community in the south of France to which he moves after Lyon, Ōtsu reveals, "since my youth, thanks to my mother the one thing I was able to believe in was a mother's warmth. The warmth of her hand as it held mine, the warmth of her body when she called me, the warmth of her love, the warmth that kept her from abandoning me."[77] For Ōtsu, God, or the sacred feminine, is a "vastly more powerful accumulation of this warmth—in other words, love itself."[78]

Mitsu had returned to the leprosarium to be, like the nuns who ministered there, a loving companion to those suffering from leprosy.[79] She did so in the knowledge that it is possible in the leprosarium for patients, as perhaps also for those ministering to them, to "no longer feel . . . abandoned,"[80] and to discover "a purpose in life . . . that you can't find outside."[81] During her ministry at the leprosarium Mitsu suffered the torment of witnessing children suffering in agony, and she sought, in Christ-like fashion, to take that suffering upon herself. Mitsuko Naruse, after her divorce from her husband, also becomes a volunteer, in a hospital. Unlike Mitsu, however, far from experiencing "solidarity in suffering" with her patients, Mitsuko's ministry to the patients in the hospital is a "make-believe charade of love,"[82] and on occasion she perversely pretends to forget to change undergarments or to dispense medicines. Whereas Endō presents Mitsu as a Christ-like figure, through Mitsuko he attempts to portray how, above all, "sin . . . disfigures"[83] humankind. But disfiguring sin can, just as suffering, lead to God, according to Endō, for whom even perversions, or the devilish side of human beings can lead to God, via the "negative" road, "a road not easily forgivable."[84] Ōtsu suggests something very similar in a letter to Mitsuko from Israel, where after France he continues his ever-struggling theological pilgrimage[85]: "quinine produces high fevers if you drink it when you are well, but it becomes an indispensable drug for a malaria sufferer. I think sin is very much like quinine."[86]

In *The Girl I Left Behind*, Sister Yamagata claims that "no amount of suffering can surpass the despair occasioned by loneliness."[87] Between the lines of Mitsuko's conviction that she "cannot truly love another person,"[88] Ōtsu "feels" how lonely Mitsuko really is and reassures her that not only that God understands her pain, but that God is always "within and beside" her.[89] Moreover, like O'Connor, for whom "in us the good is something under construction,"[90] Ōtsu remains confident that God who, "makes use of every means," including sin, will "transform" Mitsuko's "charades" ultimately.[91] First, however, she must make a deep pilgrimage into the charade of her own heart and prepare to dispense with fabrications of love. When the invisible thread "transcending herself"[92] brings Mitsuko to Varanasi, India, where Ōtsu is living, she finally becomes capable of doing so through her own encounters with lepers, and in particular with the leprous goddess Chāmundā.

It is Enami, the tour guide, who first introduces Mitsuko and the other Japanese pilgrims to Chāmundā, the goddess, who "displays all the sufferings of the Indian people," bearing every illness, and enduring every pain.[93] As he explains the suffering goddess to the Japanese tourists, Enami recalls his own mother, who had raised him through many trials of her own after she was abandoned by her husband[94]; this is another echo perhaps of Endō's mother,[95] who had suffered abandonment by Endō's father as well as her own hurdles in raising two children after divorce.

For Mitsuko, it is the wailing voices of lepers who had lost all their fingers, "men and women with their stubs of hands and their decaying skin covered with filthy rags"[96] that breaks through the masochism, borne of hunger for love, in her own heart. Above all it is Chāmundā, "festering with leprosy, encoiled by poisonous vipers, gaunt, yet nursing children from her drooping breasts,"[97] who pierces her previously only pricked heart, transforming the charade of pure and pristine love exemplified for Mitsuko by the "lofty, dignified Holy Mother of Europe," the Virgin Mary, into the grotesque reality of the "Asian mother."[98]

Chāmundā stirs in Mitsuko's heart memories of her biblical encounter with Isaiah's Suffering Servant at the Kultur Heim, when she had sought to keep Ōtsu from his God. And as if connecting the dots in some soteriological puzzle, it now dawns on her that Ōtsu, like Isaiah's Suffering Servant, had "no form nor comeliness" and had, as with the Suffering Servant, been "despised and rejected" by herself.[99] Moreover, Mitsuko has learned from other members of the Japanese tour that Ōtsu, wearing a *dhoti* and living in a Hindu ashram, carries the bodies of Hindus to the cremation grounds. When she does eventually encounter Ōtsu, it is his face—disfigured with eruptions[100] evocative of the leprous Chāmundā—that bespeaks his solidarity, like Mitsu before him, with the suffering in his midst.

Ōtsu now considers himself a "Catholic priest,"[101] even though it is far from clear he has ever succeeded in becoming one through the traditional Christian seminary ordination process. Earlier, his lack of obedience and questionable faith had been found wanting;[102] now, the Church in Varanasi takes "no responsibility" for him.[103] While he feels personally bound to the Christian Church, proclaiming, "Jesus has me in his grasp," Ōtsu nevertheless has an affinity for the view that "there are many different religions, but they are merely various paths leading to the same place."[104] This Christian pluralism has been fomenting throughout the novel, but to it Ōtsu now adds a defense against accusations of heresy.[105] Similarly, as a seminarian Ōtsu had espoused a nondualistic pantheism of God as "love itself," not "any of the other innumerable doctrines mouthed by the various churches," and had been considered heretical.[106] This nondualist love pantheism is now encapsulated, in Ōtsu's mind, by the Ganges River, which he calls his "river of love," flowing past, while "accepting all, rejecting neither the ugliest of men nor the filthiest."[107] Moreover, doctrine, as Mitsuko attests when she declares it "true that Ōtsu's words were substantiated by the life of misfortune he had led,"[108] pales in significance to the salvific import of the life Ōtsu leads in *imitatio Christi*.

If, as O'Connor suggests, "the creative action of the Christian life is to prepare" one's "death in Christ,"[109] Ōtsu embodies such a life. Ministering as he does to the Harijans, the outcast "children of God"[110] in Indian society, it is the kenotic Jesus who would "carry the fallen on his back and take them to the cremation grounds. Just as he bore the cross on his back while he was alive,"[111] which bolsters Ōtsu's faithful way of life. According to Endō, "Christ himself takes the form of Ōtsu in this novel. Perhaps I should call it an imitation of Christ, but I have tried to juxtapose the life of Ōtsu onto that of Christ."[112] Ōtsu's *imitatio Christi* is as blatant as Mitsu's was subtle, when he transports the dying and corpses of the "abandoned caste of humanity" to the funeral pyres by the Ganges River and offers up himself in prayer: "*You carried the cross upon your back and climbed the hill to Golgotha. I now imitate that act. . . . You carried the sorrows of all men on your back and climbed the hill to Golgotha. I now imitate that act.*"[113] The creative act by which Endō completes Ōtsu's "preparation for death in Christ" occurs when Ōtsu vicariously assumes the transgressions of the Japanese photographer, Sanjō,[114] and is critically wounded. Like a sacrificial lamb bleating in pain, Ōtsu endures torment for the sake of another.

For the Christian, of course, to prepare one's death in Christ is to live in the hope of resurrection, or rebirth, and it is most appropriately Mitsuko through whom Endō chooses to communicate "the assurance of things hoped for, the conviction of things not seen,"[115] in the concluding pages of *Deep River*. Clad with a sari, Mitsuko has prepared for rebirth by descending, like death itself into the grotesquely polluted baptismal waters[116] of the Holy Mother Ganges, the river of love that accepts all and rejects none, and by raising herself in prayer. Like the disciples, every one of whom, according to Ōtsu, "had stayed alive" by "abandoning" Christ and running away[117] when he was killed, Mitsuko balks at the purported "powerlessness"[118] of Ōtsu's vocation when she witnesses him lying broken on a litter prepared for the dead in Varanasi. Ōtsu had been of the conviction that Christ continued to love the disciples even though they betrayed him, and as a result, those who remained "finally understood his love and what it meant."[119] So too, does Mitsuko come to understand the meaning of the love of which Ōtsu has spoken and which he has lived; a love which becomes "etched" even into the most hardened of "guilty hearts,"[120] such as her own, so that it cannot be forgotten, or left behind.

Mitsuko's epiphany takes place neither on a road to Emmaus nor at the foot of the Holy Mother Ganges, but on the streets of Mother Teresa's Calcutta, in an encounter reminiscent of Mitsu's first meeting at the leprosarium,[121] with two nuns, one white, one Indian.[122] The purpose of these two nuns' lives is to help prepare others for death, as their "Home for the Dying," and the comment by one of the nuns, "except for this . . . there is nothing in this world we can believe in" suggests.[123] One suspects the nuns of the Catholic mission at the foot of Mount Fuji might have espoused similar convictions, as might the nuns of Our Lady of Perpetual Help in Atlanta, Georgia, who, according to O'Connor, in their love of Mary Ann, taught her "what alone could have been of importance to her."[124] It is these two nuns, embodying as they do love's suffering ministry, just as Ōtsu has with his Christ-like vocation, that make tangible for Mitsuko "that charity which grows invisibly among us, entwining the living and the dead"[125] of which O'Connor writes.

The Catholic Church calls this action by which charity grows invisibly among us, transforming the most hardened hearts no less, potentially more,[126] than those who live in *imitatio Christi*, the Communion of Saints.[127] According to O'Connor, "it is a communion created upon human imperfection, created from what we make of our grotesque state."[128] O'Connor experienced debilitating suffering and disfigurement in her own life, as did Shūsaku Endō in his, which may be part of the reason why delving deep into the grotesquery of suffering, as of sin, became a vocation for him as it was for her.[129] And, as with O'Connor,[130] who died the year *The Girl I Left Behind* was first published, the deep roots of Endō's unusual fiction, especially in his purportedly heterodox[131] final novel, still lay in religious orthodoxy.

Notes

1. Shusaku Endo, *The Girl I Left Behind*, trans. Mark Williams (New York: New Directions, 1994), 194.
2. Emi Mase-Hasegawa, *Christ in Japanese Culture: Theological Themes in Shusaku Endo's Literary Works* (Boston and Leiden: Brill, 2008), 204.
3. *The Girl I Left Behind*, 31. Cf. 26.
4. Ibid.
5. Ibid., 38.
6. Ibid., 39.
7. Ibid., 61.
8. Ibid., 52.
9. Ibid., 70.
10. Ibid., 68. She had been saving up for a yellow cardigan that she had seen in a store, and intended to buy socks for Yoshioka.
11. Ibid., 51.

12. Ibid., 117. Yoshioka would like to make use of Mitsu for sex while he is short on the funds that might more easily procure it for him.

13. Ibid., 114.

14. Ibid., 117.

15. Ibid., 129. Mitsu's account of her mother's view does not fit well with what was to become Endō's proclivity for the maternal Christ, one who suffers with us. See my essay, "Agape Unbound in *Silence* and *Deep River*," in *Approaching* Silence*: New Perspectives on Shusaku Endo's Classic Novel*, ed. Mark W. Dennis and Darren J. N. Middleton (New York: Bloomsbury, 2015), 125–38.

16. Endo, *The Girl I Left Behind*, 134.

17. Ibid., 148.

18. Ibid., 158.

19. Ibid.

20. Ibid., 159. Cf. 171.

21. Ibid., 174.

22. Shusaku Endo, *A Life of Jesus*, trans. Richard A. Schubert, S.J. (New York: Paulist Press, 1973), 85–86. A number of scholars have provided compelling accounts of this Christological motif in Endō's oeuvre. See the following: How Chuang Chua, *Japanese Perspectives on the Death of Christ: A Study in Contextualized Christology*, Dissertation, Trinity International University, 2007; Emi Mase-Hasegawa (see note 2 above); Jeff Keuss, "The Lenten Face of Christ in Shusaku Endo's *Silence* and *Life of Jesus*," *The Expository Times* 118, no. 6 (2007): 273–79; Mark Williams, *Endō Shūsaku: A Literature of Reconciliation* (New York: Routledge, 1999); and Elizabeth Wills, "Christ as Eternal Companion: A Study in the Christology of Shusaku Endo," *Scottish Journal of Theology* 45, no. 1 (February 1992): 85–100.

23. Endo, *The Girl I Left Behind*, 193.

24. Ibid., 189.

25. Flannery O'Connor, "Introduction to 'A Memoir of Mary Ann,'" in *Mystery and Manners*: *Occasional Prose*, ed. Sally and Robert Fitzgerald (New York: Farrar, Straus & Giroux, 1969), 213–28, 227.

26. Ibid. See also, Fyodor Dostoevsky, *The Brothers Karamazov*, trans. Constance Garnett, ed. Ralph E. Matlaw (New York: W. W. Norton & Company, 1976), 225.

27. I am indebted to Paul Elie for first introducing me to Flannery O'Connor's perspective in his transformative work, *The Life You Save May Be Your Own: An American Pilgrimage* (New York: Farrar, Straus & Giroux, 2003), 309–15. See, in particular, 314.

28. O'Connor, "Introduction to A Memoir of Mary Ann," 213–28.

29. Hawthorne could not determine the sex of the child. Ibid., 218.

30. Hawthorne quoted in O'Connor, Ibid., 218–19.

31. Elie, *The Life You Save*, 314.

32. Endo, *The Girl I Left Behind*, 189.

33. Ibid., 188.

34. Ibid., 189.

35. See Matt 18.3: "Truly I tell you, unless you change and become like little children, you will never enter the kingdom of heaven," in *The New Oxford Annotated Bible, New Revised Standard Version with the Apocrypha*, 3rd edition (New York: Oxford University Press, 2001).

36. Mitsu's embodiment of Christ-like love places her ultimately closer to Ivan's brother Alyosha, than to Ivan. See Dostoevsky, *The Brothers Karamazov*, 218.

37. Endo, *The Girl I Left Behind*, 191.

38. O'Connor, "Introduction to A Memoir of Mary Ann," 228.

39. Endo, *The Girl I Left Behind*, 192.

40. Ibid., 22.

41. Shusaku Endo, *Deep River*, trans. Van C. Gessel (New York: New Directions, 1993), 120.

42. Mitsu also appears in Endō's psychological thriller, *Scandal*, the novel in which nurse Mitsuko Naruse makes her vile debut. Readers might look to Justyna Weronika Kasza's *Hermeneutics of Evil in the Works of Endō Shūsaku: Between Reading and Writing* (New York: Peter Lang, 2016), for an in-depth treatment of Mitsuko and *Scandal*.

43. Endo, *Deep River*, 35. Mitsuko even felt that "within each woman lurked the impulsive drive to destroy herself." Ibid., 41.

44. Ibid., 40.

45. Mitsuko, herself a country girl, had an inferiority complex and was always buying drinks for her so-called friends. Ibid., 35, 40, and 43.

46. As Mitsuko notes, in the novel Moïra seduces the puritanical student, Joseph, who later, murders her. Ibid., 47.

47. Ibid., 36.

48. Ibid., 40.

49. Ibid., 37.

50. Ibid., 38. And like Yoshioka with Mitsu, she quotes Marx to Ōtsu. Ibid., 43. Cf. Endo, *The Girl I Left Behind*, 35.

51. Endo, *Deep River*, 39.

52. Ibid., 41.

53. Ibid.

54. Ibid., 42. See *Silence*, trans. William Johnston (New York: Taplinger, 1980).

55. Endo, *Deep River*, 47–48.

56. Ibid., 45 and 48.

57. Ibid., 42.

58. Ibid., 44.

59. Ibid., 43.

60. The author has in mind the centrality of scripture to St. Augustine's conversion, as recounted in Book VIII of his *Confessions*, trans. Henry Chadwick (Oxford: Oxford University Press, 1991), 152–53. When she meets up with Ōtsu in France later in the novel, Mitsuko learns that Ōtsu has the name "Augustine Ōtsu" at his seminary. Endo, *Deep River*, 60.

61. Ibid., 45; Cf. Isaiah 53.2–4, *The New Oxford Annotated Bible* (see note 34 above).
62. Endo, *Deep River*, 62.
63. Mitsuko finds both Ōtsu and her husband tedious. Ibid., 66.
64. Ibid., 57.
65. Ibid., 117.
66. Ibid., 63.
67. Ibid.
68. Ibid., 64.
69. Ibid., 66.
70. Endo, *The Girl I Left Behind*, 189.
71. Endo, *Deep River*, 65.
72. Ibid., 103.
73. Ibid., 200.
74. Ibid.
75. Ibid., 118. At times in *Deep River*, Endō falls into anthropomorphic language. See for instance, "By now the morning light had begun to trickle into the city, as if to suggest that God had finally noticed the sufferings of man." Ibid., 193.
76. Ibid., 118. I consider Darren Middleton's suggestion that pan*en*theism is the more appropriate appellation for what Ōtsu espouses in *Deep River* to be on the mark. See Middleton's contribution to this anthology.
77. Endo, *Deep River*, 119.
78. Ibid.
79. Endo, *The Girl I Left Behind*, 176.
80. Ibid., 153.
81. Ibid., 154.
82. Endo, *Deep River*, 124.
83. Elie, *The Life You Save*, 315.
84. Shusaku Endo, quoted in Kasza, *Hermeneutics*, 121 (see note 42 above).
85. Ōtsu has still not been able to become a priest. Endo, *Deep River*, 121.
86. Ibid., 120.
87. Endo, *The Girl I Left Behind*, 189.
88. Endo, *Deep River*, 117.
89. Ibid., 120.
90. O'Connor, "Introduction to A Memoir of Mary Ann," 226.
91. Endo, *Deep River*, 120.
92. Ibid., 116.
93. Ibid., 140.
94. Ibid.
95. Cf. Endo, *Deep River*, 41.
96. Endo, *Deep River*, 161.
97. Ibid., 175.

98. Ibid. Cf. 140–41. The stance espoused is comparable to Endō's reenvisioning of Christ in *Silence*. See my essay, "Agape Unbound in *Silence* and *Deep River*" (see note 15 above).

99. Ibid., 175.

100. Ibid., 185.

101. Ibid. 153. Cf. 181.

102. Ibid., 121.

103. Ibid., 163.

104. Ibid., 191.

105. Ibid.

106. Ibid., 119.

107. Ibid., 185.

108. Ibid.

109. O'Connor, "Introduction to A Memoir of Mary Ann," 223.

110. Endo, *Deep River*, 166. Worthy of comparison are Sister Yamagata's reflections on Mitsu and the biblical exhortation to "be like children" in Endo, *The Girl I Left Behind*, 187. Cf. Matt 18.3 (see note 34 above).

111. Ibid., 184.

112. Endo, quoted in Williams, *A Literature of Reconciliation*, 205 (see note 22 above).

113. Endo, *Deep River*, 193.

114. Ibid., 212. Compare Isaiah 53.5: "He was wounded for our transgressions, crushed for our iniquities," *The New Oxford Annotated Bible* (see note 34 above).

115. Hebrews 11.1, *The New Oxford Annotated Bible* (see note 34 above).

116. Cf. Mitsu's deathbed baptism in Endo, *The Girl I Left Behind*, 191.

117. Endo, *Deep River*, 184.

118. Ibid., 212.

119. Ibid., 184.

120. Ibid., 185.

121. The first time Mitsu had "ever set eyes on a nun" was the day she entered the leprosarium. Endo, *The Girl I Left Behind*, 142.

122. This is powerful testimony to the ground that has been covered in what Mark Williams calls Endo's *Literature of Reconciliation* between the East and the West, in his book of that name (see note 22 above).

123. Endo, *Deep River*, 215.

124. O'Connor, "Introduction to A Memoir of Mary Ann," 224.

125. Ibid., 228. Endo, *Deep River*, 215.

126. It is, after all, less the Christ-figures who need transforming love than those who, like Mitsuko, feel only the "enervation of love." Endo, *Deep River*, 124.

127. Cf. Yoshioka's retrospective interpretation that Mitsu was a saint. Endo, *The Girl I Left Behind*, 22.

128. O'Connor, "Introduction to A Memoir of Mary Ann," 228.

129. Ibid., 225.

130. Elie, *The Life You Save*, 314.

131. Some of the less charitable criticisms of Endō come in John T. Netland's "Rewriting the Death of Jesus: An Intertextual Reading of Shusaku Endo's *Deep River*," *Christian Scholar's Review* 46, no. 1 (2016): 65–78. There, Netland argues that in *Deep River*, Endō subverts the orthodox meanings of Christian texts and motifs, redefining them in therapeutic rather than theological idioms.

Chapter Eight

From "Catholic" to "catholic"
Arriving at *Deep River*

MAERI MEGUMI

Introduction

Endō Shūsaku, a Roman Catholic from an early age,[1] chose the career of a fiction writer in order to grapple with the conflict between his religious and cultural identities. During his three-year-long stay in France in the early 1950s, Endō became acutely aware of the discordance between what he called "Japanese sensibilities"[2] (*Nihonteki kansei*) and European Catholicism, and decided to pursue the path of a fiction writer because he believed that imaginative works were the best medium to express and explore his own conflict of being both a Catholic and Japanese individual. Endō's struggles were manifested most famously, perhaps, in *Silence* but also in many other works. *Deep River*, his last major work, concludes his journey of reconciling his Catholic faith and Japanese sensibilities. Here, Endō's "Catholic" perception was replaced with a newly found "catholic"[3] worldview after his persistent striving to find an answer not only to his struggles of faith, but also as a writer trying to understand and depict human beings truthfully. Although he never abandoned the Catholic faith, Endō's religious identity—what it meant for him to be Catholic—evolved. I contend that this transformation is the result of his lifelong endeavor as a writer, that is, the author's keen eye transformed his own religious identity from "Catholic" to "catholic."

In this chapter, I show in what ways *Deep River* showcases Endō's "catholicism" and what kinds of transformations are present in comparison with his earlier writings. Most notably, he dispenses with the use of dichotomy in *Deep River*, which he favored in his previous works because he had believed it to empower fiction; instead, he emphasizes and embraces the diversity of the world by organizing the novel with multiple perspectives and plots. Further, his critical view toward his own cultural or religious heritage decreased. In order to illustrate these features, a brief review of Endō's earlier ideas about religion, literature, and their interconnections appear instructive.

Endō's Early Approach to Japanese Religion and Its Influence on Literature

From the very beginning of his writing career, Endō explored the characteristics of Japanese religious traditions in contrast to Judeo-Christian tradition, and examined how the Japanese religious milieu affected the production of modern Japanese literature.[4] Believing that "Japanese sensibilities" represented the most significant difference between Japanese and Western cultures and literary traditions,[5] he insisted that Japanese pantheistic religions are the faulty foundation of Japanese sensibilities and of modern Japanese literature. According to Endō, the Christian worldview is founded upon the "order of existence" (*sonzai no chitsujo*), which divides humans, God, angels, or any other creatures. Those belonging to a certain category remain fixed, never crossing the boundaries or merging into another; for example, humans can never become God or angels or vice versa. There is no such "order of existence" in Japanese religious traditions, Endō argues; gods can easily be seen as an extension of human beings, and the Japanese do not have to fight against gods since they conceptually conceive of themselves as belonging to the same category, as a part of nature-cum-deities.[6] Consequently, the Japanese lack a conscious relationship with supernatural beings, unlike those belonging to the Christian tradition. Because even the act of rejecting God often presupposes a certain degree of recognition of Him, those in the Western Christian tradition have a much stronger and conscious relationship with Him.[7] Instead of such a conscious relationship with God, what exists in the mind of the Japanese is a "yearning to be absorbed" (*kyūshū e no akogare*); the proclivity to become "part of the whole" withers the sense of "self," "subjectivity," and even the "competitive spirit," making the Japanese lazy.[8]

Endō also believed that modern Japanese literature is structurally weaker than European literature, especially because of the innate "lack of order" and the subsequent paucity of "competitiveness."[9] He therefore proposed that Japanese authors should utilize the Christian metaphysics that had enriched European literature, identifying two important axioms of that metaphysical system that could strengthen Japanese literature: first, the assumption that a supernatural world exists beyond the real or physical world, which he credits with sharpening and widening an artist's eye; and, second, the spirit of competitiveness that stems from and is inherent in the Christian theological scheme that posits dichotomies of opposing forces such as God versus humans, good versus evil, or body versus spirit.[10] Because Japan never had a monotheistic, absolute "God" of Judeo-Christian tradition, however, Endō did not consider that using Christian dichotomies such as good versus evil or God versus humans would create meaningful oppositions in the Japanese context. Instead, he proposed the juxtaposition between the "world with God" with the "world without God" as a meaningful opposition in the Japanese context, and indeed employed this strategy in many of his earlier works.[11] In *The Sea and Poison*, for example, the inherent lack of the sense of morality and guilt of the Japanese is implied to be the result of the "Godless"[12] Japanese religious environment, and is juxtaposed with those who believe in "God" and have an absolute sense of morality. In *Silence*, the protagonist's faith in God is tested in the "Godless" Japanese religious/cultural milieu that cripples imported foreign religions. In *Deep River*, however, there is no such juxtaposition between the "world with God" with the "world without God," nor does Endō further elaborate on the two primary themes of his earlier works—his conflict between Catholic and Japanese identities and the negative assessment of Japanese cultural attributes. What becomes central in *Deep River*, instead, is the multiplicity of the world, which Endō illuminates by underscoring the "catholic" nature of the Ganges, along with the related Buddhist concept of *zen'aku funi*, which basically means that "good and evil are but two faces of the same coin."[13]

Discarding Dichotomies

The most distinctive feature of *Deep River* is Endō's use of multiple perspectives, and its lack of a dominating character or a single issue shared by all the major characters. It is not that the use of multiple perspectives is uncommon in Endō's work. Indeed, one of his earlier works, *The Sea and Poison*, contains sections that focus on different individuals; even so, each is tied to the same theme of the lack of morality of the Japanese. In this light, *Deep River*'s structural, as well as thematic, multiplicity is striking. The story has five main characters—Isobe, Mitsuko, Numada, Kiguchi, and Ōtsu—who are given their individual chapters such as "The Case of Isobe," "The Case of Mitsuko," and so on. The first four characters participate in the same tour to India and that is how they become acquainted, while Ōtsu, Mitsuko's old friend, lives in India, where she finds him after a number of years. Although there are chapters that describe these main characters' interactions during the trip in India, they do not become particularly involved with one another. Each has his/her own reason to join the tour, and their independent pursuit of their own goals is delineated in separate sections.

For instance, the novel starts with Isobe's chapter where he has just found out that his wife has cancer and details how the couple spends her last days at the hospital. He later undertakes the trip to India because his wife told him on her deathbed that she would be reborn into this world and she wanted him to find her. Isobe does not really believe in reincarnation, but he cannot ignore his wife's last wish; after getting some information that there is a girl in India who claimed that she was a Japanese in a previous birth, Isobe decides to participate in the tour to find the girl and thereby fulfill the wishes of his late wife. In another chapter, the reader is introduced to Kiguchi, a war veteran, who travels to India to console the spirits of his deceased war comrades. Kiguchi's story reveals how his friend, who saved Kiguchi's life during the war, harbored a strong sense of guilt from committing the act of cannibalism and drank himself to death haunted by these memories. Kiguchi, now a Buddhist, joins the tour and eventually finds solace by the Ganges where he conducts a personal ritual reading of Pure Land Buddhist sūtras for his deceased friend and war comrades. Each character has a different personality, life experience, and so on; the only common thread is that each has a painful past to deal with and has come to India to find some kind of closure. Even though their stories sometimes overlap, and the description of some characters is a little more detailed than others, each character's story is narrated independently, in an equally objective manner.

By stringing together these seemingly disjoined stories, Endō's intention seems to be spotlighting the complexity and multiplicity of the world. Although there is one character, the ex-priest Ōtsu, who talks briefly about the conflict between religious and cultural identities, it is just one of the novel's many elements. In this way, instead of individual issues, diversity itself is *Deep River*'s central motif, and there is no clear binary offered to create this tension. Replacing such a dichotomy of two opposing forces is the figures representing the perception that the oppositions are in fact contained in a single entity.

Replacing the Dichotomy

The only female character, Mitsuko, who volunteers at hospitals, most clearly exemplifies how Endō is now turning away from the scheme of the competition between two opposing poles. The doctors and nurses praise her devoted work, but Mitsuko herself is quite aware that her "good work" is nothing but a façade, mere "play-acting." She actually does not care about the patients after all; in fact, she is cruel at times:

> As she watched the unresisting figures of elderly women sleeping in their beds, Mitsuko would suddenly be gripped by a nebulous urge, and at times she would pretend to forget to change their undergarments or to give them the medicines they were supposed to take. On those occasions, she heard another voice identical to hers saying: *This invalid isn't going to get better whether she takes her medicine or not. This old woman isn't doing anybody any good; in fact, she's a burden to her family, and it's a far better thing to put her at ease sooner rather than later.*[14]

This misanthropic awareness is partly why she joins the tour to India; she comes to identify with the Indian goddess Kālī, who has two faces: on the one hand, she is compassionate with her eyes brimming with gentleness; but at the same time, the "smiling Kālī sucked warm blood from the blood-soaked demon Raktavīja. She held up a freshly severed head, and blood flecked her lips as she poked out her long tongue."[15]

The dual character of Mitsuko is also shared with the Ganges, which, in its own way, accommodates what seem to be polar opposites, such as life and death, or purity and pollution. In the Ganges,

> [the] women were placing flower petals they had bought at a stall.... On the stone steps the yellow-robed Brahmin beneath his large parasol was blessing a newlywed couple ... the ashes of the body that had just been cremated were being shovelled into the river.... Even though the waters bearing the ashes of the dead came flowing towards the bathers, no one thought it peculiar or distressing. Life and death coexisted in harmony in this river.[16]

The living gather to be blessed and purified and the dead gather to be received by the great river that encompasses all aspects of humanity and beyond. Even if it sounds paradoxical, the river's capacity to accommodate even filth is the essence of its holiness.¹⁷ Here, its ability to accept all kinds of humanity, including the filth and, perhaps, even evil, is underscored as "holy" and "catholic."

Mitsuko also embodies "catholicism" in the way that she threads together the disparate stories of other characters in the novel: she is the only character who has direct contact with all other main characters. She took care of Isobe's late wife while she was dying of cancer and so became acquainted with Isobe. Mitsuko also tends to Kiguchi who falls ill during the tour, and even though she dislikes Ōtsu's sentiments, she still reads Ōtsu's letters. Like Kalī, Mitsuko ultimately accepts everyone with an attitude both compassionate and contemptuous. When Mitsuko enters the Ganges and merges with its sacred waters in the later part of the novel, the gesture carries symbolic resonance. As her entire body is submerged in the river, she comes to the realization that

> What I can believe in now is the sight of all these people, each carrying his or her own individual burdens, praying at this deep river. . . . I believe that the river embraces these people and carries them away. A river of humanity. The sorrows of this deep river of humanity. And I am a part of it.¹⁸

The only thing Mitsuko, the self-proclaimed atheist, believes in is the "river of humanity" that the Ganges embodies, and that, regardless of their specific identities, all individuals are, in the end, included within it. This "river of humanity" is deemed to be bigger than any established religion, such as Christianity, and to possess its own all-encompassing logic.¹⁹ While there is a very strong indication at the end of the novel that Ōtsu's death is imminent, Mitsuko, who becomes one with the Ganges, one with the "river of humanity," survives, even absorbing Ōtsu's story.

No Longer Critical of the Japanese

In his early essays, Endō famously described his struggle to reconcile his religious and national identities in terms of "reforming ill-fitting Western clothes into Japanese clothes."²⁰ While this expression seems to indicate that he was trying to tailor his "Western clothes" to suit his Japanese body, an examination of Endō's literary works reveals that he was, in truth, questioning whether it was the Japanese body, rather than the Western clothes, that was at fault and in need of re-formation.²¹ Endō often juxtaposed Japanese religion with Catholicism and interpreted the former as negatively influencing Japanese culture. He also blamed Japan's religious heritage for deforming the Japanese people's psychological makeup; even so, he was also unable to accept European-style Catholicism wholesale because it conflicted with his own Japanese sensibilities.

Although his earlier works frequently contained at least one prominent negative characteristic of Japan that was central to the story, such criticism seems to abate in *Deep River*. In *The Sea and Poison*, for instance, the three main characters share the Japanese flaws of lacking a strong sense of morality and the willpower to act with conviction. In *Silence*, Japan was likened to a swamp that enervates foreign religions. In *Deep River*, however, Endō's characters do not share these kinds of "Japan[-]specific" flaws. Although the main characters are all Japanese, they are not presented as representatives of a flawed Japanese culture, but are depicted, rather, as people grappling with universal human problems. Isobe exemplifies those who must deal with a spouse's death, for example, and Kiguchi typifies a veteran haunted by his memories of battle.

Even though most of the major characters are depicted as conscientious people, this does not mean Endō was trying to portray all Japanese as virtuous. As discussed earlier, Mitsuko unmistakably possesses the traits of a cold-hearted woman. And the tour guide Enami, an important secondary character, describes his contempt toward the Japanese tourists who are always busy buying souvenirs and only "superficially" interested in Indian culture. At the same time, Enami himself is an example of a self-absorbed, arrogant Japanese intellectual who believes that he is better than the Japanese tourists. Another secondary Japanese character, a photographer named Sanjō, is an extremely shallow, fame-seeking, egocentric individual. Endō's intention is, therefore, not to reverse the image of Japanese people from "evil" to "good," but rather to illustrate a more nuanced and heterogeneous picture of the Japanese, or, just people—some sincere and others shallow, some pursuing fame and money while others try to deal with their painful pasts. Out of such diverse human beings, Endō chooses those who struggle with their pasts as an essential component for his story.

No Longer Worried about European Christianity

Just as Endō's criticism of Japan and its people lessens in *Deep River*, the conflict between Christianity and Japanese identity is also deemphasized. While it was often this sort of conflict that was the focus of Endō's previous works, here, the ex-priest Ōtsu, the character most clearly bound by the conflict between religious and cultural identities, finally reconciles his Catholic faith and Japanese identity. Even though European missionaries criticize his heretical, pantheistic views, Ōtsu still considers himself a Catholic and no longer cares what others think. Unlike Fr. Rodrigues in *Silence*, who was preoccupied with the question regarding God's presence in apparent absence,[22] Ōtsu does not speculate on theological questions because he believes that what he *does* with his chosen God, not whether God exists or not, is far more important. His conviction that "God is not so much an existence as a force"[23] is also clearly demonstrated by his choice of living in a Hindu ashram and carrying corpses to the cremation ground.[24] There is a strong sense of certainty in Ōtsu and his actions, as he believes that it is his given task to help those who come to the Ganges to die. As he confides to Mitsuko, "in the end, I've decided that my Onion doesn't live only within European Christianity. He can be found in Hinduism and in Buddhism as well. This is no longer just an idea in my head, it's a way of life I've chosen for myself."[25] Ōtsu, clearly Endō's double, no longer falters in his own chosen religion.

Religion and Literature

Endō was already an established author when *Deep River* was published, and even though many critics believed it would be his last literary success,[26] a few commentators criticized the novel. Consider Shimizu Masashi. He severely, but perhaps aptly, argues that the novel ends up being a "Shallow River," because it privileges theological matters over aesthetic concerns.[27] Other appraisers, like Nakamura Shinichiro, concur.[28] One possible reason for this negative feedback highlights Endō's ardent desire to use fiction to transmit his beliefs about life and religion in combination with his increasingly deteriorating physical condition.

The way the novel is structured, with five major figures, seems to have contributed to the lack of character development. In contrast, *Silence*, which is only slightly shorter than *Deep River*, had only one protagonist, Fr. Rodrigues, whose psychological and physical journey seems rewardingly detailed, unlike the five major figures in *Deep River* who are given a single chapter each. Because of the limited space, each story is delineated as though it were a summary of each character's concerns—a strategy that arguably runs the risk of robbing the reader of the depth and intimacy needed to know how each individual tackles particular difficulties under specific circumstances. Mitsuko is probably the most developed character; her chapter is the longest and she appears most frequently throughout the novel, as she is the only individual who has some connection to everyone in the story. Even so, Mitsuko cannot be taken as the protagonist.

Another explanation for the lack of character development in *Deep River* is the fact that each of the characters' stories seems to be, in one way or another, a rehashing of Endō's previously published fictional works. Numada's story resembles Endō's earlier work, "Forty Year Old Man," in which, just like Numada, the protagonist's bird dies while he undergoes surgery, and he thinks that the bird died in place of him. Mitsuko Naruse's double-sided nature is identical to that of Madame Naruse in *Scandal*. Likewise, we see Gaston, the main character from *Wonderful Fool* in the chapter linked to Kiguchi.[29] And Ōtsu is the most familiar figure, one that recurs throughout Endō's fiction, as the character caught between the Western monotheistic belief system and Japanese polytheistic culture. The use of familiar characters, however, need not necessarily negate the quality of a given artwork because, as Akutagawa Ryūnosuke, one of the most celebrated authors in the history of Japanese literature, elaborates, all works of art are re-creations of something that had already existed. But, as Akutagawa continues, it is *how* one does it that determines the artwork's quality.[30]

In all likelihood, Endō made a conscious choice to use characters from his previous works.[31] The problem seems to be not that they are familiar characters, but that each character did not have enough space or freedom to show their own lives in depth; they ended up becoming more like instruments of the author's message than living individuals. This aesthetic oversight is unfortunate because, in his early writings, Endō emphasizes the difference between propaganda and literature. In his view, characters, not dogma, should lead the story, and authors do not have the right to control their fictional creations.[32] He went so far as to claim that if a novelist uses characters to propagate religious messages, then his or her writing ceases to be literature.

I suspect that Endō's rapidly deteriorating health entailed that he could not let the characters live enough on their own. This concern raises an intriguing question about the interaction between religious faith and literary creation: Can one's religious faith or belief—however ardent or agonized—hinder one's literary creation? Mishima Yukio, in his conversation with another novelist Takeda Taijun, notes that a novelist's religious faith would destroy the form of the novel, and Takeda agrees with Mishima by saying, in reply, that "religious faith itself can never be the subject of a novel."[33] Endō achieved success in creating *Silence* and other stories in which the protagonist's faith is the theme, but it is the existential struggle that made the characters living human beings, and not the religious messages associated with them.[34] It is ironic that, when Endō seems to be conveying his belief in "humanity," his ardent desire to deliver this philosophy about religion may have spoiled the quality of *Deep River* as a work of literature.

Conclusion

To say that Endō's writing career began because he was Roman Catholic is not an exaggeration. He was drawn to French Catholic writers because he wanted to find an answer to his increasing sense of conflict between his religious and national identities. His early academic interest was eventually replaced with an acute desire to reconcile his Catholic and Japanese identities through his own fiction writing, and Endō produced numerous great literary works that uniquely focus on the issue of religious and national identity.

In *Deep River*, published just three years before his death, Endō no longer had a problem with the polytheistic and syncretistic Japanese religious heritage; his "catholicism" resembles Japanese religiosity, and even though he would still call it his own version of Catholic faith, it is probably more accurately described as "catholicism." Having experimented with various ideas and philosophies such as religious pluralism, Buddhism, as well as psychoanalysis, he ceased using the system of dichotomies as an organizational method in writing novels because he realized that "the dichotomy he learned from European Christianity is no longer of any use for observing human beings."[35] Instead of structuring the two opposing poles of God versus no God, *Deep River* consists of multiple stories and perspectives. No longer is there a struggle between his national and religious identities. His renewed perception toward religion, with which he confidently rejects orthodox "Catholicism" as narrow and embraces his more inclusive brand of "catholicism," is unmistakable. Discarding the Christian system of dichotomies does not mean Christianity became unimportant for Endō, however. As he wrote in 1989, "despite the gulf between Christianity and me, modern Catholic literature left deep imprints . . . on my literature,"[36] and Endō remained a devout Catholic, as he defined it, until the end of his life.

Notes

1. He was baptized at his mother's instigation at the early age of eleven. In this sense, it was not his conscious choice to become Catholic. Endō also describes in a number of essays that he seriously considered leaving Catholicism several times but was never able to do so. In the end, therefore, it was his own decision to remain Catholic throughout his life. See, for instance, "Awanai yōfuku: nan no tame ni shōsetsu o kakuka" [Unfitting clothes: why I write novels] or "Watashi no bungaku: jibun no baai" [My literature: in my case] in *Endō Shūsaku bungakuron shū: shūkyo hen* (Tokyo: Kodansha, 2009), 303–5, 248–55.

2. This expression is used in many of his essays, such as in the title of his essay "Nihonteki kansei no soko ni arumono" [What constitutes the foundation of Japanese sensibilities] in *Shūkyō to bungaku* [Religion and literature] (Tokyo: Nanbokusha, 1963).

3. I am using the word "catholic" defined by the Oxford Dictionary as "including a wide variety of things, all-embracing," https://en.oxforddictionaries.com/definition/catholic, accessed October 16, 2017.

4. He studied French Catholic writers such as François Mauriac and Georges Bernanos in college. See his earliest essays such as "Kamigami to kami to" [Gods and God], in *Kaze no nikusei* [Voice and wind] (Tokyo: Yamato Shuppan, 1986), 166–72. "Katorikku sakka no mondai" [The problems confronting Catholic authors], in *Shūkyō to bungaku* [Religion and literature], 153–68.

5. Endō mentions these ideas in many essays, such as "Tanjōbi no yoru no kaisō" [A reflection on the night of my birthday], in *Endō Shūsaku bungakuron shū: bungaku hen* (Tokyo: Kōdansha, 2009), 13–26. He wrote this essay at age twenty-seven right before leaving for France.

6. A number of sociologists and religious scholars as well as literary specialists have shown that the Japanese people's relationship with "religion" is qualitatively different from those in the Judeo-Christian tradition. For instance, see Daisaburō Hashizume and Masachi Ōsawa, *Fushigina kirisuto-kyō* [Wonders in Christianity] (Tokyo: Kōdansha, 2011); Ian Reader and George J. Tanabe Jr., *Practically Religious: Worldly Benefits and the Common Religion of Japan* (Honolulu: University of Hawai'i Press, 1998); Hisa Kamogami, "Akutagawa Ryūnosuke ni okeru kirisuto-kyō: kirishitan mono kara saihō no hito e," in *Hikaku bungaku kenkyū: Akutagawa Ryūnosuke*, ed. Seiichi Yoshida and Ryūtarō Fukuda (Tokyo: Asahi shuppansha, 1978), 112–45.

7. For example, Endō explains the Renaissance artists rejected God by competing with and/or attempting to overcome God. Kamogami (1978) also displays a similar view in her analysis of Akutagawa's Christian-related stories.

8. Endō wrote, "Truly, Japanese sensibilities are lazy," in "Tanjōbi no yoru no kaisō."

9. Endō also considered how the importation of Christianity affected many Japanese writers negatively. He explains that most Japanese literati who became interested in Christianity from the late nineteenth century to the early twentieth century were drawn only to the surface of Christianity; namely, the individualistic search for faith (*kojinteki kyūdō ishiki*) which was particularly emphasized in Protestantism, and the impulse of confession (*kokuhaku shōdō*). The birth of the Japanese "I-novel," which focused on "individualistic" matters and utilized the form of "confession," was the result of the adaption of these, but because they are superficial aspects of Christianity, the I-novel could never become as powerful as European naturalist novels. See "Kirisuto-kyō to nihon bungaku" [Christianity and Japanese literature] in *Endō Shūsaku bungakuron shū: bungaku hen*, 49–53.

10. Ibid.

11. Endō, "Bungaku to kirisuto-kyō" [Literature and Christianity], in *Shūkyō to bungaku* [Religion and literature], 9–19.

12. I am using "Godless" here instead of "godless" (with a lowercase "g") because there are many gods (*kami*) in the Japanese religious tradition, but not "God" in the sense of monotheistic religions such as Christianity.

13. This definition is from Weblio Dictionary. http://ejje.weblio.jp/content/%E5%96%84%E6%82%AA%E4%B8%8D%E4%BA%8C, accessed October 16, 2017.

14. Shusaku Endo, *Deep River*, trans. Van C. Gessel (New York: New Directions, 1994), 124.

15. Ibid., 115.

16. Ibid., 210.

17. Interestingly, this is the opposite of Shinto purity that is usually described with qualities such as transparent, clear, and free of dirt.

18. Endo, *Deep River*, 21; italics are in the original.

19. In the novel, it is said that "something great and eternal that could not be limited to the Onion" (*Deep River*, 211); here, the term "Onion" refers to Christ. Further, by suggesting that "holiness" includes dirt, filth, and even death, the "river of humanity" is presented as much bigger than any Japanese religion, such as Shinto.

20. For instance, Endō uses the term in "Awanai yōfuku: nan no tame ni shōsetsu o kakuka" [Unfitting clothes: why I write novels], in *Endō Shūsaku bungakuron shū: shūkyō hen* (Tokyo: Kōdansha, 2009), 303–5.

21. Literary scholar Kenzō Furuya points out that one of the most important discoveries of Endō's stay in France is the realization of his "yellow" skin. Endō's 1954 debut piece of fiction *Aden made* [To Aden] has a scene in which a Japanese man, in bed with a French woman, sees their naked bodies in the mirror and realizes his skin is "yellow," dark and somber in sharp contrast with his girlfriend's white skin. Furuya suggests that Endō decided to "accept the [Japanese] body as ugly, and confront it" (268) during his stay in France, and some of his novels, such as *Silence*, can be seen as the way to justify this "ugliness." For more detail, see Kenzō Furuya, "Endō Shūsaku ni okeru ryūgaku no imi," in *Gunzō Nihon no sakka 22: Endō Shūsaku*, ed. Jun Etō (Tokyo: Shōgakukan, 1991), 262–70.

22. Even in *Silence*, the theological question regarding God's existence ultimately becomes less important. At the very end of the story, Rodrigues says that "my life until this day would have spoken of him," indicating that Rodrigues's life is more important than the theological question regarding God's existence. He also describes that God should be seen more as a form of *hataraki* (force/work) than *sonzai* (existence), an assertion that is revisited and emphasized in *Deep River*.

23. Endo, *Deep River*, 64.

24. This perception of religion seems to correspond with how "religion" usually operates in the Japanese context. One of the characteristics of Japanese religion is that it is practice-centered, instead of faith-based.

25. Endo, *Deep River*, 184. Ōtsu begins to use this term "onion" (*tamanegi*) to refer to the Christian God because Mitsuko is an atheist and dislikes even hearing the word "God" (*kami*) in their conversation. Endō mentions that he believes that "onion"

is an apt word to describe his idea of God because there is no actual core in an onion but the layers are what constitute the onion. Likewise, the "central core" is not what is important in Catholicism; rather each layer representing how an individual has his or her own way of dealing with, or doing with, the religion is important. See Fukai kawa *sōsaku nikki* [*Deep River* composition diary] (Tokyo: Kōdansha, 2000).

26. The publisher Kōdansha advertised it as "Endō Literature: Masterpiece," "Pure literature, a full-length novel written for this publication," in the band of its first hardcover edition.

27. See Shimizu's essay: "Shimizu Masashi no Endō Shūsaku ron 2: *Fukai kawa* to Endō Shūsaku no hitogara" [*Deep River* and the personality of Endō Shūsaku] http://shimi-masa.com/?p=98, accessed August 2004.

28. Ibid.

29. Furthermore, the theme of cannibalism and the sense of guilt from the act is reminiscent of the 1951 novel *Nobi* [Fires on the plain] by Shōhei Ōoka.

30. Ryūnosuke Akutagawa, "Bungeitekina amarini bungeitekina" [Literary, all too literary], in *Akutagawa Ryūnosuke zenshū 5* [Collected literary works of Akutagawa Ryūnosuke 5] (Tokyo: Chikuma shobō, 1971), 130–84.

31. Endō wrote that the bulk of his life is certainly contained in this novel. Fukai kawa *sōsaku nikki* [*Deep River* composition diary], 115.

32. See "Shūkyō to bungaku" [Religion and literature], in *Shūkyō to bungaku* [Religion and literature], 164.

33. In this fascinating conversation, Mishima mentions that he considers religious faith as an obstacle that destroys the form of novels, and refers to Endō's *White Man* and *Yellow Man* as examples. Takeda believes that the only way for a novelist to be successful in using religious faith in a novel is to depict how it crumbles. He argues that religious faith itself can never be the subject of the novel because the act of writing means that the author is already betraying the faith. See Yukio Mishima and Taijun Takeda, "Bungaku wa kūkyoka," in *Bungei Tokuhon* (Tokyo: Kawade shobō, 1975), 144–66; see 148 especially.

34. Mishima was one of the committee members when Endō received the Tanizaki Literary Prize for *Silence* in 1966. Mishima praises *Silence* as Endō's masterpiece, but questions the inclusion of the description "He was not silent" at the end of the novel. Mishima considers that the role of literature is not to provide an answer; it would, therefore, be better to leave the question of God's silence unanswered. See Yukio Mishima, *Mishima Yukio Zenshū 32* (Tokyo: Shinchōsha, 1975), 460–61.

35. Endō, "Kirisutokyō to watashi no kuichigai" [The gulf between Christianity and I], in *Kokoro no nokutān* (Tokyo: Bunshun bunko, 1989), 114–17; see 116 especially.

36. Ibid., 117.

Chapter Nine

Deep River as Endō's *Book of Job*

Gathering a Community of Sufferers at the Water's Edge

VAN C. GESSEL

Deep River, O Lord,
I want to cross the river
And go to the land of gathering[1]

—Endō Shūsaku, "The Coming of 'Deep River'"

Introduction

Confession, they say, is good for the soul, so as I set out on a perilous journey in search of traces of theodicean inquiry in Endō Shūsaku's last serious novel,[2] *Deep River*, I admit that, as a literary scholar but certainly not as a theologian, I am marginally qualified to probe these murky depths. I feel rather like the greatest of all Japanese haiku masters, Matsuo Bashō, who, when he set out on a poetic pilgrimage to the Kashima Shrine in 1687, wrote that he was dressed in black robes like a religious pilgrim but acknowledged that he was "neither a priest nor an ordinary man of this world. . . ." Rather, he said, he "might be described as a bat, being between a bird and a rat."[3] I also want to be clear at the outset that I am not making any anachronistic suggestion that Endō ever consciously considered *Deep River* some sort of response to the Book of Job. There is no indication in anything I have seen that he had

Job in mind when he wrote the novel. (I will describe later how the idea was planted in his mind.) There is no one-to-one correspondence between Job's afflictions and either Endō's own struggles or the challenges of his characters in the novel. Nor do I want to get into the business of probing his psyche to see whether some unconscious motivation led him to weave bits and pieces of his own lifetime of physical, emotional, and spiritual sufferings into the lives of the novel's main characters.[4] What is clear from the text is that each character carries burdens of pain, loss, betrayal, loneliness, and disillusionment in the baggage they bring on their pilgrimage to India. Even if Endō did not set out to write *Deep River* as a commentary or meditation on the Book of Job, I hope to demonstrate that he most certainly lived a Job-like life (as do many of his fictional characters), and that, in a way not dissimilar to the struggles that Fr. Rodrigues faces in *Silence*, *Deep River* is a meditative response to the dilemmas of human suffering in the face of a frequently silent God who could easily be regarded as uncaring.

Personal Plagues

In September 1992, just as he completed writing the first draft of *Deep River*, Endō received rare good news from his doctor: results from tests of his kidney functions, which had been a source of concern because of his diabetes, had come back remarkably positive. This encouraging report made the last two weeks during which he completed the draft of this important novel—which he had been pondering since the early 1980s—a time of elation.[5] Within a month, however, his doctor called back to notify him that his test numbers had plummeted to dangerous levels, and that he was perilously close to needing dialysis. Endō was no stranger to afflictions of the body. His lifelong struggles with lung ailments are widely known: Youthful battles with lung disease kept him from the battlefields of the Second World War; his research stay in France from 1950 to 1953 was curtailed when he coughed up massive quantities of blood; and the last of the three lung surgeries he underwent in 1961 resulted in the removal of one entire lung.[6] During the final fifteen years of his life, however, he was assaulted by a succession of illnesses of such variety and severity that they are indeed reminiscent of Old Testament/Hebrew Bible plagues. I knew and worked with him for the last two decades of his life, and though I observed an unexceptional decline in his energy level, it was not until he entered his seventies that it became obvious that his physical body was giving out on him.

Despite what was nearly a lifetime of health struggles, Endō remained consistently prolific in his writing prior to the publication of *Deep River*. I think it's accurate to say that he enjoyed the greatest physical and creative vigor between the writing of *Silence* in 1966 and the publication of *The Samurai* in April 1980.[7] A month before the latter novel appeared, however, he was admitted to the hospital for a suspected case of cancer of the palate. A biopsy performed as part of sinus surgery ruled out cancer, but a worsening of his blood pressure and diabetes complicated recovery from the procedure.

Inspired both by his own recurring, protracted, and always agonizing experiences with doctors and hospitals and by the death from cancer in 1980 of a young woman who had worked as a housekeeper for Endō and his wife,[8] he instigated a campaign to promote "warm-hearted medical care" (*kokoro-atatakana iryō*). In subsequent years, he wrote essays and gave speeches devoted to this subject and provided encouragement to a small group of "Endō Volunteers" who continue the campaign today in local hospitals for more humane care of patients.[9]

Over a period of months following the cancer scare, Endō's kidneys worsened and he suffered a hemorrhage in one eye. His thoughts naturally turned to aging and the approach of death, and his personal reading inclined toward studies of the unconscious mind and the problem of evil. He would expand his studies into Jungian theory and the Buddhist concept of the *ālaya-*consciousness, the deepest level of the unconscious.[10] This program of study, combined with his later reading of John Hick's *God Has Many Names*[11] and *Problems of Religious Pluralism*,[12] had a profound influence on his philosophy of Christian soteriology vis-à-vis other religious traditions, which he explores in detail in *Deep River*.

As though it were a signal of his own impending death, in May 1993, Endō was admitted to the hospital to prepare his body for peritoneal dialysis. Of that surgery he wrote:

> I've had five surgeries up until now, but none has been so painful, so difficult, and so hard to bear as this one. During the surgery, I kept thinking "I wish they'd just kill me." The pain became intense, my lips and tongue were parched, and though I prayed fervently all the while that the surgery would end quickly, I had to endure it for two and a half hours. That would have been one thing for a forty or fifty year old, but it was far too grueling a day for my seventy-year-old body. The pain in my abdomen was still excruciating when I was taken back to my room, and my breathing was shallow. I know

that without the devoted care of my wife, I wouldn't have made it through. She stayed by my side all through the night, massaging my limbs . . . and though I had three injections of pain-killers, that night was one of sheer agony. . . . To divert my mind from the pain, I mulled over a passage from *Deep River*, since it's in a novelist's nature to think "I should have written it this way." But at this point all I want is for the novel to be published. I'm eager to run my fingers over the cover. Was it necessary for my skin and bones to be literally sliced away and me forced to endure today's suffering in order to produce this novel?[13]

Perhaps in response to that plaintive question, Endō would spend the remaining three and a half years of his life in and out of hospitals. However, his wish to "run [his] fingers over the cover" was swiftly granted: *Deep River* was published in June 1993, while he was still in his hospital bed recovering from the peritoneal surgery. Recognizing that his kidneys were beyond repair, Endō wondered whether he should consider a transplant. He consulted one of his dearest friends, Fr. Inoue Yōji,[14] who cautioned him that many of the kidneys made available for transplants came from the impoverished in the Philippines who sold their kidneys in order to feed their families. This information caused Endō to abandon the idea of a transplant, since he preferred to die rather than have another person barter their organs in order to keep him alive.[15]

"Hast thou considered my servant Job?" (Job 1:8)[16]

Not long after Endō's wife, Junko, had accustomed herself to administering his dialysis, he was visited by a new plague: incessant itching over his entire body.[17] Moved by the succession of afflictions her husband had to experience,[18] she tried to offer him encouragement by suggesting that he must be having all these trials because God wanted him to write a "Book of Job." At first he was doubtful that he had sufficient strength or even eyesight to undertake such a project. But only a few days later when a publisher paid him a visit, Endō said, "I want to write about Job. Not a novel, an essay." Somehow this resolve gave him renewed energy and purpose: Junko reported that though he had been murmuring and grumbling about his afflictions for many weeks, after this pronouncement she heard no further words of complaint from him.[19]

In September 1993, the journal *Kokubungaku* published an interview between Endō and his literary colleague, Kaga Otohiko,[20] centering around the recent publication of *Deep River*. In that discussion, Endō announced: "The next thing I want to write is 'The Book of Job.'" When Kaga asked, "Will Mitsuko make another appearance?" he replied, "No, it's not going to be a novel. I'm thinking of writing it as a long essay. This is a great challenge that's been foisted on me."[21] As evidence that this was not likely a passing whim for Endō, in November of that year, in response to a request from a journal to write a short piece on the topic "Even when life is tragic, every day can be a good day," Endō produced "Why Did Job Have to Suffer?" Here is the essay in its entirety:

> When people reach my age, they have to deal with the death of a friend or acquaintance at a frequency of almost one a month. Death comes to everyone, so there's no debating it. But some deaths plunge me into a depression. However I might feel about someone my age dying, it's truly painful for me to learn about the deaths of small children or youth who have not yet reached adolescence. At such times, the profound question of "Why?" naturally comes to mind. Even now, I have no idea why innocents such as small children must suffer from cancer or some other terrible ailment.
>
> Occasionally parents I've never met send me a book they have created in memory of a child who has died prematurely. Each records through their tears how their completely blameless child had to endure the pains of illness and then die, and every story clutches at my heart as I read it. Each time this happens, I think about the story of Job recorded in the Old Testament. As you know, Job was a righteous man of strong faith. Sufferings are heaped one after another on this good man. Even though he has committed no sin worthy of punishment, he is stricken with every kind of malady, loses all his riches, and ends up totally alone. Yet, even though his friends encourage him to renounce God, he refuses.
>
> For a long while I've been consumed by the question of why Job had to suffer. This question is inherent in half of the novels I have written. Why does God remain silent when Job is suffering? Or at least speak in some form other than words?
>
> I'm an optimist, and ordinarily I don't think of life as such a terrible tragedy. But when I see innocent people and children who have committed no sin having to suffer, that strikes me in the very depths of my heart as a real tragedy. That's why I've wanted to write about Job at some point in my life, and presently I am

preparing to do so. Even though I say I'm "preparing," that doesn't mean that I have already come up with answers to this dilemma. In truth, I'm still groping in the dark. Depending on how you look at it, groping in the darkness in search of answers to this greatest of all problems may well be part of the joy of living for me. That's because, no matter how hard I try to forget about it, these questions always linger at the base of my consciousness and are constantly popping up from who knows where, even if I'm trying to divert my thoughts by drinking, or by watching a play or a movie.

There is no question that suffering is painful, but at the same time I also feel the joy of grappling with an insoluble problem such as this. Perhaps, to put it in an extreme way, it is that joy which makes every day worth living for me. I have come to the conclusion that to live—and I realize this sounds like a wet-behind-the-ears literary adolescent—means to fight against the all-too-overwhelming problems that God throws in our path. I'm nothing more than a novelist, but for many years I've had the problem of Job thrust in my way without being able to come up with any conclusions. But it's precisely because I haven't reached any conclusions that I've been able to write novels—in fact, couldn't help but write novels. In that sense, the purpose of our lives is to grapple with the challenges (which may be different for every person) that God gives us.

These are the thoughts that popped into my head when the editors of this journal assigned me this topic. To be honest, I don't think I'll be able to come up with a convincing answer to this problem before I die. But at my present age, it has become my hope that I might be able to discover some clues or paths toward an answer in my own way. I'm quite sure that Dostoevsky asks these same questions in his novels.[22]

"My soul is weary of my life" (Job 10:1)

Although the issue of theodicy is implicit in many of his writings, to my knowledge, this is the first time in his career that Endō explicitly made the connection between God's silence—the very heart of his novel *Silence*, but, I would suggest, also inherent in earlier works such as *The Sea and Poison*—and his desire to seek out some divine rationale behind human suffering. Given his own rapidly declining health, however, combined with the suggestion from his wife that he write about Job, it makes sense that he would be focusing his thinking on the dilemma of universal human pain. And, of course, he had just published *Deep River*.

We cannot hope to know how Endō would have viewed the question of theodicy in his never-written Job essay. But my extensive reading of his literary works gives me the courage (or fans my foolishness) to speculate on a couple of key issues that tie the Job narrative to Endō's fiction. I can imagine Endō siding with those modern critics who consider the core narrative of Job, "the poem" (chapters 3–37), to be of different authorship than the "frame-story (chapters [1–2], [38–42])," which Robert Alter describes as "a folktale that had been in circulation for centuries, probably through oral transmission. . . ."[23] I doubt Endō would have been comfortable with a God who roars from the whirlwind; when a deity chooses to speak in his works, it is with a "still small voice."[24] It is also critical to point out that in *Silence*, the voice of Christ that speaks to Rodrigues through the *fumie* offers no *answers* to the question of suffering. Of greater importance to Endō than a solution to the theodicy conundrum is the reassurance that we are not alone in our trials, that we have an immortal companion (as well as other compassionate mortals who join us on our sojourn) who is willing to share our burdens. We continue on our journeys—and this is certainly true for Fr. Rodrigues as well as for Ōtsu in *Deep River*—as ignorant as is Job of the reasons for our pain, even when it is obvious that we have done nothing to deserve divine punishment.

Was Endō comfortable viewing each of us in a state of not-knowingness? In a sense God leaves Job, along with Endō's fictional creations, at a distance, with a gap between the human and the celestial that is neither filled with knowledge nor with what can seem, in the final chapters of the Book of Job, like outright petulance.[25] I doubt Endō would have been pleased with those last chapters, and would have preferred to side with those who choose to sever the "fable/frame-story" from the meaty debates in between Prologue and Epilogue. His literary project was, in a sense, an attempt to stand beside a Job battered from all sides and bereft of sympathetic friends, thereby exhibiting a willingness to offer love and companionship to a fellow victim of mortality's slings and arrows. Fr. Rodrigues's final pinnacle of understanding is simply—but comfortingly—a recognition that his life has "spoken of him [God]" through all he has endured.[26] Similarly, Ōtsu has no theological insights to offer to those who crawl in agony toward the banks of the Ganges; all he can do is to help carry them toward their final destination, linking his own experiences of being despitefully used to those dying in India, as well as to the sufferings and death of Christ.

"Oh, don't you want to go / To that Gospel feast, /
That promised land / Where all is peace?"[27]

In keeping with the title of chapter 8 of the novel, "In Search of What Was Lost," Endō remarked that he was depicting characters "In search of lost love."[28] It is not difficult to identify characters in *Deep River* who have lost—or never truly had—love in their lives. There is Isobe, who never gave a thought to the meaning of love in his marriage until after his wife died of cancer; Tsukada, who feels that the sin of staying alive by eating the flesh of a dead war comrade makes him unworthy of forgiveness and unfit to live among his fellow beings after the war; or the writer Numada, who, as a child, had to endure one separation after another, first from a parent and then from his beloved dog, and who can only confide his innermost feelings to the mute birds and other animals he uses as the main characters in his stories. Each of these characters has been deprived of opportunities to experience and return love to others. They dwell, as it were, in a "desert of love."[29]

This stark vision of isolated man in the modern age is common in much of Endō's writing. His displeasure with selfish ambition that leaves lonely victims in its wake is perhaps most evident in his "popular" works, including *The Girl I Left Behind* and *When I Whistle*, while his mistrust of self-serving man-made institutions—whether they be political or even religious entities—comes to the fore in both *The Samurai*[30] and *Deep River*.

Endō expounded on his critique of the self-absorbed individual—who, through his apathy and neglect, causes a great deal of pain for others—in a short article he published in August 1993, just two months after *Deep River* appeared in print:

> I think of how blessed the people of India must be, having a Mother who finally accepts them. In comparison, how unhappy the Japanese are! Even though we'll ultimately be swept away, we end up having no idea where we ought to be swept away to. It's true that we have a blueprint for our daily lives. We think about how old we'll be when we become a company section head, and what age we'll be when we become an executive. But, sadly enough, we have no blueprint for actually *living*. Hidden behind our cheery boasts that we Japanese have the longest lifespan is the fact that the elderly have grown weary of living. . . . As the end of our lives nears, we are forced into hospitals where the only goal is to extend

life, so we're robbed even of the freedom to die in our own homes. We can't do anything of our own volition as our lives draw to a close. I don't know what we could call this other than "unhappy." In the past, the Japanese had a blueprint for living. . . . I think many Japanese people in former times were able to discover at the end of their lives a place where they could finally come to rest in the midst of nature, whether beside the sea or in the mountains. But all such places have disappeared now. We have become victors in our daily lives, but losers at truly living.[31]

Given Endō's view of selfish man in late twentieth-century Japan as a "loser at truly living," it is tempting to wonder whether he had descended into cynical despair about humanity. Yet, as he noted in the 1993 essay quoted above, he remained an optimist at heart. Could/should the same be said about Job? "I know that my redeemer liveth" (Job 19:25) is not an utterance one would expect from a man without hope.

Amid all the frustrated dreams and desires of the central characters in *Deep River*, the one common source of ultimate consolation is the great leveling—or, to put it another way, the great assimilation—of all human experience that takes place at the banks of the Ganges. There, without judgment or ranking, all the pains and conflicts and betrayals that serve to define the mortal experience are absorbed into one at the moment each individual pilgrim enters the waters: some, like the Japanese pilgrims in the novel, for the first time, others at the moment of passage into eternal rest. The omniscient narrator of *Deep River* observes:

> Revenge and hatred were not limited to the world of politics, but were the same in the realm of religion. When a group is formed in this world, oppositions emerge, dissension is created, and strategies are concocted to belittle the opponent. Isobe, who had lived through the war and post-war periods in Japan, had seen so many people and groups of that inclination that he was sick of it all. He had heard the word "right" so often that he had wearied of it. At some point the vague feeling that he could never believe in anything had come to rest permanently at the bottom of his heart. . . . People were linked together more by enmity than by love. It was not love but the formation of mutual enemies that made a bonding between human beings possible. By such means had every nation and every

religion survived over the long span of years. In the midst of all that strife, a pierrot like Ōtsu had aped the behavior of [Jesus] and in the end had been discarded.[32]

Each character in the novel is, in one way or another, seeking someone or something that can fill the cavernous loneliness in their hearts and provide a loving connection as they journey across the "desert of love" that is mortality. Ōtsu tells Mitsuko that it is not the doctrines of any religion that will provide him the kind of comforting warmth he felt from his mother. "Love, I think, is the core of this world we live in, and through our long history that is all that [Jesus] has imparted to us. The thing we are most lacking in our modern world is love; love is the thing no one believes in any more; love is what everyone mockingly laughs at—and that is why someone like me wants to follow [Jesus] with dumb sincerity."[33] I am reminded here of the words of a sermon delivered by Archibald MacLeish[34] in 1955: "Acceptance of God's will is not enough. Love, love of life, love of the world, love of God, love in spite of everything is the only possible answer to the ancient human cry against injustice."[35]

In the final analysis, I don't think Endō presents any new answers to Job's dilemma in *Deep River*. I have the feeling he thinks that that is how it is supposed to be: God remains silent (not even discoursing on His own majesty as He does in the Biblical story) so that we can navigate our own course toward the deep river of immortality. Leaving the piloting to us makes us accountable for the decisions we make, especially as they impact others. We may choose selfish gain, obtainable only by despising and rejecting others, or we have the freedom to select love of others in response to all the enmity and unfairness of life.

What the novel does convey is a powerful conviction that, however different doctrines or practices might be, the end goal of every religion is the kind of (in Endō's belief system, "Christ-like") love exemplified by Ōtsu, dressed in the robes of a Hindu sādhu but still a believer in Christ, as he wanders the alleyways of Vārānasī, seeking out the dying and carrying them on his back—recalling as he does so Christ carrying his cross to Golgotha—to their final resting place in the flowing Mother Gangā. This particular scene is, I think, perhaps the most beautifully composed in Endō's entire oeuvre. In it, Ōtsu plays the role that is of greatest import to the author—the one who, like his motherly Christ figure, always walks alongside those who suffer, the "eternal companion" (*eien no dōhansha*) each lonely human craves to have. Ōtsu's own literary companions in Endō's writings include Gaston of *Wonderful Fool* (and *Deep River*), Kichijirō in *Silence*, and Yozō in *The Samurai*.

Finally, an observation perhaps most kindred to the underlying philosophy of *Deep River* comes from Rabbi Harold S. Kushner in his musings on Job:

> I have met God in the readiness of people to reach out to the afflicted, to salve their wounds not with their doctrines but with their hugs and their tears. Like Job, like Abraham, I have seen a world in flames and I have been sustained by the message that God has not abandoned His world. Having heard God say to Job, It will not be a perfect world, but it will be a world marked by great natural beauty, inspiring human creativity, and astonishing human resilience, and I will be with you in all of those times, I, like Job, respond: *Em'as v'nihamti al afar v'efer*. I repudiate my past accusations, my doubts, even my anger. I have experienced the reality of God. I know that I am not alone, and, vulnerable mortal that I am, I am comforted.[36]

Among the many who had rejected or denounced him, in ways not unlike Eliphaz, Bildad, Zophar, and even the "tedious" Elihu,[37] Ōtsu had his own experiences with latter-day "comforters": Mitsuko initially, but subsequently the French seminary priests who cannot abide his "heretical pantheism"—his superiors at a novitiate in Galilee, the Catholic fathers in India. But even when Ōtsu offers himself as a sacrificial victim for the despicably narcissistic photographer, Sanjō, and is described in the very last line of the novel as being "in critical condition" after taking "a sudden turn for the worse,"[38] his death is not solitary and meaningless, though it certainly appears as such to most observers. He has performed his last act in "imitation" of Christ for an undeserving young man, but it has been an act of love, and he surely was not without a Companion as his ashes were committed to the great, deep, all-embracing river of humanity.

Notes

1. The original English lyrics to this well-known spiritual are, of course, "Deep River / My home is over Jordan. / Deep River, Lord, / I want to cross over into campground." What Endō provides as an epigraph to the novel is not a standard, literal translation, but one that better suits the intent of his work. On the genesis of this spiritual, see Wayne D. Shirley, "The Coming of 'Deep River,'" *American Music* 14, no. 4 (1997): 493–534.

2. By "serious novel," of course, I refer to those writings that directly confront issues of religious faith; after the publication of *Deep River*, Endō also serialized and

published an historical novel titled *Onna* [The women] (1995), along with several brief essays and articles in journals and newspapers.

3. The first portion of the quotation is taken from *The Narrow Road to the Deep North and Other Travel Sketches*, trans. Nobuaki Yuasa (Middlesex: Penguin Books, 1966), 65; the second segment of the translation comes from Donald Keene, *World Within Walls: Japanese Literature of the Pre-Modern Era, 1600–1867* (New York: Holt, Rinehart and Winston, 1976), 91.

4. This is *not* to suggest that there are no snapshots from Endō's personal experience that are included in the album of each fictional character. There are most decidedly such correspondences, but identifying them is beyond my purposes here. The interested reader is referred to Justyna Weronika Kasza's chapter in the present volume.

5. His high spirits during these two weeks in Karuizawa have been described by his wife, Junko, in her book of reminiscences, *Otto no shukudai* [Homework from my husband] (Tokyo: PHP Research, 1998), 15–16.

6. During the third surgery, which lasted six hours, Endō's heart stopped for a time, and he contracted hepatitis from a blood transfusion. Yet even the stark outcome of these surgeries became a source of dark humor for him. He would later write that, despite having only one lung, he continued to smoke, since his chances of contracting cancer were only half that of a normally healthy person. He mentioned this in his first letter to me in 1974.

7. Many critics, including Katō Muneya and myself, consider Endō to have been at the peak of his literary powers with *The Samurai*. Katō told me this in a personal conversation.

8. When this unfortunate young woman, Suzuki Tomoko, was diagnosed with bone marrow cancer, Endō, in accordance with Japanese practice, decided to amplify the efficacy of his prayers on behalf of Suzuki by giving up something very dear to him: his cigarettes. Unfortunately, she succumbed to the cancer at the age of twenty-five. Mentioned in the Endō chronology compiled by Yamane Michihiro in the final volume of the *Endō Shūsaku Bungaku Zenshū* [Collected literary works of Endō Shūsaku] (Tokyo: Shinchōsha, 1999–2000), 15 volumes, 15: 371.

9. Endō's widow has not been timid in her published intimations (primarily in *Otto no shukudai*) that some of her husband's doctors made several negligent, critical errors in treating him in the years leading up to his death. To cite two examples, after he was diagnosed with serious kidney disease in late 1992, a doctor notified her that the sleeping medication her husband had been given by another physician was suspected of causing damage to the kidneys; shortly thereafter, the Japanese Ministry of Health and Welfare had the medication removed from the marketplace. In addition, after he went on peritoneal dialysis in 1993, he began (as noted in this essay) to suffer from unrelieved, intense itching all over his body. Not until January 1996 did new doctors determine that four of the prescriptions he was taking could be contributing to his itching; after these were stopped, his itching disappeared within two weeks.

10. Endō's own interpretation of this philosophical construct derived from his reading of the writings of Vasubandhu, a fourth/fifth-century Indian Buddhist priest. In Endō's view, the Ālaya, as the deepest level of the unconscious mind, is where the seeds of "latent good" and "latent evil" are "forever whirling around and erupting upwards like a raging torrent." (From a speech Endō gave at a plenary session of the International PEN Club Congress in Tokyo, May 15, 1984. Original transcript and English translation, by Janusz Karol Buda, in author's possession.) Endō was simultaneously reading Jung and was greatly influenced by the notion of a "collective unconscious." It was in bringing these Eastern and Western philosophical strains together that Endō perceived the potential for God to work at this deepest level of the human unconscious, there to cause good to sprout even from seeds of evil. In *Deep River*, the Gangā serves as the place where good and evil, life and death, sin and redemption are brought together without discrimination or judgment.

11. Translated into Japanese in 1986.

12. Endō mentions the powerful impact of reading both Hick books in his *Fukai kawa sōsaku nikki* [*Deep River* composition diary] (Tokyo: Kōdansha, 1997), 24–25.

13. Endō Shūsaku, *Deep River* composition diary, 137–38.

14. (1927–2014). He and Endō formed a warm bond of friendship and trust when both were studying at the University of Lyon in 1950. Each had a profound influence on the other as they pondered an image of Christ that might touch the hearts of the Japanese people. Among Inoue's best-known works are *Nihon to Iesu no kao* [Japan and the face of Jesus] (1976) and *Namu no kokoro ni ikiru* [Living with a heart full of praise] (2003), the latter showing traces of the same kind of religious pluralism that informs *Deep River*, since the "namu" of the title derives from the Buddhist prayer "Namu Amida Butsu" (Praise to the Amida Buddha). Inoue would further explore this religious hybridization with the concept of "Namu Abba" (Praise Abba). Interestingly, Fr. Inoue is, in addition to Endō himself, one of the chief models for the character of Ōtsu.

15. Described in Endō Junko, *Otto no shukudai*, 29–31. She adds that their son, Ryūnosuke, volunteered to donate one of his own kidneys, but Endō's response to him was, "Idiot! You've got two children of your own to take care of. I'm not so desperate to live that I'd take one of my own son's kidneys! I've lived long enough." But after Ryūnosuke left the room, Endō turned to his wife and said cheerfully, "I figured he was unreliable, but I guess we didn't do such a bad job raising him!"

16. This and subsequent translations of Job come from the King James Version.

17. Since I am discussing Endō's writings in the context of the Book of Job, I can't help thinking of this itching in relation to Job's boils.

18. Endō called himself "a virtual department store of diseases." On one occasion he drew a comic picture of a snail and attached a poem: "Thanks to T.B., I have only one lung / Yet with chronic hepatitis / High blood pressure / And diabetes / I have fought back and been writing for over twenty years / So don't underestimate your ill-

nesses / And don't surrender to them." Cited in Yamane Michihiro, *Endō Shūsaku Fukai kawa o yomu* [Reading Endō Shūsaku's *Deep River*] (Tokyo: Chōbunsha, 2010), 13.

19. Endō Junko, *Otto no shukudai*, 34–35.

20. Born in 1929, Kaga was one of several important Japanese writers who became Christians later in their lives under Endō's influence. Many, such as Kaga, asked Endō to act as godfather at their baptisms. A trained psychiatrist who focused his studies on criminal psychopathology, Kaga became a Catholic in 1988.

21. *Kokubungaku* 38, no. 10 (September 1993): 21.

22. *Shinchō* 45, 12:11 (November 1993): 41–42. Taken at face value, Endō's comments here about the Book of Job may suggest that he *did* have the Biblical sufferer in mind prior to his writing of *Deep River*. I suspect, however, that he is playing fast and loose with the timeline here to make a point about his sympathy for those who endure extreme trials.

23. Robert Alter, *The Wisdom Books: Job, Proverbs, and Ecclesiastes* (New York: W. W. Norton & Company, 2010), 4. Harold Kushner calls the two sections of the book the "Fable" and the "Poem"; Marvin Pope refers to them as the "Prologue-Epilogue." For these latter two designations, see Harold S. Kushner, *The Book of Job: When Bad Things Happened to a Good Person* (Jewish Encounters Series) (New York: Knopf Doubleday Publishing Group, 2012), 15–16.

24. 1 Kings 19:12. I am thinking here also of the gentle, reassuring voice of Christ that speaks to Fr. Rodrigues from the *fumie* in Martin Scorsese's magnificent film version of *Silence*.

25. For additional reflections on God's testy response to Job, see: Richard Elliott Friedman, *The Hidden Face of God* (San Francisco: HarperSanFrancisco, 1995), 96–117; Jim Garrison, *The Darkness of God: Theology after Hiroshima* (London: SCM Press, 1982); Jack Miles, *God: A Biography* (New York: Vintage, 1996), 308–33; and, David Penchansky, *What Rough Beast?: Images of God in the Hebrew Bible* (Louisville, KY: Westminster John Knox Press, 1999).

26. Shusaku Endo, *Silence*, trans. William Johnston (New York: Taplinger Publishing, 1980), 191.

27. Verse of "Deep River" spiritual.

28. In Japanese, "Ushinawareta ai o motomete," which is surely an echo of the title of the Japanese translation of Proust's *À la recherche du temps perdu*, "Ushinawareta toki o motomete."

29. Here again, I can't help but wonder whether Endō had in the back of his mind the title of one of the two works by François Mauriac—*Le Désert de l'amour* (1925) and *Thérèse Desqueyroux* (1927)—that had a profound influence on him. He translated both into Japanese.

30. For me, his most scathing denunciation of the Church as an institution subject to selfish motivation comes in *The Samurai*, in the scene set in Civitavecchia in which Fr. Velasco pleads with Cardinal Borghese to send more missionaries to Japan despite the anti-Christian persecutions raging there. Borghese's response ("If in

searching for the one lamb the other sheep are exposed to danger . . . , the shepherd has no choice but to abandon that lamb. It cannot be helped if one is to protect the organization")—an apparently deliberate reversal of the import of Jesus's parable of the ninety-nine sheep—is painfully ironic. *The Samurai*, trans. Van C. Gessel (New York: Harper and Row/Kodansha International, 1982), 193.

31. From the journal *Gendai*, quoted in Yamane, *Reading* Deep River, 190.

32. Shusaku Endo, *Deep River*, trans. Van C. Gessel (London: Peter Owen, 1994), 188, 195. In the original, "Jesus" is referred to as the "Onion," a euphemism that Ōtsu employs when Mitsuko rankles at his mention of the name of Jesus.

33. Ibid., 119.

34. MacLeish himself did a dramatic adaptation of the Book of Job in his verse play *J.B.* (1958).

35. Archibald MacLeish, "God Has Need of Man," in *The Dimensions of Job: A Study and Selected Readings*, ed. Nahum N. Glatzer (New York: Schoken Books, 1969), 285.

36. Kushner, *The Book of Job*, 201.

37. The designation belongs to Robert Alter, *The Wisdom Books*, 6.

38. Endo, *Deep River*, 216.

Chapter Ten

Mitsuko, That's Me

Autobiographical Space in Endō Shūsaku's Final Novel

JUSTYNA WERONIKA KASZA

Even though this was the first-time Mitsuko had laid eyes on the scenery in the Landes region, she knew all about such things from her reading of *Thérèse Desqueyroux*.[1]

—Endō Shūsaku, *Deep River*

Is it not the true reason for my laziness that our novels express the essential part of our self? Only fiction does not lie: it half-opens a hidden door on a man's life, through which slips, out of all control, his unknown soul.[2]

—François Mauriac, in Philippe Lejeune, *On Autobiography*

[All] literature, in the end, is autobiographical.[3]

—Jorge Luis Borges, "A Profession of Literary Faith"

"Portions of Self": In Search of the Author in *Deep River*

In *Fukai kawa o yomu* (Reading *Deep River*), Yamane Michihiro recalls Endō Shūsaku saying shortly before the publication of *Deep River*: "For my next project, I would like to start working on the story of Job. I shall not be working on fiction anymore but I am seriously considering writing a long essay on

Job. The story has provided me with a massive topic, and I want to challenge myself with it. I am therefore determined to write about Job."[4] There is no evidence suggesting that Endō embarked on the new project as planned, and we can only speculate what shape such a text would have taken. *Deep River* remains, therefore, his final major work of fiction. Just before his death in 1996, Endō confided to his fellow writer Yasuoka Shōtarō: "I have my doubts as to how people might understand this novel."[5] According to Yamane, "this novel" meant *Deep River*.

Though followed by texts on religious and personal topics, including the essay "Shi ni tsuite kangaeru" (My Thoughts on Death), *Deep River* is considered Endō's final work of fiction (*White Man* and *Yellow Man*, both published in 1955, are considered Endō's debut novellas), as if the author had predicted that it would be his very last literary project. Thus, it seems we are justified in reading the novel as Endō's final literary endeavor, one of a deeply confessional nature, completing his life and a career that spanned almost fifty years, starting with the essays and critical works, "Kamigami to kami to" (The gods and God, 1947), "Katorikku sakka no mondai" (Dilemmas of Catholic Writers, 1954), through the novels *The Sea and Poison*, *Silence*, *The Samurai*, and *Scandal*. These works, without any exaggeration, made him one of the most widely translated Japanese writers of the twentieth century.

I believe that the current volume, *Navigating* Deep River, not only provides an opportunity to reconsider and evaluate the perspectives from which the novel has been read to date, but also to reveal its unidentified and hidden dimensions. My very own "navigating" of the novel brings me back to words spoken by Endō during his conversation with Yasuoka and his anxieties regarding *Deep River*'s reception: "I have my doubts as to how people might understand this novel." Lacking further interpretive guidance for these words, we might then ask: Have we read the novel in accordance with the author's wishes?

But to consider the author's intention in our analysis would have us ignore the so-called death of the author, which asserts that he or she remains irrelevant to the interpretive process. Yet, does that *death* mean that we must entirely ignore or erase the author, the writing persona, and the subject from our reading practice? And if not, would such an approach be limited to a search of biographical traces in the narrative? In other words, are we interested in evidence suggesting that the characters, motifs, or plot mirror, in some way, the author's life? And if so, how does this move us toward a fuller appreciation of the *text*?

As such, my chapter seeks to answer a seemingly simple yet challenging question: Could *Deep River* be read, in some way, as Endō Shūsaku's autobiography? But we might also ask: What is the significance of such a question? How could interpreting the novel as a piece of life writing that focuses on the author enrich our reading? Methodology is equally important. We can effortlessly prove that each character—whether Ōtsu, Mitsuko, Isobe, Numada, or Kiguchi—embodies a trace of the author; even so, does this prove that *Deep River* is an autobiography or autobiographical novel?[6] Furthermore, does the novel "fit" into the framework of Japanese *shishōsetsu* (the "I" novel) writing?[7]

Literary criticism has made a number of attempts to overcome similar dilemmas. In *The Return of the Author*, Eugen Simion challenges the removal of the writing persona from postmodern literary discourse; although he acknowledges that biographical criticism may not be fully relevant to present day research, he provides us with sufficient evidence that an author's life affects the works he or she creates.[8] On the other hand, Sean Burke maintains that the problem of the "author" and "authorship" is still an open issue in literary studies but identifies the key limits of theories proclaiming the removal of the author (or "authorial intention"). He argues, "The decision as to whether we read a text with or without an author remains an act of critical choice governed by the protocols of certain ways of reading rather than any 'truth of writing.' Which is to say that authorial absence can never be a cognitive statement about literature and discourse in general, but only an intra-critical statement and one which has little to say about authors themselves except in so far as the idea of authorship reflects on the activity and status of the critic."[9]

David Lodge approaches the problem differently by switching the focus to the question of "literary truth," but he too points out an inner inconsistency:

> What does the truth mean in this context? . . . If we grant that writers often deal with painful and disturbing personal experience in their fictions . . . does this not usually involve departing from the empirical facts such as experience—alerting them, even inverting them, reinterpreting them, and combining them with purely fictional material? If so, is there not a danger in trying to pin down the sources of characters and events of novels too literally in the writer's own life? Does the novel become more "believable" when we succeed in doing this? Or less?[10]

James Wood, in *How Fiction Works*, argues that what is "believable" in a novel refers—in most cases—to the question of "referentiality"; hence, he argues we must differentiate between "living a life" and "narrating a life."[11] Despite attempts to "restore" the *subject* in literary criticism, we seem to remain reluctant to confirm that "someone" is behind the text. We question not only the entire notion of "authorship," but, not infrequently, the singularity or distinctiveness of a literary genre itself.

The point of departure for my investigation of *Deep River* is Philippe Lejeune's concept of "autobiographical space" (*l'espace autobiographique*), which enables us to approach the novel comprehensively, through relation and interdependence with Endō Shūsaku's other works, without being beholden to the conventional classifications of autobiography or the autobiographical novel. To read *Deep River* through the lens of "autobiographical space" is to acknowledge that the life of the writing persona is dispersed among other narratives and the author's selfhood becomes, to use Paul John Eakin's words, the "storied self,"[12] because "the centre of all autobiographical narrative is necessarily a fictive structure."[13] Endō's own words are also inspiring in this regard: in the Introduction to the English edition of the short stories titled *The Final Martyrs*, he writes, "The characters . . . are reflections of a portion of myself."[14] I am convinced that the methodology proposed by Lejeune offers insight into what I term "the inner workings of Endō's novel," and the extent to which the novel remains in strong interdependence and dialogue with his other works, particularly his nonfiction texts.

The focal point of my investigation is the female character Naruse Mitsuko, whom I treat as the axis of the entire narrative; she binds together the plot and is tied to the other characters and to Endō himself. Through her, we can immerse ourselves again into the author's experience of reading the novel he loved: *Thérèse Desqueyroux* by François Mauriac. In Mitsuko, Endō included an essential part of his own personal experience. That is, like Endō, she studies French literature at university and then travels to France. Though *Deep River* depicts the journey to India, Mitsuko continuously recalls the moments when she was wandering around the forests of Bordeaux. The images of dense forests, so impressively evoked by Endō in the diary he kept in the early 1950s during his first trip to France, and in the essay "Terēzu no kage o otte" (Following the Shadow of Thérèse, 1952), constitute an indispensable part of her memory. Her route toward, and through, France resembles the route undertaken by the young Endō: his reading of Mauriac's novel and his subsequent journey to the Landes region of France is reflected in the portrayal of Mitsuko. This is the journey that profoundly shaped Endō. In the same way, the experience of reading Mauriac and the journey to France shapes the personality of Mitsuko. My analysis of *Deep River* is complemented by references to those texts that noticeably resonate in the novel, especially "Following the Shadow of Thérèse" and *Fukai kawa sōsaku nikki*, which is the diary that records the creation of the novel *Deep River*.

Lejeune's understanding of "autobiographical space" converges with Paul Ricoeur's *narrative identity*, a concept grounded in hermeneutical thinking. For Ricoeur, story is the most important form of mediation. Like Ricoeur, Lejeune perceives selfhood to be unstable, constantly being remade. Autobiographical space shows that the autobiography is, therefore, dispersed and always incomplete. In this way, Lejeune's understanding of our lives as narrative lives echoes Ricoeur's words: "Just as it is possible to compose several plots on the subject of the same incidents . . . so it is always possible to weave different, even opposed, plots about our lives."[15]

The Autobiographical Space, *Shishōsetsu*, and the Ambiguity of the "I"

Philippe Lejeune begins his study *On Autobiography* by asking: "Is it possible to define autobiography?"[16] He concludes that autobiography is a "retrospective prose narrative written by a real person concerning his own existence when the focus is his individual life, in particular the story of his personality."[17] The studies that followed Lejeune, however, stress the limitless and *indefinability* of the genre: "What could be simpler to understand than the act of people writing about what they know best, their own lives? But this apparently simple act is anything but simple, for the writer becomes, in the act of writing, both the observing subject and the object of investigation, remembrance, and contemplation."[18]

Lejeune argues that autobiographical space accommodates a writer's investment in autobiography without privileging autobiography over fiction. He observes that when authors claim their fiction is more truthful than their autobiography, "they designate the autobiographical space in which they want us to read the whole of their work."[19] Referring to André Gide and François Mauriac, he points out:

> It is no longer necessary to know which of the two, autobiography or novel, would be truer. It is neither one nor the other; autobiography will lack complexity, ambiguity, etc.; the novel, accuracy. So, it would be one, then the other? Rather, one *in relation* to the other. What becomes revealing is the space in which the two

categories of texts are inscribed, and which is reducible to neither of the two. This effect of contrast obtained by this procedure is the creation, for the reader, of an "autobiographical space."[20]

Therefore, to read *Deep River* as a piece of life writing is to "invite" into our investigation other texts that not only compose (in a narrative way) the plot of the novel but also, through a network of references, recreate those motifs, topics, and, possibly, characters who reoccur in other works. "Autobiographical space" thus offers us a comprehensive lens through which to read the totality of texts and a single text as a totality.

Eakin provides a similar definition. He speaks of autobiography as an *inter-subject*, and the story he or she creates is the story of the *other*. For Eakin, this counterbalances the "death of the subject": "I write my story; I say who I am; I create myself."[21] At the same time, when highlighting that "all narrative is relational" and that the act of self representation is conditioned by the relational identity, Eakin distinguishes the "space of autobiography, the space of the self . . . occupied by the self and the other."[22]

The source of modern selfhood is, as Eakin reminds us, not a Cartesian "I," the confident *cogito*, but what he terms the "non-I." Similarly, in his analysis of the development of the Japanese *shishōsetsu* (and the shape it took in post war conditions), Akiyama Shun emphasizes the *other* (*tasha*) as the source of self-narration. Referring to the characteristics of the Japanese language, Akiyama indicates the avoidance of expressing the first person pronoun "I": "It is almost certain that everyone has experienced the situation when using the third person pronoun that, in fact, he or she was expressing the 'I,' and this is the peculiarity of the Japanese language. . . . When expressing the 'I' in Japanese we struggle between making it visible and, at the same time, diminishing it."[23] Similar comments were made by Katsumata Hiroshi: "There is nothing more misleading than thinking that the Japanese *watashi* equals the English *I*, French *je*, or German *ich*. . . . *Watashi* is not the *I*. . . . Western individuals and the societies they create are made up of *I*'s . . . The problem consists in the fact that the Japanese *watashi* and the Western *I* are structurally and fundamentally different."[24] From the literary point of view, *shishōsetsu* refers, by default, to others and gestures toward these two perspectives—the "death of the author" and "the (re)emergence of the author"—that converge and condition each other.

Shishōsetsu is not the reflection of the self(subjectivity). In Japanese, the third person pronoun could be (and is) in many instances read as "I." As much as the discovery of the confessional literary form (Akiyama refers to Rousseau's *Confessions* as the example) was a turning point for Japanese literature in the second half of the nineteenth century (bringing it to the platform of world literature), Katsumata speaks of "a thousand years of *shishōsetsu*," clearly suggesting that the genre has been (in a way) an indigenous convention in Japanese literature. Here we see the same dilemma in defining Lejeune's autobiography and the *shishōsetsu*. In both cases, we might ask: Is it possible to define these literary genres?

This lack of a clearly delineated framework still makes it possible to look at *Deep River* beyond the conventional classification into autobiography or the Japanese *shishōsetsu*. Let us reconsider yet another type of life writing, namely *autofiction*. The term was created by the French writer, Serge Doubrovsky, to describe a work of fiction that involves recognition of moments and events in the writer's life experience that turned out to be crucial in the process of re-creating his or her identity. In defining *autofiction*, Doubrovsky maintains, "Writing is a never-ending search for sense: it consists in constructing this sense. . . . The sense of life does not exist; it simply does not exist anywhere. It cannot be discovered, it needs to be invented. The process of inventing is carried out not by all the parts but the traces. The sense must be constructed."[25] Identifying the author who "has returned" as a *broken subject*—equivalent to Ricoeur's *shattered cogito*—Doubrovsky claims that "memory itself is fictive, is fictitious, memory itself may harbour screened memories. . . . The meaning of life in certain ways escapes us, so we have to reinvent it in our writing, and that is what I personally call *autofiction*."[26]

Like Doubrovsky, Eakin recognizes the processual character of life writing and treats autobiography "not as a literary genre but instead as an integral part of a lifelong process of identity forming."[27] Eakin's approach resonates with the words of Georges Gusdorf that "autobiography is . . . never the finished image or fixing forever of an individual life: the human being is always a making, a doing; memories look to an essence beyond existence, and in manifesting it they serve to create it."[28] From this perspective, *Deep River* is, to use Gusdorf's words, "a second reading of experience."[29]

Lastly, what remains significant in an approach that emphasizes the *indefinability* of autobiography as a literary genre and also justifies the application of "autobiographical space" in reading any novel, like *Deep River*, that resists conventional classification, is what Lejeune terms "an indirect pact." That pact is the mechanism addressed to the readers who know that the authors have "chosen to leave their autobiography incomplete, fragmented full of holes and open."[30] Following this short description of selected methodological premises, let us now examine more closely the idea of "autobiographical space" in *Deep River* with reference to some of Endō's other texts.

From Thérèse to Mitsuko: Textual Hauntings in *Deep River*

> Mitsuko stared at her own rather grim face reflected in the window glass and at her large eyes, and could feel almost painfully how Thérèse had felt. *In the past I was Moïra; now I am Thérèse.* [She] felt that, unlike other women, she was unable truly to love another person. . . . *Just what is it you want? . . . Just what is it you're searching for?*[31]

The passages that describe Mitsuko's journey through Landes were based on the journey undertaken by Endō in the summer of 1951. The outcome of this trip was the essay "Following the Shadow of Thérèse," which constitutes a specific form of nonfictional writing offering an account of his journey in relation to the settings of Mauriac's novels. In terms of textual composition, we are dealing with a wide-ranging and multilayered piece of work consisting of various sorts of subject matter. The journey assumes a twofold character: the "actual" and the "imaginary" as well as the simultaneous "physical" and the "metaphysical." The reality that Endō finds in the southwest corner of France is filled by his imagination (as a reader of *Thérèse Desqueyroux*) and his own creativity (as a writer to be). Endō turns into Endō the storyteller, recounting Mauriac's novel, and at the same time creating his own version of Thérèse's tale. And by conducting the constant dialogue with the character in this mythological land of Mauriac (Landes), he himself, like Mitsuko in her wanderings, becomes an essential participant in the story. On the one hand, Mitsuko recreates the narrative reality of Mauriac's novel; on the other hand, she is being immersed into the same *world* where Thérèse was to live.

However, the world that Mitsuko encounters during her solitary trip appears in texts that precede *Deep River*. First, in "Following the Shadow of Thérèse" and later in "Aku, shi no hon'nō" (Evil, the Instinct of Death), which constitutes the final chapter of the collection *The Novel I Have Loved*. Here we read, "Thérèse remains submerged in the darkness, and is not, as Mauriac hoped, saved."[32] She remains in "an inanimate state"[33]; "Once she becomes submerged in it, it takes the quality of a rejection that consists of a longing to lose oneself in the endlessness of sleep."[34] Thérèse is trapped in the "forest of darkness,"[35] "unending night,"[36] and the only "audible" sound for her is "silence of a much blacker, much more frightening emptiness,"[37] "the silence of the night in the marshes."[38]

Describing Thérèse's appearance, Endō stresses her "emotionless eyes" as most strongly expressing her sensitivity and her passivity toward the world and her reluctance to resist it. During his journey, he cannot rid himself of the question: "Why couldn't I, for many years, expunge the charm of this middle-aged woman?"[39] When he attempts to answer this question, he notices a parallelism of fate between Thérèse and himself: "Thérèse grew completely tired living in a feudalistic home situated in a village in the marshes. In the same way, I grew tired of war and the darkness of the times. I could not help but adopt a passive attitude to everything."[40]

During her journey through France, Mitsuko is confronted with the question "Who am I?" She cannot forget the "charm of Thérèse." And like Endō, she, too, gradually begins to identify with Thérèse. Mitsuko literally interrogates reality through a comparison with an imagined world. The parts depicting Mitsuko's lonely travel around Bordeaux, reality (Mitsuko's reality), and the narrative world (the fictional world of Mauriac) are interwoven. The following passage encapsulates this trait:

> Mitsuko realized that the train in the novel that had transported Thérèse into the forest of darkness had been Mauriac's invention. If that were the case, then Thérèse had not passed through an actual forest in the dark, but in fact travelled through the darkness in the depths of the human heart. . . . At this realization, Mitsuko knew that . . . she had come to this rustic area in order to search out the darkness in her own heart.[41]

Here, the fictional character of Thérèse is incorporated into the narrative. This time it is Mitsuko who, in her recollection of the past, conducts an analysis and examination of Thérèse. Mitsuko's conversations with herself are a prolongation of the dialogue Endō himself had experienced with Thérèse in his own essay. For Mitsuko, therefore, though these elements are clearly visible, it turns out to have a more complicated dimension if we consider how her life is reminiscent of the fate of Thérèse. On the one hand, Mitsuko is the creation of Endō, a character in his fiction; on the other, Endō seems to continue his reading of Mauriac. That is, through the figure of Mitsuko, he is once again reading Mauriac's novel; the comments Mitsuko makes about Thérèse are close to those that appear in Endō's nonfictional texts. In the following passage, Mitsuko reflects Endō's experience of reading the novel.

> She suddenly recalled a scene from *Thérèse Desqueyroux*. It was the night Thérèse tended her ailing husband Bernard. . . . It was a scene Mitsuko was fond of. It was the same impulse she had felt not only tonight but on her honeymoon as she had studied her

husband's sleeping face. . . . Every time she stared into his face, she thought of the scene from *Thérèse Desqueyroux*. Those pages she had read over and over again, those pages wherein she had discovered a reflection of something dark within herself.[42]

While the essay "Following the Shadow of Thérèse," written over forty years before the novel, prefigures Endō's lasting attachment to Mauriac's work, the collection of essays *The Novel I Have Loved* provides an evaluation and reassessment of Mauriac's literary techniques. Predominantly, what occupies Endō's mind (and becomes an important topic) is the question of a "character's freedom" and the possibility for "salvation." According to Endō,

> Mauriac wants to rescue Thérèse from the world of the darkness; he wants to move her towards the world of the light. That is why Mauriac creates the figure of a priest. . . . But Thérèse acts against Mauriac's will. Until the very end, she remains in the world of the darkness. . . . It seems that for Mauriac, the character's freedom is a deception, it does not exist.[43]

The question of a "character's freedom" and the possibility for salvation is, in my view, the essential dilemma that informs the work but at the same time binds and completes the space of Endō's "autobiography." Posed for the first time in the essay "Dilemmas of Catholic Writers," these questions return in his last novel, in the tale of his very own Thérèse—Mitsuko. However, when reading *Fukai kawa sōsaku nikki*, we discover the path to creating Mitsuko was complex and circuitous. On September 29, 1991, Endō makes the following note, "Mrs. Naruse. Thérèse Desqueyroux. Her intentions will turn into evil. I must start writing this story."[44] Endō's process of creating Mitsuko includes extensive reading and rereading of Mauriac, but also the novels of Graham Greene (*The Human Factor* and *The End of the Affair*), and, of course, Julien Green's *Moïra*. This juxtaposition of the writers who undoubtedly contributed to the development of Endō's literary workshop (whose names appear and reappear in a number of his essays and critical works, years before *Deep River*) point to the intertextual dimension of the novel.[45] Mitsuko does not instantly become *Thérèse*; rather, she evolves with Endō's process of rereading the novels of Western writers; her attitude toward Ōtsu reminds us first of Sarah from *The End of the Affair*, then of Julien Green's *Moïra*. Finally, she becomes Thérèse. Remarkably, Graham Greene seems to play an important part in this creative process. While Mauriac provides Endō with the topic ("Can Mitsuko be saved?"), Greene, as Endō confirms in one of the diary entries, contributes literary techniques.[46]

When we read *Fukai kawa sōsaku nikki* together with *Deep River*, we can observe how the outline of the novel (drafts being prepared by the writer) constantly transitions from Mauriac to Greene, from Thérèse to Sarah. Initially, the relationship between Mitsuko and Ōtsu was to be based on that of Sarah and Bendrix (many of the sections of the diary analyze Greene's novel), but on March 19, 1992, Endō confesses, "Finally I have started writing the part in which she [Mitsuko] meets him [Ōtsu]. I used parts of Julien Green's *Moïra*," hence the words spoken by Mitsuko in the novel, "*In the past I was Moïra; now I am Thérèse.*"[47]

Regarding the development of the leading character, Takemoto Toshio suggests that we can interpret Mitsuko as being "Moïra socially but Thérèse existentially."[48] Takemoto categorizes the novel as *bunshin monogatari* ("the story of the alter ego" of the author) and claims that as much as Thérèse was a kind of obsession throughout his literary career, Mitsuko becomes the modus vivendi of this entire narrative. However, he also points to fundamental differences between the two characters: While Thérèse remains passive (as she does in Endō's essays), Mitsuko abandons her husband, thereby triggering the dynamics of the plot and becoming the point of departure for her spiritual journey. Mitsuko begins her trip, both physical and emotional, in France, in the mythical land of Mauriac's Landes, but she literally "disembarks" in India. While Thérèse was unable to escape the "world of the darkness," Mitsuko's movement from darkness toward the light leads through the trip to India[49]; thus, Takemoto names Mitsuko "anti-Thérèse."

In one of his final entries in the diary on April 23, 1992, Endō notes, "I have reached a deadlock with my novel. I am now concerned that the readers might not appreciate the motif of the Catholic seminary, [but] I managed to complete the section regarding Mitsuko's stay in Lyon. Ōtsu . . . he will later become lonely . . . he will live only through love . . . and finally he will live in the world of Teresa (Mother Teresa)."[50] Searching for the path leading toward salvation for Mitsuko, Endō seems to guide her from Thérèse Desqueyroux to Mother Teresa upon the Ganges River.

Conclusion: Mitsuko, That's Me:
In Search of the Real End

Deep River reconstructs the hermeneutical circle, the circle of understanding,[51] and explanation of the self. The *self* is not stable or confident; it is the "I" in the making and is being recreated through the stories that "demand to be told." While Lejeune sees this process within the concept of "autobiographical space," Paul Ricoeur states that "narrative . . . is not only a way of representing past facts that are themselves in part independent of narrative modes of thought and speech, but a way of forming expectations about future events."[52]

The approach offered by Lejeune recreates the path traveled by the writer, his lived experience, but it is also the experience of all books read. The autobiographical space is the space of the Endō Shūsaku library, spread out across the texts he read and wrote. We rediscover *Deep River* as an unusual form of autobiography that takes the shape of *the universe* as imagined by Borges. In the *total library of all existing books*, possessed by Endō it is *Thérèse Desqueyroux*, the novel he has loved, which occupies the central position. Through the figure of Mitsuko, Endō *re*-creates his autobiography around the questions: How have I read Mauriac's novel? How does the text speak to me? It seems to attest that "[T]here is an unbridgeable chasm between the book that tradition has declared a classic and the book (the same book) that we have made ours through instinct, emotion, and understanding: suffered through it, rejoiced in it, translated into our experience."[53] Mauriac was once asked if "he could say, as Flaubert had said of *Madame Bovary*: '*Thérèse, c'est moi.*'" He replied, "[Thérèse] is made up of everything . . . that I have been obliged to overcome, or circumvent, or ignore,"[54] but adds, "Thérèse remained a mystery: [she] did not know why she had been tempted to poison her husband, and I don't know why I wrote *Thérèse Desqueyroux*."[55]

The 1951 summer journey toward the fictional land of Mauriac to follow in the footsteps of Thérèse had its destination in India in 1990. There, Mitsuko experienced "the deathlike Indian night, a night that in Buddhism would be called the darkness of the soul. A night lacquered in a black so absolute it would be unthinkable in Japan."[56] In *Thérèse Desqueyroux*, it is the image of an endless night that overwhelms the character. In the final passage of Mauriac's novel, we read that "Thérèse . . . could not read now."[57] Her last words in the novel are: *I just do nothing. I hear the clocks strike, I wait for the end . . . The night seemed endless.*"[58]

Analyzing the similarities between characters, Takemoto remarks that "both women abandon their husbands and ask themselves what they are looking for; in other words, they are embarking on the journey toward their own inner selves. But in the case of Thérèse there seems to be no rescue from her loneliness. In the fictional world created by Mauriac, there is no end of the night. In *Deep River,* all meaningful events begin during the night. But Mitsuko's night is destined to end."[59]

While working on this final novel, struggling with anxieties and with the topic that haunted him since his very first encounter with Mauriac, Endō notes in his diary: "I have no confidence whether the novel will ever become my masterpiece. Nevertheless, it is certain that this work contains most of myself."[60]

Notes

1. Shusaku Endo, *Deep River*, trans. Van. C. Gessel (Tokyo: Tuttle Publishing, 1994), 58.

2. François Mauriac, in Philippe Lejeune, *On Autobiography*, ed. Paul John Eakin, trans. Katherine Leary (Minneapolis: University of Minnesota Press, 1989), 26.

3. Jorge Luis Borges, "A Profession of Literary Faith" (1926), in *The Total Library* (London: Penguin, 2001), 23.

4. Yamane Michihiro, *Endō Shūsaku: Fukai kawa o yomu* (Tokyo: Chōbunsha, 2010), 15.

5. Ibid., 16.

6. "The autobiographical novel includes personal narratives (identity of narrator and protagonist) as well as *impersonal* narratives (protagonist designated in the third person)." Lejeune, *On Autobiography*, 13.

7. *Shishōsetsu* (also known as *Watakushi shōsetsu*) is an autobiographical form that flourished in the Taishō period (1912–1926). For more details, see Edward Fowler, *The Rhetoric of Confession: Shishōsetsu in Early Twentieth Century Japanese Fiction* (Berkeley: University of California Press, 1988).

8. Eugen Simion, *The Return of the Author*, trans. Lidia Vianu (Evanston: Northwestern University Press, 1996), 90–91.

9. Sean Burke, *The Death and Return of the Author: Criticism and Subjectivity in Barthes, Foucault and Derrida* (Edinburgh: Edinburgh University Press, 2008), 169.

10. David Lodge, *Lives in Writing* (London: Vintage Books, 2015), 2.

11. James Wood points to Philip Roth's *The Counterlife* as the example of the text that "provides the metafictional game-play to make a grave and fundamentally metaphysical argument about the different ways of living, and narrating life." James Wood, *How Fiction Works* (New York: Picador, 2008), 119.

12. Paul John Eakin, *How our Lives Become Stories: Making the Selves* (Ithaca, NY, and London: Cornell University Press, 1999), 18.

13. According to Eakin, "autobiographical truth is not a fixed but an evolving content in an intricate process of self-discovery and self-creation and . . . self that is a centre of all autobiographical narrative is necessarily a fictive structure . . . materials of the past are shaped by memory and imagination to serve the needs of present consciousness." Paul John Eakin, *Fictions in Autobiography: Studies in the Art of Self Invention* (Princeton, NJ: Princeton University Press, 1985), 3 and 5.

14. Endō, Preface to the English edition of *The Final Martyrs* (London: Tuttle, 1994). Quotation slightly modified.

15. Paul Ricoeur, *Time and Narrative*, vol. 3, trans. David Pellauer (Chicago: The University of Chicago Press, 1988), 248.
16. Lejeune, *On Autobiography*, 3.
17. Ibid., 4.
18. "Defining Kinds of Life Narratives," in *Reading Autobiography: A Guide For Interpreting Life Narratives*, Sidonie Smith and Julia Watson, eds. (Minneapolis: University of Minnesota Press, 2010), 1.
19. Lejeune, *On Autobiography*, 27.
20. Ibid.
21. Eakin, *How Our Lives Become Stories*, 43. Emphasis mine.
22. Ibid., 61.
23. *Shishōsetsu handobukku* [The handbook of *shishōsetsu*], ed. Akiyama Shun and Hiroshi Katsumata (Tōkyō: Watakushi shōsestu kenkyūkai, 2014), 16–17.
24. Hiroshi Katsumata, *Nikki bungaku kara kindai bungaku made. Shishōsetsu sen'nen shi* [From diary literature to modern literature. A Thousand years of *shishōsetsu*] (Tōkyō: Bensei shuppan, 2015), 173, 182, 184.
25. Serge Doubrovsky, *Autobiographies: de Corneille à Sartre* (Paris: Presses Universitaires de France, 1988), 77.
26. Roger Celestine, *Interview with Serge Doubrovsky*, March 1997, 400.
27. Eakin, "Breaking Rules: The consequences and self-narration," in *Biography* 24, no. 1 (Winter 2001): 114.
28. Quotation from Gusdorf in Mark Freeman, "Autobiographical Understanding and Narrative Inquiry," in *Handbook of Narrative Inquiry*, ed. D. Jean Clandinin (Alberta: SAGE Publishing, 2007), 138.
29. Ibid., 131.
30. Lejeune, *On Autobiography*, 28.
31. Endo, *Deep River*, 57.
32. Endō, "Aku, shi no hon'nō," in *Endō Shūsaku Bungaku Zenshū* [Complete works by Endō Shūsaku], vol. 14 (Tōkyō: Shinchōsha, 2004), 120. English translation of the essay in my monograph *Hermeneutics of Evil in the Works of Endō Shūsaku: Between Reading and Writing* (Oxford: Peter Lang, 2016), 341.
33. Ibid., 343.
34. Ibid., 339.
35. Ibid.
36. Endō, "Terēzu no kage o otte," vol. 12, 153. English translation, ibid. 311.
37. Ibid.
38. Ibid., English translation, 310.
39. Endō, "Terēzu no kage o otte," 151.
40. Ibid.
41. Endo, *Deep River*, 58.
42. Ibid., 152.
43. Endō, *Watashi no aishita shōsetsu*, in *ESBZ*, vol. 15, 111.

44. Endō, *Fukai kawa sōsaku nikki*, in *ESBZ*, vol. 15, 291.

45. Akifu Kasai, "*Sukyandaru* kara *Fukai kawa* e. Sōsaku nikki o yomitokinagara" [From *Scandal* to *Deep River*: reading the diary], in *Endō Shūsaku Kenkyū*, vol. 7 (2014), 54–69.

46. Endō, *Fukai kawa sōsaku nikki*, 305–8.

47. Endo, *Deep River*, 57. An interesting analysis of female characters in Endō's works is offered by Yōko Abe in her essay, "Moïra to Sāra—Endō Shūsaku to futari no Gurīn" [Moïra and Sarah: Endō Shūsaku and two Green(e)'s], in *Endō Shūsaku. Chōhatsu suru sakka* [Endō Shūsaku. a provocative author], ed. Tsuge Teruhiko (Tōkyō: Shibundo, 2009), 82–91.

48. Toshio Takemoto, "*Fukai kawa* no Naruse Mitsuko" [Naruse Mitsuko in *Deep River*], in *Endō Shūsaku kenkyū*, vol. 6 (2013), 15.

49. Kōsuke Fukuda points out that the passages of the novel concerning Mitsuko and her real and imaginative (fictive) journey through France and the translated version of the novel (though, as often confirmed by Endō, not linguistically accurate) blur, fuse, and become one narration. The "autobiographical space" is, therefore, complemented by Endō's own translation of Mauriac's novel published in 1966. Fukuda Kōsuke, "Terēzu o sōkei—yūwaku to bosei" [Modeling on Thérèse: temptation and motherhood], in *Endō Shūsaku. Chōhatsu suru sakka*, 81.

50. Endō, *Fukai kawa sōsaku nikki*, 311.

51. For information on the hermeneutical (or hermeneutic) circle, also known as the circle of understanding, see Karl Simms, *Paul Ricoeur* (London: Routledge, 2006), 87.

52. Deiter Teichert, "Narrative, Identity and the Self," *The Journal of Consciousness Studies* 11, no. 10–11 (2004): 183.

53. Alberto Manguel, *The Library at Night* (New Heaven: Yale University Press, 2010), 218.

54. Robert Speaight, *François Mauriac: A Study of the Writer and the Man* (London: Chatto and Windus, 1976), 87. See also Edward J. Gallagher, *Textual Hauntings: Studies in Flaubert's Madame Bovary and Mauriac's Thérèse Desqueyroux* (Lanham: University Press of America, 2005).

55. Mauriac's letter to Édouard Champion on April 4, 1927. François-George Maugarlone, *La traversée du désert de Mauriac* (Paris: Pierre-Guillaume de Roux Editions 2011), 76. Translation mine.

56. Endo, *Deep River*, 152.

57. Mauriac, *The End of the Night*, trans. Gerald Hopkins (London: Penguin Books, 1972), 319.

58. Ibid.

59. Takemoto, "*Fukai kawa* no Naruse Mitsuko," 21–22.

60. Endō, *Fukai kawa sōsaku nikki*, 321.

Chapter Eleven

Imagining India

Traversing *Deep River* with Enami and Ōtsu

P. A. GEORGE

Introduction

Deep River is perhaps the most recent Japanese novel on the theme of India's unique spirituality, which has served as the foundation of Indian civilization for several thousand years. Endō Shūsaku had always been attracted to the mystic, cosmic view of Hinduism, a polytheistic religion, which can usefully be compared, in some ways, to Shintō, Japan's own indigenous religion. Although Hinduism has a complex philosophical system based on a long-standing scriptural tradition that Shintō lacks, both religions are generally inclusive in nature and have countless number of gods and goddesses in their respective pantheons. Endō, a Japanese brought up as a Catholic, always viewed Christianity, especially Catholicism, as practiced and monopolized by the West, as highly institutionalized, dogmatic, and exclusive. He believed that this kind of Christianity could not take root in the "marshland of Japan."[1] In support of this view, Ōtsu, the Catholic protagonist of *Deep River*, failed to satisfy his superiors in the seminary in France because of his upbringing in the pantheistic, or polytheistic, religious environment of Japan. His religious sensibility came into constant conflict with the Western Christian concept of a transcendent God who is both absolute and omnipotent.

Why did Endō choose India, especially Vārānasī and the Ganga, as the location for the climax of his story, especially given that *Deep River* is Endō's only novel that features India? The author made a few trips to India prior to writing the novel in order to better understand its society and culture, though he lamented, in a scholarly discussion with Motoki Masahiro after *Deep River*'s publication, "I don't know much about India."[2] Even so, the novel reveals a depth and clarity of understanding of Indian society and its culture that belies this claim, which we can attribute to the author's natural modesty. In comparing Indian society to the West, he states unequivocally that he tires quickly of cities like Paris because of their excessive order; on the contrary, the chaotic and disorderly world of India fascinates him.[3]

Endō had also read whatever materials were available on India in Japanese and appears to have been particularly moved by *Thoughts from India* (*Indo de kangaeta koto*) by Hotta Yoshie and *The Temple of Dawn* (*Akatsuki no tera*), the third part of Mishima Yukio's famous tetralogy *The Sea of Fertility* (*Hōjō no Umi*). *The Sea of Fertility* deals mainly with the concepts of karma and reincarnation, though Mishima himself did not believe in these Buddhist notions. Endō is said to have been greatly moved by Mishima's description of the cremation of dead bodies at the *ghāts* on the banks of the Ganga in Vārāṇasī and by the concepts of karmic retribution and reincarnation. He writes, "Faith in transmigration, or karmic rebirth, is a commonly held notion among Indians; this is truly enviable from the Japanese point of view. This notion differs from the Japanese way of thinking where each individual thinks only about 'his own death' or 'thinks only about one's own life after death.'"[4] Endō seems to have delved deeply into the Indian psyche, dissected it carefully, and fully grasped this commonly held notion upon which the whole Indian worldview is based. In *Deep River*, Endō tries to map this Indian notion through Enami, the tour guide. Before analyzing Enami's characterization, it seems appropriate to briefly delineate the special significance of the Ganga.

Vārāṇasī and the Ganga

Vārāṇasī, also known as Benares and Kashi,[5] is the most sacred place for Hindus, similar to the Holy Land for Christians and Mecca for Muslims. It is situated along the banks of the Ganga and has innumerable temples and other religious symbols located near the *ghāts* for cremating the dead. Gautama Buddha, after attaining enlightenment, preached in Vārāṇasī at several spots on the banks of the holy river Ganga, and at Sarnath, where he first taught the Dharma, thereby "setting in motion the wheel of dharma." Sarnath is situated about eight miles northeast of Vārāṇasī near the confluence of the Ganga and Varuna rivers. The city is also important for Jainism, as four of its *tīrthaṅkaras* were born there.[6] Ādi Śaṅkarācārya, the key exponent of Advaita Philosophy and great reformer of Hinduism in the eighth century,[7] traveled to Kashi from his hometown in Kerala in southern India and established the Kashi Vishwanath Temple, the first temple dedicated to Lord Śiva, in the city. This temple is the center of all religious activities in the city even today.

In modern times, Vārāṇasī, often referred to as "the eternal city," has become synonymous with Hinduism and Hindu culture. One of the oldest cities in the world, Vārāṇasī has been a long-standing and stable center of cultural florescence, remaining the holiest pilgrimage center for Hindus. "Banaras is older than history, older than tradition, older even than legend, and looks twice as old as all of them put together," commented Mark Twain in 1897.[8] The pilgrimage to Kashi at the end of one's life is considered to be the ultimate aim of all Hindus, who believe that taking a dip in the holy waters of the Ganga at Kashi absolves all one's sins and leads to *mokṣa*, freedom from the clutches of karma and rebirth. Hindus also believe that if one is born in the city itself, one is guaranteed freedom from rebirth. Endō was clearly aware of the significance of Vārāṇasī as a Hindu pilgrim center; Tiziano Tosolini notes that in Vārāṇasī, "Endo saw a place with symbols, divining an echo of that collective unconscious in which the life of all humanity, regardless of one's cultural or religious heritage comes together in the single, peaceful flow of the great river."[9]

At the same time, Vārāṇasī is also a place of mundane human activities, offering residents and visitors alike a flourishing material life. Thousands of people find their means of sustenance in Vārāṇasī by engaging in various business and service activities supporting the pilgrims. The city offers a vibrant mixture of the usual commotion and lawlessness on roads and ugly interior lanes juxtaposed to beautifully decorated and air-conditioned shops selling expensive products like Benares saris; one finds five-star hotels and roadside food stalls, high-tech cars and manually pulled rickshaws, or millionaires and beggars. All coexist peacefully. In other words, Kashi is not only the center of Indian spirituality but it is also a place of "merry making, enjoyments and reckless flings."[10] However, the Vārāṇasī that Endō depicts in his novel is mainly the Hindu spiritual center through which the all-absorbing Ganga and its *śakti* (force) flow endlessly. Pilgrims and faithful devotees have been visiting this city for several thousand years to attain liberation and they will continue to visit as long as their faith remains strong. According to the *Skanda Purāṇa*, Lord Śiva reassured Viṣṇu, saying, "This sacrosanct place is very dear to me and no event takes place here against my wish. Even if a person living here happens to be a sinner he has nothing to fear because I protect him. One who lives far from Kashi but remembers it with reverence becomes absolved of all his sins."[11]

According to Hindu beliefs, it is normally Yama, the god of death, who, with the help of his assistant Chitragupta, controls the life span of every individual. He maintains the complete record of all living human beings and knows when an individual's life should be taken back, and sends Chitragupta to that individual to get his soul. However, in Vārāṇasī it is not Yama but Kālabhairava who keeps the books. Kālabhairava is a manifestation of Śiva, the god of annihilation. He keeps the account book of every individual's sins and gives each one his or her appropriate punishment, subjecting them to various levels of torment according to the nature of their sins. Since he has the accounts of everyone's deeds, he knows in advance who is going to be one with him from among those who come to Vārāṇasī for the atonement of their sins by taking a holy dip in the waters of Ganga. Once a devotee is inside Kashi, irrespective of his or her taking a holy dip in the river, Lord Śiva goes to him or her and whispers the holy *Tāraka mantra* in the right ear at the time of death.[12] Soon the devotee will be rid of all his or her sins and torments, and will also be free from the cycle of birth and death, attaining *mokṣa*. This belief is precisely why millions of Hindus throng to the holy Ganga at Vārāṇasī.

The Ganga is called "Mother (Goddess) Ganga" and its waters are considered sacred, having the mystical power to purge the sins of humankind. It is considered a *tīrtha*, a crossing point between heaven and earth. When devotees make prayers and offerings at a *tīrtha*, they will, without fail, reach the gods and heaven will immediately shower blessings on them. It offers liberation to all who take a dip or bathe in its healing waters, or who simply sprinkle its water on themselves. This sanctifying effect of the river and its mystical power of absolution help free human beings from the bondage of karma and rebirth, leading to the liberated state of *mokṣa*, which is why many Hindus travel to Kashi toward the end of their mortal life. This concept of obtaining *mokṣa* through the sacred river Ganga, the purgation of one's sins, may be compared with the Christian concept of deliverance from one's sins through Jesus Christ, who, according to Christianity, died on the cross to absolve humankind's sins so that all would be able to enter the Kingdom of God. Taking a holy dip in the river for atonement of sins is the ultimate wish of any devout Hindu. The holy water of the Ganga is used virtually for all Hindu rituals, and if Ganga water is not readily available, water from the local rivers is used after making it sacred by invoking the Ganga. Normally, when pilgrims travel to Gangotrī, Vārāṇasī, Haridwar, or Prayag—the four most important *tīrthas* for taking a holy dip or for immersing ashes—they typically return home with some holy water from the Ganga.

Enami's Understanding of India

Before coming to India as tourists, all the characters in *Deep River* hold a particular preconceived notion of the country, which they may have acquired through books, mass media, or from friends and relatives who had visited. Having such preconceived ideas is natural for all the Japanese tourists who visit India; some bring with them a very positive image that influences how they view the reality of Indian society, experiencing wonder even when encountering India's extremes that often exist side by side without apparent contradiction or conflict. For instance, just outside a five-star hotel, one may find a slum; high-tech cars speed along the roadway, which may be blocked by herds of cows, past rickshaws and bullock carts; and the rich and poor shop at the same roadside vegetable vendors. Groups of people may be found at street corners or in the shade of trees in the villages and even in towns, spending their free time, sipping hot *chaai* (milk-tea) and smoking hookah while chatting, joking, or discussing politics. Those tourists who are not ready to give up their preconceived notions often come away, like the Sanjōs in the novel, with an extremely negative image of India.

Unlike the Sanjōs, Enami holds a highly mature and nuanced view of Indian society that began to develop during his four years as an exchange student. His perception of India is unbiased and sympathetic, and he teaches the tour group how to behave while in India, warning them about the risks of drinking ice water or unboiled water. Even many Indians, the author included, hesitate to drink unfiltered or unboiled water. This does not mean that water everywhere in India is contaminated, but that there is a great chance, relative to countries in colder climates, of getting sick because of conditions conducive to the growth of bacteria and viruses. Barring the monsoon season, moreover, much of India receives little rainfall; thus, the air becomes quite polluted with dust and other particles. The Japanese tourists who come to India with little knowledge of its cultural diversity might be shocked when they encounter this reality directly since it is quite different from the order found in Europe and Japan. Fully aware of this fact, Endō has Enami prepare his tour group for this reality so that they can see it in a positive manner and come to a fuller understand of Indian sociocultural values.

Enami also tries to educate his guests about the centuries-old caste system that has prevailed in India. He tells the group, "In India there is a religious system of social ranking known as the caste system. They call it *varna jati*. It is very complex, and I can't explain it in simple terms."[13] The caste system, which has often been misunderstood, has been misused and abused by the same people who instituted it. It originally served as a kind of social classification based on one's occupation that was created with the good intention of insuring the smooth functioning of society by enabling everyone to carry out his or her assigned duties, or *dharma*, in society. Like the *shi-nō-kō-shō* (samurai, peasants, artisans, and merchants) class system in Japan during the feudal Tokugawa period, Indian society in the Vedic period divided people into four distinctive categories: Brahmins, Kśatriyas, Vaiśya, and Śūdras. Each class was allocated specific duties (*dharma*): the Brahmins were to engage in intellectual and religious pursuits, the Kśatriyas in military activities, the Vaiśyas in business and trade, and the Śūdras in manual labor in households and fields. Besides these four classes, which came under the *varna* system,[14] there were the untouchables who performed all kinds of menial jobs, including scavenging and the disposal of the carcasses of dead animals. Over time, this system was used by society's upper strata to discriminate against and oppress the weak and marginalized, eventually taking on its present-day form.

Enami is certainly an outstanding observer, his eyes catching the detail of typical street scenes, including the child beggars. The ubiquitous beggars of Indian cities are often the children of senior beggars who have migrated from villages to the large cities or may have been kidnapped and forced into begging; they also include immigrants from neighboring countries. These kids, often found half naked and wearing torn and shabby cloths, are trained to change their facial expressions as the situation demands so that they will get the empathy of passersby. Enami was fully aware of their tricks, warning the Japanese tourists: "The panting for breath and the pleading expressions and gestures were all for show, and that once you gave money to one child, you would be endlessly thronged by the other children."[15] These beggar children, though they are more active in front of tourists, also approach Indians at traffic signals. However, since the local people understand their gimmicks, they are often chased away. This is indeed one of the major social menaces found in Indian cities, although some local governments have forbidden begging in their area.

When the tourist bus heading to Vārānasī passed through a village, Enami tells the Japanese guests: "This is a typical evening in an Indian village. Cows are sprawled out everywhere. Beside them everyone sits and drinks tea. The milk they pour into their tea is squeezed from those same cows."[16] In this age of information technology and globalization, Indian villages still maintain the age-old cultural traditions that bond people of different caste and creed, race and faith. As such, they differ with the neat and clean modern towns and villages found in Japan or other developed countries in the West where social decorum, etiquette, and formal human relationships are valued highly. Of course, these values are also important for Indian community life, but there is always a space provided for flexibility. Indian villages are more or less peaceful and harmonious, though occasionally one might hear about intercaste or communal clashes and atrocities that are infrequent considering the size of the country and its population. Enami is attracted to this lifestyle, admitting that he "fell in love" with India.[17] Indeed, he argues that the tourists who come to India can be classified into two groups: those who "despise the place after only one visit" and those who "want to come back over and over again."[18] Then he happily reveals himself, saying, "I'm one of the latter."[19]

Enami considers India, especially Vārāṇasī, to represent a unique world that had been known to all Japanese but has been forgotten. Perhaps this view emerged from his conviction that India was the birthplace of Buddhism and that the Japanese people had, until premodern times, looked to India with reverence as *Tenjiku*,[20] the Western Paradise. However, in modern times, especially during the Cold War, India lost its glamor in the eyes of the Japanese people due mainly to the bifurcation of states into those allied with the United States and the others aligned with the USSR. Japan supported the United States, while India took a neutral stand as one of the founders of the nonaligned movement, though it actually tilted toward the Soviet Bloc. Such geopolitics gave rise to a feeling of alienation among the Japanese people toward Indians, and gradually they forgot *Tenjiku* and its people for some three decades starting in the 1960s.

Endō must have been concerned about this shift in the relationship between the two countries. Even during his visit to India prior to the conception of *Deep River*, Indo-Japanese relations were stagnating. This situation started to improve soon after the liberalization of India's economy and the opening of its markets in the early 1990s. Until that time, the Land of the Buddha had been completely forgotten by the people from the Land of the Rising Sun, though hundreds of books on India from a Buddhist perspective continued to be written and published in Japan even during that period of stagnation. Such books imparted to Japanese readers the general impression that India remained an overwhelmingly Buddhist nation. Hence, most of the Japanese tourists arrived in India with this notion and were naturally disappointed when they realized that the reality was quite different from the accounts of these books.

Endō uses Enami as a vehicle for discussing this issue, having his character tell the group, "In India today, adherents of the Hindu religion make up an overwhelming majority, followed by Muslims, while Buddhism has all but disappeared."[21] He is also aware of the preference of some marginalized Indians, such as the untouchables, who fall outside the caste system, to convert to Buddhism since it teaches the equality of all human beings. Indeed, mass conversions to Buddhism by the so-called scheduled castes (Dalits) happen occasionally in some parts of India due to various sociopolitical reasons. However, even when we take into account these cases, the number of Buddhists in India is negligible. When the former soldier Kiguchi asks Enami about a temple where he could offer a memorial service to the war victims, Enami could not give him a quick reply since he was unsure whether Kiguchi was asking for a Hindu or a Buddhist temple, recognizing that there were only a small number of the latter in ordinary places.

At times, Enami becomes indignant when defending India and its culture. The Sanjōs, a newly married couple, have chosen India for their honeymoon although both seem to dislike the country. The main reason for selecting India was Mr. Sanjō's interest in photography. He had been told that there were several unique historical and cultural spots as well as panoramic scenes in India that might, if he could capture them on film, fetch him an award and help establish himself as a professional photographer. When the Sanjōs make a derogatory comment about the Hindu belief system related to reincarnation and fail to recognize the holiness of the Ganga, Enami bursts out in anger, forgetting his role as tour guide. "There is nothing disgusting about it," Enami snaps back, telling them:

> If you find India disgusting, then you should have chosen a pleasant tour of Europe. But since you're here in India, please make the effort to enter into this unique world, a realm utterly removed from Europe or Japan. No, that's not correct. Let me rephrase that. We're about to enter into a unique world that we once knew but have now forgotten. That's the attitude I'd like you to have as we travel through India. Of course, this is just my personal opinion, but. . . ."[22]

Here we see not Enami the tour guide but a defender and custodian of Indian culture and religious customs. In other words, Endō is openly admitting the uniqueness of Indian culture, which is entirely different from the Christian world of the West or other Asian countries, including Japan. He is trying to draw a line between the highly dogmatic, orderly, inflexible, and exclusive Western culture and the disorderly, chaotic, flexible, pluralistic, and inclusive Indian culture.

Hinduism is often viewed as a way of life rather than a religion. It has no supreme spiritual head or patriarch like the Catholic Pope, nor a single authoritative religious book like the Holy Bible or Quran. Instead, it has several sacred books like the Vedas, Purāṇas, Rāmāyaṇa, and Mahābhārata, and a highly sophisticated philosophy of life and death. Its philosophy, social customs, and religious practices have evolved over the millennia into the present form. Through meditation and study, the sages and ṛṣis (ascetics) of ancient India gained intuitive insight into the very purpose of human existence. Over time, they realized that whatever existed outside in the cosmos could also be found within each individual. This discovery became the cornerstone of the Indian belief of the oneness between nature and human beings. Since our internal world and external environments are one and the same, there should thus be no conflict between them. This thinking has inculcated the qualities of tolerance, compassion, and love in the minds of individuals, while also teaching them the importance of peacefully coexisting in a pluralistic society wherein distinct lifestyles are seen to manifest a unique form of divine presence. This fundamental cosmic view held by many Indians informs their philosophical outlook on society and nature, which emphasizes coexistence and coprosperity. To an outsider, however, Indian society may appear to be mired in utter chaos and lawlessness, filled with contradictions. On the one side, it may be perceived to be extremely spiritual and mystical, while simultaneously appearing to be highly materialistic. Likewise, other apparently contradictory factors—good and evil, cleanliness and pollution, prosperity and poverty, for instance—coexist within Indian society.

Even the gods and goddesses embody this dichotomy, as they may appear to be extremely merciful and benevolent at times, while ferocious and vengeful at others. Take the case of the goddess Kālī. She is the ferocious form of the otherwise gentle and benevolent goddess Pārvatī, the spouse of Lord Śiva, who took the form of Kālī to annihilate evil forces. On the other hand, the goddess Chāmundā, who is portrayed in the novel, symbolizes suffering and mercy. Enami tells the tour group, "She displays all the sufferings of the Indian people. All the suffering and death and starvation the people of India have had to endure over many long years come out in this statue. She contracted every illness they have suffered through the years. She has tolerated the poison of cobras and snakes. Despite it all . . . as she pants for breath, she offers milk to mankind from her shrivelled breasts."[23] Mercy, benevolence, love, and perseverance are universal truths and are an integral part of the teachings of any religion. Through the portrayal of the goddess Chāmundā, Endō tries to emphasize the spiritual strength of the Indian people to face destructive forces like poverty, famine, illness, natural calamities, and external threats, even when it lacked the basic material resources to confront such situations.

The all-inclusive nature of Indian civilization has withstood all kinds of foreign aggressions from ancient to modern times, including its colonization by the British, by safeguarding its spiritual and social values based on concepts such as peaceful coexistence, unity in diversity, *atithi devo bhava* (the guest is equivalent to god),[24] and *vasudhaiva kuṭumbakam* (the world is one family).[25] Just as the Ganga accepts whoever comes to it—poor or rich, educated or illiterate, high or low caste—and atones for their sins, India, too, accepts everybody and everything reaching its shore and tries to feed them like the goddess Chāmundā in the novel. Of course, one might occasionally hear about communal clashes and intercaste or interreligious clashes in India. For example, the atrocities committed against the Sikh community soon after the assassination of Indira Gandhi, as mentioned in the novel, is one such case. Generally, the Hindu-Sikh relationship has been extremely cordial and peaceful. But the evil deeds of some members of a particular religious community may betray the mutual trust and disrupt that peaceful coexistence, especially when it has a political undertone, the situation may take a turn into darkness and violence. The clash that occurred after the assassination of Indira Gandhi was not exactly between Hindus and Sikhs, but between a particular political orientation and a particular religious community.

In the novel, Mr. Sanjō takes photographs of bodies being carried to the burning *ghāts* for cremation. Although there is no written rule against taking photos of such funeral processions, conventionally it is prohibited in Vārānasī. According to Hindu belief, death offers the opportunity to attain *mokṣa* after gaining deliverance from one's karmic bondage; hence any attachment to this world should be avoided. According to these beliefs, moreover, nothing in this world save the soul is permanent. All other things, including the human body, are *māyā*, or mere illusions. Since the soul naturally leaves the body, the dead physical body need not be preserved and so is cremated.

Enami is aware of this Hindu outlook on life and death, and he cautions his guests, saying, "As we get closer to the cremation grounds, you will see a number of bodies being carried to the ghats. Please don't take any pictures of the bodies. You'll make the families very angry."[26] Despite Enami's repeated warnings of Mr. Sanjō to refrain from photographing funeral processions, Sanjō ignored them and violated the custom. Even Ōtsu had warned him when he was about to take out his camera to photograph an earlier funeral procession. However, Sanjō waited for his chance and finally took a photograph, which gave rise to a great commotion. Ultimately, it was the innocent Ōtsu, not Sanjō, who had to pay for it with his own life. However, Indian society is able to overcome such disruptions because of its worldview based on the above-mentioned notions of peaceful coexistence, *vasudhaiva kuṭumbakam*, and so on. Indeed, such cases of communal clashes or violence are rare, and, considering India's size, population, and diversity, these are uncommon occurrences. And Endō, through his tour guide Enami, has skillfully captured this uniqueness of Indian culture in his novel.

Ōtsu's Discovery of India

Ōtsu, the Japanese Catholic priest who was found unfit for the highly dogmatic and institutionalized Catholic church in the West, discovers an entirely new world in Vārāṇasī. Although a devout Catholic, he was branded a heretic by his superiors in the West and was often criticized for his pantheistic views that he had acquired from the Japanese sociocultural and religious environment in which he had grown up. In that view of Christianity, a monotheistic religion, there is no space for accepting any god other than the omnipresent and omnipotent almighty God. As Ōtsu discovers, one must conform to the doctrines and rites of the Western Catholic church if one wants to get admitted to the fold. When the Jesuit missionaries led by St. Francis Xavier started their evangelical activities in Japan, they were warmly welcomed by some of the feudal lords. However, that initial reception did not continue for long because the missionaries breached the trust of the government. Tokugawa officials started viewing the missionaries with suspicion, as they perceived their prosyletizing as a threat to the people's peaceful co-existence, the fundamental principle of an all-inclusive polytheistic or pantheistic society, by intentionally persuading the converts to give up the cardinal values of Japanese culture.

The Japanese people are known for their religious tolerance and broad-minded attitude to alien cultures, though there were occasions in history when they persecuted the followers of Christianity. When Buddhism reached Japan in the middle of the sixth century, it was welcomed wholeheartedly and propagated ardently under the patronage of the state and the nobility in the court who ruled the country. The indigenous folk religion of the people did not put up any noteworthy resistance to Buddhism's propagation, thanks to its characteristic nature of being a polytheistic belief system. Of course, at times, the state and its rulers had shown undue patronage to protect either Buddhism or Shintō as the sociopolitical situation in the country demanded. As it tried to gain a foothold in this historical context, the monotheistic and alien religion of Christianity underwent a number of persecutions. The persecution of Christians in the Tokugawa period happened because of certain sociopolitical upheavals, which could have been avoided had the Christian missionaries shown due respect to the cultural and ethical values of Japan. Endō made this issue a central theme in his famous novel *Silence*.

India had a similar experience with the Jesuits during the Middle Ages when the Portuguese missionaries reached its shores, accompanied by traders. The history of Christianity in India goes back to the first century of the Christian era. According to popular belief, St. Thomas, one of the disciples of Jesus Christ, came to Kerala in South India in AD 52 to preach the teachings of Jesus Christ to inhabitants of the subcontinent. He converted to Christianity many Hindus from the upper strata of society, constructed seven churches, and codified a set of rules for Christians. The local kings and nobles accorded him a warm welcome, granted him various rights, and offered him free land for constructing churches. This traditional Christian sect, called St. Thomas Christians, is still prominent in India today. Scholars have been hesitant to accept this account at face value since there is no contemporaneous written testimony corroborating it, only an oral tradition asserting its truth. But there are extant historical documents and monuments suggesting the presence of Christianity in Kerala from the third century onward; in short, India had a well-established Christian church even before its teachings had arrived in Europe.

Even so, the Portuguese missionaries who arrived on Indian shores in the middle of the sixteenth century found the rites, prayers, and such of the Indian church entirely different from their own. Hence, they branded the Indian church as a non-Christian heretical and paganistic sect and tried to forcibly convert its members into the fold of the Latin (Western) Church. These attacks led to the first schism in the centuries-old Indian church, which finally split into two: one group accepted papal governance and authority while the other group remained in the old church.[27] In response, the kings and other rulers of India never persecuted the Christians; rather, they offered support and protected the interests of the community. At the same time, the St. Thomas Christians never engaged in anti-Hindu activity that would have undermined the fundamental Indian virtue of peaceful coexistence.

Besides Christianity, other religions like Islam, Judaism, and Zoroastrianism met little resistance when they reached the shores of India, bringing distinct teachings and customs. They were accepted as different "paths that led one to the only one God. These cultures that wafted in brought their own distinct fragrances and they also became part of the Indian way of life and a harmoniously blended culture has emerged as the Indian culture."[28] This harmonious and peaceful coexistence is the hallmark of Indian civilization; in short, ordinary Hindus do not differentiate religions on the basis of their scriptures or teachings because all religions are seen to lead to the same god, and said god does not judge his devotees on the basis of his religion since he does not belong to any particular religion. According to Mahatma Gandhi, "the different religions are beautiful flowers from the same garden, or they are branches of the same majestic tree. Therefore, they are equally true, though being received and interpreted through human instruments equally imperfect."[29] Gandhi, a devout Hindu, used to carry with him the Holy Bible and Quran along with the *Bhagavad Gītā*, the holiest book of Hinduism, and tried to live according to the teachings of all three religions. Even so, the monotheistic religions of the world may not agree with this outlook. Endō, being a Catholic from a pantheistic-polytheistic environment, was fully aware of this difference in outlook and tried to highlight it by juxtaposing the monotheistic and exclusive Christian world of Europe with the polytheistic and inclusive world of India through Ōtsu, the Japanese Catholic priest in *Deep River*.

Ōtsu was a pious Catholic who had the noble intention of serving humanity. Having been born and brought up in the predominantly pantheistic Buddhist society of Japan, his outlook on religion and god did not match that of his superiors in the seminary in France. According to Hindu and Buddhist beliefs, good and evil are inseparable: that is, every person has elements of both qualities and it can be difficult to distinguish what is good from what is evil—they are like two sides of the same coin. Many Hindus and Buddhists would argue that one's environment and attachment to certain sorts of worldly things can lead one to commit evil deeds. Christianity, on the other hand, makes clear distinctions between good and evil, and directs its followers to adhere to the teachings of the church in order to avoid committing sins. But Ōtsu could not accept this clear-cut Western conception, saying, "I can't make the clear distinction that these people make between good and evil. I think that evil lurks within good, and that good things can lie hidden within evil as well."[30] Ōtsu reveals his anger with the Western Catholic Church to Mitsuko, his classmate who visited him at his seminary in Lyon, France. In one of the letters Ōtsu wrote to Mitsuko, he mentions his painful experience with his superiors in the French seminary and reveals to her his understanding of God, writing, "God has many different faces. I don't think God exists exclusively in the churches and chapels of Europe. I think he is also among the Jews and the Buddhists and the Hindus."[31]

According to Ōtsu, God is love and is universal. God in the form of love is manifest in all religions. Endō had realized this truth after going through various experiences in his life as a Japanese Catholic. According to Emi Mase-Hasegawa, "Endo reveals his own image of Christ in the life of Ootsu, who has failed in authoritarian Christianity, yet ended up living in India following Jesus' Way. Endo finally comes to the reflection on his religious experience that the Love of God through Jesus Christ is present in this world not only in European Churches, but can be found in Hinduism and Buddhism."[32]

Ōtsu was severely criticized by his superiors for his unorthodox Christian views based on an Asian and Japanese ethos and values. He was branded a heretic holding pantheistic views, unsuitable for taking the oath of the Catholic priesthood. In holding to these beliefs, he ultimately underwent many hardships, suffering humiliation and rejection. Finally, Ōtsu realized that the West was not the proper place for his priestly vocation and that God, whom he describes as the Onion, "doesn't live only within European Christianity. He can be found in Hinduism and Buddhism as well."[33] This realization compelled him to leave the West and come to Vārānasī where he was warmly welcomed by the Hindu *sādhus*. Although Ōtsu was not reluctant to give up his cassock and other Christian symbols for this purpose, he never gave up his Catholic faith, never abandoned his "Onion."[34] Rather, he reasserted his conviction that "love," as taught by Christ, is the most important thing—all other things are secondary. And based on such love, which is not restricted to any one religion, Ōtsu went to work among the poorest of the poor in and around Vārānasī. During the day, he carried the desolate and dying pilgrims on his shoulders to the banks of the river, offered them the Ganga's holy water, and let them die with dignity. He also carried the bodies of poor people who had died inside the city to the cremation *ghāts* at the banks of the Ganga. The image of Jesus Christ carrying the cross on his shoulders in atonement for all the sins of humanity would appear in Ōtsu's mind whenever he carried a dead body on his shoulders. While carrying these corpses or placing them on the funeral pyre, he would offer a prayer saying, "*O Lord . . . you carried the cross upon your back and climbed the hill to Golgotha. I now imitate that act. . . . You carried the sorrows of all men on your back and climbed the hill to Golgotha. I now imitate that act.*"[35] His being a Catholic priest did not act as a psychological barrier preventing him from executing such humanitarian services filled with love and compassion at the *ghāts* because he believed that he was destined by the divine to render such service. Ōtsu firmly believed that if his

God, in the form of Jesus Christ, a synonym for love, had come to Vārānasī, he, too, would have done the same thing. In this way, he found, at last, the true meaning of the life he wanted to live.

In the night, he comes back to his room, washes himself, eats his supper, and says the Holy Mass before going to sleep. He did not encounter any resistance from the *sādhus* or from the Hindu pilgrims he met with daily in the course of his social service. Nobody scolded him or discriminated against him because of his different look and complexion. As long as one conforms to the customs and practices of the society, as long as one does not fail to respect another's religious practices and belief system, as long as one does not disturb the community's peaceful coexistence, no one will interfere. This is one of the defining characteristics of Indian culture. Ōtsu never did anything that would have disturbed the peace, tranquility, and equanimity of society. Rather, he discovered the true meaning of the teachings of Christ after coming to Vārānasī, equating the Ganga with Christ. He says, "Every time I look at the River Ganges, I think of my Onion. The Ganges swallows up the ashes of every person as it flows along, rejecting neither the beggar woman who stretches out her fingerless hands nor the murdered prime minister, Gandhi. The river of love that is my Onion flows past, accepting all, rejecting neither the ugliest of men nor the filthiest."[36] Ōtsu did not feel awkward in juxtaposing the Ganga with Christ, as he realized that both Christ and the Ganga treat everything and everybody equally, accepting all human suffering and pathos without any discrimination of high or low, rich or poor, Brahmin or outcast. Ōtsu's realization of this truth not only helped him discover the uniqueness of India's spiritual greatness but also helped him to be reborn as a true Christian.

Conclusion

Ultimately, it can be said that Ōtsu voluntarily became a *sādhu*. To become a *sādhu*, one must renounce all worldly attachments and family ties, abandoning also any yearning for the pleasures of the material world and sensual life. The *sādhu*'s mind must always be focused on prayers and spiritually guided activities that will ultimately lead to *mokṣa*. Unlike the West, however, Indian spirituality does not consider the things of the material world as something to be avoided early in life. Rather, the renunciation of worldly matters in Hinduism comes only in the last stage of the four stages of life, known as the *āśramas*,[37] that is, it is only in this final stage wherein most of one's time is spent in meditation and prayer. The *āśrama* system is one facet of *dharma*, whose ultimate goal is liberation, or *mokṣa*, from worldly bondage and karmic rebirth. This dynamic system has enabled Indian society to assimilate various outside religions, philosophies, and cultural traditions while still maintaining its essential spiritual and cultural nature. This inclusiveness, this coexistence of religions and cultures, evolved into a *deep river* of spirituality giving solace to every seeker, irrespective of caste, creed, race, or religion.

Enami's experience of having lived in India for many years helped him to grasp the age-old customs, religious beliefs, character, and ethos of the Indian people objectively. Through his occasional warnings and reminders to the tourists, he tries to reaffirm the positive qualities of Indian society's inclusive attitude toward all and India's readiness to absorb everything into its fold like the river Ganga or the goddess Chāmundā. His explanations of Indian culture and religion greatly changed the outlook of all the tourists in his group except for the young Sanjōs. Even Naruse Mitsuko, the female atheist and protagonist of the novel, who had always found pleasure in teasing Ōtsu, changed her outlook after visiting the Ganga and seeing the image of the goddess Chāmundā. The emaciated image of Chāmundā, the embodiment of all sufferings and torments, pierced Mitsuko's heart and she discovered the Asian mother "utterly different from the lofty, dignified Holy Mother of Europe."[38]

Endō Shūsaku's *Deep River* may be read through this unique Indian view on human liberation and its conceptual similarities with Christianity. This connection may have been the motive force that drove Ōtsu, the failed seminarian, to run away from the West—which he perceived as degenerate and inflexible—to India. Ōtsu possesses a deep-seated understanding of the flexible, all-inclusive nature of Indian culture. Similarly, Enami, the tour guide, has a balanced understanding of Indian pluralism. In *Deep River*, Endō uses these two characters to offer readers an unconventional interpretation of Indian mysticism and a new dimension of its cultural ethos and social and religious plurality.

Notes

1. Endō used the expression "marshy land of Japan" in his famous novel *Silence*.
2. Shūsaku Endō, *Fukai Kawa o Saguru* (Tokyo: Bungei Shunju, 1994), 1 (my translation).
3. Ibid., 12.
4. Ibid., 23.
5. The *Skanda Purāṇa* includes a chapter on Kashi that explains the city's origins and significance. See section. 1.4 Kashi Khand of the *Skanda Purāṇa*, available at: http://hinduonline.co/Scriptures/Puranas/SkandaPurana.html, accessed October 4, 2017.

6. *Tīrthaṅkara* means a savior and spiritual teacher of *dharma*, or the righteous path.

7. In Advaita philosophy, Ādi Śaṅkarācārya argues that *ātman* (the true self) and *Brahman* (the highest metaphysical reality) are one and the same, meaning that an individual's soul and God are inseparable.

8. Mark Twain, *Following the Equator: A Journey around the World* (Hartford, Connecticut: American Pub. Co., 1897), 480.

9. Tiziano Tosolini, "Japan," in *God between the Lines*, ed. Tiziano Tosolini (Osaka Japan: Asian Study Centre, Private edition, 2016), 110.

10. M. T. Vasudevan Nair, *Varanasi*, trans. N. Gopalakrishnan (New Delhi: Orient Blackswan Private Limited, 2014), 55. The novel, translated into English from Malayalam by N. Gopalakrishnan, was published in Malyalam in 2002 by Current Books, Thrissur, Kerala.

11. *Skanda Purāṇa*, 1.4.5.

12. The Tāraka mantra has two main mantras: *Oṃ Śrī Rāma Jaya, Rāma Jaya Jaya Rāma* (Oṃ, Victory to Śrī Rāma, Victory to Rāma, Victory to Rāma) and *Rāma rāmāya namaḥ*, or *Oṃ rāmāya namaḥ* (Oṃ, Lord Rāma, I worship you). The latter is found in the *Rāmottaratāpaniya Upaniṣad*, 1st Khanda. It is believed that when a person is about to die, Lord Śiva himself recites one of these mantras into his or her ears, helping the spirit of the person to get free of *saṃsāra*.

13. Ibid.

14. In the caste system, the Brahmins, Kṣatriyas, Vaiśya, and Śūdras were called the *savarnas*, a reference to the higher castes, while the others were called *avarnas*, the outcastes or untouchables.

15. Shusaku Endo, *Deep River*, trans. Van C. Gessel (New York: New Directions Publishing Company, 1994), 105.

16. Ibid., 106.

17. Ibid.

18. Ibid.

19. Ibid.

20. *Tenjiku* (天竺) is the Japanese pronunciation of the Chinese word *tianzhu*, meaning the heavenly center of Buddhism. In Japanese, this word also refers to India, the Western Paradise. However, it is not used much in modern Japanese.

21. Endo, *Deep River*, 30.

22. Ibid., 108.

23. Ibid., 140.

24. *Atithidevo bhava* is a part of the mantra *mātrudevo bhava, pitrudevo bhava, āchāryadevo bhava, atithidevo bhava*, found in the *Taittirīya Upaniṣad*, which suggests, according to traditional Indian thinking, one should treat one's *mother, father, teacher,* and *guest* as god.

25. *Vasudhaiva kuṭumbakam* is yet another integral part of Indian traditional thinking meaning "The world is one family."; it is found in *Mahā Upaniṣad* and other Hindu texts.

26. Endo, *Deep River*, 144.

27. Until the advent of Western Christianity in the sixteenth century, the Saint Thomas Christians of Kerala—also known as Syrian Christians and Nasrani Christians—remained one church. However, after the first schism caused by the interference of the Latin (Western) Catholic Church in the sixteenth Century, it experienced several splits. The major factions of the contemporary Saint Thomas Christians include the Syro-Malabar Catholic Church, The Syro-Malankara Catholic Church, The Malankara Orthodox Chruch, The Malankara Jacobite Syrian Orthodox Church, and the Mar Thoma Church.

28. Surendralal G. Mehta, *Rich Tradition Richer Heritage* (Mumbai: Bharatiya Vidya Bhavan, 2016), 29.

29. *Harijan*, January 30, 1937, 407.

30. Endo, *Deep River*, 65.

31. Ibid., 121.

32. Emi Mase-Hasegawa, "Image of Christ for Japanese—Reflections on Shusaku Endo's Novels," in *Inter-Religio* 43 (Summer 2003): 29.

33. Endo, *Deep River*, 184.

34. Ōtsu calls Christ, his God, "Onion" during his conversation with Naruse Mitsuko.

35. Endo, *Deep River*, 193.

36. Ibid., 185.

37. The *āśramas* are the four stages of life a man should undergo according to Vedic scriptures: *brahmacharya* (student life), *gṛhastha* (family life), *vanaprastha* (retired life), and *saṃnyāsa* (life of renunciation).

38. Endo, *Deep River*, 175.

Chapter Twelve

Endō Shūsaku and Religious Pluralism

EMI MASE-HASEGAWA

Introduction

In accordance with Endō Shūsaku's will, copies of *Chinmoku* [*Silence*, 1960] and *Fukai kawa* [*Deep River*, 1980] were placed in his coffin since both novels epitomize his lifelong struggle with faith's meaning. This struggle displays itself in Endō's foremost literary-theological theme, which may best be grasped as *mishōka*, or Christianity's inculturation on Japanese soil.[1] I think Endō's image of Christ as the savior of the spirit, an all-embracing maternal presence, and the One who empathizes with broken men and women, which he developed in *Silence*, is consistent until the close of Endō's life. However, Endō's model of Christ seems weakened in *Deep River*. Here, Endō reimagines faith as an existential response to the work of the Holy Spirit, and he rethinks the Spirit's functions in diverse ways. This chapter explores this reimagining, especially in the broader context of Endō's untiring leitmotif of boundless love and universal salvation in life's spiritual dimension. These and other core ideas in Endō's work were influenced by the British theologian John Hick (1922–2012), whose ideas I will use to argue for a Japanese religious pluralism (harmony in diversity) coursing through *Deep River*.

Main Characters

Battling old age and recurring illnesses, Endō took three years to write *Deep River*, and the composition process appears to have been an arduous one. "I am losing confidence whether this novel will become a representative work of mine. However, there is no doubt that I have incorporated most of my thoughts into this novel," Endō reveals in the diary he kept.[2] Endō interweaves those thoughts into the backgrounds of his characters whose individual chapters are titled "The Case of ~." I begin by offering brief explanations of those characters—Isobe, Naruse Mitsuko, Numada, Kiguchi, Ōtsu, Sanjō, and Enami—which include the themes that Endō assigns to each.

The chapter on Isobe begins with a nostalgic invocation of "*Yaki imō, Yaki imō.* Piping hot sweet potatoes."[3] In the corner of a park, Isobe sits, stunned by news of his wife's terminal cancer. We learn that he resembles many Japanese men, devoted to his work and content to leave his wife to assume all home responsibilities, eager for a relationship of unspoken understanding with no tangible expressions of love. His wife's diagnosis confronts Isobe with an explicit sense of death's urgency, and he is troubled by the deep emptiness that takes over his spirit as he ponders outliving his wife. After her death, he tries to fulfill his wife's last wish by finding her reincarnation in India; this search gives his life purpose and leads him to join the tour group to India. Based on a letter from scholars researching reincarnation at the University of Virginia, Isobe searches for an Indian girl who claims to have been Japanese in her former life. Through this character, Endō addresses animism, marital love, synchronicity, past life memories, and the Buddhist view of life and death.[4] It is worth noting that Endō has Isobe's dying wife use the word *Umarekawari* (reincarnation or rebirth), which means she eschews the technical Buddhist word *saṃsāra* as well as the Christian word "resurrection."[5] This word choice hints at Endō's sense of a universal soteriology.

Mitsuko Naruse's chapter shows her volunteering at the hospital where Isobe's wife was being treated. Mitsuko, we discover, was born after the war, and she seems materially wealthy but spiritually bankrupt. During her university days, Mitsuko seduced Ōtsu, a seminary student who daily prayed to God (Jesus) in the university chapel, an act of faith that seemed pointless to her.[6] For Mitsuko, seduction began as a way to challenge God's or Jesus's influence in Ōtsu's life, though eventually she realizes that getting involved with Ōtsu changes her worldview. Through Mitsuko's characterization, then, Endō addresses existential as well as metaphysical concerns, such as agnosticism, subverting social norms, the internal struggle of women in patriarchal societies, and emotional deception.

An author of children's books, Numada spent his childhood in Dalian and only returns to Japan when his parents' divorce. In Japan, though, he often falls ill and is hospitalized. During one operation, Numada experiences an acute sense of his pet bird dying in place of him (a scene that evokes Endō's own history). Shaken by this feeling, he joins the other pilgrims and tours India in order to repay the dead myna bird. Animals roam throughout Numada's books, and several times they appear as companions, somehow able to grasp and minister to the sadness and loneliness of humans, and this characterization gestures toward a recurring theme in Endō's literary art: Jesus, the Eternal Companion.

The chapter on Kiguchi reveals him to hail from the generation that lived through the battles in Burma during World War II. When Tsukada, Kiguchi's survivor-comrade, is hospitalized, Kiguchi learns of the memories tormenting Tsukada, especially his memory of eating the flesh of a dead Japanese soldier to survive. After returning from the war, he sent the envelope, which had wrapped the human flesh he had desperately consumed, to the victim's grieving family as a token of his apology. About two months later, the victim's widow and a child visited Tsukada. On the visit, the boy looked at Tsukada. The child's timid look reminded Tsukada of his deceased comrade and, in his despair, Tsukada drank to forget. Kiguchi, who hears Tsukada's deathbed confession about his cannibalism, tours India to memorialize his comrades as well as his enemies. Through his characterization of Kiguchi, Endō ponders sin's nature and function in the broader context of Christian theological anthropology.

Ōtsu resembles Endō. The character and his author are persons of faith, conscientious Christians taught by their mothers to believe in God's salvific agency through Jesus of Nazareth and the Holy Church. More specifically, Ōtsu emulates the model of Jesus by tending lovingly to India's untouchables. Misunderstood and maligned, like Jesus, Ōtsu's life ends in a form of compensatory death when he is attacked for the sins of another—Mr. Sanjō. Through Ōtsu, then, Endō investigates the theological themes of Christian realism, orthodoxy and heterodoxy, faith as *fiducia*, exemplaristic soteriology, and religious diversity as well as spiritual pluralism.

Sanjō travels with his wife to India on his honeymoon. An inconsiderate and egotistical character, he seeks to become an award-winning photographer by capturing scenes from India but violates the prohibition of photographing the dead bodies of Hindus. Alarmed by Sanjō's selfish and intrusive behavior, indignant relatives of the deceased chase after him. He successfully gets away without realizing that Ōtsu, who had stepped in to mediate the situation, was seriously injured in his place. Sanjō then heads for home feeling neither remorse nor repentance, only the self-satisfied feeling that came from possessing his photographs. Sanjō epitomizes a self-serving, profit-based lifestyle, even at the cost of exploiting or oppressing others; by showing him to have suffered no ill consequences, Endō seeks to question whether justice is a delusion in the modern world.

Enami, after spending four years living and studying in India, works part-time as a guide for the India tour. He has a special affection for the Hindu goddess Chāmundā, devotion that issues from the special feeling that Enami has for the mother who raised him while bearing various trials after being deserted by her husband (a scene that evokes Endō's own history). The goddess Chāmundā, whose image Enami carries with him at all times, and the Ganges River reflect the story's sub-plot, coming together to display Endō's yearning for the sacred feminine or the divine's maternal presence throughout life. It is impossible to overstate Endō's attachment to this way of modeling or picturing God.

India as the Stage Setting

For the main characters who travel from Japan to India in the late autumn, India is a completely different world, surrounded by "a humid, lukewarm wind. They breathed in a tepid wind that blew, the smell of the earth, and a battlefield smelling of jungle."[7] Isobe sees India as "the world of reincarnation," while Mitsuko describes it as a "dark and total blackness; it was a solitary journey in the moonless night." Kiguchi remembers the "pathetic jungle of Burma," and Numada thinks of its bird sanctuaries and wildlife preserves.[8] Finally, the group enters the city of Vārānasī on the banks of the Ganges River, which is sacred ground to Hindus, whose views on the sacred differ in important ways from Japanese Shintō's models of purity and impurity. The key Hindu doctrines of karma, *saṃsāra*, and *mokṣa* are distinct; within the Hindu worldview, one seeks to break free (*mokṣa*) from the endless cycle of transmigration (*saṃsāra*) by accumulating good karma and reducing bad karma. But this is possible in other ways; for instance, simply by bathing in the holy River Ganges one escapes rebirth's cycle and attains freedom.

By moving the novel's stage from Japan to India, Endō shows a key development in his understanding of the nature and function of evangelism. Not all but many of Endō's previous books—from the first stage of his literary career—consistently portrayed Christianity's missionary activities as one directional, moving from the West to Japan. Within this traditional framework, Endō depicted in stark contrast the conflicts that arose between the evangelizer and evangelized.[9] But in *Deep River*, Endō alters this pattern through Ōtsu. Although he had questioned his faith, Ōtsu journeys to Lyon, France, in hopes of becoming a priest. His ecclesiastical superiors label his ideas heretical, however, and do not approve his ordination. Ōtsu travels far and wide, including Israel, and then, after much turmoil and hardship, arrives in India where its many peoples, cultures, and faith traditions begin reshaping his theological and pastoral views.

Images of Christ

Endō grounds his fiction in Christian theology and ethics. And *Deep River* displays three dominant images for Christ as the Savior—the suffering servant, the companion, and the maternal presence.[10] For the first of these, the image of the suffering servant, we can identify several items in Endō's story: How Mitsuko perceives Ōtsu; Numada's myna bird; Rouault's jester; and Gaston, who comforts Kiguchi's comrade, Tsukada. Such characters, even the myna bird, may be likened to "clowns," who provoke laughter without hurting anyone and, in the final analysis, make others feel good.[11] Clowns denote someone meek and naïve, a person who respects others even as those others mock them, and clowns can often be seen as individuals who walk the path of goodness to the very end without seeking personal gain. Endō seems to see the origins of this clown figure in the Hebrew Bible (Isaiah 53), in the Suffering Servant Song.[12] Traditional Christians hold that Isaiah 53 is the place in scripture where, for lack of better phrasing, Jesus's job description may be found, even though the text makes no explicit reference to him. Today, Christian soteriology underlines Jesus's role as the long-awaited suffering servant, attested in God's Word. Like a clown, Jesus is treated with contempt, is rejected and despised by the people, and bears sorrow and grief.

The second image, Jesus the companion, surfaces in Endō's characterization of Numada, the writer of children's stories. In Dalian, where Numada spent his childhood, his puppy Kuro (Blackie) was "the one who understood his sadness, the only living thing that would listen to his words and was his companion."[13] Later, during Numada's hospitalization for tuberculosis, he confessed his soul to the myna bird that his wife had given him.[14] For his part, Endō's own sensitivity to animals, such as birds and dogs, helped him craft the image of Christ as nonhuman companion. In *Deep River*'s last part, though, he pushes this image beyond the customary limits of Christian theological speculation and applies it to non-Christian faith traditions:

> When my friend was about to die in his despair, having done a thing no human should ever do, that man [Gaston] came to be

with him. That man . . . for my friend, was a *living buddha* who walked with him along the pilgrimage.[15]

As a part of Japanese folk belief, there is a pilgrimage known as the *Shikoku henro*, on which pilgrims travel to temples in eighty-eight locations. As they walk, they believe that *Kōbō-Daishi* (Kūkai), who became "a living buddha," accompanies them on their journey. For Endō, there is more to Christ's companionable presence than Jesus of Nazareth; that is, Christ may be found throughout creation.

Enami, the tour guide, takes the Japanese group to see images of the Hindu goddess Chāmundā and to the banks of the Ganges River, which brings us to Endō's third image for Christ. This emphasis on the sacred, holy, and feminine may reflect Endō's own feelings. Chāmundā *is* an analogy for Christ, and she mirrors the Holy Mother Mary. Roman Catholicism's Holy Mother Mary symbolizes tender mercy and deferential duty, yet India's goddesses are often, states Enami, depicted as mother-earth goddesses. Chāmundā is a case in point. She assumes India's suffering, ministering to life's vulnerable and broken inhabitants, even though there is nothing comely about her. Chāmundā is the mother of India—she is not gentle, pure, or refined, but is actually fearsome, ugly, and old. Though the statue the tour groups sees of Chāmundā was carved in the twelfth century, the suffering of India's people, and thus the suffering she bears, continues unabated. After introducing Chāmundā to the group, Enami accompanies the pilgrims-tourists to the Ganges River. Finally, the image of India's maternal presence overlaps the river, as the mother Ganges, who accepts all living creatures.

In learning from Chāmundā and the mother Ganges, moreover, Mitsuko finds that her thoughts turn to the Bible's "suffering servant," and Ōtsu's way of life surfaces in her mind. Ōtsu symbolizes the act of loving wastefully, Christ-like kenosis, and the spirit of self-sacrifice. The major world religions endorse such qualities, and John Hick, whose pluralistic theology Endō admired, believes a morality marked by the self's surrender in service of others' flourishing acts like connective tissue uniting different faiths. It is to Hick's influence on Endō that I now turn.

John Hick's Influence on Endō

While writing *Deep River*, Endō was greatly influenced by Hick's general approach to religious diversity. On September 5, 1992, Endō states:

> It was a coincidence that the book that had been forgotten by a store clerk or customer in the corner of the shelf upstairs at Taishōdō a few days ago was Hick's *Problems of Religious Pluralism* [in Japanese]. More than a coincidence, it was, rather, that what my subconscious was seeking called forth the book. . . . This shocking book has overwhelmed me since the day before yesterday. Also, I received *God Has Many Names* [in Japanese] by the same author from a visitor from Iwanami Shoten who just happened to visit and I am absorbed reading it.[16]

Based on the notion that diverse religions exist, Hick proposed a hypothesis for the understanding of religions centered on "ultimate Reality." Endō was surprised and moved that this ultimate Reality was perceived in most global religious traditions in either personal or nonpersonal ways; that various forms of human response to this presence appears acceptable in an age of religious cosmpolitanism; and, Endō valued Hick's insistence that the various world religions equally provided a path/place of salvation.

In *Deep River*, Ōtsu claims, "If you don't like the word God, you can call it by other names, 'a tomato,' 'an onion,' or 'a lump of love.' "[17] Such phrasing evokes the title of one of Hick's books—*God Has Many Names*.[18] Ōtsu's faith was rejected as pantheistic, and thus heretical, thinking by the Western world that professes the absoluteness of traditional Christianity.[19] After going through a life full of twists and turns, Ōtsu not only gains the assurance that Jesus accompanies him with maternal acceptance of love at all times but also is accepted by the Hindu *sādhus* even though he had been like an unwanted puppy. Once there, he just follows and serves Jesus Christ, carrying the dying outcasts who had fallen by the wayside to the Ganges River on his back. For Ōtsu, this is an imitation of Jesus climbing the hill of Golgotha carrying the cross on his back. In this way, Ōtsu, again and again, carried the people's sorrows to the Ganges—the river as mother, the river of love. The terminus of Ōtsu's faith is expressed in his words that can be taken as a prayer:[20] "In the end, I've decided that my Onion lives not only in European Christianity but also in Hinduism or Buddhism. It is not just an idea, it is a way of life I chose for myself."[21]

Jesus's way of life, imitated by Ōtsu, is the ultimate self-sacrifice; in Hick's words, "the transformation of human existence from self-centredness to Reality centredness."[22] That is, without pressing or forcing his own faith, wearing an *achara* (a soiled robe) along with the believers of many other religions, Ōtsu carries those who have fallen by the wayside to the river mother. Hick's approach to religious pluralism contends that God/Ultimate Reality is working in all religions. God is understood as a sanctifying, rather than a self-revelatory, entity—one who repudiates those forms of religious authoritarianism that consider only one form of revelation to be the highest truth.

Additionally, Hick's religious pluralism promotes the notion of ultimate Reality's universal salvific will. The lifestyle, followed by priests and believers, of trusting in God's love and imitating Christ appears to be pointless to the people who live in thrall to capitalism, Endō complains.[23] In *Deep River*, Endō pours out his anger through Mitsuko, the narrator, and Enami. When Numada sees the children begging close to the *ghāts* as well as the men and women who have lost all their fingers to leprosy, he declares, almost in tears, that these people are human, just like us. However, Mitsuko fails to reply. She no longer wants imitations of love or cheap sympathy. She wants real love, nothing less. Later, Endō's narrator talks of the conflict between various religions, and Mitsuko once again expresses her anger and sadness.[24] In a society where the logic of "strength wins over all" runs rampant, the weak are eliminated. However, Christianity transforms such logic.[25] As God's Son in the flesh, Jesus died on the cross and brought about the reconciliation between the holy God and an errant mankind, atoning for the sins that mankind itself could not make right. This model of self-sacrificial love begins with Jesus but is not confined to Him, Endō, following Hick, holds. Christ-like loving wastefully is revived in Ōtsu, who dies as a scapegoat for Sanjō, and reappears in the nuns who work in the Home for the Dying.[26] Even Mitsuko learns about Jesus through Ōtsu's self-sacrificial love and, by the novel's close, she seems to be thinking about the universal salvific will of Ultimate Reality.

The Framework of Salvation in *Deep River*

It is important to mention that the title of the novel was *Kawa* [River] in the beginning. The river is the presiding symbol for Christians, helping them to understand rebirth through the ritual of baptism. Endō changed the title to *Fukai kawa* [Deep River] after the first galley proofs were finished, and in the final stage of printing when he heard and was moved by the faith encapsulated in the African American spiritual of the same name[27]: "*River* is the river of Love, and the river of Spirituality," he later wrote in his diary.[28] Through the metaphor of rivers leading to the ocean, Endō sought to situate Christianity within the soteriological framework of Hick's hypothesis of religious pluralism.

One of the presuppositions of Hick's hypothesis of religious pluralism is the idea that it is more rational to believe that various forms of religious experience—*nirvāṇa*, *satori*, or liberation—can be seen throughout the world. They are not purely projections by humans but responses to the universal presence of ultimate Reality. The fundamentally ineffable ultimate Reality is *experienced* by people as a human response, and, in the end, the stories accompanying their experiences can be shared.[29] This framework of salvation is presented in *Deep River*, and we see it again in the Endō-facilitated debates involving Mase Hiromasa (1938–) and Fr. Kadowaki Kakichi (1926–), which were convened during the novel's composition process.[30] Fr. Kadowaki held the position that "religious experiences are shared," and he made an appeal from his own experience: in coming alongside another person through meditation, religious experience can or may be shared by nonverbal communication. On the other hand, Mase Hiromasa, my own father, insisted from the standpoint of critical realism that "religious experiences cannot be shared." To Endō, their different positions were both understandable, but he was torn between them. My father remembers the day that Endō was very serious, listening to their argument.[31]

As Mase Hiromasa's daughter, I would like to elucidate my father's imprecise "cannot be shared" argument. In the 1980s, our family was traveling across the lands of different Native American groups. It was pouring rain when my mother, who was driving the car at the time, stepped on the breaks and skidded, hydroplaning on the swiftly running water. The car spun sideways three times and barely stopped at the edge of the embankment with three flat tires. The Native American policeman who rushed to the scene in his patrol car exclaimed, "It's a miracle that no one in the car was hurt and that the car didn't fall off the embankment!" Three days later, we resumed our trip without mishap and, shortly after we started out, a large rainbow appeared in the sky. Seeing the stunningly beautiful rainbow, my devout mother uttered a word of thanks to God. The rest of the family remained silent. Ten years later, my father addressed a Keiō University research meeting, at which I was present, and he claimed that my mother's religious experience was her own, something unique to her. Although I was young and immature at the time, I recall that for some reason I shed tears of annoyance at his statement. Were we not there, in the car, and thus aware of her experience? In the end, my father has taught me that a religious experience has *meaning* as an individual's unique experience and can never be shared wholly and completely; that said, an effort must always be made to speak of it, believing that it ought to be verbalized and then shared.

Conclusion

From the above experience, I conclude with one last observation concerning Endō's framework of religious pluralism in *Deep River*.[32] Kiguchi, a Japanese

Buddhist man, stands on the banks of the mother Ganges and "looks toward the river's flow," chanting the *Amida Sūtra* for the repose of the souls of his friends and other fallen war comrades. Standing beside him is an Indian girl "who kept her large black eyes fixed on him and did not move a bit."[33] The girl does not understand the sūtra that the man chants nor does she grasp its deeper meaning; however, both are "looking in the same direction."[34] Here, Endō places two protagonists of different nationalities, religions, generations, and genders by the Mother Ganges. Without verbal communication, they are looking *toward* the ocean, *the Ultimate Reality*. Both appear to embrace hope for salvation, their spirituality seems comprehensible, then, but neither one of them wholly and completely grasps the religious experience of the other.

In this scene, I think Endō displays his faithfulness to the framework of Hick's religious pluralism. And this concluding scene, I understand, *is* Endo's interpretation of the debate between Fr. Kadowaki and Professor Mase.[35]

As a Christian, Endō used literary art as a vehicle for his understanding of religious pluralism. And he wrote in what I take to be the form of a confession. I see *Deep River* as a story of love and salvation as well as hope, and I think it upholds what our world most needs: a theology of *harmony in diversity*.

Notes

1. Emi Mase-Hasegawa, *Christ in Japanese Culture: Theological Themes in Shūsaku Endō's Literary Works* (Leiden and Boston: Brill, 2008).

2. Shūsaku Endō, Fukai kawa *sōsaku nikki* [*Deep River* composition diary] (Tokyo: Kōdansha, 1997), August 16, 1992, entry, 118. English translations of quotations are by the author.

From August 26, 1990, until May 25, 1993, while writing *Deep River*, Endō was also writing in a notebook to keep a record of his daily life and the twists and turns of his novel. This notebook was discovered posthumously and was published as *Fukai Kawa Sōsaku Nikki* by Kōdansha Publishing Company. Later, it was included in *Endō Shūsaku Bungaku Zenshū* [The complete works of Shūsaku Endō], vol. 15 (Tokyo: Shinchōsha, 2000).

3. Shūsaku Endō, *Fukai kawa* [*Deep River*] (Tokyo: Kōdansha, 1993), 9. English translations of quotations are by the author.

4. Shūsaku Endō, Fukai kawa *o saguru* [Searching for *Deep River*] (Tokyo: Bungei Shunjū, 1994). The book includes the dialogues held among nine experts from various fields. These dialogues were held from the preparation period of *Fukai kawa* to after its completion (1986, 1994). Endō received many hints from these dialogues in creating his story.

5. Shūsaku Endō, *Fukai kawa*, 26. *Umarekawari* is translated as "reborn" by translator Van C. Gessel (New York: New Directions Publishing Company, 1994), 17.

6. Mitsuko is portrayed as a villainess rather like Eve. (Cf. Shūsaku Endō, *Fukai kawa*, 65: "Mitsuko thought of Eve who seduced Adam and caused the eternal banishment of mankind from the garden of Eden. There is an impulsive power to destroy oneself in every woman."). Within traditional Christian culture, Mary and Eve are presented as the symbols of "light and darkness," "purification and contamination," "innocence and corruption."

7. Shūsaku Endō, *Fukai kawa*, 169.

8. Ibid. Image of India for Isobe: 175, Mitsuko: 176, 185, Kiguchi: 176, Numada: 212.

9. Shūsaku Endō, *Chinmoku* [*Silence*] (Tokyo: Shinchōsha, 1966) and *Samurai* [*The Samurai*] (Tokyo: Shinchōsha, 1980).

The evangelical policy emphasized in the seventeenth century of "imposing Western culture for the expansion and development of the church" was revised by the Second Vatican Council of 1962–65. However, the conventional missionaries' evangelical activity of "proclaiming the gospel" was affected by the viewpoints of two distinct groups: the evangelizers and the evangelized. In this oppositional relationship, the missionaries became the "providers" of the teaching and the Japanese were seen, therefore, as the "receivers." Here, the full acceptance of the side being evangelized was not taken seriously. In this way, after the Meiji era, the Christianity that was transplanted by the missionaries, although playing a role in promoting Westernization and emphasizing the importance of faith, never went so far as to affect the culture, religious consciousness, or psychic depths of the Japanese.

10. Emi Mase-Hasegawa, "Love and Salvation," in *For People Learning about Religious Pluralism*, ed. Mase Hiromasa (Kyoto: Sekai shisōsha, 2008), 227–44.

11. Shūsaku Endō, *Fukai kawa*. For the link to clowns for Mitsuko: 51, 286, Numada: 121–22, 126–27. Kiguchi: 124, 160. Also, see Endō's earlier work, *Obaka-san* [*Wonderful fool*] (Tokyo: Chūōkōron, 1959). The main character, Gaston, represents the image of a clown.

12. Ibid., 71, 285, 339. Endō quotes the verse three times in the novel. Shūsaku Endō, Fukai kawa *sōsaku nikki* (August 26, 1992), 122: "Needless to say, this verse is the key theme of my novel for now."

13. Ibid., 118.

14. Ibid., 128. Endō developed the image of Jesus, the companion, in his second period of literary work (1966–1980). The image of Jesus as the eternal companion was established in the climactic scene of *Samurai* (1980), where the samurai, sentenced to life imprisonment, is told by his retainer, "that person will accompany you from this point."

15. Ibid., 323.

16. Shūsaku Endō, Fukai kawa *sōsaku nikki*, 24.

17. Shūsaku Endō, *Fukai kawa*, 103–4.

18. John Hick, *God Has Many Names* (Philadelphia: The Westminister Press, 1980/82), *Kami wa Ōku no Namae o Motsu*, trans. Hiromasa Mase (Tokyo: Iwanami Shoten, 1986).

Incidentally, when Endō had reached an impasse in his story, he encountered the two books by Hick. Later, Endō was invited to a *getsuyō-kai* (Monday study group) with Mase Hiromasa, the translator of Hick's books and also a junior colleague from the university from which Endō himself had graduated.

Ref. Shūsaku Endō, *Fukai kawa sōsaku nikki* (September 6, 1991), 25: "After reading Hick's shocking books, I find other books tasteless."

See also, Hiromasa Mase, "Endō Shūsaku to Shūkyo Tagenshugi: *Fukai kawa Sōsaku nikki* o megutte" [Shūsaku Endo and religious pluralism: in relation to his journal of *Deep River*] (Tokyo: The Hiyoshi Review of the Humanities, Keiō University 1999), 147–56.

19. Ōtsu and his panentheistic theological thinking is based on Endō's lifelong friend Father Yōji Inoue (1927–2014). I once asked Fr. Inoue: "Is Ōtsu you?" With a gentle smile, he answered "No." He then gave me a DVD of *Fukai kawa*.

20. Shūsaku Endō, *Fukai kawa sōsaku nikki* (January 6, 1992), 55: "I want to write a novel that traces human sorrow, or prayer would not arise."

21. Shūsaku Endō, *Fukai kawa*, 300.

22. John Hick, *An Interpretation of Religion* (London: Macmillan, 1989), 301.

23. Shūsaku Endō, *Fukai kawa*, 263.

24. Ibid., 307, 316, 338–39.

25. Psalms 147:10–11 (NKJ): "He does not delight in the strength of the horse; He takes no pleasure in the legs of a man. The Lord takes pleasure in those who fear Him, in those who hope in His mercy."

26. Shūsaku Endō, *Fukai kawa sōsaku nikki* (July 30, 1992), 112–13: "Mother Theresa wrote for me 'God bless you through your writing.'"

27. Shūsaku Endō, *Fukai kawa sōsaku nikki* (November 9, 1992), 131.

28. Ibid. (May 2, 1992), 92.

29. John Hick, *Problems of Religious Pluralism*, trans. Hiromasa Mase (Kyoto: Hōzōkan, 2008), 173. Hick also pays attention to the word "revelation." He says, "All pure religious perception is a response to the subsuming reality and the preemptive pressure of a divine presence."

30. Shūsaku Endō, Fukai kawa *sōsaku nikki*, 38. Also see John Hick, *An Autobiography* (Oxford: Oneworld Publications, 2002), 286–87.

31. Ibid., 38, "Oct. 7, 1992 Monday Group Meeting, Talk of Hick's theology. A heated debate between members of the panel, Professor Mase and Father Kadowaki, regarding Christology. Or, rather, a battle-argument. Pouring outside. As the moderator, I was perplexed, torn between Hick's way of thinking and conventional Christology." Ref. Emi Mase-Hasegawa, "Haha naru mono o Motomete" [In search for the maternal] (Tokyo: Mita Bungaku Winter Edition 2006), 186–97.

32. Emi Mase-Hasegawa, *Christ in Japanese Culture*, 168–74.

33. Shūsaku Endō, *Fukai kawa*, 326.

34. *Kawa o mitsumenagara* is translated literally as "Staring into the river" by translator Van C. Gessel (New York: New Directions Publishing Company, 1994), 201. However, this translation does not lead readers to pay attention to the direction that Kiguchi and the girl are facing, thus Endō's framework of religious pluralism is not readily apparent.

35. Emi Mase-Hasegawa, "John Hick no Shūkyo Tagenshugi Saikō" [Reconsidering John Hick's religious pluralism] (Tokyo: The Journal of J.F. Oberlin University, Studies in Humanities vol. 7, 2016), 117–36.

Chapter Thirteen

Endō Shūsaku's Process Panentheism

DARREN J. N. MIDDLETON

Introduction

Endō Shūsaku's literary art bears an anguished theological character. His stories show him wrestling, that is, with the uneasy alliance between sin and redemption as well as Christian distinctiveness and the catholicity of divine grace. Jesus and interreligious dialogue troubled him, as the present volume upholds, and yet he often sensed that the God who fashioned our evolving world from formless chaos did not squeeze diversities and uncertainties out of it. Endō struggled theologically, and never more so than when he would brood over European theism and Japanese pantheism.[1] Throughout *Deep River* it is the character of Ōtsu—a Japanese Roman Catholic who lives in India but once trained for the priesthood in France—who typifies this transcultural aspect of Endō's anguished theology. Ōtsu focalizes my chapter.

Pantheism signifies God-is-all-ism. And a case can be made for Ōtsu's pantheism. But in this chapter I suggest that the failed seminarian's religious reflections, which appear in chapters 6 and 10 of *Deep River*, may best be seen as disclosing process panentheism—the participating of everything in God. Process panentheism's advocates often paint the theological picture of God's transcendence-within-immanence, viewing the sacred as everywhere, the circumambient divine presence within which all created realities experience their becoming. I outline this way of visualizing God and the world in the sections that follow. While it is instructive for an adequate image of process panentheism to take the measure of this theological overlay's intellectual development, an examination of the contemporary as well as classical thinkers is not undertaken here because it would render my task too unwieldy and because others have already undertaken such a summary.[2] I paint with broad brushstrokes. Some British and North American thinkers surface. But process panentheism is not simply a Western wonder. Rather, its history reaches back into an ancient and diverse (i.e., non-Western) religious past, as studies show, and, more specifically, this intricate worldview is not alien or foreign to Japan.[3] Viewable as nature-mysticism, *koshintō*, known as Basic Shinto, resembles process panentheism, and a "*koshinto*-influenced religious sensibility" flecks Endō's fictions, as Emi Mase-Hasegawa notes.[4] European, as well as Japanese, Christian theologians, some of whom Endō read and admired, have promoted process panentheism's claim that God or the divine is part of the processes of evolution, actively involved in the world of mutability and flux, touched by world events, sometimes to the point of changing the divine or God's mind. In the end, though, I focus on *Deep River*, interpreting it panentheistically. Ōtsu's spirituality flows from his mystical sense that an energetic God—whom the wise call by many names—in each fresh moment quickens the longing for continued becoming through creation, because the divine desires all life to become new. This God inspires Ōtsu to load the dying Hindu woman on his back—like Christ carrying the wooden cross, mounting Golgotha's summit of extravagant love—and convey her to the cremation grounds.[5] It is also the evolving God of Ōtsu who absorbs, like the Ganga, each completed experience of every self-creative event in the processes of reality, because God wants to know (and, where possible, appreciate) what those events have become.

Western Process Panentheism

Emerging in the early decades of the last century in the work of several thinkers—Henri Bergson, Alfred North Whitehead, Pierre Teilhard de Chardin, and Charles Hartshorne—eager to use Charles Darwin's evolutionary theory to imagine new models of God and the world, process panentheism promotes the idea that change brands everything.[6] We do not occupy a static milieu. From elementary particles like bosons to complex organisms like ourselves, all reality discloses itself to us as lively. Rivers flow, stars burn, gravity bends light, space curves, and our universe expands. Yet this universe is unlike the one scientists, philosophers, and theologians of previous generations had thought they knew, process panentheists declare. Take Christianity's emergence, for example, and its influence across time. The shapers of Christian orthodoxy matched ancient Greek philosophy with Christian faith, since Parmenides and Plato seemed as convincing to the Patristics as Stephen Hawking and Darwin are today, even if such Parmenidian-Platonic thinkers soon argued that the really Real does not change. For those who take this line of thought, what follows might be styled "theological determinism." A fixed and passionless Absolute, God serves as the ground and grammar of a static, invariable cosmos.[7]

Such thinking triumphed for centuries. When the process panentheists arrived on the scene in the 1910s, though, they began to grumble about Christianity's reliance on the ageless idea of permanence and change. On this view, whatever changes decays, to state the issue briefly, and so the ancient Greeks not only tied change to imperfection, they visualized the perfect God as changeless. Medieval theologians took up this Aristotelian logic and imaged the divine as the Unmoved Mover—capable, that is, of initiating change in others but remaining unchanged in Godself. In the centuries that followed, this Scholastic model of God became Christianity's main theological picture. Unhappily, as process panentheists note, this picture not only places the divine beyond the messy verities of embodied existence, in order to preserve God's absolute sovereignty, as well as unilateral power, it runs the risk of diminishing Christianity's incarnational theology. Whitehead claims that

> the doctrine of an aboriginal, eminently real, transcendent creator, at whose fiat the world came into being, and whose imposed will it obeys, is the fallacy that has infused tragedy into the histories of Christianity and Mohametism [Islam]. When the Western world accepted Christianity, Caesar conquered. . . . The brief Galilean vision of humility flickered throughout the ages, uncertainly. In the official formulation of the religion, it has assumed the trivial form of the mere attribution to the Jews that they cherished a misconception about their Messiah. But the deeper idolatry, of the fashioning of God in the image of the Egyptian, Persian, and Roman imperial rulers, was retained. The church gave unto God the attributes which belonged exclusively to Caesar.[8]

If Endō perhaps came across such traditional theism during his postgraduate studies in France in the 1950s, then Ōtsu categorically heard about it in his Lyon-based seminary.[9] Today's Christian process panentheists, like Paul Fiddes and Ann Pederson, dispute this conventional construal of God's changeless perfection, however, and they do so by thinking worshipfully as well as analogically.[10]

We are not inflexible entities that trek unchanged through time. Rather, we are the many experiences and changes we have had; thus, we are relational and processive. The same is true of God. If our tears twirl humanity's water mills, for example, but fail to move the divine, then this passionless Absolute appears unworthy of worship, theologians like Donna Bowman and David Pailin hold.[11] God is subject to change as we are subject to change, they say. The divine is part of life's insubstantiality, inextricably intertwined with our world, to the point of being affected by what occurs within it. The Unmoved Mover is unrelated to us, Joseph A. Bracken declares, and this absence of relationality seems as existentially ruinous as it is biblically unsound:

> Whitehead's thought is in many ways better attuned to the conventional understanding of Holy Scripture than the philosophy and theology of Thomas Aquinas, the Dominican monk whose thought has been the benchmark for Roman Catholic thought since the thirteenth century. Where Aquinas emphasized God's transcendent reality as Creator of heaven and earth, Whitehead proposes that God is necessarily involved in an ongoing, ever-changing relationship with creatures. Just as pictured on the pages of sacred Scripture, Whitehead's God responds with feelings of joy or sadness to what is happening in the world. God thus shares in our world in a way that is logically impossible for the somewhat distant, unchanging God of traditional Thomistic philosophy and theology.[12]

Whereas Thomists promote an unchanging God, operating on the cosmos from outside, process panentheists stress divine transcendence-within-immanence. God is the world's soul, life's arche and telos, ontologically independent from and yet evolving or developing through God's cosmic body, beckoning all things forward, continuously receiving and responding to the body's shifting states. The divine personality develops through collaboration with the cosmos God embodies, and the cosmos affects God.

This is an eye-catching vision that is often linked to experiences of an intensely mystical, or what might be called process panentheistic, character. And perhaps "the river" is an instructive trope for such spiritual sensibilities. Everything in life flows (*panta rhei*), like the Ganga, which seeps from its source in the Himalayan glaciers and runs through the plains of northern India, joined by numerous tributaries until it spills out and into the Indian Ocean. Everything flows. Everything also seems constant. "It is as true to say that God is permanent and the World fluent, as that the World is permanent and God is fluent," Whitehead muses, almost prayerfully. Furthermore: "It is as true to say that God is one and the World many, as that the World is one and God many."[13] Mitsuko's own entreaty, which she haltingly intones at the close of Endō's novel, virtually reiterates this process panentheistic vision:

> *What I can believe in now is the sight of all these people, each carrying his or her own individual burdens, praying at this deep river.* At some point, the words Mitsuko muttered to herself were transmuted into the words of a prayer. *I believe that the river embraces these people and carries them away. A river of humanity. The sorrows of this deep river of humanity. And I am a part of it.*
>
> She did not know to whom she directed this manufactured prayer. Perhaps it was towards the Onion [God] that Ōtsu pursued. Or perhaps it was towards something great and eternal that could not be limited to the Onion.[14]

Spirituality in our changing, often-troubled world thus involves heeding and then responding to the adventurous, many-named God who disturbs and urges us with the desire to seek creation's flourishing.

Everything flows, and everything matters. And our sense that our effort to seek personal and systemic transformation, higher goals, and ever new possibilities matters to God can serve to foster our commitment to human togetherness and ecological sensitivity. Orthopraxis thus flows out of a discernment of our role as inventive co-creators with the divine in the creative advance. Whitehead once more: "It is as true to say that God creates the World, as that the World creates God."[15] David Pailin elaborates:

> We are to be neither contented cows nor regimented robots. The ideal life is one which never ceases to be creative, in which people both experience aesthetic joy and contribute those experiences to the fulness of the divine being. It is a disturbing goal. The life of the artist is uncomfortable. Others may be hostile because their bovine complacency is threatened; the artist's own experience is unsettled because there is no final satisfaction to the pursuit of aesthetic joy. At the same time it is also a profoundly satisfying mode of being when it is appreciated that 'all objects are internal' to God. Whatever is achieved is thereafter enjoyed cosmically and everlastingly.[16]

Endō found this vision of a world in which God ("this Onion") is continuously at work, chiefly through companionable tenderness or respectful persuasion, invigorating. "God is not so much an existence as a force," Ōtsu notifies Mitsuko. "This Onion is an entity that performs the labours of love."[17] Expressed differently, *Deep River*'s dynamic deity is a personalized activity (*hataraki*), whose panentheistic presence may best be seen in the experience that arises in the created processes of reality as they travel forward from creative possibility, through inanimate and animate nature, to conscious agents like ourselves. "This *hataraki* pushed Shūsaku Endō throughout all his life," according to Adelino Ascenso; and thus, as Makoto Fujimura claims, Endō's God is "constantly *hataraku Kami* (active and moving God)."[18]

Before I outline the basic features of non-Western process panentheism, let me conclude this section by observing that some of the Western theologians that Endō read and admired also view God as dynamic, evolving, and related to the world of change. Among them is John Hick, whose Christian pluralistic theology courses through *Deep River*, according to Mark B. Williams and others.[19] Endō's diaries and other, related writings mention Hick and his Japanese translator, Mase Hiromasa, repeatedly.[20] Hick also acknowledges Endō as well as Whiteheadian thought in his autobiography.[21] And more recently, Yujin Nagasawa persuasively argues for a panentheistic reading of Hick's work.[22]

For most of his life, Hick was a member of the United Reformed Church (Protestant). Regarding Catholic Christianity, which Endō also was keen to adapt to Japanese culture, critics think it is instructive to situate Endō within the broad context of post Vatican II thought, which displays marked panentheistic considerations, as Robert L. Kinast and Illtyd Trethowan note.[23] Vatican II theologians celebrate as well as affirm God's ubiquitous grace; and generally speaking, they hold that creation's aim is to serve divine becoming. Note that I said "creation's aim." The church is a pilgrim people, and the evolution of the church is the evolution of its parishoners, and part of God's evolution, but the church does not and need not monopolize divine grace.[24] After 1965, relational and dynamic models of the God-world alliance surfaced in the new theologies of Hans Küng, Wolfhart Pannenberg, and Karl Rahner.[25] Even though Endō does not cite such thinkers explicitly, he shares their desire to transcend Western, Aristotelian-inspired theologies.[26] And their version(s) of Catholic process panentheism became part of the post–Vatican II cultural agenda, implicit in European and North American Catholic fictions in the last century's second half.[27]

Non-Western Process Panentheism

When one thinks about "panentheism outside the box," to use Lorilial Biernacki's phrase, one soon encounters its transcultural dimension(s), appearing as it does in everything from Neo-Confucianism to Tibetan Buddhism, from Jainism to Islam, and from Hindu Tantra to the Jewish biblical/rabbinic tradition.[28] For the purposes of this section, though, I attend to selected Japanese affirmations of panentheism, highlighting specific thinkers as well as wide-ranging sensibilities. I make three observations, which space precludes probing in detail.

First, I use John J. Keane's recent account of the Japanese quest for divinity, which mines several seams to the meaning of the word *kami*, regularly translated as "god" or "gods."[29] While *kami* signifies, in a historical sense, an extraordinary presence(s) that has been deemed ineffable, sheer mystery, even transrational, Keane views his subject from a social scientific perspective, showing how and why ancient Japanese people revered divine spirits or forces (*kami*), which were thought to energize as well as abide within all things.[30] Buddhism and Confucianism, as well as Daoism and Christianity, eventually supplied "four separate layers, namely, animatism, animism, panentheism and monotheism" to *kami*'s initial meaning. Only one layer, monotheism, which rests on Aristotelian thought, "contradicts the other three," Keane claims.[31] I shall discuss one of the other layers, Japanese panentheism, shortly. For now, though, it is perhaps enough to follow Emi Mase-Hasegawa in perceiving that before other countries imported their religious traditions into Japan, the Japanese people institutionalized their lively sense of life's sacrality into Basic Shinto, the way of the *kami*. Mase-Hasegawa also uses the word *koshinto*, "a modern analytical concept," to signify this Basic Shinto.[32]

Second, Endō found *kami* and *koshintō* troubling, if his first published essay is to be believed, though both terms appear to compare with Nishida Kitarō's Whiteheadian process panentheism. Consider Endō's "Kamigami to kami to" (Gods and God), which appeared in 1947. This journal article reveals a youthful Endō, twenty-four and not yet studying abroad, wrestling with perceived incongruities between Western Christianity and the Japanese religious overlay, which he treats as pantheistic.[33] "The term 'gods' [in the essay's title] is a symbol for Japanese culture," Mase-Hasegawa remarks, "and 'God' for that of the West."[34] But thinking in this way simply confuses pantheism with polytheism, she laments, even if this first foray into publication sees Endō determined to find a viable way to adapt Western Christianity to Japanese religiosity. "Endo does not mention Shinto," she acknowledges. "He only claims that Japan is a pantheistic world, without explaining the theological arguments."[35] Endō's compatriot, Nishida Kitarō, who died just two years before Endō's essay appeared, also desired an East-West rapprochement, and Nishida found it in Alfred North Whitehead's philosophy. Nishida disfavors pantheism; he does not perceive the world as God without remainder. Nishida's mystical sense images God and the evolving cosmos in an alliance of co-inherence in which both act according to their degrees of autonomy and thus co-create, even if their tragic vulnerability follows as a consequence. In his final essay, Nishida refers to his mystical overlay with the word *banyūzaishinron*, which may best be translated "panentheism," in contrast to "pantheism," *banyūshinron*.[36] While there is no indication of any Nishida books in the Machida Literary Museum, where many of Endō's books were donated, Van C. Gessel holds that "Nishida was so esteemed and so widely read and the Kyoto School of philosophy he founded so influential that it is hard to imagine that any well-educated Japanese of the postwar period hadn't had an introduction to his writings. Nishida's rejection of Western-like dualism would have appealed to Endō in his later years, I think."[37] Interestingly, John J. Keane invokes Shinto scholars and Christian theologians to claim that Nishida's process panentheistic model of Japanese divinity or *kami* is anti-dualistic and mystical, an overlay that blends Western and Japanese traditions.[38] William Johnston, the Jesuit translator of Endō's *Silence*, invites a similar comparison: "After many years in this country I believe that the Japanese can accept the God of the Christian contemplatives and mystics. This is the God who is present at the depths of the universe, giving existence to all things. This is the God we meet in the silence of contemplative prayer. I am grateful to Shusaku Endo for stressing this aspect of God."[39] In summary, Endō's 1947 essay clearly shows his early struggle to adapt or inculturate his Christian faith, yet this particular tussle became less of an issue much later in his widely read life, and especially in *Deep River*, which may be read as a parable of process panentheism gesturing toward an East-West consanguinity.

Third, Fr. Inoue Yōji, an influential Catholic Japanese thinker, was on the same boat that took his friend Endō to France in 1950 and, like Endō, he has sought to adapt Catholic Christian theology to Japanese culture. Inoue is a process panentheist. And he inspired Endō's portrayal of Ōtsu.[40] Yoshihisa Yamamoto's recent study shows that while Fr. Inoue spent his time in Europe studying Thomistic theology, like most pre–Vatican II seminarians, he quickly sensed its limited appeal to "ordinary Japanese people not acquainted with European culture."[41] He abandoned the Thomistic model of God's immutability or unchangeableness, like Western process panentheists before him, fearing it promoted a view of divine transcendence that renders God unconnected or indifferent to our experience. Fr. Inoue eventually took refuge in the writings of Christian mystics, contemplatives like St. Thérèse of Liseux, and he warmed to their sense that God participates in the world's sorrow as in its joy. God counts in ordinary life, in other words, and is not remote or distant from all that is of existential value to us.

Christian mystics were not alone in stimulating Fr. Inoue. Catholic theologian Henri de Lubac inspired his international students, like Fr. Inoue, to return home after their studies and construct local, situational, or contextual theologies. Back in Japan, Fr. Inuoe set about this task of inculturation by engaging three thinkers—Watsuji Tetsurō, Suzuki Daisetsu, and Kobayashi Hideo—who seemed united, for the most part, by their desire to reconcile Western and Japanese culture. In time Fr. Inoue combined his many, varied influences and crafted his own version of process panentheism. This West-East, mystical-theological overlay is "a panentheism in which nature never exists without the action of God and in which God and nature are neither the same nor separate," he says.[42] God is not the unsmiling, obstinate, and seemingly despotic ruler in the Hebrew Bible. God is the genuinely revered, dependable well-spring of sustenance and strength, who respects life's messy and stubborn facts yet purposes novel and imaginative events through the agency of created causes, who draws into the divine life whatever good is realized, and above all who collaborates with God's continuing creation in its battle against evil. An energetic and empathic theology of God as *abba*, *agape*, and *pneuma* carries this process panentheism forward, Yamamoto reveals, and for our purposes it seems instructive to note that Jesus of Nazareth, as *agape*'s and *pneuma*'s paradigm, is Fr. Inoue's symbol for not tarrying to count the cost involved in ministering to life's unlovely, the least of these (Matt 25:40).[43] Ōtsu's process panentheistic reflections resemble Fr. Inoue's, perhaps Endō's, too, and therefore I now turn to describe Ōtsu's properly Christic response to his evolving God through his many acts of loving wastefully by the banks of the Ganga.[44]

A Parable of Process Panentheism

Deep River signifies one of Endō's last attempts to articulate something he had felt his entire life, an intense or mystical experience of God's sustaining and stimulating presence in all things. Four textual moves gesture toward such process panentheism; and each move represents an important feature of his final fiction.

First, Endō uses chapter 3's terse discussion between Ōtsu and Mitsuko regarding God or the Onion to question the theological adequacy of European

Catholic Christianity.⁴⁵ Mitsuko feels distant from Thomism's remote God, we learn; and later, in chapter 6, Ōtsu bemoans Catholicism's desire for "excessive clarity," which fosters a faith that appears both "conscious and rational" yet disaffecting.⁴⁶ Ōtsu's seminary studies are heavy on God-talk's conceptual coherence, in other words, and light on spiritual joy. This struggle inspires Ōtsu to recast or inculturate his theology.⁴⁷

Second, the God of *Deep River* is a benevolent energy event, fructifying, as well as surrounding, life's changeability. "God is not so much an existence as a force," Ōtsu states.⁴⁸ Likewise: "I don't think God is someone to be looked up to as a being separate from man, the way you [Mitsuko] regard him. I think he is within man, and that he is a great life force that envelops man, envelops the trees, envelops the flowers and grasses."⁴⁹ Numada concurs, albeit for different reasons, and he implies that a process panentheistic deity sacralizes our emerging eco-system: "Nature had to be the medium that facilitated the interaction between man and the life force," Numada remarks.⁵⁰ On this view, the God-creation alliance is not one-sided. Rather, God influences and affects the world and the world affects and influences the divine. To accept this overlay, to try to live in terms of it, is to experience our becoming within an evolving world in which a dynamic and interrelated God is ceaselessly at work. All references to "force" do not mean the divine dominates and overrides creation; rather, they mean that an energetic God mobilizes and then invites cooperation from the world that God in each new moment calls forward to reflect the divine truth, beauty, and goodness.

Third, Ōtsu is an analogical theologian, which appears fitting for someone trained in Thomism, even if Ōtsu's panentheistic thinking pushes back against the traditional European descriptions of God as *impassibilis*, *actus purus*, and *ens realissimum*.⁵¹ Marked by "unbounded gentleness,"⁵² Ōtsu's God is circumambient love, the warmth of which takes different as well as many forms, yet it may best be seen in a mother's tireless affection for her child:

> Since my youth, thanks to my mother the one thing I was able to believe in was a mother's warmth. The warmth of her hand as it held mine, the warmth of her body when she cradled me, the warmth of her love, the warmth that kept her from abandoning me even though I was so much more dumbly sincere than my brothers and sisters. My mother told me all about the person you call my Onion, and she taught me that this Onion was a vastly more powerful accumulation of this warmth—in other words, love itself. I lost my mother when I got older, and I realized then that

what lay at the source of my mother's warmth was a portion of the love of my Onion. Ultimately what I have sought is nothing more than the love of that Onion, not any of the other innumerable doctrines mouthed by the various churches.[53]

A trace of Thomism in Ōtsu's allegedly heretical soul thus inspires him to ruminate analogically when thinking theologically. Later, he moves in his mind's eye from his mother to "my Onion," then from God to Jesus, "the warmth of life," and finally, from Jesus to Christians across time, the followers who have found themselves energized by their Master's example to serve others, by the banks of the Ganga or, indeed, anywhere where suffering holds people in thrall.[54] "And Ōtsu lifted such people on to his back as though shouldering a cross and brought them here to the river . . ."[55] This overlay might be styled "exemplarist soteriology."

Fourth, Ōtsu's exemplarist soteriology ties Christian discipleship to the act of loving wastefully, which explains *Deep River*'s serial allusions to Second Isaiah's Servant Song.[56] Ōtsu also frames his desire to imitate Christ through a process panentheistic lens: God or the Onion stirs within all created things as the inexhaustible source of life's surge, and all realities are in the divine life as contributors to God's open-ended experience of our emerging cosmos.[57] The whole of creation is internal to the divine, who upholds as well as receives all things, like the Ganga, Endō's image for God's creative-responsive love:

> Every time I look at the River Ganges, I think of my Onion. The Ganges swallows up the ashes of every person as it flows along, rejecting neither the beggar woman who stretches out her fingerless hands nor the murdered prime minister, Gandhi. The river of love that is my Onion flows past, accepting all, rejecting neither the ugliest of men nor the filthiest.[58]

Conclusion

In "Some Theological Mistakes and Their Effects on Modern Literature," the process panentheist Charles Hartshorne traces theological determinism as an implied metaphysic in the literary fiction of Thomas Love Peacock, Robinson Jeffers, William Wordsworth, Robert Frost, Thomas Hardy, and others.[59] I do not view Endō as determinist. On the contrary, Endō's God is giving-and-receiving love. Or, to use again the phrase I have suggested several times, Endō is a process panentheist. Saying this does not turn *Deep River* into some special kind of narrativized dogma or preachment. To assume that Endō's novel is basically tractarian is to evacuate it of its fictive power, and I do not wish to delimit *Deep River* in this fashion. I remain convinced, though, that theological accuracies (rather than, say, mistakes) are present in Endō's story, and that his way of thinking of ourselves as co-creators with God is an instructive place from which to reassess Endō's imaginative prose and its effects today.

Notes

1. For instructive coverage of this dimension, see Adelino Ascensio, *Transcultural Theodicy in the Fiction of Shūsaku Endō* (Roma: Editrice Pontifica Università Gregoriana, 2009), 12, 29–31, 47–49, 90, 139, 182–209; Emi Mase-Hasegawa, *Christ in Japanese Culture: Theological Themes in Shusaku Endo's Literary Works* (Leiden and Boston: Brill, 2008), 3–9, 61–91; and Mark B. Williams, *Endō Shūsaku: A Literature of Reconciliation* (London and New York: Routledge, 1999), 25–57.

2. Although the literature on panentheism is voluminous, one instructive survey may be found in John W. Cooper, *Panentheism—The Other God of the Philosophers: From Plato to the Present* (Grand Rapids, MI: Baker, 2006).

3. On panentheism's non-Western heritage, see Loriliai Biernacki and Philip Clayton, eds., *Panentheism Across the World's Traditions* (Oxford and New York: Oxford University Press, 2014).

4. Mase-Hasegawa, *Christ in Japanese Culture*, 7.

5. Shusaku Endo, *Deep River*, trans. Van C. Gessel (New York: New Directions, 1994), 192–93.

6. On the similarities and differences between these and other, related process thinkers, I am indebted to Douglas Browning and William T. Myers, eds., *Philosophers of Process* (New York: Fordham University Press, 1998); David Ray Griffin, et al., *Founders of Constructive Postmodern Philosophy: Pierce, James, Bergson, Whitehead, and Hartshorne* (Albany: State University of New York Press, 1993); and Charles Hartshorne and William L. Reese, *Philosophers Speak of God* (Chicago: University of Chicago Press, 1953).

7. For the unavoidably impressionistic account that follows, I use Daniel A. Dombrowski, *A History of the Concept of God: A Process Approach* (Albany: State University of New York Press, 2017); Bruce G. Epperly, *Process Theology: A Guide for the Perplexed* (London and New York: T&T Clark, 2011); Jay McDaniel and Donna Bowman, eds., *Handbook of Process Theology* (St. Louis, MO: Chalice Press, 2006); and Roland Faber, *God as Poet of the World: Exploring Process Theologies*, trans. Douglas W. Stott (Louisville and London: Westminster John Knox Press, 2004).

8. Alfred North Whitehead, *Process and Reality: An Essay in Cosmology*, corrected edition, ed. David Ray Griffin and Donald W. Sherburne (New York: The Free Press, 1978), 342.

9. Ōtsu's professors urge him to write a thesis on "scholasticism in the modern age." See Endo, *Deep River*, 49.

10. Ann Pederson, *Where in the World is God?: Variations on a Theme* (St. Louis, MO: Chalice Press, 1998), 1–16, 97–111, 144–48. Also see Paul S. Fiddes, *Participating in God: A Pastoral Doctrine of the Trinity* (Louisville, KY: Westminster John Knox Press, 2000), 131–37, 144–45, 180, 208, 278–302.

11. Donna Bowman, "God for Us: A Process View of the Divine-Human Relationship," in *Handbook of Process Theology*, ed. Jay McDaniel and Donna Bowman 11–24. Also see David A. Pailin, *God and the Processes of Reality: Foundations of a Credible Theism* (London and New York: Routledge, 1989), 76–95.

12. Joseph A. Bracken, S.J., *Christianity and Process Thought: Spirituality for a Changing World* (Philadelphia and London: Templeton Foundation Press, 2006).

13. Whitehead, *Process and Reality*, 348–49.

14. Endo, *Deep River*, 211. Mitsuko appears to internalize Ōtsu's earlier point: "I think the real dialogue takes place when you believe that God has many faces, and that he exists in all religions" (122). Although I recognize that Endō is writing literature and not theology, I am not alone in noting that John Hick's Christian pluralistic theology of religions runs through *Deep River*. One of the most instructive places to probe this theology is John Hick, *God Has Many Names* (Philadelphia: The Westminster Press, 1980), even if many Endō critics note that Endō read and admired the Japanese translation of Hick's *Problems of Religious Pluralism*. See Williams, *Endō Shūsaku*, 255n9.

15. Whitehead, *Process and Reality*, 351.

16. Pailin, *God and the Processes of Reality*, 174.

17. Endo, *Deep River*, 64.

18. Ascensio, *Transcultural Theodicy*, 48. See also Makoto Fujimura, *Silence and Beauty: Hidden Faith Born of Suffering* (Downers Grove, IL: InterVarsity Press, 2016), 85.

19. On the broader history of this question, see Mark B. Williams, "Crossing the Deep River: Endō Shūsaku and the Problem of Religious Pluralism," in *Xavier's Legacies: Catholicism in Modern Japanese Culture*, ed. Kevin Doak (Vancouver: UBC Press, 2011), 115–33; Mase-Hasegawa, *Christ in Japanese Culture*, 168–84; Ascensio, *Transcultural Theodicy*, 10–12, 15, 183, 193; and Anri Morimoto, "The (More or Less) Same Light But From Different Lamps: The Post-Pluralist Understanding of Religion from a Japanese Perspective," *International Journal for Philosophy of Religion* 53 (2003): 163–80. Finally, Endō addresses Hick's influence in Endō Shūsaku, *Fukai kawa sōsaku nikki* [*Deep River* composition diary] (Tokyo: Kōdansha, 1997), 24–25.

20. For details on the alliance between Hick, Endō, and Mase Hiromasa, see Mase-Hasegawa, *Christ in Japanese Culture*, 11, 139–80. A Keiō University professor of philosophy, Hiromasa is Mase-Hasegawa's father; intrigued readers should also probe Mase-Hasegawa's chapter in the present volume for additional reflections on the relationship between Hick, Endō, and her father.

21. John Hick, *An Autobiography* (London: Oneworld, 2002), 15, 117, 252–59, 271, 283, 285–87, 294, 316.

22. Yujin Nagasawa, "John Hick's Pan(en)theistic Monism," in *Religious Pluralism and the Modern World: An Ongoing Engagment with John Hick*, ed. Sharada Sugirtharajah and John Hick (Houndmills, Basingstoke, Hampshire, UK: Palgrave Macmillan, 2012), 176–89.

23. On Catholic process panentheism after 1965, see Robert L. Kinast, *Process Catholicism: An Exercise in Ecclesial Imagination* (Lanham, MD: University Press of America, 1999); and Illtyd Trethowan, *Process Theology and the Christian Tradition: An Essay in Post Vatican II Thinking* (Still River, MA: St. Bede's Publications, 1985). On Endō and post–Vatican II Catholic thought, see the essays by Mark Bosco, S.J., Christopher B. Wachal, Christal Whelan, and Elizabeth Cameron Galbraith in Mark W. Dennis and Darren J. N. Middleton, eds., *Approaching* Silence*: New Perspectives on Shusaku Endo's Classic Novel* (New York and London: Bloomsbury Academic, 2015).

24. Paul Lakeland, *The Wounded Angel: Fiction and the Religious Imagination* (Collegeville, MN: Liturgical Press, 2017), viii.

25. Interested readers should see Cooper, *Panentheism*, 224–27, 259–81. The work of Pierre Teilhard de Chardin lies behind their theologies; de Chardin is a process panentheist. William Johnston credits de Chardin with initiating valuable change in Roman Catholic thinking during the 1940s and '50s. See William Johnston, *Mystical Journey: An Autobiography* (Maryknoll, NY: Orbis Books, 2006), 77–90. Van C. Gessel reveals that Endō appears to have read de Chardin "since he [Endō] mentions him twice in *Watashi ni totte kami to wa* (What God Means to Me)." Personal e-mail to the author, July 7, 2017.

26. William Johnston, "Shusaku Endo discusses faith with his Jesuit translator," available online: https://www.americamagazine.org/issue/vantage-point/interview-shusaku-endo, September 30, 2016, accessed November 13, 2017.

27. Graham Greene, who inspired Endō in many ways, found such theologies fascinating. For details, see Mark Bosco, S.J., *Graham Greene's Catholic Imagination* (Oxford and New York: Oxford University Press, 2005). Also see Darren J. N. Middleton, "Endo and Greene's Literary Theology," in *Approaching* Silence, ed. Dennis and Middleton, 61–75. On Greene's own process panentheism, see Darren J. N. Middleton, "A Touch of Evolutionary Religion," in *Dangerous Edges of Graham Greene: Journeys with Saints and Sinners*, ed. Dermot Gilvary and Darren J. N. Middleton (New York and London: Continuum, 2011), 181–92. Finally, Anita Gandolfo's survey of how new theology influenced Catholic fiction repays close attention. See *Testing the Faith: The New Catholic Fiction in America* (Westport, CT: Greenwood Press, 1992).

28. Loriliai Biernacki, "Introduction: Panentheism Outside the Box," in Biernacki and Clayton, eds., *Panentheism*, 1–17.

29. John J. Keane, *Cultural and Theological Reflections on the Japanese Quest for Divinity* (Leiden and Boston: Brill, 2016).

30. Ibid., 3–43.

31. Ibid., 57.

32. Mase-Hasegawa, *Christ in Japanese Culture*, 7.

33. Ibid., 8–9.
34. Ibid., 63.
35. Ibid., 66n17.
36. Keane, *Cultural and Theological Reflections*, 47. "In order to make sure that his meaning would not be misunderstood," Keane adds, "Nishida wrote into his Japanese text the English word 'panentheism' " (47).
37. Personal e-mail to the author, July 10, 2017.
38. Keane, *Cultural and Theological Reflections*, 48–54. It is worth noting that Keane discusses Nishida's admiration for Jesus of Nazareth, as the exemplification of the tragic vulnerability that marks the God-world co-inherence, and that Keane considers Endō's *A Life of Jesus* and *Silence* instructive starting points for any future, fruitful dialogue between Christianity and Shinto (53, 150–55).
39. Johnston, *Mystical Journey*, 111.
40. Emi Mase-Hasegawa writes: "The character of Ōtsu is based on Endō's best friend Fr. Inoue Yōji. Endō trusted Fr. Inoue's theology." Personal e-mail to the author, July 2, 2017. Van C. Gessel adds: "It's pretty commonly said among Endō critics in Japan that Ōtsu is modeled after Fr. Inoue, but as I indicate in my essay [in the present volume], Ōtsu really is an interesting blend of Inoue and Endō himself. Though I haven't read deeply in Fr. Inoue's writings, I would venture to say that Ōtsu's perambulations are a lot like Fr. Inoue's, but many of his attitudes toward Western Christianity match those of both Inoue and Endō." Personal e-mail to the author, July 10, 2017.
41. Yoshihisa Yamamoto, "The Theory and Practice of Inculturation by Father Inoue Yōji: From Panentheism to *Namu Abba*," in *Xavier's Legacies*, ed. Doak, 147.
42. Ibid., 149.
43. Ibid., 151–62.
44. On the links between Fr. Inoue and Endō, see this volume's chapter nine.
45. Endo, *Deep River*, 63.
46. Ibid., 117, 121.
47. Ibid., 66.
48. Ibid., 64.
49. Ibid., 118.
50. Ibid., 133. Also see 131.
51. These three Latin theological terms, popular in the Scholastic period, refer to God as: incapable of suffering; pure actuality; and, the most real being.
52. Endo, *Deep River*, 67.
53. Ibid., 119.
54. Ibid., 124.
55. Ibid., 162.
56. Ibid., 44, 116, 175, 190–93, 205–16. Note that when Hindu nationalists beat Ōtsu, he emits a "cry of pain that sounded like the bleating of a lamb," which accentuates both Ōtsu's role as *alter Christus* and Endō's exemplarist soteriology (212).
57. Ibid., 162, 184, 190–93, 215.

58. Ibid., 185.

59. Charles Hartshorne, "Some Theological Mistakes and Their Effects on Modern Literature," *Journal of Speculative Philosophy* 1, no. 1 (1987): 55–72.

Chapter Fourteen

Japanese Sensibility and Transcendence in *Deep River*

DENNIS HIROTA

[A]nybody who did not know about the basic principles on which the religions [of the Japanese] are founded, might often well think that both we and they are preaching the same thing. . . . [Y]ou would think that they are talking about the one, supreme, true God, Saviour of the world.[1]

—Luis Frois, S.J. (1532–1597), *Historia Eclesiastica*

[Japan] never, to this day, has become an axial civilization. . . . Japan has absorbed several major axial traditions: Confucianism, Buddhism, Christianity . . . yet, I would argue, it is non-axial, because it has used, with great brilliance and success, axial culture to defend its archaic presuppositions.[2]

—Robert Bellah, *Religion in Human Evolution*

Introduction

Shūsaku Endō's final novel, *Deep River*, engages two major themes. One is the discord between the native "sensibility characteristic of the Japanese,"[3] on the one hand, and Christianity, at least as shaped by a Western or "European" mode of thought, on the other. This is a matter that occupied Endō throughout his career, from his first published fiction nearly four decades earlier.[4] The second is the depiction in contemporary terms of a relationship to transcendence as a quality of human existence. This entails the delineation of an overarching pattern that embraces different ways of understanding the quest for transcendence and its significance, a model that may be seen as shared and embodied by the world's major religious traditions.

While each of these themes raises a variety of questions, in this chapter I will focus on a further issue: What, for Endō, is the relationship between the two themes? Are there features of the "Japanese sensibility" depicted in *Deep River* that, despite the indifference to cardinal concerns of European Christianity that Endō attributes to that sensibility, allow him finally to reconcile being Japanese and being Christian? And can such elements enable a broad acknowledgment of the religious aspirations harbored in diverse traditions? While the urgency of such questions was deeply personal for Endō, he also recognized its emerging global immediacy. This urgency is implied in the novel itself, which interweaves, as backdrop to its closing scenes, the assassination of Indira Gandhi, an act of religious violence occurring scarcely a decade before the novel's publication.[5] As the narrator says: "Revenge and hatred were not limited to the world of politics, but were the same in the realm of religion."[6] We may further ask, then: What does Endō's resolution of his dilemma in *Deep River* say to us today?

Japanese (In)sensibility and Christianity

Endō acutely experienced the rift between common Japanese attitudes and Christian beliefs from childhood, and his quandary finds direct expression from his earliest works. In the novella *Yellow Man*, the narrative takes the form of a long letter to a French Catholic priest by a Japanese medical student suffering illness and spiritual malaise near the end of World War II. The student, raised as Christian, recalls playing in an old burial mound as a boy in the Kansai region: "Within the darkness of the burial mound, I experienced a strange fascination. A quiet you know nothing of—the stillness of a heathen faith, without any fear of death, any trembling at sin, or eternal hell—came over even a child's mind."[7] The "stillness of a heathen faith," characterized here as freedom from "fear of death, any trembling at sin," belongs in Endō's mind to the "Japanese sensibility" that has rendered the Japanese impervious to the guilt and anxieties he sees entrenched in the hard logic of European Christian teachings and attitudes. As the student confesses earlier in this passage: "I don't care anymore whether or not God exists."[8]

This point is reiterated in *Yellow Man* in the diary of the Frenchman Durand, a defrocked priest living in Japan, which, interwoven with the student's letter, forms the second major element of the novella. The former priest describes the Japanese people among whom he had proselytized: "Theirs are the eyes of a people indifferent to God and to sin and impassive in the face of death."[9] Further, the diary continues, "That *nan-mai-da* that Kimiko [the priest's common-law wife] sometimes utters is not in the least like our prayer; it's a spell convenient for their insensitivity to sin."[10] Here, Endō alludes to Japanese Pure Land Buddhism, particularly Shin Buddhism (*Jōdo Shinshū*), which teaches that saying the Name of Amida Buddha, *Namu-amida-butsu*, with trust in the Buddha's vow of universal salvation brings one into the power of his compassionate working. Shin Buddhism serves throughout Endō's works as the preeminent native religious tradition that stands in comparison to European Christianity.[11] It both reflects and informs Japanese perceptions and thinking.

Endō's insights here regarding the ambiguity of Japanese attitudes toward God, sin, death, and damnation are corroborated by the acerbic remarks of Christian missionaries from the time of earliest contact. The Portuguese Jesuit Luis Frois, who spent more than thirty years in Japan from 1563 and recorded astute observations of Japanese social life, writes, probably with Shin Buddhist priests in mind: "[I]f you accepted their terms and propositions at face value without any further discussion, you would think that they are talking about the one, supreme, true God, Saviour of the world. But in their reasoning and conclusions, all this is a delusion."[12]

The Existence of God, Repentance, and Prayer

Three centuries later, the American Protestant M. L. Gordon (1844–1900), an experienced missionary leader fluent in Japanese, noted with frustration "the difficulty of bringing the Buddhist to an adequate conception of God":

> If we were to ask the priest who preaches this [Japanese Pure Land Buddhist] doctrine of "Salvation by faith in the power of another [i.e., Amida Buddha]," whether Amida really exists or not, he would perhaps after some squirming admit that either view of the case is perfectly admissible.[13]

Gordon recognizes Buddhism, and Shin Buddhism in particular, as the major obstacle to Christian proselytization in Japan and is at pains to convey to his fellow missionaries the nature of the difficulties faced in addressing the Japanese outlook shaped by Shin teachings. Just as the Pure Land Buddhists are apparently comfortable without confirming the existence of Amida Buddha, so they aspire to be born into Amida's Buddha-field in the west, the Pure Land, without need to assert its physical reality. Gordon writes:

> [Pure Land Buddhist priests] do not believe the Western Paradise has an objective existence, but they encourage thousands to live and die with that as the chief object of their hopes. They threaten the wicked with . . . innumerable hells, but believe all the while that the human heart is the only hell.[14]

Challenging Pure Land beliefs with the ontological presuppositions of Western rationality is thus problematic.

Moreover, Gordon continues: "The inevitable result of all this is utter skepticism and indifference to sin."[15] For Gordon, the "objective existence" of God is the lynchpin not only of genuine religious faith but also of moral life. He reflects in his autobiography, "Christianity brings a sense of sin which the other religions [of Japan: Shintōism, Buddhism, Confucianism] . . . do not produce," and writes:

> One old lady testified that she had hardly thought of herself as a sinner, until she began to hear this "new way" [of Christianity]. Then her sins stood up before her in strong condemnation. . . . If the old religions bring no adequate sense of sin, how can they produce a genuine repentance? . . . [If there is] no sense of sin and deep repentance, true prayer by sinful man is impossible.[16]

This is precisely Durand's point in *Yellow Man*: the Japanese have vocal *nembutsu*, saying the Name of Amida, instead of the heartfelt practice of earnest prayer that Western Christians know.

I have quoted from influential Christian missionaries to Japan to indicate that the evident dissonances Endō identifies and thematizes between Japanese perspectives and the imported Christianity—the Japanese indifference to issues of the existence of God and the absence of grave anguish at sin or foreboding at death and damnation—are neither a merely personal response nor exaggerated by the novelist. How, then, can the discord between such sensibility and Christianity be understood and resolved? How is the aspiration of Ōtsu in *Deep River*, and of Endō himself—"I want to contemplate a Christianity that accords with the minds of the Japanese"[17]—to be achieved?

Endō and Pre-axial Religion

In considering the implications regarding religion of the "sensibilities of the Japanese" as depicted in *Deep River*, it will be useful to bear in mind a larger concept that, though not embraced by Endō, almost certainly engaged him during the composition of the novel. This is the notion of the "axial age" as a transformative period for religious awareness, with far-reaching consequences for civilizational history globally. In 1991, when over a year into the writing of *Deep River*, Endō happened on books by the theologian John Hick, whose work on religious pluralism seeks to provide a conceptual framework for grasping particular religious traditions in terms of a broad human religiosity.

Underpinning Hick's thinking is Karl Jaspers's concept of the "axial age," the middle centuries of the first millennium BCE during which new conceptions of the nature of reality and human existence arose. In *God Has Many Names*, one of two books by Hick that Endō explicitly mentions during the composition of *Deep River*, the theologian discusses "the axial period, in which seminal moments of religious experience occurred in each of the four principal centers of civilization—Greece, the Near East, India, and China—out of which the higher religions [e.g., Buddhism and Christianity] have come."[18] The impact of Endō's discovery for *Deep River*'s themes is apparent in Hick's assertion of a unifying vision of religious traditions: "In this period all the major religious options, constituting the *different forms of human awareness of the Eternal One*, were identified and established."[19]

As Endō notes excitedly in his diary, this paradigm for understanding the historical emergence of the major religious traditions enables Hick to "call for the relinquishing of the theology of Jesus as the Christ and the clearing up of such issues as Jesus's incarnation and the problems of the trinity"; "the religions of the world seek the same God through different paths, cultures, symbols."[20] In *Deep River*, Endō traces in his narrative a turn from the God of the theologians to the Eternal One of human religiosity—the transcendent to which the Japanese also can respond. In naming the central character involved in this turn *Augustine*, Ōtsu, Endō surely had in mind the words Augustine of Hippo addressed to God: "Our hearts are restless until they rest in you."[21] The novel depicts the human aspiration for the Eternal One taking form in the minds of a handful of modern Japanese.

Hick's use of the concept of axial religion provides a model for seeking to go beyond the absolutization of doctrinal particulars to a ground of commonality among religious traditions. At the same time, however, it conceptualizes the impasse that Endō long discerned in the case of Christianity in Japan. This is because the native religiosity, which reflects and informs the "sensibilities of the Japanese," displays the typical characteristics of religious life prior to the axial transformation. Japan and Christianity fall on opposite sides of the axial divide.

The contrast between pre-axial and axial religion has been discussed in various ways. A convenient outline of the main points of much recent thinking may be found in Charles Taylor's *A Secular Age*.[22] Taylor speaks of pre-axial self-awareness as characterized by a threefold embeddedness: "Human agents are embedded in society, society in the cosmos, and the cosmos incorporates the divine," so that there is a multi-faceted "embedding in existing reality."[23] In essence, the cosmos of existing reality is whole and all-encompassing; there is no conception of something beyond. Thus, persons are embedded in the society to which they belong, so that their identity is conceived in terms of interrelationships within that society: as a member of a family, clan, tribe, and so on. In Taylor's portrayal of the pre-axial mind, people "couldn't conceive of themselves as potentially disconnected from this social matrix."[24] Here, "religious life is inseparably linked with social life . . . the primary agency of important religious action . . . was the social group as a whole."[25] People "relate to God as a society."[26]

Second, the society and all its members are embedded in the cosmos, an "enchanted world" with "intracosmic spirits" and "causal powers which were embedded in things: relics, sacred places, and the like."[27] Third, human flourishing is understood in terms of the goods of ordinary life: "What the people ask for when they invoke or placate divinities and powers is prosperity, health, long life, fertility; what they ask to be preserved from is disease, dearth, sterility, premature death."[28]

The axial revolution is commonly described as the emergence of notions of transcendent reality beyond the immediately apprehended and experienced "existing reality." The advent of the transcendent works toward "a break in all three dimensions of embeddedness: social order, cosmos, human good."[29] This "disembedding" enables a critical, revisionary stance that calls "into question the received, seemingly unquestionable understanding of human flourishing, and hence inevitably also the structures of society and the features of the cosmos through which this flourishing was supposedly achieved."[30]

Japan and Axial Religion

In *God Has Many Names*, Hick describes pre-axial religion in similar terms but more concretely than Taylor as "above all a force of social cohesion,"[31] with "an immense variety of tribal gods and spirits, in many cases personifying the forces of nature."[32] In a slightly later work he describes the pre-axial communal life in which "forest, hills, streams, rocks, sky are full of unseen beings and forces. . . . There are the local gods and spirits, sometimes ancestors . . . to be variously worshipped. . . . In the new year festival there was an 'annual expulsion of sins, disease, and demons,'" and so on.[33] For readers familiar with Japan, such descriptions leap to life as the still vital traditional folk religious practices now identified as Shintō.

Endō had already from his early works incorporated the ambience of the native religiosity as contrasting with Christian modes of thinking: for example, the ancient burial mound of *Yellow Man*, or, in *Silence*, the social embeddedness of the Christian villagers and the enchanted cosmos of the *obon* "festival of lanterns" rituals.[34] It is not surprising that his work has been seen in the context of larger questions of Japan's relationship with axial traditions. The sociologist S. N. Eisenstadt writes in his study, *Japanese Civilization: A Comparative View*:

> Numerous external influences . . . have been incorporated into Japanese culture. . . . [A] central aspect of Japanese historical experience has been that most such borrowings, while very influential, have been thoroughly "Japanized," that is, organized or *structured according to principles specific to the Japanese experience or modes of life*. This capacity of the Japanese to absorb . . . has been vividly described by Endō Shūsaku, in his novel *Silence*, in the powerful metaphor of the Japanese swamp. This "swamping" capacity can be identified in . . . the transformation of Christian beliefs.[35]

The swamp image is of course a recurring motif throughout Endō's works (in *Deep River*, the name of the author of children's literature—the character who shares Endō's childhood and medical experience—includes the word "swamp" or "marsh," *numa*).[36]

In perhaps his last extensive treatment of Japan, "The Japanese Difference," Robert Bellah expresses a view close to Eisenstadt's:

> Since at least the seventh century Japan has been deeply influenced by Buddhist and Confucian ideas. . . . And since the sixteenth century Japan has been influenced by Christianity and Western civilization. But in the face of these religious and civilizational influences the Japanese have not rejected their pre-axial civilizational

premises; instead they have continuously revised them without abandoning them.[37]

While Eisenstadt speaks of the restructuring of external influences, Bellah speaks of a "continuous revision" of Japan's civilizational premises in engagement with religious thought from abroad. These two aspects of interfusion appear to be Endō's focal interest in considering Christianity in Japan. Thus, although he finds corroboration for his thinking in Hick's views, he does not follow Hick in adopting the notion of a fundamental break between pre-axial and axial awareness. Rather, Endō points toward a mutual enhancement or evolution stemming from the encounter of what might be categorized as the pre-axial and the axial, as in Ōtsu's suggestion to his examiners in Lyon that Europeans around Chartres "sublimated a belief in their local earth mother goddess to a belief in the Holy Mother," so that they "fostered a Christianity that has its roots in their faith in the earth mother goddess."[38]

Further, throughout Endō's novels, the chief foil or comparative model in Japan for Christianity is not the native Shintō, but Pure Land Buddhism, a tradition recognized as fundamentally axial. Thus, the question unformulated by Endō but implied in *Deep River* is not merely whether Japanese culture, with its "non-axial" religious and sociopolitical practices in tact, can relate to and accommodate Christianity, but whether by doing so, it not only offers an innovative vision of "a Christianity that accords with the minds of the Japanese," but further manifests a paradigm by which axial traditions can re-attune their apprehension of transcendence in a manner that frees them from traces of an inherently irreconcilable exclusivism.

Endō and Shinran

In the remainder of this chapter, I will take up several facets of what Endō calls "the sensibilities characteristic of the Japanese," as indicated or evoked in *Deep River*, and consider them briefly in relation to the non-axial–axial divide. These attitudes and perspectives may be taken as coordinates in configuring a general mode of thought and perception, and they function as structuring principles in the adoption or adaptation of axial religious traditions. Further, as "touchstone" to substantiate Endō's portrayal of native attitudes, I will refer in each case to the thought of Shinran (1173–1263), from whom the Shin Buddhist tradition stems. This is not an arbitrary choice. We have already seen that Catholic missionaries in the sixteenth century and Protestants in the nineteenth noted the prominence and influence of Shin Buddhism in the Japanese religious landscape. More significantly for our concerns here, from Endō's own references and allusions in his essays to *Tannishō*, a thirteenth-century record of Shinran's spoken words that is probably the most widely read religious writing in modern Japan, it is evident that he was not only familiar with the work, but had reflected seriously on Shinran's thought.

Moreover, in 1979, halfway between the publications of his best-known novels, *Silence* and *Deep River*, Endō produced a book titled *Shinran Lectures* together with a well-known scholar of Buddhism, Masutani Fumio.[39] The book is a transcript of lectures by Masutani delivered in a private seminar, interspersed with questions and comments by Endō. We can assume from this book that at least by mid-career, Endō possessed a broad knowledge of Shinran's life, writings, and Buddhist thought, one that went well beyond the familiarity with *Tannishō* clearly apparent in his essays.

Shinran Lectures opens with a comment by Endō together with a general question to start off the lectures. His question stems from his historical interest in the conditions that gave rise to a number of new Buddhist schools in the twelfth and thirteenth centuries. His comment, however, is meant to frame the entire seminar and reveals the focus of his concerns: "I am primarily interested in why it is that Shinran's Buddhist path—Jōdo Shinshū—has spread so pervasively and so deeply among the Japanese people."[40] Shin Buddhism, in other words, is for Endō that religious tradition that most fully manifests—whether through influence or through assimilation—the deep-rooted sensibilities of the Japanese.

"Eastern Pantheism"

In *Deep River*, "pantheism" is a term Ōtsu's teachers in Lyon use to denounce his views, and that Ōtsu himself employs in counterargument:

> I said: "God has many different faces. I don't think God exists exclusively in the churches and chapels of Europe. I think he is also among the Jews and the Buddhists and the Hindus" . . . to my teachers it sounded like an outright rejection of the Christian Church. I was viciously reprimanded: "these are the notions born of your pantheistic error!"[41]

For Ōtsu's French examiners, his views are a species of atheism, a denial of the absolute, transcendent God in the form of asserting that all is a divine unity. Ōtsu's declaration that "God has many faces," however, echoes Hick,[42] and his statements here suggest that his view might be better characterized as a *panentheism*,[43] with the divine existing not as, but *within* all beings and things of this world. The central issue, however, remains the pivotal axial assertion of a transcendent reality and an ultimate concern lying outside of the world of ordinary interests and experience. Pantheistic beliefs may be seen as symptomatic of pre-axial views of an enclosed cosmos that encompasses divine spirits and forces.

In his early essays, Endō identifies the native Japanese apprehension of a cosmos populated by myriads of *kami* as an "*Eastern* pantheism" distinct from the Western concept.[44] In *Yellow Man*, the defrocked former missionary states, "Though the Japanese have had gods (*kami-gami*), they have absolutely never had one God."[45] In the passage quoted above, Ōtsu goes on to claim that the faith of many early Christian converts in Japan in the sixteenth and seventeenth centuries "was different from that of the people of Europe"; he adds, "There were Buddhist elements, and elements of the pantheism that you just now condemned, intermingled in their attitude of faith."[46] Here, Endō suggests integration in the Japanese engagement with Christianity that lies between simple acceptance and complete absorption into Japanese life.

A central aspect of Christianity for Endō is the concept of love, which he recognizes is congenial to Japanese intuitions but not a Buddhist term. Thus, Ōtsu seeks to distance himself from commonplace Western notions of God as an existence standing apart from and above created things and at the same time to indicate a mode of understanding the Christian conception of love in a manner compatible with native perceptions: "Rather than an existence, God is a working. The Onion is simply the congealment of love performing its work."[47] The Onion is, of course, Ōtsu's symbol for the nonsubstantialist divine, the God compatible with Japanese perceptions and aspirations. From a newspaper column published during the period of the composition of *Deep River*, it is clear that these thoughts given to Ōtsu are Endō's own. There Endō states: "God is not an existence, but a working. Moreover, I have been able to experience this working in various ways in my own life."[48]

All-Pervading Life

There are two prominent themes in *Deep River* by which Endō emphasizes the implications of an "Eastern pantheism" and its contrast with modern Western presuppositions. One is the rejection of the anthropocentricism of much Western religious thought. The same newspaper column in which Endō asserts that God "is not an existence, but a working" opens with his report of learning that the citizens of a coastal community in Kyūshū profess that their deceased became fish in the local waters. This altogether plausible anecdote, which includes the ecological concern of the people regarding a polluting factory, is fully woven into *Deep River* as the example of Numada's work as an author of children's literature.[49] It is consistent with the narratives of Numada's relationships with a pet dog and myna bird, and also with the narrative of Isobe's wife and her conviction of rebirth. Further, as the wife's dialogue with a tree outside the hospital window indicates, in Endō's conception of pantheism in Japan, divinity as "life" extends to plants and trees. In a letter to Mitsuko, Ōtsu writes:

> As a Japanese, I find it unbearable that [Europeans] pay no heed to the immense life of nature. . . . In the Christianity of Europe, there is a hierarchy among living things. These people will never be able to understand [Bashō's haiku]: "On looking closely/ shepherd's purse is blooming /under the hedge."[50]

Ōtsu's reference to Bashō may appear tenuous, but elsewhere in *Deep River*, Numada mentions the traditional association of cherry trees with the spirits of the dead in Japan, and he further notes the resonance with the Hindu belief "that trees bear within them the life force that produces rebirth."[51] He comments that his next story will feature the interchanges between trees and children, asserting the notion of trees as chief characters that already occurs in Japan in the medieval *nō* plays.

Endō refers directly to the Pure Land Buddhist tradition through the character of Kiguchi, who wishes to have a memorial service performed for comrades who perished in the senseless and disastrous campaign to invade India during World War II.[52] At critical points of epiphany in *Deep River*—in the cave of Chāmundā and on the banks of the Ganges—Kiguchi recites from the *Amida Sūtra*, bringing Japanese Buddhism into the ground of religious encounter. As Mitsuko says, "It's a deep river, so deep I feel as though it's not just for the Hindus but for everyone."[53] At the river, Kiguchi intones: "In that Buddha-land there are always many kinds of exquisite, multicolored birds. . . . When a gentle breeze stirs the rows of jeweled trees and jeweled nets, they send forth delicate sounds."[54] He chants the short sutra in its entirety, the traditional Pure Land deathbed ritual, from which Endō quotes two brief passages that resonate with his "pantheistic" themes of all-pervasive and all-encompassing life.

Cosmocentric Awareness

Turning to Shinran's writings in order to consider the inflection of the Japanese development of Pure Land tradition, we find:

> Nirvana is called extinction of passions, the uncreated ... true reality, ... suchness, ... Buddha-nature. ... Tathagata. This Tathagata [Buddha as reality] pervades the countless worlds; it fills the hearts and minds of the ocean of all beings. Thus, plants, trees, and land all attain Buddhahood.[55]

Shinran emphasizes the essential character of the Mahāyāna Buddhist conception of wisdom as fundamentally nondiscriminative and nondualistic, speaking here of the working of Buddha-wisdom to compassionately bring all beings to the same awakening. Although the mode of thinking is divergent at its roots, Endō's notion of God as the working of love holds clear resonances. In the highlighting of the dimension of immanence, both Pure Land Buddhism and Christianity draw back from an unmitigated "disembedding" from the cosmos, to borrow Taylor's expression for the hallmark of the axial stance.

Shinran's words extend to the second prominent theme of Endō's "Eastern pantheism," for the passage continues, "Since it is with this heart and mind [pervaded by Tathāgata, or Buddha-wisdom] of all sentient beings that they entrust themselves to the Vow of the dharma-body as compassionate means, their entrusting is itself none other than Buddha-nature."[56] The identification of beings' entrusting of themselves to Amida's Vow with the Buddha-mind that fills all beings reflects a view of mental faculties that the philosopher Nishitani Keiji describes as "cosmocentric." Here, "the 'minds' which exist within all individual living things or human beings are individualizations of the great 'mind' extending throughout the world."[57] According to Nishitani, there are generally "two ways of viewing the mind, cosmocentric and self-centric."[58] While "ever since Christianity became dominant, the main axis of thought in the West has to this day been the egocentric way," both the cosmocentric and self-centric views "have been inseparably preserved throughout Buddhism, in marked contrast to the West."[59]

As a prime example of the Buddhist understanding of mind, Nishitani discusses the concept of the *ālaya*-consciousness:

> Constituting the basis of our minds, [*ālaya*-consciousness] is at the same time of the nature of what may be called a cosmic consciousness, or rather a cosmic unconscious ... the *ālaya*-consciousness

is understood to include the aspect we call universal "life" on the world-plane. . . . At the root of and at one with cosmic "mind" is a "life" . . . which encompasses the entire process of being conceived . . . being born . . . a "life" embracing the entire spectrum of the life of the flesh, the unconscious, and consciousness. Such an *ālaya*-consciousness lies latent at the base of the human mind and of the minds of all living things.[60]

I quote at length here because Endō was himself deeply interested in this thought:

I was startled at how closely the way of thinking about the unconscious in Mahāyāna Buddhism resembles that of contemporary Christian novelists. . . . In the same way as with Christian novelists, in Buddhism also the human *ālaya*-consciousness (the unconscious) is regarded as the womb of evil acts. But not only that. . . . The Buddha's working is also considered to be the unconscious. In the *ālaya*-consciousness . . . the latent power of karma from previous lives and of afflicting passions and self-attachment is swirling, but at the same time there is also a power working to purify the seeds of evil acts.[61]

Ōtsu's identification of God with a working both of "life" and "love" is connected with an acknowledgment of the unconscious latent in living things in ways he finds denied by "the clarity and logic of the way Europeans think."[62] As he states: "My Japanese sensibilities have made me feel out of harmony with European Christianity. . . . The faith of the Europeans is *conscious* and rational."[63] It is in India that the nature of "life" functioning in human existence becomes manifest, in the cave of Chāmundā, the storehouse of turmoil that is the womb of human existence, and at the deep river that draws all to its banks and in its currents "embraces everything about mankind."[64]

The Nondualism of Good and Evil

Endō's diary entries touching on the composition and publication of *Deep River*, beginning on August 26, 1990, have been published as a book.[65] The entries begin with simply a telegraphic list of three characters. The second entry to mention concretely the eventual contents of the novel, albeit only in a few lines, dates from August 28, where a list of three characters begins:

> Mrs. Yoshikawa [later Naruse Mitsuko] sees a statue of a Hindu goddess at the New Delhi museum and ponders how it is possessed of a dual nature—that what is good and what is evil exist together in it. Gradually, she considers that this is what it means to be human. However, she aspires for something immense that encompasses such human existence. Mother Teresa.[66]

At the very outset of the composition process, Endō enshrines the Indian goddess Chāmundā and the encounter with her at the heart of the novel. At some point, he situated the statue in a cave-temple, where "the repulsiveness of the statues called forth the loathing that human beings experience when they squarely catch sight of what is writhing in the underside of their own consciousness, what secretes itself beneath their conscious minds,"[67] in their unconscious. The Japanese visitors entering the cave distance themselves from the images as "unconnected to their own lives."[68] But propelled by the nascent awareness of her quest for the transcendent, "Mitsuko had the impression that she was beginning a descent into the depths of her heart."[69] The cave-temple is the re-embodiment, after forty years, of the ancient "heathen" burial mound of *Yellow Man*.

The axial-age disembedding of the individual from the society becomes possible because a way unfolds for a person to assume a stance in the transcendent and accord with its nature. This enables the critical distance for assessing actions within and by the social milieu. The integrity of the individual and the critical perspective on the world are crucial elements of the thinking regarding axial traditions. Ōtsu, however, senses the danger of usurpation by the merely human-created, perhaps a form of idolatry:

> The ways of thinking that [Europeans] have kneaded with their own hands and fashioned to meet the workings of their hearts . . . are ponderous to an Asian like me. . . . I can't make the clear distinction that these people make between good and evil. I think that evil lurks within good, and that good things can lie latent within evil as well. That's the very reason God can wield his magic. He made use even of my sins and turned me toward salvation.[70]

Later, in a letter to Mitsuko, Ōtsu reiterates his distress with his teachers' sharp differentiation of good and evil and declaiming of moral judgments as though universal and unconditional: "I was scolded for this notion ('God makes use not only of our good acts, but even of our sins in order to save us') at the novitiate. . . . I was told that good and evil are polar opposites and absolutely mutually exclusive."[71] The oppressive atmosphere that Ōtsu (and Endō) reacted against in France has been characterized by Taylor as a "moralism," which he sees as gradually developing in European Christian tradition so that "modern liberal society tends toward a kind of 'code fetishism.'"[72] It is an inversion of the original axial priorities, which a French nun describes in analyzing a nineteenth century catechism: "morality takes precedence over everything, and religion becomes its servant. Faith and the sacraments are no longer understood as the basis of the moral life, but as duties . . . to help us fulfill these moral obligations."[73] We may note that what Taylor calls "the perils of moralism" were already noted by Shinran: "If it were only by observing precepts and upholding rules that we should entrust ourselves to Amida Buddha's Primal Vow, how could we ever gain freedom from samsaric existence?"[74]

At bottom, the rift between the perspectives labeled "Eastern" ("Asian") and "European" by Ōtsu turns on the understanding of human existence. The Japanese outlook, as Endō characterizes it, is one of ineluctable embeddedness, both social and cosmic. This does not disallow transcendence, but it is not that an individual, through intellect and will, breaks through the social and cultural embeddedness to attain the genuine good that lies beyond. Rather, the transcendent must inject itself into the embeddedness and enter into beings, becoming nondifferent from them, transforming rather than eradicating their afflicting passions. It must possess the dynamic character of nondiscrimination, so that it draws and ultimately embraces them in their finitude. In this context, notions of the autonomous individual resolutely casting off the bonds of situatedness and achieving the stance of the transcendent carry little persuasive power.

Near the conclusion of *Deep River*, Kiguchi, about to chant the *Amida Sūtra* in memory of his war comrades, reflects: "What I've been thinking . . . is what in Buddhism is called 'the nonduality of good and evil,' that there's nothing a human being does that can be called absolutely right. To put it the opposite way, the seeds of salvation lie latent within every act of evil."[75] Endō, in his essays, quotes the words of Shinran expressing the religious self-awareness of incapacity: "It is impossible for us, filled as we are with blind passions, to free ourselves from birth-and-death through any practice whatever. Sorrowing at this, Amida made the Vow, the essential intent of which is the attainment of Buddhahood by the person who is evil."[76]

Cosmic Embeddedness

The sense of embeddedness that underlies the Japanese outlook depicted by Endō fundamentally tempers the modern Western individualism and the conviction of personal autonomy and the powers of discretion and will. It is the awareness that one cannot know the deepest forces and conditions that shape one's person and inhabit one's psyche. Further, one's existence is an interplay of dynamics that extend outward in all directions and into the past far beyond any capacity to fathom.

There are various facets of the embeddedness in nature or the cosmos. For example, Shinran states: "All sentient beings, without exception, have been our parents and brothers and sisters in the course of countless lives in the many states of existence. On attaining Buddhahood after this present life, we will be able to save every one of them."[77] Each person has personal bonds with all other life forms going back into the unknowable past. Endō evokes this intuition in Isobe's search for his wife's reincarnation, during which he comes to grasp the nature of "the bond uniting a husband and wife: the bond that brought two people to become lifelong companions from amidst the countless men and women in the world. . . . Isobe now had the feeling that those bonds had existed even before birth."[78]

Shinran's awareness of embeddedness, however, is not the pre-axial enclosed cosmos of Shintō, shared with gods and spirits of the dead. Rather, it coexists with the working of the transcendent. Thus, he closes his major treatise with the words:

> I have collected true words . . . in order that the process be made continuous, without end and without interruption, by which those who have been born [into Amida's Buddha-field] guide those who come later, and those who are born later join those who were born before. This is so that the boundless ocean of birth-and-death be exhausted.[79]

In her budding realization, Mitsuko similarly comes to speak of "a river of humanity," although she intimates an apprehension of the transcendent as she confesses: "I still don't know what lies at the end of that flowing river. But I feel as though I've started to understand what I was yearning for."[80]

This embeddedness includes a moral dimension, as we have already seen. Because our very existence is conditioned by myriad past causes and interconnected with the lives of all other beings, we cannot know fully the moral quality of the acts—whether good or evil—we may have committed in the past or what, given the circumstances, we may be capable of in the future. Shinran states: "If the karmic cause so prompts us, we will commit any kind of act."[81] Endō develops this theme in the context of warfare, sickness, and starvation, in the plight of Kiguchi's war comrades.

Thus, the transcendent occurs as an encompassing, dynamic power. Ōtsu speaks of God as "the river of love . . . accepting all, rejecting neither the ugliest of men nor the filthiest."[82] Shinran prefers the image of the ocean: "the Buddha's nondiscriminating, unobstructed, and nonexclusive guidance of all sentient beings is likened to the all-embracing waters of the great ocean."[83] There is no trace of an absolutized moralism, but rather a transformation. Thus Enami speaks of the all-accepting "maternal waters," "a holy, motherly river," where "holy" means to embrace all without differentiation, "both the living and the dead."[84] As Mitsuko states, "This river embraces everything about mankind."[85] Shinran states, "Rivers of blind passions, on entering the ocean/ of Amida's great, compassionate Vow . . . become one in taste with that sea of wisdom."[86]

In Shinran's thinking, there is at once the recognition of a kind of cosmic embeddedness that is characteristic of pre-axial worldviews, for human existence is inexorably conditioned. Simultaneously, however, the transformative dynamic of transcendent reality draws beings to self-awareness. Thus, "When Amida's active means toward us reaches fulfillment/we realize the trust and practice of the compassionate Vow/Then birth-and-death is itself nirvana."[87] Something of this nondual structure informs Endō's Christian understanding of religious awakening. Thus Mitsuko reflects, "the Onion died in the distant past, but has undergone rebirth within other human beings. Even after a span of nearly two thousand years . . . he underwent rebirth within Ōtsu."[88]

Communal Embeddedness

The Japanese outlook acknowledges the inherent cultural particularism in human life. Human beings do not fundamentally exist as free floating individuals, but rather as members of a particular society, situated culturally and historically. Our thinking and perceptions are informed by the language and social practices that we have acquired from infancy. Regarding religious life, Ōtsu states in a letter to Mitsuko, "It seems perfectly natural to me that many people select the god in whom they place their faith on the basis of the culture and traditions and climate of the land of their birth."[89] This cultural particularism stands in tension with axial assertions of universally valid standards and values. Thus, Ōtsu's French classmates and teachers maintain that "the truth knows no distinction between Europe and Asia,"[90] while Ōtsu insists, "I do not believe that the European brand of Christianity is absolute."[91]

The danger of an acknowledgment of cultural embeddedness is a guarded exclusivism. Mitsuko expresses such an attitude in her first meeting with Ōtsu after college: "You're Japanese, aren't you? It makes my teeth stand on edge, just to think of you as a Japanese believing in the European Christianity nonsense."[92] This exclusivism is not without intellectual justification ("I know that Western Christianity plundered many lands and killed many people in the name of spreading their gospel"[93]), but it serves Mitsuko as a shield against "the darkness in her own heart."[94]

Endō portrays this tension in his fiction from the early *Yellow Man*, in which a French missionary tells his defrocked former colleague: "Catholicism transcends all races, and embraces everyone."[95] There, the answer comes back: "Except for apostates like me."[96] It is here that we see the crux of Endō's resolution. Christianity in "non-axial" Japan must be tempered by the forms of conditionedness and finitude recognized by the traditional culture. Its focus must be shifted from unfaltering individuals cleaving to the transcendent as absolute and universal and molding their conduct according to its moral imperatives. It must turn to the person weak in self-will—"the person who is evil," in Shinran's words, characterizing the focal center of Amida's working.[97] It must guide through the self-awareness of embeddedness.

Human Flourishing

According to Taylor, the most striking contrast between pre-axial religion and axial religion relates to "a third form of embedding in existing reality"[98]: the conception of human flourishing. As we have seen, the concerns of pre-axial religion (such as Shintō) center on flourishing in terms of physical prosperity and being "preserved from disease, dearth, sterility,"[99] and so on. "Central to the later 'higher' religions, is the idea that we have to question radically this ordinary understanding."[100] Thus, "With Christianity or Buddhism . . . there is a notion of our good which goes beyond human flourishing, which we may gain even while failing utterly on the scales of human flourishing, *even through such a failing*."[101] Taylor notes that modern humanism shares with early religion an image of flourishing that "involves no relation to anything higher,"[102] anything that transcends existing reality.

If human existence as embedded means that one's perceptions of the world and of life within it are informed by one's social and cultural environment, how is it that commonsense ideas of the good in human life can be broken through? How can one abandon the values prized by one's society and presumed to be in conformity with existing reality? For Shinran, the answer lies wholly in the working of reality that transcends the horizon of human thought and perception. This is not only a rejection of any capacity within a person to sever the attachments of the ego-self; awakening to and attaining genuine good occurs as itself the negation of self-will. It is, in Shinran's terms, the falling away of our ordinary "calculative thinking" and of our clinging to the capabilities of the ego-self. From the perspective of the embedded person, it is a disembedding that occurs "of itself" or "naturally and spontaneously" (*jinen*). Shinran explains *jinen* to mean "one is brought to become so."[103]

In *Deep River*, as Mitsuko seeks to bring Ōtsu into realignment with commonsense norms and values, advising him "to get a little more adept at living,"[104] Ōtsu tries to explain that his religious awakening was not his own choice or decision: "It was the work of the Onion [God] transcending my own will."[105] "I didn't change myself. I was made to change by the conjuring of God."[106] "It just happened."[107] Above all, it was a call: "A voice, saying 'Come to me.'"[108] Shinran employs much the same language. We are far here from notions of heroic religious resolve or unbending conviction. Instead, we return to the awakening to weakness and evil that we have considered earlier.

In his final conversation with Mitsuko in Vārānasī, Ōtsu concisely sets forth the structure of the transformative disembedding that occurs in the arena of Japanese sensibilities:

> When the Onion was killed . . . every one of his disciples had stayed alive by abandoning him and running away. Even though he had been betrayed, he continued to love them. As a result, his existence was etched into each one of their guilt-ridden hearts, and became an existence they could never forget. The disciples set out for distant lands to tell others the story of his life. . . . He continued to live in the hearts of his disciples.[109]

For the Onion to "have died, and yet undergo a rebirth within the disciples" is for them to be possessed simultaneously of the weakness of inconstancy and the presence of the divine. It is an embeddedness and finitude pervaded by a dimension of disembedding. As Mitsuko perceives, "Ōtsu's way of life and his talk were literally of 'a different world' from her own."[110] He had become "the complete antithesis of her old college friends and her husband,"[111] absorbed in mundane concerns; he was "of an utterly far removed, separate world" from them.[112]

This disembeddedness is not transmitted through the imposition of alien doctrines or scriptures, which possess their own cultural rootedness; there can be no universal formulation of an absolute truth in assertions and concepts, as Ōtsu's teachers imagine. Within the embeddedness of persons within society and culture, the divine can be transmitted only by embodiment and enactment, and by encounter. In *Deep River*, it is depicted in Ōtsu's encounter with Christ and his call, Mitsuko's encounter with Ōtsu, Numada's encounter with his hornbill, and the encounter of Kiguchi's war comrade with Gaston, all "clown-like" figures that step outside of accepted common sense. Such encounter functions not like archaic religion, for the preservation of the social and cosmic order, but precisely to enable a new perception of human flourishing, one in which the horizon that defines the habituated embeddedness is broken through. It is not necessarily the destruction of the old embeddedness, but an apprehension of a new dimension of reality, one that tempers and pervades the accustomed order but does not displace or obliterate it.

The Significance of Japanese Sensibilities

Endō locates the conclusion of his novel in India. There, each of his loosely assembled band of protagonist-travelers arrives at a stage of closure in their separate spiritual quests. At the Ganges, which "embraces everything about mankind,"[113] Mitsuko finds acceptance and an apprehension of the meaning of love that she had sought: "With each of the people in the river praying with palms pressed together, each of their hearts possessed a drama. . . . And the river embraced them all, the river Ōtsu had called the river of love that is itself his Onion."[114] Mitsuko reflects that "each of the people who came to the river had a past like the goddess Chāmundā . . . stung by scorpions and bitten by cobras," in each "there resided a past that had compelled" their journey.[115] Here, we reach the initial center of the novel that Endō first tentatively sketched at the beginning of his diary of composition: "what is good and what is evil exist together . . . this is what it means to be human."

The setting in India is not a reiteration of Okakura Kakuzō's notion that "Asia is one" (Endō finds cultural nationalism as well as moral self-righteousness abhorrent), but perhaps it resonates with another aspect of Okakura's vision, that of Japan as repository and preserver of diverse traditions that reach its shores, of material and performative culture as well as intellectual. Japanese civilization may be called "non-axial" in relation to its openness to foreign influence fused with an ability to maintain a stable stance in traditional culture. But in its probing self-reflection on the limitations of human existence—on our necessary embeddedness and limitations—it may also suggest, in a period of both globalization and fragmentation, the need for a temperate respect for the other—the other cultures, other wisdoms, other experiences that must be the accumulated cultural treasure of humankind.

Notes

1. Luis Frois, *Historia Eclesiastica*, f. 2, in trans. and ed. Michael Cooper, *They Came to Japan: An Anthology of European Reports on Japan, 1543–1640* (Berkeley: University of California Press, 1965), 373–74.

2. Robert Bellah, *Religion in Human Evolution: From the Paleolithic to the Axial Age* (Cambridge, MA: Harvard University Press, 2011), 654–55.

3. Shusaku, Endo, *Deep River*, trans. Van C. Gessel (Boston: Tuttle Publishing, 1994), 117; translation modified here and in later quotations. See also *Fukai kawa* (Tokyo: Shinchōsha, 1996 [originally published 1993]), 190.

4. *White Man, Yellow Man* (*Shiroi hito, Kiiroi hito*, 1955), two novellas originally published separately in journals, then together as a book titled *White Man, Yellow Man: Two Novellas*, trans. Teruyo Shimizu (New York: Paulist Press, 2014), 82, and in *Endō Shūsaku bungaku zenshū* [The literary complete works of Endō Shūsaku], 15 vols. (Tokyo: Shinchōsha, 2000).

5. It is notable that *Deep River* appeared the same year, 1993, as Samuel P. Huntington's prescient and controversial article, "The Clash of Civilizations." See *Foreign Affairs* 72, no. 3 (Summer 1993): 22–49.

6. Endo, *Deep River*, 188; *Fukai kawa*, 307.

7. Endo, *White Man, Yellow Man*, 6; *Shiroi hito, kiiroi hito*, 102. Translation modified.

8. Ibid., 81; 101.

9. Ibid., 112; 121.

10. Ibid., 112; 121. Translation modified.

11. See Dennis Hirota, "Discerning the Marshland of This World: *Silence* from a Japanese Buddhist Perspective," in *Approaching* Silence*: New Perspectives on Shusaku Endo's Classic Novel*, eds. Mark W. Dennis and Darren J. N. Middleton (New York: Bloomsbury, 2015), 139–58.

12. Frois, *Historia Eclesiastica*, 373–74.

13. M. L. Gordon, "The Religious Influence of Buddhism as an Obstacle to the Reception of the Gospel in Japan," in *Proceedings of the General Conference of*

the Protestant Missionaries of Japan Held at Osaka, Japan, April, 1883 (Yokohama: R. Meiklejohn and Company, 1883), 97.

14. Ibid., 96.

15. Ibid.

16. M. L. Gordon, *An American Missionary in Japan* (Boston: Houghton Mifflin, 1893), 213–14.

17. Endo, *Deep River*, 66; *Fukai kawa*, 107.

18. John Hick, *God Has Many Names* (Philadelphia: Westminster Press, 1982), 71.

19. Ibid., 46; emphasis added.

20. Endō Shūsaku, Fukai kawa *sōsaku nikki* [Diary of the Composition of *Deep River*], in *Endō Shūsaku bungaku zenshū* (Tokyo: Shinchōsha, 1999), 15: 287; entry for September 5, 1991.

21. Augustine, *Confessions*, Book I, Chapter 1.

22. Charles Taylor, *A Secular Age* (Cambridge, MA: Harvard University Press, 2007).

23. Ibid., 152, 150. See also Charles Taylor, "What Was the Axial Revolution?," in *Dilemmas and Connections* (Cambridge, MA: Harvard University Press, 2011), 370–71.

24. Taylor, "What Was the Axial Revolution?," 368.

25. Ibid., 369.

26. Taylor, *A Secular Age*, 147–48.

27. Ibid.

28. Ibid., 369–70.

29. Ibid., 371.

30. Taylor, *A Secular Age*, 152.

31. Hick, *God Has Many Names*, 45.

32. Ibid., 43.

33. John Hick, *An Interpretation of Religion: Human Responses to the Transcendent* (New Haven: Yale University Press, 1989), 24.

34. See Hirota, "Discerning the Marshland of This World."

35. S. N. Eisenstadt, *Japanese Civilization: A Comparative View* (Chicago: University of Chicago Press, 1996), 303; emphasis added.

36. Endō appears to have employed some name symbolism in the novel. Although not apparent in translation, the Japanese reader will note that Ōtsu (great harbor) and Mitsuko (beauty-harbor) share a Chinese character. Their surnames in early versions were Fukatsu (deep-harbor) and Yoshikawa (good-river). There are a number of names with words related to bodies of water: Mitsuko's surname becomes Naruse (become-rapids); Isobe (seashore-surroundings); and Enami (inlet-wave). Kiguchi's name (tree-mouth) also resonates with the narrative.

37. Robert Bellah, "Introduction: The Japanese Difference," in *Imagining Japan: The Japanese Tradition and Its Modern Interpretation* (Berkeley: University of California Press, 2003), 7.

38. Endō, *Deep River*, 122; *Fukai kawa*, 197.

39. Masutani Fumio and Endo Shūsaku, *Shinran: Shinran kōgi* (Tokyo: Asahi Shuppansha, 1979), 241. This volume is part of an extended series on a wide variety of topics by well-known authors employing the format of lectures by a specialist interspersed with questions and comments by a nonspecialist having particular interest in the topic.

40. Ibid., 6.

41. Endo, *Deep River*, 121–22; *Fukai kawa*, 196–97.

42. Cf. John Hick, *God Has Many Names*, 52: "The concept of deity, or of God, takes concrete form, and a 'local habitation and a name,' in the life of a particular human community and culture as a specific divine persona or face or image or icon of the Eternal One."

43. See Darren J. N. Middleton's "Endō Shūsaku's Process Panentheism" (chapter 13).

44. Endō Shūsaku, "Katorikku sakka no mondai," in *Endō Shūsaku bungaku zenshū*, 12:22.

45. Endo, *Yellow Man*, 126, 129.

46. Endo, *Deep River*, 122; *Fukai kawa*, 197.

47. Ibid., 64, 104.

48. Endō Shūsaku, *Mangekyō* (Tokyo: Asahi Shinbunsha, 1993), 145. This volume collects essays published in a weekly column in the Asahi newspaper from November 1991 to October 1992. The examples from his own experience that Endō gives are a characteristically Japanese perception with roots in traditional culture: the absorption in writing, when the writing takes over the conscious self ("someone takes my hand and makes it write") and produces a superb, completely unforeseen result beyond his own capabilities.

49. Ibid., 143; Endo, *Deep River*, 146–47; *Fukai kawa*, 236–37.

50. Ibid., 118; 191.

51. Ibid., 131; 211.

52. Known as the infamous Imphal campaign that resulted in the horrific retreat through the Burmese jungles that Endō describes. Endō names the general Mutaguchi who, seeking personal glory, drove his soldiers to pursue a prolonged, futile attack and afterwards denied responsibility. See *Deep River*, 87; *Fukai kawa*, 139.

53. Ibid., 195; 317.

54. Ibid., 201; 326.

55. *Notes on "Essentials of Faith Alone*," in Dennis Hirota et al., trans. and ed., *The Collected Works of Shinran* [hereafter: CWS] (Kyoto: Honpa Hongwanji, 1997), 461.

56. Ibid.

57. Nishitani Keiji, "The Standpoint of Zen," trans. John Maraldo, in *The Eastern Buddhist* (new series) 17:1 (1984): 14.

58. Ibid., 16.

59. Ibid., 15.

60. Ibid., 18.

61. Endō Shūsaku, "Watakushi ni totte kami to wa" [God as I see him], in *Kami to Watakushi*, ed. Yamaori Tetsuo (Tokyo: Asahi shinbun shuppan, 2010), 220–21.

62. Endo, *Deep River*, 117; 190.

63. Ibid.

64. Ibid., 199; 323.

65. Fukai kawa *sōsaku nikki*, 285–328.

66. Ibid., 285.

67. Endo, *Deep River*, 138; *Fukai kawa*, 222.

68. Ibid.

69. Ibid.

70. Ibid., 65; 106.

71. Ibid., 119; 192.

72. Charles Taylor, "The Perils of Moralism," in *Dilemmas and Connections: Selected Essays* (Cambridge, MA: Harvard University Press, 2014), 351.

73. Sister Elisabeth Germain, *Parler du salut?* (Paris: Beauchesne, 1967), quoted in Charles Taylor, *A Secular Age*, 498.

74. *Tannishō*, §13, CWS I: 671.

75. Endo, *Deep River*, 199–200; *Fukai kawa*, 324.

76. *Tannishō*, §3, in *Tannishō: A Primer*, trans. and ed. Dennis Hirota (Kyoto: Ryukoku University, 1982), 24. See also CWS I: 663. Cf. also Shinran's well-known words: "I know nothing at all of good or evil. For if I could know thoroughly, as Amida Tathagata knows, that an act was good, then I would know good. If I could know thoroughly, as the Tathagata knows, that an act was evil, then I would know evil. But with a foolish being full of blind passions, in this fleeting world—this burning house—all matters without exception are empty and false, totally without truth and sincerity. The nembutsu alone is true and real" (*Tannishō*, Postscript, CWS I: 679).

77. *Tannishō: A Primer*, 25; CWS I: 664.

78. Endo, *Deep River*, 159; *Fukai kawa*, 258.

79. Daochao, quoted in *The True Teaching, Practice, and Realization of the Pure Land Way*, CWS I: 291.

80. Endo, *Deep River*, 210; *Fukai kawa*, 342.

81. *Tannishō: A Primer*, 34; CWS I: 671.

82. Endo, *Deep River*, 185; *Fukai kawa*, 302.

83. Shinran, *Notes on Once-calling and Many-calling*, CWS I: 486.

84. Endo, *Deep River*, 142; *Fukai kawa*, 229.

85. Ibid., 199; 323.

86. CWS I: 371.

87. "Hymns of the Pure Land Masters," 35; CWS I: 370.

88. Endo, *Deep River*, 215; *Fukai kawa*, 350–51.

89. Ibid., 121; 195.

90. Ibid., 65; 106.

91. Ibid., 121; 195.

92. Ibid., 64; 105.
93. Ibid., 42; 69.
94. Ibid., 58; 94.
95. Endo, *Yellow Man*, 126; 129.
96. Ibid.
97. Quote *Tannishō*, §3, CWS I: 663.
98. Taylor, *A Secular Age*, 150.
99. Ibid. and Taylor, "What Was the Axial Revolution?" 370.
100. Taylor, "What Was the Axial Revolution?" 370.
101. Ibid.
102. Ibid.
103. CWS I: 427.
104. Endo, *Deep River*, 66; *Fukai kawa*, 108.
105. Ibid., 64; 104.
106. Ibid., 63; 103.
107. Ibid., 62; 101.
108. Ibid.
109. Ibid., 184–85; 301–2.
110. Ibid., 185; 303.
111. Ibid., 68; 111.
112. Ibid., 116; 188.
113. Ibid., 199; 323.
114. Ibid., 200; 325.
115. Ibid., 197; 319.

Afterword

Deep and Wide

Tourists and Pilgrims in the Shallows

S. BRENT PLATE

"Deep and wide. Deep and wide.
There's a fountain flowing deep and wide."

—Christian children's hymn

The most spiritually dry day of my life was the day I visited the Taj Mahal. I had gone to India for research, to take note of the ubiquity of religious images in the Hindu traditions and the ways people responded to those images: from shoebox shrines at bus stops with tiny Ganesha figures nestled within, to watching the *Rāmāyaṇa* on television, to pilgrimaging to Vrindavan for *Janmashtami* (Krishna's birthday). I was the observer, scribbling notes and snapping pictures, examining how the others acted out their *darshan*, that spiritual-sensual interaction between devotee and deity. Even so, as one of my Indian friends smartly gathered, I was also there to take a bit of my own *darshan*. Born in the 1960s, I was still traveling the paths to enlightenment, even after my rational brain had long ago given up on "systems of belief."

But resting on the bluffs above the holy Yamuna River, the Taj Mahal left me high and dry. To be sure, it was nothing about that resplendent tombstone that disappointed me. Nor was it the high temperatures, nor my resultant sweat-soaked clothes. In retrospect I think it was just that point in my journey, a couple weeks into traveling, away from my home and my companion. The honeymoon period of visiting "exotic" new lands was over. Homesickness had set in. I left Agra, returned to my sleeping quarters at the home of an uncle of a friend who said I'd be welcome to stay, and broke down in tears. I've never had an experience where I felt so alone, so parched.

Traveling is a way to open oneself up to the world, to experience new cultures, people, languages, foods, histories, and geographies. At least we like to tell ourselves that. So do travel agencies, inspirational self-help books, and tour guides like Enami in Shusaku Endo's *Deep River*. Travel should change you, nay, *transform* you, provide you with enough different, challenging experiences that you'll never be the same, never go home again, never cross the same river twice.

And it's true often enough.

Yet there are plenty of times, like mine at the Taj Mahal, like the characters at various points in *Deep River*, when the currents are dammed, leaving us shriveled and blown away. Moments of travel where experience itself seems to cease, the hoped-for profundity of the journey becoming ungraspable, leaving us unable to swim in the depths of other lands. We get homesick, or physically sick like Kiguchi, or tired like Mrs. Sanjō, or depressed like Isobe failing to find his reincarnated wife, or confused like Mitsuko trying to figure out what she's doing in India. These are the times we don't hear much about when tour guides are announcing the trip, and even less after the journey is over and the traveler returns with pictures to show (off). But these are the times that begin to tell us something about the nature of travel, and even hint at some of the relations between tourism and pilgrimage.

Shallows

Endo's winding narrative depicts tourists and pilgrims at a confluence. We could say, and I think Endo wants us to recognize, that there are differences in travel, that Mitsuko and Kiguchi are not the same as the Sanjōs. These distinctions get muddied in that great river. The river is deep, as Mitsuko says, "so deep I feel as though it's not just for the Hindus but for everyone."[1] The metaphor is profusely pluralistic, providing a place of learning for Japanese Buddhists, nonbelievers, and devout Christians alike. Readers may want, as Endo does, to find the river sufficiently deep.

Yet I wonder: Can it be wide as well? So wide that it rolls out beyond its banks to create pools of knee-deep water? That is, can it include those who don't want or can't take the full immersion, but instead want to wade around in the shallows? The tourist? The infirm? The doubter? The one with no pious intentions? The *"river of humanity"* includes Christians, Buddhists, and Hindus, but it also includes tourists and pilgrims, blending the sacred and profane.[2] Pious or party-hardy, out for devotion or diversion, the tourist and the pilgrim walk side by side, regardless of interior intent. The river is deep and wide.

I experienced the shallows on my Taj Mahal day, but it didn't really sink in until years later along the Camino de Santiago. The Camino is an ancient pilgrimage route that leads to the old bones of St. James, the apostle of Jesus. The bones were "re-discovered" in the ninth century, just in time to help muster Christian forces against the progression of the Muslim Moors (its political mixings are beyond the scope of this Afterword). In medieval times it was one of the "big three" pilgrimages of Christianity—the other two heading toward Rome and Jerusalem—and pilgrims from all over Europe journeyed to this far Western edge of the European continent as penance for sins, or as pious action that reaped more rewards for the next life. The chronically ill kissed their loved ones goodbye and set out on the Camino as their final journey, knowing they'd never return. Plenty of others saw it as a way to get out of town and see some new sights. Still others discovered a built-in economic market where business opportunities abounded.

Today's Camino is its own deep river. When I made the trip, I walked alongside Korean Buddhists, Korean Protestants, Mexican Catholics, Spaniards out-for-a-weekend-with-friends, and a great variety of that most contemporary of religious groups, the spiritual-but-not-religious congregation. Some went to be alone, others to find the party. Many went for health reasons, or to get over a break up, or to meet a new partner, or to experience a different kind of travel across the beauty of northern Spain. A startling number of people have done the journey before and/or are going to do it again. People still die along the way, though nowadays death comes unexpectedly.

Into the third week of my Camino I fell ill, probably a result of too many different water sources, too many different types of food, and sometimes unsanitary conditions. My homesick days were behind me; this was purely gastrointestinal. Like Kiguchi, I lay in bed for a couple days trying to keep sustenance in my body, and not caring a bit for the remainder of the Camino. Pain is an anesthetic. It shuts down sensual feeling, desire, just as it shuts out past and future, leaving one in an excruciating now. Such experiences in the shallows—sickness, desperation, lack of interest, loneliness—are wedges that show the dominance of the body, of the physical world, in spite of ethereal attempts at finding profound, life-changing meaning in the realm of the interior soul. This is where, I've begun to believe, I need to pay attention.[3]

Bodies

To understand the spiritual journey we need to understand the importance of the shallows. The journey's dynamic hinges on the fact that it is a skin deep, "superficial" experience, as much as it occasionally promotes deep thoughts. External actions often mean more than contrite hearts, which is also to say the journey, undertaken by pilgrim *or* tourist, is thoroughly and unfailingly a physical process that our linguistic narratives and metaphors often only serve to cover over. Once the journey is captured in words, put into forms of rational knowledge (as I'm doing here), the body is left behind, the sensual engagements cut off. Uncovering the deeper meaning of the superficial lets us learn in the face of things, like a poetic physiognomy.

The body precedes thought—indeed, gives rise to thought. Sensed impulses at the level of our skin filter through us, the stirrings of emotions and chemicals course through the veins, interlace with muscle fibers well before the brain gets a chance to deliberate. Prior to knowing fully why we want to go, we sometimes go anyway. Before leaving, Mitsuko "had no real sense of what she wanted to see in India."[4] Even after arriving, in her hazy search for Otsu, in the midst of her "senseless actions," she "vaguely perceived that she yearned for *something*."[5] Her body knew something before her brain caught up.

Three days into my journey on the Camino de Santiago, I had fallen in with a spirited bunch: three Koreans of varying ages who had only just met each other on the way, a heavily tattooed Italian lawyer, and a middle-aged Spaniard who seems to have been on and off the Camino for years and still yearning, like Mitsuko, for *something*. At one point I had a slight out of body experience watching us all huddled around a spaghetti dinner the Italian had made for us in a little hostel. I heard us laugh together as we asked each other why we were here. Secretly, I suspect, we all had our own reasons, though these remained concealed, again I suspect, because we ourselves didn't know how to fully formulate them. The reasons stayed vague, making our actions seem senseless. But what happy fools were we.

The journey, then, is a ship of fools, on errands we know cannot be fulfilled, from Sanjō's winning the Pulitzer Prize for his incessant picture taking to Isobe's quest for his dead wife's reincarnated soul. (Otsu, the biggest fool of all.) It's all the glorious foolishness of the religious quest, the absurd and illogical deeply felt as compelling.

My pious Korean Protestant friend memorized bible verses as he walked. The Italian lawyer who made spaghetti for us attached a speaker to his belt and blasted rock-and-roll along the path. An agnostic Korean university student

I walked alongside for a while noticed how the landscapes often looked like the background image of Windows XP. One co-walker had recently fled the California tech industry. Trying to find his way again he opted for a radically new and simpler life with his young family; he kept a GPS device firmly attached to his shoulder straps, even though the Camino is heavily marked. We all walked the same route. And walked some more.

People have their own reasons for heading out to distant lands, even when they don't know what they are. The loss of someone dear is common, like Kiguchi and Numada. I met a man on the Camino who lost his wife and started walking, going to Santiago, and then on south to Fatima, east to Lourdes, and finally Rome. Another had lost his farm through a foreclosure and started walking . . . from the Czech Republic. We hear such stories and are moved, witnessing the profundity of the symbolic gesture.

But let's not forsake the shallows, the illogic, and the foolishness of it all. A symbol, in its simplest definition, is a material thing that stands in for an immaterial meaning. There is generally a culturally or biologically embedded connection that links the material to the immaterial, like love being expressed through hearts, or the color red grabbing our attention and making us stop, or water being purifying. But what does the material sign of walking hundreds of kilometers, or bathing in a river, have to do with dead spouses or memories of war or anything else? There is no logical connection. We don't know why we have come, but something pre-symbolic compels us to move. Not only is it "pre-symbolic," it is often resolutely *non*-symbolic, not even fitting within the symbolic register.

To me, the pivotal scene in *Deep River* is when Enami takes a few of the tourists down into the subterranean *bhaga* of the Vishvanatha Temple. Down in the dank shadows, the darkness of Mitsuko's heart is symbolically met when she encounters Chāmundā, the great gruesome goddess who is both like and entirely unlike the Christian Mary. In the narrative, this is a key symbolic point for unraveling Mitsuko's secrets, her place on the journey.

More importantly, this is a key scene because of what it tells us about travel, about the experiences of both pilgrim and tourist, and expresses the non-symbolic. The visit to the *bhaga* is first and foremost a bodily experience, where symbolic language does not tread. As they descended, the tourists heard the word "goddess," and thus "had been expecting something tender, something maternal. And the sweltering heat of this underground chamber had left their faces and necks stained with sweat."[6] They were expecting something symbolic: the immaterial meaning of "goddess" would be matched by a material image that looks tender and maternal. Yet Endo doesn't follow the line about "expecting something tender" with a substituted thought like, "what they realized instead was that goddess is X." That is, Endo doesn't have them change their mind, or find a new symbol. He simply disregards their symbolic thought processes and returns to the shallow reality of "faces and necks stained with sweat."

Like "goddess," the terminology of "journey" makes us expect things that simply aren't there, and when we get to the path we are left sweating from the heat or a fever, confused in the shallows. These non-symbolic, body-based points of the journey are real, common, and not to be overlooked in a quest for depth. They are profoundly superficial.

Recently, I was reading through one of the many online Camino forums. Someone posted a deceptively simple question about whether doing the Camino actually changes lives. (The responses are an overwhelming "yes.") One response, by a sixty-year-old woman from the United States caught my eye for the evidence it gave: "Before the Camino I would say "tree" or "bird" or "food" and they were nouns with no color or taste or soul. After I walked a few weeks I began to see the tree as a living being . . . I heard the bird calling." This woman implicitly turned symbolic words back into their material, sensual existence. This is not to pit the body against language, or against thinking itself, but it is to find meaning from another direction, from the skin deep experiences of sensing humans who are seeing, hearing, tasting, faces full of sweat.

The physicality of the journey extends to the things we carry. Sanjō's camera, Numada's myna bird, and Mitsuko's sari all become vibrant matter, objects without which the journey would lose its effectiveness. The Camino itself is lined with votives, shrines, cairns, crosses, and pictures. Over a quarter million people walk some part of it every year, so it's bound to get a bit messy, littered with things sacred and profane. Travelers feel the need to leave stones, pictures, notes, poems, prayers, and promises all along the way. In the absence of objects, a few just start in on graffiti. Some of the scrawled words tend toward the profound, like the Schopenhauer-Buddhist aphoristic koan I saw in La Rioja: "Without pain there is no satisfaction," or simple expressions of love: "K.C. ♥ L.M"—all superficial, physical impulses that make no sense.

Confluence

Other forms of graffiti pushed toward the provocative, like the scribbled "Real pilgrims walk in silence," on the edge of Galicia. This was a constant implicit refrain: the authenticity of the trip. From graffiti to guidebooks to the evening conversations in the hostels, opinions were expressed about the real-ness of one's travels, provoking ponderings as to whether I should feel bad about getting on a bus and skipping a day of walking because of a hurt knee. Doubt ensues: maybe you're not really a pilgrim; maybe you're *just* a tourist.

Tourists may be centered on comfort, finding beautiful scenery, and spending time taking pictures of those lovely landscapes, which sounds fine but I doubt many people who read *Deep River* want to be like Mr. Sanjō. When Enami wants to take the tour group to the *ghāts* early one morning, Mr. Sanjō wonders if it's more "interesting" at that time, and he's surely thinking of what pictures he might be able to take then. It's Enami's response that strikes a chord: "It's not 'interesting,' it's holy."[7] It's a great distinction, to be sure. Nicely put. And yet it matches the analytic work of many scholars who over the years have worked to create a tourist-pilgrim distinction, supplying a binary logic for maintaining difference. We might be tempted to say that the tourist seeks the interesting, while the pilgrim that which is holy. We might even see Mitsuko transforming from tourist to pilgrim when in the final pages she begins to believe in the deep "*river of humanity*."[8]

These categories get jumbled in the shallows, and Endo is attentive to the muddy water. In a letter to Mitsuko from France, Otsu complains about European logic, its "excessive clarity," and "way of explaining everything in such clear-cut terms." As an Asian, he has a hard time with this, ultimately surmising that "there is something they have lost sight of."[9] The need to divide tourist from pilgrim falls directly into such "lucid logic," leaving us wondering: What do we lose sight of when we are intent on our clear-cut terms, separating the sheep and goats, real pilgrims from selfie-snappers?[10]

It's not that Person A is ontologically a "pilgrim" and Person B is ontologically a "tourist." Rather, these identities are fluid, and along the way we become one and/or the other as we stand on the wide riverbanks, dip our toes in, or dive in head first. A lot happens in the shallows; it's not just a transition zone between depth and regular life. Indeed, some of the problems with travel come when we expect too much and don't realize that the shallow water is also part of the river: the homesickness, gastrointestinal sickness, boredom, sweat, confusion, and doubt are all felt in and through the body that has a tendency to be stopped up and dried out. The reality is that we travelers—tourist and pilgrim alike—all spend a lot of time, in fact the majority of our travel time, in the shallows. The shallows are constantly folding travelers into their flows.

As a sometime tourist, sometime pilgrim, I'm beginning to think that pilgrimage and tourism are nested inside of each other, always burgeoning, ready to emerge in the midst of the other. We are tourists at times and pilgrims at others, and often a bit of each simultaneously. To come to grips, and terms, with the journey, in body and mind, means we need to get a little wet, but also a little dry. Resist the notion that the real experience is only in the depths.

Notes

1. Shusaku Endo, *Deep River*, trans. Van C. Gessel (New York: New Directions, 1994), 195.
2. Ibid., 211.
3. For additional details, see S. Brent Plate, *By the Way: Dispatches, Devotions, and Deliriums on the Camino de Santiago. Killing the Buddha* e-book, 2016.
4. Endo, *Deep River*, 32.
5. Ibid., 180.
6. Ibid., 139.
7. Ibid., 141.
8. Ibid., 211.
9. Ibid., 117.
10. Ibid.

For Further Reading

Shusaku Endo (English Texts)

White Man/Yellow Man. Translated by Teruyo Shimizu. New York: Paulist Press, 2014.

———. *Kiku's Prayer.* Translated by Van C. Gessel. New York: Columbia University Press, 2013.

———. *Song of Sadness.* Translated by Teruyo Shimizu. Ann Arbor: University of Michigan Center for Japanese Studies, 2003.

———. *The Girl I Left Behind.* Translated by Mark Williams. London: Peter Owen, 1994; New York: New Directions, 1995.

———. *Deep River.* Translated by Van C. Gessel. London: Peter Owen, 1994; New York: New Directions, 1994.

———. *The Final Martyrs: Stories by Shusaku Endo.* Translated by Van C. Gessel. London: Peter Owen, 1993; New York: New Directions, 1994.

———. *Foreign Studies.* Translated by Mark Williams. London: Peter Owen, 1989; New York: Simon & Schuster, 1990.

———. *Scandal.* Translated by Van C. Gessel. London: Peter Owen/New York: Dodd, Mead, 1988.

———. *Stained Glass Elegies: Stories by Shusaku Endo.* Translated by Van C. Gessel. London: Peter Owen, 1984; New York: Dodd, Mead, 1985.

———. *The Samurai.* Translated by Van C. Gessel. London: Peter Owen; New York: Harper & Row/Kodansha International, 1982.

———. *When I Whistle.* Translated by Van C. Gessel. London: Peter Owen/New York: Taplinger, 1979.

———. *A Life of Jesus.* Translated by Richard A. Schuchert. New York: Paulist Press, 1978.

———. *Volcano.* Translated by Richard A. Schuchert. London: Peter Owen, 1978; New York: Taplinger, 1980.

———. *Wonderful Fool.* Translated by Frances Mathy. London: Peter Owen, 1974; New York: Harper & Row, 1983.

———. *The Sea and Poison*. Translated by Michael Gallagher. London: Peter Owen, 1972; New York: Taplinger, 1980.
———. *The Golden Country*. Translated by Frances Mathy. Tokyo: Tuttle, 1970.
———. *Silence*. Translated by William Johnston. Tokyo: Sophia University & Tuttle, 1969; London: Peter Owen, 1976; New York: Taplinger, 1979.

Endō Shūsaku (Japanese Texts)

———. *Endō Shūsaku bungaku zenshū* [The collected works of Endō Shūsaku; often cited as *ESBZ*], 15 volumes. Tokyo: Shinchōsha, 1999–2000; an 11-volume series that first appeared in 1975.
———. *Fukai kawa sōsaku nikki* [*Deep River* composition diary]. Tokyo: Kōdansha, 1997.
———. *Fukai kawa* [Deep River]. Tokyo: Kōdansha, 1993.
———. *Sukyandaru* [Scandal]. Tokyo: Shinchōsha, 1986.
———. *Samurai* [Samurai]. Tokyo: Shinchōsha, 1980.
———. *Kuchibue o fuku toki* [When I whistle]. Tokyo: Kōdansha, 1974.
———. *Iesu no shōgai* [A life of Jesus]. Tokyo: Shinchōsha, 1973.
———. *Bara no yakata, ōgon no kuni* [The rose pavilion and the golden country]. Tokyo: Shinchōsha, 1969.
———. *Chinmoku* [Silence]. Tokyo: Shinchōsha, 1966.
———. *Ryūgaku* [Foreign studies]. Tokyo: Bungei Shunjū Shinsha, 1965.
———. *Watashi ga suteta onna* [The girl I left behind]. Tokyo: Bungei Shunjū Shinsha, 1964.
———. *Kazan* [Volcano]. Tokyo: Bungei Shunjū Shinsha, 1960.
———. *Obakasan* [Wonderful fool]. Tokyo: Chūō Kōronsha, 1959.
———. *Umi to dokuyaku* [The sea and poison]. Tokyo: Bungei Shunjū Shinsha, 1958.

Critical Studies (English Texts)

Albinia, Alice. *Empires of the Indus: The Story of a River*. New York: W.W. Norton, 2010.
Ascensio, Adelino. *Transcultural Theodicy in the Fiction of Shūsaku Endō*. Roma: Editrice Pontifica Università Gregoriana, 2009.
Berkouwer, G. C. *The Second Vatican Council and the New Catholicism*. Translated by Lewis B. Smedes. Grand Rapids, MI: Wm. B. Eerdmans, 1965.
Biernacki, Loriliai, and Philip Clayton, eds. *Panentheism across the World's Traditions*. Oxford and New York: Oxford University Press, 2014.
Björnström, Daniel. *What Has Tokyo to do with Jerusalem? Towards a Japanese Theology via Shusaku Endo's Literature*. Middletown, DE: Independently Published, 2017.
Bosco, Mark, S.J. *Graham Greene's Catholic Imagination*. Oxford and New York: Oxford University Press, 2005.

Boyer, Nicholaus. *Sacred and Secular Scriptures: A Catholic Approach to Literature.* Notre Dame, IN: University of Notre Dame Press, 2005.
Bracken, Joseph A., S.J. *Christianity and Process Thought: Spirituality for a Changing World.* Philadelphia and London: Templeton Foundation Press, 2006.
Bussie, Jacqueline Aileen. *The Laughter of the Oppressed: Ethical and Theological Resistance in Wiesel, Morrison, and Endo.* New York: T & T Clark International, 2007.
Coenradie, Sigrid. *Vicarious Substitution in the Literary Work of Endō Shūsaku: On Fools, Animals, Objects and Doubles.* Publications of the Department of Philosophy and Religious Studies 93, Utrecht University, 2015.
Cooper, John W. *Panentheism—The Other God of the Philosophers: From Plato to the Present.* Grand Rapids, MI: Baker, 2006.
Crowe, Marian E. *Aiming at Heaven, Getting the Earth: The English Catholic Novel Today.* Lanham, MD: Lexington Books, 2007.
Dalrymple, William. *Nine Lives: In Search of the Sacred in Modern India.* New York: Vintage, 2011.
Daughrity, Dyron B. *Rising: The Amazing Story of Christianity's Resurrection in the Global South.* Minneapolis: Fortress Press, 2018.
Davis, Lanta. "Embracing Paradox: A Dialogue of Suffering between John Paul II and Shusaku Endo." *Intégrité: A Faith and Learning Journal* 11, no. 1 (2012): 27–40.
Dennis, Mark W., and Darren J. N. Middleton, eds. *Approaching* Silence*: New Perspectives on Shusaku Endo's Classic Novel.* New York and London: Bloomsbury Academic, 2015.
Doak, Kevin M., ed. *Xavier's Legacies: Catholicism in Modern Japanese Culture.* Vancouver: University of British Columbia Press, 2011.
Dombrowski, Daniel A. *A History of the Concept of God: A Process Approach.* Albany: State University of New York Press, 2017.
Eck, Diana L. *India: A Sacred Geography.* New York: Harmony, 2013.
Faessel, Victor A. "Spirit of Christ Inculturated: A Theological Theme Implicit in Shusaku Endo's Literary Works." *Japanese Religions* 30, no. 1–2 (2005): 148–51.
Fehler, Brun. "Re-defining God: The Rhetoric of Reconciliation." *Rhetoric Society Quarterly* 33, no. 1 (2003): 105–26.
Ferreter, Luke. *Towards a Christian Literary Theory.* Houndsmills, UK: Macmillan Press, 2003.
Flannery, Austin, ed. *Vatican Council II: The Conciliar and Post-Conciliar Documents.* Wilmington, DE: Scholarly Resources, 1975.
———. "Shusaku Endo: Japanese Catholic Novelist." *Religion and Intellectual Life* 3, no. 3 (1986): 101–13.
Fujimura, Makoto. *Silence and Beauty: Hidden Faith Born of Suffering.* Downers Grove, IL: InterVarsity Press, 2016.
Furuya, Yasuo, ed. *A History of Japanese Theology.* Grand Rapids, MI: Wm B. Eerdmans, 1997.
Gallagher, Michael. "For These the Least of My Brethren: The Concern of Endō Shūsaku." *Journal of the Association of Teachers of Japanese* 27, no. 1 (1993): 75–84.

Gandhi, Leela. *Postcolonial Theory: A Critical Introduction*. New York: Columbia University Press, 1998.
Gandolfo, Anita. *Testing the Faith: The New Catholic Fiction in America*. Westport, CT: Greenwood Press, 1992.
Gessel, Van C. "The Road to the River: The Fiction of Endō Shūsaku." In *Oe and Beyond: Fiction in Contemporary Japan*, edited by Stephen Snyder and Philip Gabriel, 36–57. Honolulu: University of Hawai'i Press, 1999.
———. "Hearing God in Silence: The Fiction of Endo Shusaku." *Christianity and Literature* 48, no. 2 (Winter 1999): 149–64.
———. "Endō Shūsaku: His Position(s) in Postwar Japanese Literature." *Journal of the Association of Teachers of Japanese* 27, no. 1 (1993): 67–74.
———. *The Sting of Life: Four Contemporary Japanese Novelists*. New York: Columbia University Press, 1989.
———. "Voices in the Wilderness: Japanese Christian Authors." *Monumenta Nipponica* 37, no. 4 (1982): 437–57.
Gessel, Van. C., ed. *Japanese Fiction Writers Since World War II*. Detroit, MI: Gale Research, 1997.
George, P. A., ed. *East Asian Literatures: An Interface with India*. New Delhi: Northern Book Centre, 2006.
George, Sam. *Diaspora Christianities: Global Scattering and Gathering of South Asian Christians*. Minneapolis: Fortress Press, 2018.
Gilvary, Dermot, and Darren J. N. Middleton, eds. *Dangerous Edges of Graham Greene: Journeys with Saints and Sinners*. New York and London: Continuum, 2011.
Greeley, Andrew. *The Catholic Imagination*. Berkeley: University of California Press, 2001.
Grigore, Rodica. "Shusaku Endo: From the Silence of the East to the Silence of God." *Theory in Action* 3, no. 1 (2010): 7–23.
Hagiwara, Takao. "Return to Japan: The Case of Endō Shūsaku." *Comparative Literature* 48, no. 2 (2000): 125–54.
Haines, Daniel. *Rivers Divided: Indus Basin Waters in the Making of India and Pakistan*. Oxford and New York: Oxford University Press, 2017.
Hartshorne, Charles. "Some Theological Mistakes and Their Effects on Modern Literature." *Journal of Speculative Philosophy* 1, no. 1 (1987): 55–72.
Hick, John. *Faith and Knowledge*. Eugene, OR: Wipf & Stock, 2009.
———. *An Autobiography*. Oxford: Oneworld, 2002.
———. *The Fifth Dimension: An Exploration of the Spiritual Realm*. Oxford: Oneworld, 1999.
———. *A Christian Theology of Religions: The Rainbow of Faiths*. Louisville, KY: Westminster John Knox Press, 1995.
———. *An Interpretation of Religion: Human Responses to the Transcendent*. New Haven: Yale University Press, 1989.
———. *Problems of Religious Pluralism*. New York: St. Martin's Press, 1985.

———. *God Has Many Names*. Philadelphia: Westminster Press, 1982.
Hick, John, ed. *The Myth of Christian Uniqueness*. New York: Orbis Books, 1988.
Higgins, Jean. "East-West Encounter in Endo Shusaku." *Dialogue & Alliance* 1, no. 3 (1987): 12–22.
———. "The Inner Agon of Endo Shusaku." *CrossCurrents* 34 (1984–1985): 414–26.
Hill, Christopher. "Crossed Geographies: Endō and Fanon in Lyon." *Representations* 128 (2014): 93–123.
Hirota, Dennis, ed. *Toward a Contemporary Understanding of Pure Land Buddhism: Creating a Shin Buddhist Theology in a Religiously Plural World*. Albany: State University of New York Press, 2000.
Hoekema, Alle G. "Vicarious Substitution in the Literary Work of Shusaku Endo: On Food, Animals, Object and Doubles." *Exchange* 46, no. 2 (2017): 218–20.
———. "The 'Christology' of the Japanese Novelist Shusaku Endo." *Exchange* 29, no. 3 (2000): 230–48.
Hoeveler, Diane Long. "Shusaku Endo's *Deep River*: Trauma, Screen-Memories, and Autobiographical Confessions." *CEA Critic* 67, no. 3 (2005): 28–40.
Hoffer, Bates. "Shusaku Endo and Graham Greene: Cross-Cultural Influences in Literary Structure." *Language and Literature* 28 (2003): 127–33.
Hollick, Julian Crandall. *Ganga: A Journey Down the Ganges River*. Washington, DC: Island Press, 2007.
Inoue, Masamichi. "Reclaiming the Universal: Intercultural Subjectivity in the Life and Work of Endo Shusaku." *Southeast Review of Asian Studies* 34 (2012): 153–70.
Inoue, Yoji. *The Face of Jesus in Japan*. Translated by Hisako Akamatsu. Tokyo: Kindai Bungeisha, 1994.
Jay, Paul. *Global Matters: The Transnational Turn in Literary Studies*. Ithaca, NY: Cornell University Press, 2010.
Jenkins, Philip. *The Next Christendom: The Coming of Global Christianity*. Oxford: Oxford University Press, 2002.
———. "The Journey of the Suffering Servant: The Vulnerable Hero, the Feminine Godhead and Spiritual Transformation in Endo Shusaku's *Deep River*." *Exchange* 41, no. 4 (2012): 320–34.
Johnson, Patricia Altenbemd. "Kierkegaard and Endo: The Dialectic of Religiousness." *Union Seminary Quarterly Review* 39, no. 1–2 (1984): 85–99.
Johnston, William. *Mystical Journey: An Autobiography*. Maryknoll, NY: Orbis Books, 2006.
———. "Endo and Johnston Talk of Buddhism and Christianity." *America* 171, no. 16 (1994): 18–20.
Kadowaki, Kakichi. "Nichiren and the Christian Way." *Dharma World* 26 (1999): 14–22.
Kasza, Justyna Weronika. *Hermeneutics of Evil in the Works of Endō Shūsaku: Between Reading and Writing*. Oxford & Bern: Peter Lang, 2016.
———. "Polysemy of the Other: Endō Shūsaku's Encounter with the West." *The IAFOR Journal of Literature and Librarianship* 2, no. 1 (2013): 43–55.

———. "The Cognitive Functions of 'Distanciation': the Image of Japan in the Works of Endō Shūsaku." *Regioninės Studijos* 4 (2010): 35–50.
Keane, John J. *Cultural and Theological Reflections on the Japanese Quest for Divinity*. Boston and Leiden: Brill, 2016.
Keuss, Jeffrey F. *Freedom of the Self: Kenosis, Cultural Identity and Mission at the Crossroads*. Eugene, OR: Pickwick Publications, 2010.
———. "The Lenten Face of Christ in Shusaku Endo's *Silence* and *Life of Jesus*." *The Expository Times* 118, no. 6 (2007): 273–79.
Kim, JinHyok. "The Wounded Grace: Memory, Body and Salvation in Endō Shūsaku and Rowan Williams." *The Expository Times* 124, no. 8 (2013): 374–83.
———. "The Journey of the Suffering Servant: The Vulnerable Hero, the Feminine Godhead and Spiritual Transformation in Endō Shūsaku's *Deep River*." *Exchange* 41, no. 4 (2012): 320–34.
Kinast, Robert. *Process Catholicism: An Exercise in Ecclesial Imagination*. Lanham, MD: University Press of America, 1999.
Kitamori, Kazoh. *Theology of the Pain of God*. Richmond, VA: John Knox Press, 1965.
Koyama, Kosuke. *Mount Fuji and Mount Sinai*. London: SCM Press, 1984.
Lakeland, Paul. *The Wounded Angel: Fiction and the Religious Imagination*. Collegeville, MN: Liturgical Press, 2017.
Lakshmi, M. V. "India as Portrayed in Modern Japanese Literature: A Study of Shusaku Endo's *Deep River*." In *East Asian Literatures: An Interface with India*, editd by P. A. George, 223–31. New Delhi: Northern Book Centre, 2006.
Lazarus, Neil, ed. *The Cambridge Companion to Postcolonial Literary Studies*. Cambridge: Cambridge University Press, 2004.
Leigh, David J., S.J., "The Ultimate Way: Apocalypse and Pluralism in the Postcolonial Fiction of Salman Rushdie and Shusaku Endo." In *Apocalyptic Patterns in Twentieth-Century Fiction*, 206–24. South Bend, IN: University of Notre Dame Press, 2008.
Lewell, John. *Modern Japanese Novelists: A Biographical Dictionary*. Tokyo: Kodansha, 1993.
Li, David Leiwei, ed. *Globalization and the Humanities*. Seattle: University of Washington Press, 2004.
Link, Christopher A. "Bad Priests and the Valor of Pity: Shusaku Endo and Graham Greene on the Paradoxes of Christian Virtue." *Logos: A Journal of Catholic Thought and Culture* 15, no. 4 (2012): 75–96.
Mallet, Victor. *River of Life, River of Death: The Ganges and India's Future*. Oxford and New York: Oxford University Press, 2017.
Mase-Hasegawa, Emi. *Christ in Japanese Culture: Theological Themes in Shusaku Endo's Literary Works*. Boston and Leiden: Brill, 2008.
———. "Religion and Contemporary Japanese Novelists: Endo's Concept of God Reconsidered." *Interreligious Insight* 4, no. 4 (2006): 20–27.
———. "Endo Shusaku's *Deep River*—An Interpretation." *The Japan Mission Journal* 59, no. 3 (2005): 191–95.

———. "Image of Christ for Japanese: Reflection on Theology Implicit in Shusaku Endo's Literary Works." *Inter-Religio* 43 (2003): 22–33.
Matata, J.P. Mukengeshayi. "Endo Shusaku's Novels and Religious Pluralism: A Reply to Prof. Emi Mase-Hasegawa." *Inter-Religio* 43 (2003): 34–38.
Mathy, Francis. "Shusaku Endo: The Second Period." *Japan Christian Quarterly* 40, no. 4 (1974): 214–20.
———. "Shusaku Endo: Japanese Catholic Novelist." *Thought* 42 (1967): 585–614.
Matsuoka, Fumitaka. "The Church in the World: The Christology of Shusaku Endo." *Theology Today* 39 (1982): 294–99.
Middleton, Darren J. N. "Dead Serious: A Theology of Literary Pilgrimage." *CrossCurrents* 59, no. 3 (2009): 300–318.
Middleton, Darren J. N., ed. *Mother Tongue Theologies: Poets, Novelists, Non-Western Christianity*. Eugene, OR: Cascade, 2009.
Morimoto, Anri. "The (More or Less) Same Light but from Different Lamps: The Post-Pluralist Understanding of Religion from a Japanese Perspective." *International Journal for Philosophy of Religion* 53, no. 3 (2003): 163–80.
Murphy, Michael P. *A Theology of Criticism: Balthasar, Postmodernism, and the Catholic Imagination*. Oxford and New York: Oxford University Press, 2008.
Netland, John T. "From Cultural Alterity to the Habitations of Grace: The Evolving Moral Topography of Endo's Mudswamp Trope." *Christianity and Literature* 59, no. 1 (2009): 27–48.
———. "Rewriting the Death of Jesus: An Intertextual Reading of Shusaku Endo's *Deep River*." *Christian Scholar's Review* 46, no. 1 (2016): 65–78.
———. "'Who Is My Neighbor?' Reading World Literature through the Hermeneutics of Love." *Journal of Education and Christian Belief* 11, no. 2 (2007): 67–82.
———. "From Resistance to *Kenosis*: Reconciling Cultural Difference in the Fiction of Endo Shusaku." *Christianity and Literature* 48, no. 2 (1999): 177–94.
———. "Encountering Christ in Shusaku Endo's Mudswamp of Japan." In *Christian Encounters with the Other*, edited by John C. Hawley, 166–81. New York: New York University Press, 1998.
Newby, Eric. *Slowly Down the Ganges*. New York: Lonely Planet, 1998.
Ni, Zhange. *The Pagan Writes Back: When World Religion Meets World Literature*. Charlottesville: University of Virginia Press, 2015.
———. "Japan's Orient and Animal Theology in Endo Shusaku's *Deep River*." *Journal of the American Academy of Religion* 81, no. 3 (2013): 669–97.
Ninomiya, Cindy. "Endō Shūsaku: Bridging the Gap between Christianity and Japanese Culture." *Japan Christian Quarterly* 56, no. 4 (1990): 227–36.
Noble, Colin. "Endo Shusaku's Jesus: Introduction to a Japanese Christology." *Crux* 27, no. 4 (1991): 28–32.
Odin, Steve. *Tragic Beauty in Whitehead and Japanese Aesthetics*. Lanham, MD: Lexington Books, 2016.
Okada, Sumie. *Japanese Writers and the West*. Basingstoke, England: Macmillan Press, 2003.

Orpett, Susan. "Silences and Voices: The Writings of Endo Shusaku." *Journal of the Association of Teachers of Japanese* 27, no. 1 (1993): 57–58.

Pearce, Joseph. *Literary Converts: Spiritual Inspiration in an Age of Unbelief.* San Francisco: Ignatius, 2000.

Pellegrino, Joe. "Endo's Ethics." *Kentucky Philological Review* 15 (2001): 44–48.

Prior, Karen Swallow. *On Reading Well: Finding the Good Life through Great Books.* Grand Rapids, MI: Brazos Press, 2018.

Reichardt, Mary R. *Exploring Catholic Literature: A Companion and Resource Guide.* Lanham, MD: Rowman & Littlefield, 2003.

Reinsma, Luke M. "Shusaku Endo's River of Life." *Christianity and Literature* 48, no. 2 (1999): 195–211.

Rimer, J. Thomas. "That Most Excellent Gift of Charity—Endō Shūsaku in Contemporary World Literature." *Journal of the Association of Teachers of Japanese* 27, no. 1 (1993): 59–66.

Rimer, J. Thomas and Van C. Gessel, eds. *The Columbia Anthology of Modern Japanese Literature*, two volumes. New York: Columbia University Press, 2005–7.

Robinson, Lewis. "Images of Christianity in Chinese and Japanese Fiction." *American-Asian Review* 3 (1985): 1–61.

Said, Edward. *Orientalism.* New York: Vintage, 1994.

Sanneh, Lamin. *Whose Religion Is Christianity? The Gospel Beyond the West.* Grand Rapids, MI: Wm. B. Eerdmans, 2003.

Sanneh, Lamin and Michael J. McClymond, eds. *The Wiley Blackwell Companion to World Christianity.* Chichester, United Kingdom, and Malden, MA: Wiley Blackwell, 2016.

Sanyal, Sanjeev. *Land of the Seven Rivers: A Brief History of India's Geography.* New York: Penguin, 2013.

Schreiter, Robert. *Constructing Local Theologies.* New York: Orbis Books, 1985.

Shafer, Ingrid. "Shusaku Endo and Andrew Greeley: Catholic Imagination East & West." *Midamerica* 18 (1991): 160–73.

Shaw, Samuel, and Joel Carpenter, eds. *Christianity in India: Conversion, Community Development, and Religious Freedom.* Minneapolis, MN: Fortress Press, 2018.

Sherry, Patrick. "The End of the Catholic Novel?" *Literature and Theology* 9, no. 2 (1995): 165–78.

Shirley, Wayne D. "The Coming of 'Deep River.'" *American Music* 15, no. 4 (1997): 493–534.

Smart, Ninian. *Buddhism and Christianity: Rivals and Allies.* Basingstoke, United Kingdom: Macmillan Press, 1993.

Somers, Sean. "Passion Plays by Proxy: The Paschal Face as Interculturality in the Works of Endō Shūsaku and Mishima Yukio." In *Through a Glass Darkly: Suffering, the Sacred, and the Sublime in Literature and Theory*, edited by Holly Faith Nelson, et al., 327–46. Waterloo and Brantford, Ontario: Wilfrid Laurier University Press, 2010.

Song, C. S. *Jesus in the Power of the Spirit.* Minneapolis, MN: Fortress Press, 1994.
Sugirtharajah, Sharada, and John Hick, eds. *Religious Pluralism in the Modern World: An Ongoing Engagement with John Hick.* Houndmills, Basingstoke, Hampshire, UK: Palgrave Macmillan, 2012.
Suzuki, Tomi. *Narrating the Self: Fictions of Japanese Modernity.* Palo Alto, CA: Stanford University Press, 1996.
Takayanagi, Shunichi, S.J. "River, Symbol, Plot, and Narrative in Shusaku Endo's *Deep River.*" *Ultimate Reality and Meaning* 24, no. 4 (2001): 292–304.
———. "Christianity in the Intellectual Climate of Modern Japan." *The Chesterton Review* 14, no. 3 (1988): 385–93.
Toma, Johnny V. *A Study of the Catholic Priest in Shusaku Endo's Novels: A Rare Glimpse into the History of Japan and Christianity.* Saarbrücken, Germany: Lap Lambert, 2011.
Tracy, David. *The Analogical Imagination: Christian Theology and the Culture of Pluralism.* New York: Crossroad, 1981.
Turnbull, Stephen. "From Catechist to Kami: Martyrs and Mythology among the Kakure Kirishitan." *Japanese Religions* 19, nos. 1/2 (1993): 58–81.
Wakabayashi, Bob Tadashi, ed. *Modern Japanese Thought.* Cambridge: Cambridge University Press, 1998.
Walls, Andrew F. *The Missionary Movement in Christian History: Studies in the Transmission of Faith.* Maryknoll, NY: Orbis Books, 1996.
Washburn, Dennis. "The Poetics of Conversion and the Problem of Translation in Endō Shūsaku's *Silence.*" In *Converting Cultures: Religion, Ideology and Transformations of Modernity*, edited by Dennis Washburn and A. Kevin Reinhart, 345–63. Leiden, Netherlands: Brill Publishers, 2007.
———. *Translating Mount Fuji: Modern Japanese Fiction and the Ethics of Identity.* New York: Columbia University Press, 2007.
———. *The Dilemma of the Modern in Japanese Fiction.* New Haven, CT: Yale University Press, 1995.
Whitehouse, J. C. *Catholics on Literature.* Dublin: Four Courts, 1997.
Williams, Mark. "Crossing the Deep River: Endō Shūsaku and the Problem of Religious Pluralism." In *Xavier's Legacies: Catholicism in Modern Japanese Culture*, edited by Kevin M. Doak, 115–33. Vancouver: University of British Columbia Press, 2011.
———. "Endō Shūsaku: Death and Rebirth in *Deep River.*" *Christianity and Literature* 51, no. 2 (2002): 219–39.
———. *Endō Shūsaku: A Literature of Reconciliation.* London and New York: Routledge, 1999.
Williams, Philip. "Images of Jesus in Japanese Fiction." *Japan Christian Quarterly* 49, no. 1 (1983): 12–22.
Wills, Elizabeth. "Christ as Eternal Companion: A Study in the Christology of Shusaku Endo." *Scottish Journal of Theology* 45 (1992): 85–100.

Yamagata, Kazumi. "Mr. Shusaku Endo Talks about His Life and Works as a Catholic Writer." *The Chesterton Review* 12, no. 4 (1986): 493–506.

Yamaoka, Sanji. "Religious Sentiment as a Japanese Catholic: Shusaku Endo's Perspective: Transforming Christianity for the Japanese." *Fujen Religious Studies* 3 (2001): 227–57.

Yancey, Philip. *Soul Survivor: How Thirteen Unlikely Mentors Helped My Faith Survive the Church*. New York: Doubleday; Colorado Springs, CO: Water Brook Press, 2003.

Yuki, Hideo. "Christianity and Japanese Culture." *Japanese Religions* 25, nos. 1/2 (2000): 28–35.

Contributors

Mark Bosco, a Jesuit priest, is vice president for mission and ministry at Georgetown University, United States, and teaches in the English department. His research focuses on theological aesthetics and the intersection of religion and art, especially the twentieth-century Catholic literary tradition. He is the author of *Graham Greene's Catholic Imagination*; *Academic Novels as Satire: Critical Studies of an Emerging Genre*; and *Revelation and Convergence: Flannery O'Connor and the Catholic Intellectual Tradition*. Other publications include essays on Gerard Manley Hopkins, Margaret Atwood, and Endō Shūsaku. He is a producer and director of the upcoming documentary feature film *Flannery*.

Mini Chandran is a professor of English at the Indian Institute of Technology Kanpur, Uttar Pradesh, India. She works on Indian literature and aesthetics, translation studies, and literary censorship, often translating between English and Malayalam, a south Indian language. Besides publishing articles in national and international journals, she is the author of *The Writer, the Reader and the State: Literary Censorship in India* and she co-edited *Textual Travels: The Theory and Practice of Translation in India*.

Mark W. Dennis is a professor of religion at Texas Christian University, United States, where he teaches courses in Buddhism, Daoism, and Confucianism, religion and violence, and world religious traditions. He earned his PhD in Buddhist studies at the University of Wisconsin in 2006, focusing on early Japanese Buddhism, and has a PhD minor in Japanese literature. He lived in Japan and India for eight years where he studied Buddhism and Hinduism, and he has traveled widely in Asia. His first book was an English translation of the *Shōmangyō-gisho*, a Japanese Buddhist text written in classical Chinese. He is co-editor of *Approaching* Silence*: New Perspectives on Shusaku Endo's Classic Novel* with Darren J. N. Middleton. He is also co-editing *Voices of Freedom from Asia and the Middle East* with his TCU colleague Rima Abunasser.

Elizabeth Cameron Galbraith was educated at the universities of Nottingham, Durham, and Cambridge, completing her divinity doctorate in 1992. She taught at Coe College from 1992 to 2002, where she held the Joseph E. McCabe chair in religion. Durham theologian Ann Loades' book *Kant and Job's Comforters* had a formative influence, not only upon the book that Galbraith published while at Coe, *Kant and Theology: Was Kant a Closet Theologian?*, but also upon what became long-standing teaching and research interests on the problem of suffering for Galbraith during the eleven years she went on to teach at St. Olaf College. It had also been at Coe that Galbraith's burgeoning interest in Asian Catholicism was both nourished and, all significantly, institutionally supported through field research and teaching opportunities in both India and Japan. Galbraith discovered in Endō Shūsaku an author whose novels inextricably combine the problem of suffering and Asian Catholicism. Galbraith currently resides in Collegeville Minnesota, with her husband and three children. She has returned, on a part-time basis, to the idyll of studenthood, delighting in offerings in Monastic studies at the School of Theology and Seminary at Saint John's University.

P. A. George is a professor of Japanese language and literature and the current chairperson of the Centre for Japanese Studies, School of Language, Literature and Culture Studies, Jawaharlal Nehru University, New Delhi, India. A native of Kottayam in Kerala, India, he had his university education at the Jawaharlal Nehru University, and he has done extensive research in modern Japanese literature, especially on Shimazaki Tōson, Miyazawa Kenji, and Ishikawa Takuboku. He has served as visiting scholar to Waseda University, Iwate University, International Research Centre for Japanese Studies and visiting professor to Kwansei Gakuin University, Nishinomiya, Japan. He has published sixteen authored, edited, or translated books. In 2016, George was awarded the Japanese Foreign Minister's Commendation in recognition of his contribution to Japanese studies in India. In 2002, the City Government of Hanamaki bestowed upon George the coveted Miyazawa Kenji Shoreisho Award in recognition of his research. Presently, he is engaged in research on supernatural beings in Miyazawa Kenji's works. He lives in New Delhi with his wife, Sophia George, a postgraduate in physics, and their daughter, Haruka George, a B.Tech. in engineering physics.

Van C. Gessel was born in California but was raised in Salt Lake City, Utah, United States. He has an undergraduate degree from the University of Utah and MA and PhD degrees from Columbia University. He has taught modern Japanese literature at Columbia, Notre Dame, and the University of California, Berkeley, and in 1990 he joined the faculty at Brigham Young University (BYU). At BYU, he has served as department chair and dean of the College of Humanities. He has published seven translations of works by the Japanese Christian novelist Endō Shūsaku, including *The Samurai*, *Deep River*, and *Kiku's Prayer*. A translation of another Endō novel, *Sachiko*, is forthcoming. With J. Thomas Rimer, he co-edited *The Columbia Anthology of Modern Japanese Literature*. Recently, he was literary consultant for Martin Scorsese's film adaptation of Endō's best-known novel *Silence*. In 2016, he received a commendation (*Gaimu Daijin Hyōshō*) from the foreign minister of Japan, and in 2018, he was awarded the Order of the Rising Sun (*Kyokujitsu chūjushō*) decoration from Japan for contributing to mutual understanding between Japan and the United States. He and his wife, Elizabeth, live in Orem, Utah, and are the parents of three children and have five grandchildren.

Ronald Green received an MA in Japanese literature from the University of Oregon, United States, as well as an MA in South Asian studies and a PhD in Buddhist studies from the University of Wisconsin-Madison, United States. He is currently an associate professor of religious studies at Coastal Carolina University in Conway, South Carolina. His book publications include *Buddhism Goes to the Movies* and *Gyōnen's Transmission of the Buddha Dharma in Three Countries*. He has written a number of articles examining representations of religions in novels, including a recent piece titled "Konkōkyō Religious Ideas in the Writings of Ogawa Yōko."

Dennis Hirota is professor of Shin Buddhist studies, emeritus, and a senior research fellow at Ryukoku University, Kyoto, Japan. He was the head translator of *The Collected Works of Shinran* and has published books and articles in both Japanese and English on Japanese Pure Land Buddhist tradition, particularly the thought of Shinran and Ippen. He has served as a visiting professor at the International Research Center for Japanese Studies (Kyoto, 1996–1997) and Harvard Divinity School (1999, 2008). His books include *Asura's Harp: Engagement with Language as Buddhist Path*, *Shinran: Shūkyō gengo no kakumeisha* [Shinran and Religious Language], and *No Abode: The Record of Ippen*. He is co-author, with Ueda Yoshifumi, of *Shinran: An Introduction to His Thought* and has published on Buddhist aesthetics in Japan, including *Wind in the*

Pines: Classic Buddhist Writings of the Arts as Way. He is currently completing a book on Shinran and Heidegger and is at work on a book on Shinran and moral anthropology (with Charles Hallisey).

Julian Crandall Hollick has produced many award-winning radio documentaries for National Public Radio and BBC Radio 4 on India, including *The World of Islam*, *Passages to India*, *Letters from Jitvapur*, *Apna Street*, *Monsoon*, and *Ganga*. In 2004 to 2005, he traveled the entire length of the Ganga by country boat. He has also written two books: *Ganga* and *Apna Street*. He has contributed to several volumes about aspects of India, including *Travellers Tales*, *Samskara*, *When Peacocks Dance*, and *Our National River Ganga*. Since 2012, he has taught an annual workshop on cross-cultural journalism at Xaviers College in Mumbai and is developing a ten-part mass-open online course for the college, to be released in 2019 to 2020. He lives with his wife in Provence, France.

Justyna Weronika Kasza is an assistant professor in Japanese studies at Nicolaus Copernicus University in Torun, Poland, where she teaches courses in Japanese literature, literary studies, and translation. She received her PhD from the University of Leeds, England, in 2013 and was a visiting scholar at the Institute of Comparative Culture at Sophia University in Tokyo from 2008 to 2009. Between 2011 and 2015, she was an associate lecturer in Japanese at the University of Central Lancashire, Preston, England. She is the recipient of two prestigious awards, from the Japan Foundation Fellowship and the Great Britain Sasakawa Foundation. In 2016, her doctoral thesis was published as the monograph *Hermeneutics of Evil in the Works of Endō Shūsaku: Between Reading and Writing*. As part of her recent research activities, in 2016 she attended the Sixth Seminars in World Literature hosted by the Institute for World Literature at Harvard University. Currently she is working on a new book project: *The "I" in the Making: Rethinking Japanese shishōsetsu in a Global Age* for which, in 2018, she was awarded a scholarship from the Japan Foundation.

Emi Mase-Hasegawa is associate professor at J. F. Oberlin University in Tokyo, Japan, where she teaches in the field of religious studies. She holds a ThD in missiology and ecumenical studies from Lund University, Sweden. Besides contributing to several volumes and academic journals, she is the author, in English, of *Christ in Japanese Culture, Theological Themes in Shusaku Endo's Literary Works*.

Maeri Megumi was born in Kagoshima, Japan, and earned her MAs from the University of Iowa and the University of Southern California (USC), United

States, where she studied linguistics, Japanese language pedagogy, and East Asian cultures. After having taught Japanese at USC, she completed her doctorate at the University of Texas in Austin with a dissertation titled "Religion, Nation, Art: Christianity and Modern Japanese Literature." Currently, she teaches at St. Edward's University (SEU) in Austin, Texas. While teaching Japanese language courses at SEU, she has also been taking part in the summer program between SEU and APU (Asia Pacific University in Japan), promoting cultural communication between the United States and Japan. Her research interests include modern Japanese literature, religion, and Japanese language pedagogy.

Darren J. N. Middleton serves as the John F. Weatherly professor of literature and theology at Texas Christian University (TCU), United States. He also directs TCU's Master of Liberal Arts program. A native of Nottingham in the English East Midlands, he was educated at the universities of Manchester, Oxford, and Glasgow before teaching in Memphis, Tennessee, and in Fort Worth, Texas, where he has been since 1998. He has authored or edited ten books, the most recent of which is *Rastafari and the Arts: An Introduction*. Studies of George Eliot, the Victorian novelist, and on global Rastafari spirituality, are forthcoming. He lives in Fort Worth with his wife, Elizabeth Flowers, an American religious historian, and their son, Jonathan. For additional information, see www.darrenjnmiddleton.com.

Zhange Ni is associate professor of religion and culture at Virginia Tech, United States. She teaches courses in Asian religions, religion and literature, and critical theory. She received her PhD in religion and literature at the University of Chicago Divinity School and, in 2010 to 2011, she was a research associate at Harvard Divinity School's Women's Studies in Religion program. Endō Shūsaku is one of the authors she studied in her first book *The Pagan Writes Back: When World Religion Meets World Literature*. She is currently working on religion and speculative fiction in the United States and East Asia.

S. Brent Plate's teachings and writings explore relations between sensual life and spiritual life. He is a writer, editor, public speaker, and associate professor of religious studies by special appointment at Hamilton College, United States. He has authored or edited fifteen books, and his writing has appeared in Newsweek.com, Salon.com, the *Washington Post*, the *Christian Century*, the *Islamic Monthly*, *America*, the *Los Angeles Review of Books*, *Religion Dispatches*, and elsewhere. He is president of CrossCurrents/The Association of Religion and Intellectual Life, and co-chair of the board of the Interfaith Coalition of Greater Utica, New York. Recent books include *A History of Religion in 5½*

Objects: Bringing the Spiritual to its Senses; *Religion and Film: Cinema and the Re-Creation of the World*; and the co-edited *Religion in Museums*. See more at www.sbrentplate.net.

Christopher Wachal received his PhD from Loyola University Chicago, United States. His dissertation, *Pax Ecclesia: Globalization and Catholic Literary Modernism*, examines the evolution of Catholic literary aesthetics under the pressures of globalizing modernity. He has previously published scholarship on Flannery O'Connor's "The Displaced Person" and Endō Shūsaku's *Silence*. He lives in Chicago with his wife and dog.

Mark Williams is currently vice president for International Academic Exchange at International Christian University in Tokyo, Japan. Born in the United Kingdom, he received his BA in Japanese studies at the University of Oxford and his PhD in Japanese literature at the University of California, Berkeley. He then taught Japanese studies at the University of Leeds from 1988 to 2017, where he served as chair of the School of Modern Languages and Cultures and, from 2008 to 2011, as president of the British Association for Japanese Studies. Between 2011 and 2014, he was on secondment to Akita International University, Japan, where he served as vice president for academic affairs. He has published extensively, in English and Japanese, on postwar Japanese literature and Christianity in Japan. He is also the translator of two novels by Endō Shūsaku.

Index

Abe, Yōko, 211
Abhinavagupta, 70
Adi Granth (also *Guru Granth Sahib*), 9–10, 93
Ādi Śaṅkarācārya, 59, 215, 229n7
Advaita Philosophy, 215, 229
agape, 253
Agni, 6
Agra, 10, 288
Akal Purakh ("Immortal, Timeless Being"), 9
Akal Takht ("the Throne of the Timeless One"), 95–96, 104
Akali Dal (Sikh political party), 11, 94–95
Akbar, Emperor (1542–1605), 10
Akiyama, Shun, 36, 202, 210
Akutagawa Prize, 2
Akutagawa, Ryūnosuke, 105n18, 175
ālaya–consciousness, 183, 193, 272–73
Allahabad, xvi, xx–xxi, 69
alter Christus, 18, 259n56
Amarnath, 13
Ambedkar, 12, 25
Amida Buddha, 41, 81, 85, 193, 263–64, 272, 275–78, 284; Amitābha, Buddha, 16–17, 52
Amida Sūtra (also, *Amida sutra*), 14, 17, 25, 43, 52–53, 84, 116, 240, 271, 275

Amitayurdhyana Sūtra (Contemplation Sūtra), 25
Amritsar, 10, 93, 95
anātman (selflessness), 35
anti-Sikh riots, 3, 89, 92–97, 103, 104n16
apostasy, 2, 48, 128, 155
arhat ("worthy one"), 16
Asahara, Shōkō, 23
ātman (self or soul), 6, 35, 42, 229
avarṇa ("without a *varṇa*"), 229n14
avatār (also, avatar; "descent"), 7, 24, 64
Axial religion, 266–68
Ayyappan pilgrimage, 8, 24

Bangalore, 60
Barron, Robert, 17
Bashō, Matsuo, 90, 104, 181, 271
Bein, River, 9
Bernanos, Georges, 128, 177n4
Bhabha, Homi, 57, 63
Bhagavad Gītā, 64, 66, 70, 225
Bhagīratha (also Bhagirathi), xvi, 59
bhajans (singing hymns dedicated to a deity), 7
bhakti (devotion), xvi, 7–8, 10
Bhattacharya, Haridas, 70
bhavacakra ("wheel of life"), 35
Bhindranwale, Jarnail Singh, 10–11, 93–96, 104

Bhiṣma, 59
Bihar, 14, 58, 104
Bodh Gayā (the site of the Buddha's enlightenment), 14
bodhi (wisdom) tree, 15
bodhicitta (mind of enlightenment), 16
bodhisattva (wisdom being), 16–17
bodhi tree ("wisdom" tree), 15
Borges, Jorge Luis, 197, 208, 209n3
Bosco, Mark, viii, 18, 33, 47, 50, 127–48 passim, 296, 305
Brahmā, 90
Brahman (ultimate reality), 6, 229
Brahmin (priestly caste), 6–7, 24–25, 44, 171, 218, 227, 229
Brar, Kuldip Singh, Lieutenant General (Sikh officer), 95–96
British East India Company, 10–11
Brothers Karamazov, The, 49, 89–103
Buddha ("Awakened One," also Gautama Buddha; see also Shakyamuni Buddha), 14–17, 24n27, 34–35, 49, 50–52, 61, 84, 128, 214; Buddhahood, 16, 39, 272, 275–76; Buddha-dharma, 51; Buddha-field, 276; Buddha-land, 271; Buddha-mind, 272; Buddha-nature, 272; Buddha-wisdom, 272; Gautama Buddha, 219; living buddha, 236
Buddha Amitābha (also Amida Buddha), 16–17, 41, 52–53, 81, 85, 193, 263–64, 272, 275–78, 284n76; Amida's Buddha-field, 276
Buddha Lokeśvararāja, 16
Buddhaghoṣa, 42
Buddhism, 5–6, 13, 15–17, 25n27, 25n37, 34–35, 40, 52, 61, 77–78, 81, 84, 92, 121, 129, 131, 134, 136, 145n6, 146n18, 147n43, 154, 174, 176, 208, 219–20, 223–24, 226, 229n20, 237, 251, 261, 263–65, 269, 272–73, 275, 278, 305, 307; Japanese Buddhism, 271; Mahāyāna Buddhism, 16, 272–73; Tibetan Buddhism, 251. *See also* Pure Land Buddhism
Bungakkai (Literary world), 76
Bunka Kunshō (Order of Culture), 4
bunshin monogatari ("the story of the alter ego"), 207
Burma, 2, 13, 16, 40, 53, 76, 79–81, 101, 116, 156, 233–34

Calcutta, 67, 70, 159
Camino de Santiago, 19, 289–90
caste system (also outcastes), 6–7, 9, 14–15, 25n27, 30, 43, 66, 91, 144, 159, 218–19, 220, 222, 228, 229n14
Catholicism: and interfaith relations, 18, 136; Asian form of, 306; Communion of Saints doctrine, 149, 160; European form of, 138, 167, 173, 213; Mariology, 236; sacramentalism, 17–20; Scholastic form of, 138, 154; Second Vatican Council, 130, 133–36
Cavanaugh, William, 32
Chāmuṇḍā (a manifestation of Devi, the Hindu Divine Mother), 7–8, 21, 33, 51, 61, 63, 74, 76–77, 85, 89, 91, 101–3, 120, 157–58, 221–22, 228, 234, 236, 271, 273–74, 280, 291
Chandran, Mini, xxn1, 8–9, 14, 33, 43, 57–71, 305
China, 16, 74, 76, 78–79, 131, 142, 265
Chinmoku, 3, 231. *See also* Silence
Chitragupta, 216
Christianity: European, 48, 64, 101, 118, 136–39, 142, 173–74, 176, 226, 237, 262–63, 273, 278; history in India, 224–27; traditional theism, 156–58, 168–69, 173–74, 246–50
Confucianism, 251, 261, 264
Congress Party, 12, 94–96
Cosmocentrism, 272–73

Covill, Linda, 51

Dakshineshwar temple, 8
Dalian, 1, 40, 78–81, 232, 235
Dalit, 12, 25n27, 220
Dalit Buddhist movement, 25n27
Damdami Taksal (Sikh educational group), 94
darshan, 287
darśanas, 6
Deep River: African American spiritual, 5, 49–50; Buddhist themes, 30–55 passim; creative process, 41, 111–12, 206–9, 214; cultural difference, 57–69; filmic adaptation, 3; interfaith theme, 136–44; Japanese-language scholarship, 20–21, 109, 119–20, 174, 197; Japanese sensibilities, 168–69, 176, 261–81 passim; Job theme, 181–91 passim; John Hick's influence on, 19, 38, 112, 129, 183, 231, 236–38, 250, 257n14, 265; name symbolism, 55n20, 282n36; omniscient narrator, 189; pilgrimage theme, xviii, 1–4, 20, 22, 31, 61, 63, 73, 90, 116–19, 128, 154, 157, 182, 288; process panentheism theme, 245–56 passim; rebirth theme, 5–7, 14, 18, 34, 41–45, 63, 90, 97, 100, 116, 119–20, 159, 214–15, 238, 271, 277; self-realization motif, 107–23; textual hauntings, 204–7 passim; theodicy theme, 181–91 passim; theology of harmony in diversity, 231–39. See also *Fukai Kawa*
Delhi, 10, 79, 95–96, 274, 306
Delhi Sultanate, 10
Dennis, Mark W., 1–25 passim, 29–55 passim, 305–6
Derrida, Jacques, 82
deva (male deities), 7, 54
devī (female deities), 64

dharma, 6, 16, 51, 214, 218, 227, 229, 272, 307; Wheel of Dharma, 15, 214
Dharmākara, Bodhisattva, 16–17
Dharmaśāstra, 6–7
Dharmasūtra, 6
Din-i-Ilahi ("Religion of God"), 10
dōhansha ("constant companion"), 115, 123, 190
Doms, 33, 66
duḥkha, 30–31, 34, 38, 49, 52–53
Durgā, 61
dvija ("twice born"), 7, 43
Dostoevsky, Fyodor, 49, 89–103 passim

Elie, Paul, 32, 153
Enami (character, *Deep River*): arrogant Japanese intellectual, 173; attitude toward India, 7, 62, 173, 213–30 passim; caste system, 6–7, 15, 91, 218; Chāmundā, 33, 61, 101, 157, 221, 234, 236; contempt for Japanese tourists, 173; Ganges River, 90, 101, 277; Hinduism, 91; name symbolism, 55n20, 282n36
Endō, Ikuko (Shūsaku Endō's mother), 108
Endō, Junko (Shūsaku Endō's wife), 108, 184, 192–94
Endō, Ryūnosuke (Shūsaku Endō's son), xii, 193
Endo, Shusaku (also Endō Shusakū): and Eastern pantheism, 269–70; and Shinran, 268–69; animal theology, 82–85; biblical motifs, 21, 31, 43, 92, 103, 109, 114, 155, 159, 181–91 passim, 235–36, 253; Catholic/catholic faith, 167–76; Christian inclusivist, 129–44 passim, 190–91; critical essays, 108–9, 172–73, 183, 188, 204–6, 251–53; European Catholic literary revival, 78, 110–11, 127–44 passim; France, 2, 45, 78,

Endo, Shusaku *(continued)*
107, 128–32, 167, 177n5, 178n21, 182, 200, 204, 247, 252, 275; funeral, 4; general themes, 2–3, 18–19, 21, 100; heterodoxy, 160; image of India, 213–28 passim, 234–35; I-novel tradition, 36, 39, 41, 177n9, 197–209 passim; identification with his characters, 44–46, 157, 175, 188, 192n4, 233, 270; illness, 1–4, 175, 182–84; interviews, 184–86; Jungian influence, 113–15, 183; life and literary art, 1–4; literary critic, 110–15; mentors, 76; model of God, 250, 253–55; mother's influence, 154, 157, 176n1; pre-axial religion, 265–66 passim; soteriological themes, 43, 78–85 passim, 113–14, 183, 232, 235, 238–39, 255; theocentrism, 19, 121, 236–38; theological anthropology, 102, 169, 233, 273–75; theology of encounter, 136–44 passim

End of the Affair, The, 45, 206, 207

Five Ks of Sikhism, 10
Four Noble Truths of Buddhism, 15
Four passing sights of Buddhism, 14
Fr. Ferreira (character, *Silence* novel), 48, 83
Fr. Rodrigues (character, *Silence* novel): alienated from God, 119, 174; believing apostate, 178n22; decision to trample, 112, 187; *kenosis* of the self, 37; spiritual transformation, 44, 47, 54; suffering, 31, 174, 182; taming of the ego, 36
Fujimura, Makoto, 250
Fukai kawa, 1, 22n3, 23n7, 50, 122n4, 122n5, 122n8, 122n9, 122n19, 123n59, 179n27, 211n45, 211n48, 211n59, 231, 238, 240n3, 240n4, 241n5, 241n6, 241n7, 241n11, 241n17, 281n3, 281n6, 282n17, 283n38, 283n41, 283n46, 283n46, 283n49, 283n52, 284n67, 284n75, 284n78, 284n80, 284n82, 284n84, 284n88, 285n104, 296. See also *Deep River*
Fukai kawa o saguru (In search of the Deep River), 122n25, 123n63, 228n2, 240n4, 242n19, 242n20, 242n21, 242n23, 243n33
Fukai kawa o yomu (Reading Deep River), 194n18, 197, 209n4
Fukai kawa sōsaku nikki (Deep River composition diary), 41, 86n10, 122n10, 123n63, 179n25, 179n31, 193n12, 201, 206–7, 211n44, 211n46, 211n50, 211n60, 240n2, 241n12, 241n16, 242n18, 242n26, 242n27, 242n30, 257n19, 282n20, 284n65, 296
Fukuda, Kōsuke, 211n49
Fukuda, Tsuneari, 140, 155
Fukuzawa, Yukichi, 2
fumie (an image of Jesus or Mary used in the ritual of apostasy), 47, 83, 92, 112, 155, 187, 194n24
Furuya, Kenzō, 178n21
fumu ga ii ("It is all right to trample" [on the *fumie*]), 47

Galbraith, Elizabeth Cameron, 18, 22, 32, 44, 149–65 passim, 306
Gandhi, Indira: ashes of, 13; linked to Chāmundā, 102; "Mother of India," 102; murder of, 2–5, 9, 13, 35, 44, 47, 67, 89, 92–93, 96, 101–2, 144, 222, 227, 255, 262; Operation Blue Star, 11, 94, 96
Gandhi, Mahatma, 12, 142, 225
Gandhi, Rajiv, 13, 95
Ganesha, 287

Gaṅgā (also Ganga), vii, xiii–xxiii, 1–3, 7–9, 13–15, 17–22 passim, 30–31, 33, 35, 38, 41, 43–45, 47, 49–51, 58–61, 66–69, 128–29, 136, 140–41, 144, 148n65, 193, 213–17 passim, 220, 222, 226–28, 246, 248, 253, 255; *Ganga* (Julian Crandall Hollick), 57–58, 69n3, 299, 308; Ganga Devi, 8; Mother Ganga, 53, 59, 190, 216; *Ganga jal* (also *gangājal*), xiv, xviii, xix, xxin3, xxiiin49, 59; *Ganga ki Bahan* ("sister of Ganga"), xxiin23; *Ganga Lahari*, 59; *Ganga Stotram*, 59; Gangaprasad, 61. See also Ganges

Ganges, xiii–xvi, xxin7, 13, 22, 30, 38, 44, 47, 52, 58, 67, 73, 81, 84, 90, 99, 101–2, 109, 114, 116–117, 120, 141, 143–144, 158–159, 169, 170–172, 174, 187, 189, 207, 227, 234, 236–237, 240, 255, 271, 280, 299, 300–1

Gangotrī (also Gangotri), xv, 216

Gaston (characters, *Deep River* and *Wonderful Fool*), 14, 44, 102–3, 117, 156, 175, 190, 235, 280

George, P. A., 5, 41, 43, 213–30 passim, 306

Gessel, Van C., 1–4, 31, 36, 44, 47, 54n10, 54n15, 55n20, 181–95 passim, 252, 258n25, 259n40, 307

ghāṭ (also *ghat*), xx, 3, 7, 9, 30, 33, 35, 41, 63, 65–66, 143, 214, 222, 226, 238, 293

Godavari, xv–xvi, xvii, xix, xxin4, xxin16, xxin17

Godse, Nathuram, 13

Golden Country, The, 48, 83

Golden Temple. See Harmandir Sahib

Gopalakrishnan, N., 229n10

goptṛī (the Protector), 64

Government of India Act (1858), 11

Green, Julien, 45, 78, 91, 154, 206–7

Green, Ronald, 5, 9–10, 32, 42, 46, 49, 89–105 passim, 307

Greene, Graham, 21, 128, 206, 258n27

gurbāni ("the speech of wisdom"), 10

gurdwara (Sikh temple), 10, 93–94

Gurmukhī ("[from the] mouth of the guru"), 9

Guru Amar Das (1479–1574; third Sikh guru), 10

Guru Gobind Singh (1666–1708; tenth and final human Sikh guru), 10

Guru Granth Sahib (also known as the *Adi Granth*), 9–10, 93

Guru Nanak (1469–1539; first Sikh guru), 9, 93, 95

Guru Ram Das (1534–81; fourth Sikh guru), 10

Guru Tegh Bahadur (1621–75; ninth Sikh guru), 10

Hagiwara, Takao, 85n2, 298

haiku, 104n3, 108, 181, 271

Hara, Tamiki, 75

Haridwar, xv, xxin17, xxiiin44, 69n8, 216

Harijan, 7, 9, 91, 159, 230n29

Harmandir Sahib (Temple of God; known as the Golden Temple in English), 10–11, 93–96, 104n13

Hasekura, Rokuemon, 82, 112

Hashizume, Daisaburō, 177n6

hataraki (force, work), 178n22, 250

Hawthorne, Nathaniel, 32

Hesse, Hermann, 5

Hick, John, 19, 38, 85n3, 112–14, 129, 142–43, 193n12, 231, 236–38, 242n18, 250, 257n14, 257n20, 265–68, 270

Himalayas, 13, 58, 248

Hinduism, xvii, xx, 5–7, 14–15, 50, 61, 64, 91–92, 103n1, 128–29, 134, 141, 143, 174, 213, 215, 221, 225–27, 237, 305

Hindu Mahasabha, 24n23
Hirayama, Ikuo, 74
Hirohito, Emperor, 23n7
Hiromasa, Mase, 239
Hiroshima, 76
Hirota, Dennis, 16, 39, 47–49, 52, 55n20, 261–85 passim, 307–8
Hollick, Julian Crandall, xiii–xxiii passim, 20, 57–58, 60, 63, 68, 308
Hōnen (1133–1212), 25n30
Hosokawa, Morihiro, 23n7
Hotta, Yoshie, 41, 214

Igarashi, Hitoshi, 23n7
Imphal campaign, 283n52
Inabata, Teiko, 108
inculturation, 127–28, 231, 253
India, viii, xv–xvii, xx, xxiin18, 2–3, 5–12, 15, 19, 21, 24n20, 24n23, 25n27, 31, 33, 38, 41–42, 45, 58, 60–63, 68, 73–76, 78–79, 82, 84, 90, 93–94, 96, 100–1, 114, 116, 120, 128, 131, 135, 140–42, 154, 157, 170–71, 182, 187–88, 191, 200, 207–8, 213–15, 217–26, 228, 229n20, 232–36, 241n8, 245, 248, 265, 271, 273, 280, 287–88, 290, 305–6, 308; All India Radio, 95; Mother India, 61; Mother of India, 102; "Passage to India," 73; *Times of India*, xviii, xxiin40
Indian, 9, 13, 24, 35, 42–43, 57–61 passim, 68–69, 74, 80, 90, 93, 121, 160, 208, 214, 218, 224, 228; Indians, xxin7, 12, 33, 41, 58, 60, 68, 101, 157, 214, 217–222, 228; Indian art, 74; Indian author, xix; Indian Buddhists, 15; Indian civilization, culture, and society, 15, 21, 40, 43, 100, 129, 159, 173, 213–14, 217–23 passim, 225, 227–28, 232, 240, 248, 287, 305; Indian independence movement, 12, 24n20; Indian Insurrection, 24n23; Indian literature and texts, 57, 305; Indian military and soldiers, 10–11, 13; Indian Peace Keeping Force (IPKF), 13; Indian mind and thinking, 68, 71n54, 214, 229n24, 229n25; Indian rivers, xix; Indian Rebellion of 1857; Indian religions, spirituality, and holy sites, 90, 109, 171, 193, 215, 224, 227–28, 274; Indian scientists, xix; Indian subcontinent, 9–10, 12, 24n14; *The Indian War of Independence, 1857*, 24n23
Indo-Japanese relations, 219
Indonesia, 131
Indra, 6, 64
Indus (also Sindhu), xv, xvii, xxin2, xxin4, xxin16, 24n14, 296, 298
Inoue (character, *Silence* novel), 48
Inoue, Fr. Yōji, 184, 193n14, 242n19, 252–53, 259n40
Interdependence, 30, 35, 39–41, 100, 200
Ishikawa, Takuboku, 306
Isobe (character, *Deep River*): connection to Mitsuko, 42, 90, 100, 102, 113; Japan, 189; image of India, 234; loss of his wife, 31, 35, 100, 173, 188, 232; name symbolism, 55n20, 282n36; nature-mysticism, 39; reincarnation hope, 2, 5, 39, 42–43, 63, 116, 119, 128, 232–34, 271, 276, 288, 290; salvation motifs, 116; Shirley MacLaine, 43; University of Virginia, 5, 232
Issa, 29–30, 35, 52
Iwanami, Gō, 107
Iwate University, 306
Iyer, V. Subrahmanya, 65–66

Jagannātha Paṇḍita, 59
Jahangir, Emperor (1569–1627), 10

Jāhnavī (daughter to Jahnu and Ganga ma), 59
Jainism, 24n27, 34, 215, 251
Janmashtami (Krishna's birthday), 287
Japan, 2–4, 25n30, 30, 36, 40, 48, 61–62, 73–79, 81–83, 108, 117, 128–29, 131, 141, 155, 169, 173, 189, 194n30, 208, 213, 217–20, 223–25, 228n1, 232, 234, 246, 251–53, 259n40, 261–64, 266–71 passim, 278, 280, 282n37, 305–10 passim
Japanese, v, 1–2, 4–6, 16, 20–22, 36n36, 31, 36, 40–42, 44, 48–50, 53, 54n10, 55n20, 61–62, 73–82 passim, 85, 89–90, 92–93, 99, 108, 116, 127–30, 136–37, 139, 157–59, 167, 169–70, 172–73, 175, 177n6, 178n21, 178n24, 188–89, 192n8, 193n14, 194n28, 194n29, 213–14, 217–19, 229n20, 232, 236–37, 241n9, 250–52, 261–65 passim, 267, 269–71, 274, 278, 282n36, 306, 308–310; Japanese army and militarism, 13, 21, 31, 35, 76, 78, 81, 233; Japanese body and clothes, 172; Japanese Buddhism, 14, 16–17, 25n30, 29, 50, 77, 239, 263, 271–72, 288, 305, 307; Japanese Catholicism, xiii, 2, 75, 132, 223, 225–26, 245; Japanese Christians, 37, 44, 77, 83, 92, 246, 307; Japanese colonialism, 79–80; Japanese culture, identity, people, and society, 23n7, 49, 75, 82, 128, 136, 169, 173–74, 176, 223, 236, 250–53, 263, 267–69, 281; Japanese government, 192n9; Japanese history, 127; Japanese language, 202, 306, 309; Japanese literature and writers, 2–3, 168–69, 175, 177n9, 181, 194n20, 198–99, 202–3, 213, 305–310 passim; Japanese mind, 48, 138, 214, 226, 241n9, 262–64, 268; Japanese nationalism, 40, 76, 81, 85, 86n14; Japanese nativist, 74; Japanese Orientalism, 75, 80; Japanese religion, 47, 168–69, 172, 176, 177n8, 178n12, 178n19, 178n24, 231, 234, 245, 251–52, 259n36, 269; Japanese Romantic School (Nihon Romanha), 75–76, 86n12; Japanese sensibilities, outlook, and attitudes, ix, 167–68, 173, 177n2, 261–66 passim, 268, 273, 275–77, 279–80, 283n48; Japanese soil, 127, 231; Japanese swamp, 48, 267

jāti, 6, 22, 24n16, 218
Jayamuni, xvi
Jesuit, 36, 131–32, 135, 145n14, 223–24, 252, 263, 305
Jesus: and aesthetics, 18–19; and Endō's God-Onion concept, 49, 195n32; and Mitsu, 44–45, 149; animals aligned to, 41, 46, 81–85, 91, 102; biblical portrait of, 99, 101, 103; Eternal Companion, 152, 191, 233, 235, 241n14; maternal tropes for, 33, 152, 237, 255; panentheism, 236; pluralistic interpretations of, 129, 245; redemptive suffering, 32, 150–54; 190, 226–27, 238; Rouault's clowns linked to, 46, 83, 102; St. Thomas and India, 224; Vatican II, 135
Jinnah, Muhammad Ali, 12
jiriki ("self power"), 17
Jōdo Shinshū. *See* Pure Land Buddhism
Jōdoshū. *See* Pure Land Buddhism
Johnston, William, 121, 127, 146n14, 252, 258n25
Jung, Carl G., 38, 112–13, 122n21, 183, 193

Kadowaki, Kakichi, 239
Kaga, Otohiko, 119, 122n19, 123n59, 184–85, 194n20

Kālabhairava, 216
Kālī (goddess), xix, xxiin43, 7–8, 61–62, 91–92, 101–2, 120, 171, 221
Kamakura era (1185–1333), 16, 25n30
Kamei, Katsuichirō, 75–78, 84, 84n13, 86n18
Kami, 178n12, 178n25, 242n18, 250–52, 303; "Kamigami to kami," 108, 177n4, 198, 251, 270; *Watashi ni totte kami to wa*, 258n25, 284n61
Kamloji (village in *Deep River*), 42
Kamogami, Hisa, 177n6, 177n7
kanji (Chinese character), 22, 55n20
Kanpur, xviii, xxiin43, 305
karma, 6, 15, 34, 41–42, 66, 100, 214–16, 234, 273
Karnataka, xv, xviii
Kasai, Akifu, 211n45
Kashi Vishwanath Temple, 215
Kasza, Justyna Weronika, 2, 36, 41, 44–45, 197–211 passim, 308
Katō, Muneya, 192n7
"Katorikku sakka no mondai" (The issues confronting the Catholic author), 108, 177n4, 198, 283n44
Katsumata, Hiroshi, 36, 202–3, 210n23, 210n24
Kaveri River (also Cauvery River), xv, xvi–xix, xxin4, xxin16
Kawamura, Minato, 120, 122n5, 123n60
Keane, John J., 251–52, 258n29, 259n36, 259n38, 300
Kei, Kumai, 3, 89
Keiko (Isobe's wife in *Deep River*), 35, 39, 42, 90, 100, 102
Keio University, 2, 108, 239, 257n20
kenosis, 37, 137–38, 236
Kerala, 24n19, 57, 215, 224, 230n27, 306
Khair, Tabish, 68
Khalistān (Land of the Pure), 94

Khalsa, 10
Kichijiro (also Kichijirō; character, *Silence* novel), 44, 54n15, 190
Kiguchi (character, *Deep River*): and animals, 40, 80; cannibalism, 21, 78–81, 170; and Chāmundā, 101–02; chanting Buddhist scriptures, 2, 13–14, 17, 43, 52–53, 84, 170, 271, 275; friendship with Tsukada, 31, 34–35, 80, 83, 103, 156, 233, 235; Highway of Death, 31, 40, 52–53, 63, 78; name symbolism, 55n20, 282n36; Occidentalism, 62; river trope, 52; trauma of war, 3, 128, 173, 234, 277
Kindai no Chōkoku (*Overcoming Modernity*), 75
kirtan (the recitation of sacred hymns), 9
Kitamori, Kazō, 83
Kobe, 2
kojinteki kyūdō ishiki ("individualistic search for faith), 177n9
kokoro-atatakana iryō ("warm-hearted medical care"), 183
kokuhaku shōdō (impulse of confession), 177
Kondabagil, Kiran, xviii
Korea, 16, 142, 289, 290
Krishnadas, xvi
Kṛṣṇa (also Krishna), xvi, 7–8, 287
kṣatriya (warriors), 7, 218, 229
Kūkai (Kōbō-Daishi), 236
Kultur Heim, 92, 137, 155, 158
Kumai, Kei, 3, 89
Kumbh Mela, 60, 69n8
Kurukshetra, xvii, xxin7
Kuśīnagara (site of Buddha's death), 14
Kwansei Gakuin University, 306
Kyoto, 152, 307
Kyoto School, 76, 252
Kyūshū, 271

kyūshū e no akogare ("yearning to be absorbed"), 168

Lahore, 9–10
Lalitāsahasranāma, 64
Laos, 16
Lejeune, Philippe, 36, 41, 197, 200–3, 208, 231
Liberal Democratic Party (LDP), 23n7
Liberation Tigers of Tamil Eelam (LTTE), 13
Life of Jesus, A, 152, 259n38
Lodge, David, 199
Longer Sukhāvatīvyūha Sūtra (Infinite Life Sutra), 25n31
Lumbinī, 14

Machida Museum of Literature (Tokyo), 130, 132, 252
Mahā Upaniṣad, 229n25
Mahābhārata (also Mahabharata), xxin7, 6, 59, 221
Maharasthra, xxi
Mahāsthāmaprāpta, 16
Malaya Mountains, xvi
Malayalam, 57, 229n10, 305
Manchuria, 1, 3, 31
Manikarnikā Ghāt, 30, 66, 143
Manshū-koku (1932–45), 79
mantra, 17, 229n24
Manusmṛti, 6
Māra (Death), 15, 34–35
Mardana, 9
Maritain, Jacques, 76, 145n8
martyrdom, 2, 37, 128
Mary, the Mother of Christ, 8, 21, 61, 63, 83, 91, 158, 236, 241n6, 291
Mase, Hiromasa, 239–40, 241n10, 242n18, 242n29, 242n31, 250, 257n20
Mase-Hasegawa, Emi, 19, 43, 49, 109, 226, 231–43 passim, 246, 251, 259n40, 308

Mauriac, François, 22n1, 36, 45, 78, 110–11, 128, 155, 177n4, 194n29, 197, 200–1, 204–8, 211n49
māyā ("illusion"), 6, 222
Megumi, Maeri, 19, 37–38, 167–79 passim, 308–9
Meiji, 2, 241n9
metaphor: Buddhist thought, 51–53; function, 45–49; rivers, 49–51, 58–60
Middleton, Darren J. N., 1–25 passim, 33, 36, 47, 54n7, 163n76, 245–60 passim, 309
Minamikawa, PFC (character, *Deep River*), 31, 40
Mishima, Yukio, 41, 175, 179n33, 214
mishōka (Christianity's inculturation on Japanese soil), 231
Missionaries of Charity, 3, 43, 67, 142, 159, 207, 274
Mitsuko (character, *Deep River*): and Isobe, 42, 90, 100, 113; anxiety, 31, 92, 117, 140, 154, 190, 274, 278, 288; cold-hearted figure, 173; connection to other Endō novels, 45, 111, 154–56; encounter with Ōtsu's Christian faith, 43, 47, 99, 101, 112, 118, 138–39, 157–59, 225, 238, 250, 253–54; Endō's most developed character, 174, 197–211 passim; failed marriage, 3; Ganges, 33, 45, 81, 140, 172, 228; Hinduism, 8, 13, 67, 91, 101–03, 157, 274; mother-figure, 102, 138; name symbolism, 55n20, 282n36; pluralistic sensibilities, 69, 120, 129, 172, 249, 271, 277, 288; reader of literature, 197–211 passim; seduction of Ōtsu, 33, 63, 97–98, 100–1, 109, 140, 232; view of India, 234, 290; work with the poor, 3, 66; yearning for transcendence, 261–85 passim
Miyazawa, Kenji, 306

Mohinī (female avatar of Viṣṇu), 24n19
Moïra, 45, 78, 154, 204, 206–7
mokṣa (also moksha), xvii, 6, 9, 43, 59, 215–16, 222, 227–28, 234
Motoki, Masahiro, 214
Mughal Empire, 10, 24n22
Mughal era (1526–40 and 1555–1857), 9, 11
mukti, xvi, 6
Muslim, 9–12, 289
Mutaguchi, General, 283n52

Nadī sūktam, 59
Nagasawa, Yujin, 250, 258n22
Nagpur, xxiiin49
Nakamura, Hajime, 92
Nakamura, Shinichiro, 174
Nakshar Bhagavatī temple, 62
nām japō (the repetition of God's name), 9
namu Amida Butsu (I pay homage to the Buddha Amitābha), 17, 193n14
Narada, xvi
Narasiṃha, 64
Narmada, xv–xix, xxin4, xxin16
Nasadīya-sūkta, 66
Nasik (also Nashik), xvii, xxi, 69n8
Nawab of Bengal, 24n22
Nehru, Jawaharlal, xv, 12, 24n20, 306
Nhat Hanh, Thich (Vietnamese Zen Buddhist monk), 39, 54n9
nembutsu (chanting the Name of Amida Buddha), 17, 264, 284n76
Netland, John T., 137, 139, 165n131
New Age spirituality, 43
Ni, Zhange, 16, 21, 32, 34, 40, 46, 73–88 passim, 309
Nihonteki kansei ("Japanese sensibilities"), 167, 177n2
Nimishamba, xviii

nirvāṇa (also nirvana), 6, 14–15, 34, 46, 51, 67, 238, 272, 277; parinirvāṇa, 14
Nishida, Kitarō, 251–52m 259n36, 259n38
Nishitani, Keiji, 272, 283n57
niṣkāma karma, 66
numa ("swamp" or "marsh"), 48, 267
numachi ("mudswamp," "swampland," and "marshland"), 48
Numada (character, Deep River): birds, 3, 46, 63, 79, 82–83, 102, 117, 235, 271, 280, 292; childhood, 3, 78; dog named Blackie, 31, 78–79, 83, 188, 271; friendship with Li, 79–81 passim; Japan, 40, 80–81, 271; Jesus as Eternal Companion, 233, 235; name symbolism, 55n20, 282n36; nuanced view of India, 40, 234, 238; panentheism, 254; physical ailments, 31, 46, 82, 102, 117, 232–33, 235; rebirth concept, 119; Rouault's paintings, 46, 83, 102; writer of children's stories, 31, 78, 80, 82, 188, 232–33, 235, 271

Obayashi seishin joshi gakuin, 108
obon ("festival of lanterns"), 267
O'Connor, Flannery, 18, 21, 32, 149–65 passim, 305, 310
Occidentalism, 62–63
Ōe, Kenzaburō, 1
Okakura, Kakuzō, 280
Ōoka, Shōhei, 179n29
Operation Blue Star, 11, 95–96
Order of the Rising Sun (Kyokujitsu chūjushō), 307
Orientalism, 62, 73–76, 79–80, 85
Ōsawa, Masachi, 177n6
Ōtsu (also Otsu; character, Deep River): and Chāmuṇḍā, 103, 157–58, 228;

and scripture, 91, 143–44, 155, 158, 236; and Sikhism, 94; and Vedānta, 63–68; attacked by mob, 9, 35, 67, 93, 109, 172; discovery of India, 223–27; failed seminarian, 3, 33, 64–66, 129, 141, 156, 158, 170–73, 213, 223, 228, 234, 280; God–Onion concept, 33, 49, 64–67, 77, 97–103, 118–19, 142, 174, 236–38, 249–54, 273, 277, 279–80; Hindu disinterestedness, 66, 121, 227; imitation of Christ, 3, 7, 9, 18, 30–33, 44, 48, 66, 101, 114, 119, 140–43, 149, 158–60, 187, 190, 226–27, 233, 236–38, 246, 255, 280; interfaith spirituality, 129, 136, 139, 142, 144, 170, 231–33, 236, 240; Japanese Christianity, 48, 175, 264–68, 279; name symbolism, 55n20; 282n36; panentheism, 3, 19, 39, 47, 138, 156, 245–60, 270; relationship with Mitsuko, 33, 78, 90–99, 109, 117–18, 136–41, 154, 157, 159, 225, 232, 252–54, 271, 280; rebirth concept, 43–44, 67, 119, 277; sad clown, 103, 190, 290; Thomism, 33, 138, 254

Pakistan, 5, 9–10, 12, 94
pan-Asian, 68, 73, 75
panentheism, 36, 54n7, 163n76, 245–60 passim, 270, 283n43
pantheism, 129, 158, 191, 245, 251–52, 269–72
paradox, 29, 37, 58, 68, 84, 172
Partition, 11–13
Pārvatī (goddess), 59, 221
Pāṭaliputra (modern-day Patna), 14
patristic theology, 131
Pierrot, 32, 46, 49, 82–83, 89, 91, 97, 102–3, 190

Plate, S. Brent, 19, 50–51, 287–94 passim, 309–10
posthumanist, 41, 81, 84–85
postsecular, 41, 76, 85
Prahlāda, 64
pratītyasamutpāda ("dependent co-arising"), 39
Prayag (also Prayaga), xv, xvi, 216
pūjā (the ritual bathing of statues), 7
Puniral, Rajini (character, *Deep River*), 42, 116
Punjab, xx, 10, 93–95, 104n13
Punjabi language, 9
Purāṇas, xiv, xvii, xxiin18, 6–7, 221; *Matsya Purāṇa*, xxiin36; *Padma Purāṇa*, xvii, xxiin18, xxiin27, xxiin32; *Skanda Purāṇa*, xv, xxiin20, xxiin35, 215, 228n5, 229n11
Pure Land Buddhism, 13–17 passim, 25n30, 29–30, 39, 52–53, 77–78, 84, 170, 263–64, 268, 271–72, 307; Jōdoshū, 25n30; Jōdo Shinshū, 16, 25n30, 263, 269; Pure Land Buddhist sūtras, 170; Shin Buddhism, 29, 263, 268–69, 307

Raktavīja, 171
Ramanujan, A. K., 68, 71n54
Rāmāyaṇa, 6, 221, 287
Rāmottaratāpaniya Upaniṣad, 229n12
rangaku (Western learning), 2
rebirth, 5–7, 9, 14, 18, 30, 34–35, 41–45 passim, 50, 58–59, 63, 90, 97, 100, 116, 119–20, 159, 214–16, 228, 232, 238, 271, 277, 279, 303
reborn, 5, 16–17, 34, 42–45, 67, 116, 170, 227, 241n5
Reichardt, Mary R., 18
reincarnation, 2, 5, 21, 33, 39, 41–43, 54n14, 90–91, 100, 103, 116, 119, 128, 170, 214, 220, 232, 234, 276

religious pluralism, 2, 21, 43, 50, 113, 129–33, 135–36, 142, 147n27, 176, 183, 193n14, 231–43 passim, 265
Ricoeur, Paul, 36, 201, 203, 208
Rig Veda, xiv, 59
Riksha Mountains, xvi
Rishikesh, xviii
Rouault, Georges Henri, 46, 83, 102, 235
ṛsis (ascetics), 221
Rupa Gosvamin, xvii

sādhu, 66, 141, 146, 190, 226–27, 237
Sagira, King, xiv
Sahya Mountains, xvi
śakti (divine feminine energy and power), 7, 215
Śākyamuni ("Sage of the Śākya"; also Sakyamuni and Shakyamuni), 13–16, 52, 61, 116. See also Buddha
samhāriṇi (the Destroyer), 64
saṃsāra, 5–6, 9, 15, 21, 30, 34–35, 39, 42–43, 51, 54n6, 90, 229n12, 232, 234, 275
Samurai, The, 82, 112, 119, 183, 190, 192n7, 194n30, 198, 241n14
Sanjō (character, *Deep River*): egocentric character, 62, 173, 233; name symbolism, 55n20, 282n36; negative image of India, 62, 68, 217, 220, 228; photography and cremation, 222–23, 233, 290, 293; saved by Ōtsu, 101, 112, 159, 223, 238
Saraswati, xv, xvii, xx, xxin4, xxin16, xxiin37
Sarnath (site of Buddha's first teaching), 14–15, 214
Satan, 64
Satō, Yasumasa, 109, 122n8, 122n9, 123n25
Satnām ("True Name"), 9

satori, 238
"Saul" (three-act drama), 107–23 passim
Savarkar, Vinayak Damodar, 24n23
savarnas (higher castes), 229n14
Scandal, 97, 111, 122n21, 162n42, 175, 198
Scorsese, Martin, 3–5, 23n6, 44, 47, 54n15, 154n24, 307
Sea and Poison, The, 112, 169, 173, 186, 198
seishin kyōdōtai (spiritual commonality), 77
Sepoy Rebellion, 11
Sepoy Mutiny, 24n23
Seven Sacred Rivers, xiv–xviii, xxin2, xxiin21, xxiin39
Shantanu, King, 59
Shantao (Pure Land Buddhist patriarch), 52
Shikoku henro, 236
Shimazaki, Tōson, 306
Shimizu, Masashi, 174, 179n27
shi-nō-kō-shō (samurai, peasants, artisans, and merchants), 218
Shin Buddhism (*see* Pure Land Buddhism)
Shinran (1173–1263), 16, 25n30, 39, 55n25, 77, 268–69, 272, 275–79, 284n76, 307–8
Shinto (also Shintō), 136, 178n17, 213, 224, 234, 246, 251–53, 264, 267–68, 276–79, 284n76, 307–8
Shipra River, xxin17
shishōsetsu (the "I" novel), 199, 202–3, 209n7, 210n23, 210n24, 308
Shivaliks, xx
Shōtoku, Prince (573–621), 77
"Shūkyō to Bungaku" (Religion and literature), 76, 86n17, 87n21, 177n2, 177n4, 177n11, 179n32
shūtaisei (definitive work), 108

Index

Siddhārtha, Prince, 14–15
Sikh (Sikhism), 3, 5–6, 9–12, 36, 93–96, 103n1, 104n13, 222
Silence (see *Chinmoku*): biblical motifs, 37; Buddhist readings, 5; climactic scene, 47, 112, 155; comparisons with *Deep River*, 4, 36, 75, 92, 231; Dennis and Middleton anthology, 2–5, 21–48 passim; diversity of reading practices, 20, 252, 267; Endō's casket, 4, 231; feminine Christ, 231; maternal religion, 47; narrative structure, 36, 174; religious hybridity, 134, 252; soteriological themes, 37; swamp metaphor, 48, 173, 267; theodicy, 31, 128, 169, 182, 186–88; title symbolism, 4; translation issues, 47
simran (meditation on passages from the text), 9
Sindhu. *See* Indus
Singh, Beant, 96
Singh, Rana B., 63
Singh, Satwant, 96
Singh, Master Tara, 12
Śiva (also Siva), xiv, xvii, 7, 24n19, 59, 64, 90–91, 215–16, 221, 229n12
skandhas (five elements), 35
Smith, Lee, 22
smṛti ("that which is remembered"), 6–7
sōkessan (overall reckoning on his oeuvre), 108
Sophia University, 127, 145n14
sonzai (existence), 178n22
sonzai no chitsujo ("order of existence"), 168
śramaṇa ("striver"), 24n27
Sri Lanka, 13, 16, 131
sṛishṭi kartṛi (the Creator), 64
śruti ("that which is heard"), 6
Steiner, George, 4

śūdra (laborers), 7, 218, 229n14
Sukhāvatī (the Pure Land of the West; literally, "Land Filled with Bliss"), 16–17, 52
sūtra (also *sutra*), 52, 127, 240, 271
Suzuki, Daisetsu, 253
Suzuki, Tomi, 303
Suzuki, Tomoko, 192n8
Swift, Graham, 22

Taishō period (1912–26), 209n7
Taiwan, 142
Taj Mahal, 287–89
Takeshita, Noboru, 23n7
Takeda, Taijun, 175, 179n33
Takemoto, Toshio, 207–8, 211n48, 211n59
Tamil Nadu, xv, 24n19
Tanaka, Stephen, 74, 86n8
Tandava dance, xvii
Tanizaki Prize, 3, 179n34
Tannishō, 269
Tāraka mantra, 216, 229n12
tariki ("other power"), 17
tarpaṇa (rites for dead ancestors and friends), 67
Tathāgata, 51, 272, 284n76
Tenjiku, 219, 229n20
Teresa, Mother, 87n22, 142, 159, 207, 274; Mother Teresa's Missionaries of Charity, 3, 67
Thailand, 16
Theology of the Pain of God, 83
Theravāda (School of the Elders), 16
Thérèse Desqueyroux, 22n1, 45, 78, 155, 194n29, 197, 200, 204–8
thirodhānakari (the One Who Causes the Disappearance of Things), 64
Thomas Aquinas, 248
three poisons of Buddhism: greed, anger, and ignorance, 15, 35, 52

tīrtha (also *tirtha*, pilgrimage destinations), xv, xvii, 8, 59, 216
tīrthaṅkaras, 215, 229n6
Tokyo, 1, 4, 23n7, 117, 130, 145n14, 152
tōyō (literally "the Eastern Ocean," but also Japan's orient), 74, 76; *tōyō-gaku* (Oriental studies), 74; *tōyō no haha* (Asian mother), 74
Trimbekashwar Temple, xxiin38
Trimūrti, 90
Triveni (junction of three rivers), xx
tṛṣhṇā ("thirst"), 34
Tsuji, Mitsuhiko, 109, 122n6
Tsukada (character, *Deep River*): cannibalism, 80, 116, 188, 233; dying, 14, 31, 34–35, 83, 117, 156; friendship with Kiguchi, 31, 34–35, 80, 83, 103, 156, 233, 235; forgiveness, 102, 188, 235; funeral, 84; salvation, 156; sickness, 3, 44
Twain, Mark, 4, 22, 215

Uchimura, Kanzō, 77, 87n21
Uddhava-Gīta, 66
Ueda, Yoshifumi, 307
Uehara, Kazu, 74
Ujjain, xxin17, 69n8
Unno, Taitetsu, 29, 52
untouchable, 7, 129, 218, 220, 229n14, 233
Upaniṣads, xiv, 6
Uttar Pradesh, 58, 305
Uttarakhand, 58–59

Vaiśālī, 14
vaiśya (merchants and farmers), 7, 218, 229n14
varṇa jāti (also *varna jati*), 6–7, 22, 218, 229n14
Varanasi (also Vāranāsī), xiv–xv, xviii, 1, 3, 8, 13, 15, 31, 35, 41–42, 44, 50, 58–60, 63, 67–68, 69n2, 116–17, 128–29, 141, 143, 157–59, 190, 213–16, 218–19, 222–23, 226–27, 234, 279; *Varanasi* (novel) 57, 60, 65–66
Vasubandhu, 193n10
Vasudevan, M. T., 57–69
vasudhaiva kuṭumbakam (the world is one family), 222–23, 229n25
Vedānta, 63, 65
Vedas, xx, 6, 221
Vedic, xv, 6, 24n27, 25n27, 218, 230n37
Vietnam, 16, 142
Viṣṇu, 7, 64
Vishvanatha Temple, 291
Vrindaban (also Vrindavan), xvi, 8, 287
Vyasa, xxin7

Wachal, Christopher B., 18, 33, 47, 50, 127–48 passim, 310
Waheguru (the "Wonderful Lord"), 9
Waseda University, 306
watashi ("I"), 36, 39, 202
Watashi no ai shita shōsetsu (A Novel I Have Loved), 22n1, 122n21, 210n43
Watsuji, Tetsurō, 74, 253
Waugh, Evelyn, 21
West Bengal, 58
White Man/Yellow Man, 2, 198
Whitehead, Alfred North, 246–47
Williams, Mark, 13, 14, 6, 19, 38, 45, 52, 107–23 passim, 250, 310
Wonderful Fool, 44, 84, 127, 156, 175, 190

Xavier, Francis, 223

Yama (the god of death), xv, 216
Yamagata, Sister (character in *The Girl I Left Behind*), 32, 151–53, 157
Yamamoto, Yoshihisa, 252, 253
Yamane, Michihiro, 197, 198

Yamuna, xv–xx, xxin16, xxiin23, xxiin29, 58, 287
Yamunashtakam, xvi–xvii
Yasuoka, Shōtarō, 198
yātrā (pilgrimage), 7, 43, 59
Yoga Sūtras, 6

Yoshimitsu, Yoshihiko, 75–78
Yozō (character in *The Samurai*), 190

Zen Buddhism, 16, 17, 39, 145n6
zen'aku funi, 169
Zoroastrianism, 224

www.ingramcontent.com/pod-product-compliance
Lightning Source LLC
Chambersburg PA
CBHW030001240426
43672CB00007B/775